AF521741

7 Days in DeKalb

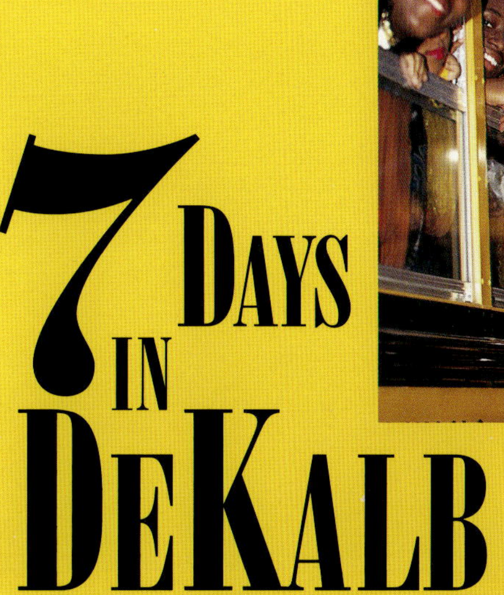

PHOTO BY KEN HAWKINS

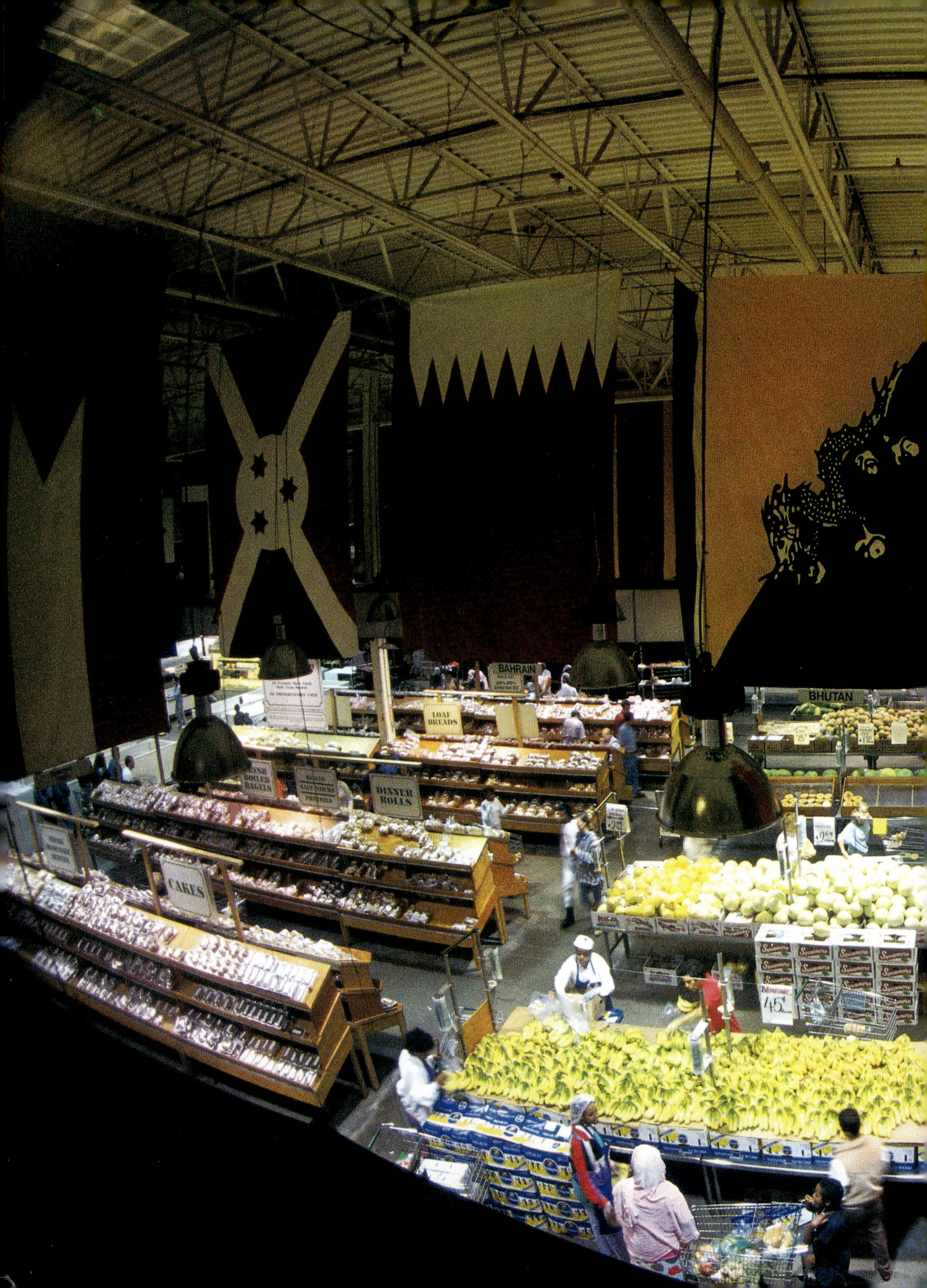
BAHRAIN
BHUTAN
LOAF BREADS
DINNER ROLLS
CAKES

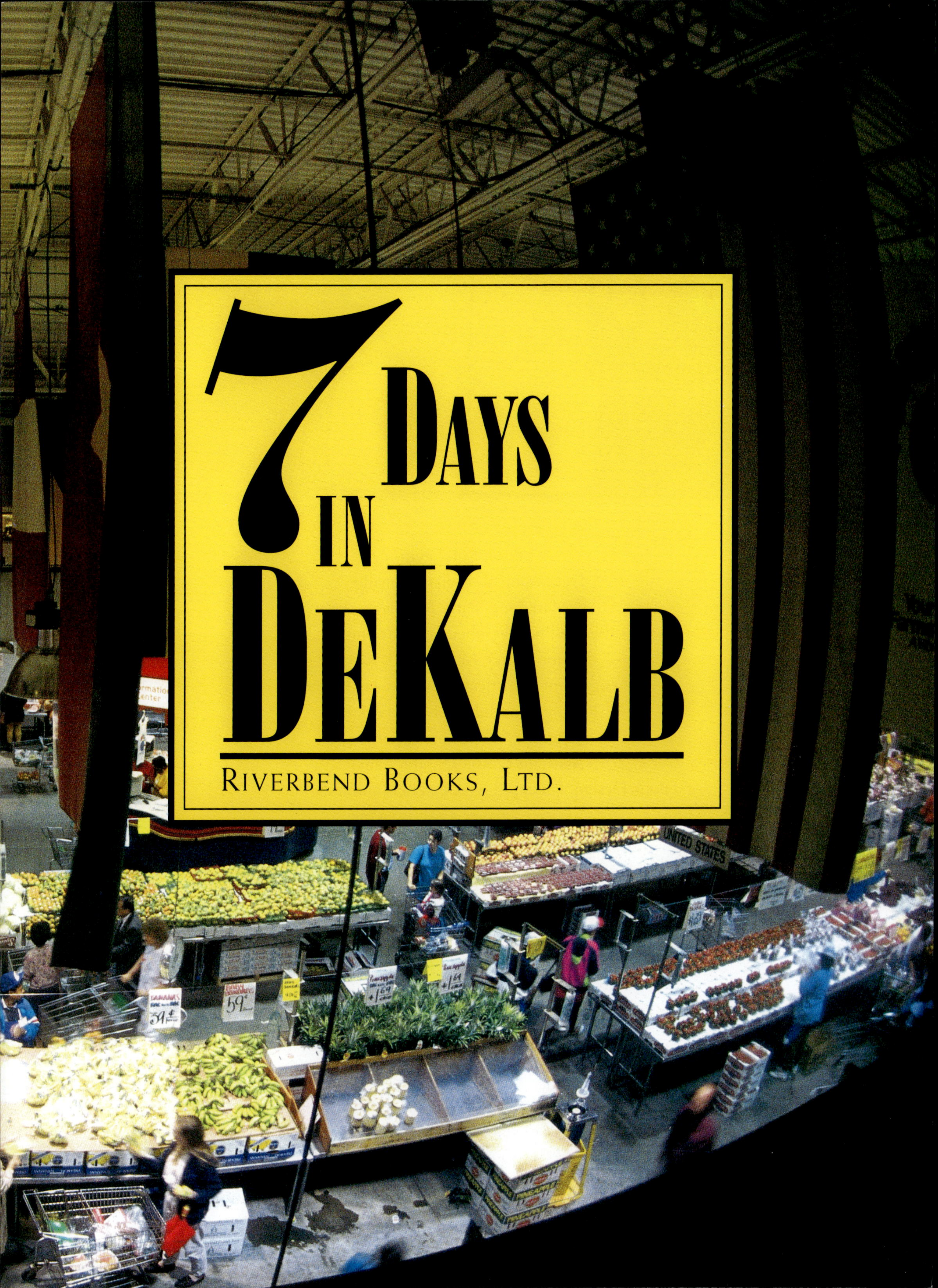
7 Days in DeKalb
Riverbend Books, Ltd.
United States

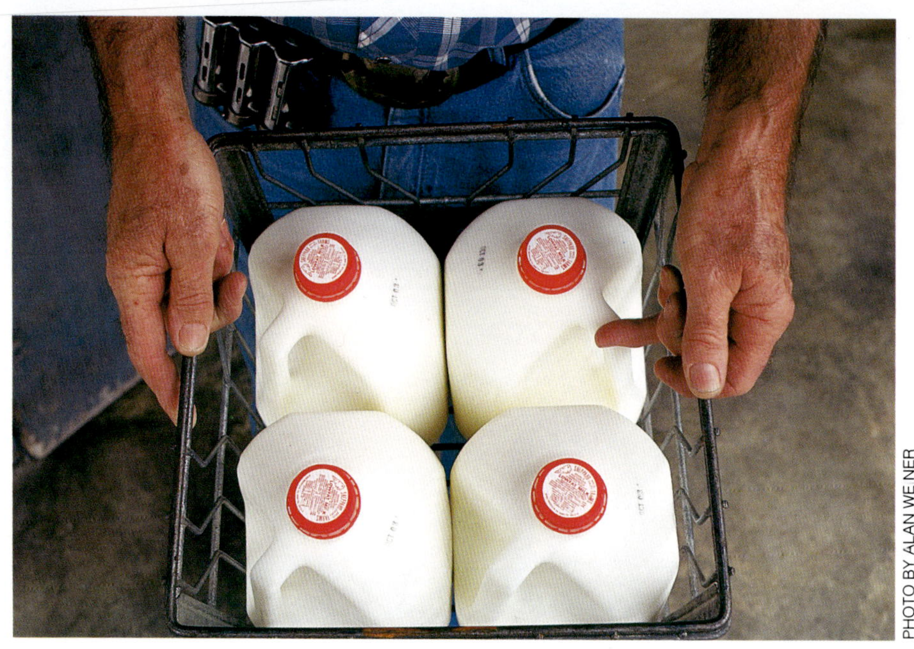
PHOTO BY ALAN WEINER

Editor, Rob Levin
Development, Melanie Smallie
Marketing, Barry M. Levin
Senior Photographer, Scott Robinson
Senior Writer, Margaret O. Kirk
Assignment Logistics, Mary Lee, Jan Pogue
Photography Editor, Ken Hawkins
Photography Captions, Vivian Price
Assistant Editor, Jennifer Eanes
Book Design, Paulette Livers Lambert and Judy Purvis
Office Manager, Leahbeth Yap

Printed in Hong Kong

Title Page Photo: Alan S. Weiner

Published by Riverbend Books, Ltd.
512 Means Street, N.W., Atlanta, Georgia 30318

ISBN 1-8839787-00-8

Acknowledgments

It was only one week in the life of DeKalb County. But it took two years (counting the time before and afterwards) to make a book about those seven days.

Our thanks go to dozens of people who gave generously of their time and effort. Among these heroes are, of course, our writers and photographers, whose credits and bios are listed in the back of this book. But I especially want to cite Scott Robinson of Los Angeles whose photographic expertise and talent laid the foundation for future similar projects. And to Margaret O. Kirk, of Philadelphia, who tackled the writing and accomplished what had never been done before in this country.

The list goes on. Mary Lee, who spent weeks tracking down assignments, taking the most wistful of ideas for a photograph and finding the reality to match it; Jan Pogue, who followed in Mary Lee's path and flushed out numerous assignments for us on short notice; Leahbeth Yap, who managed the ad hoc news room from daybreak to midnight, kept a hundred details in order and never complained; to the countless people (but most specifically Linda Harris and Vivian Price) whom we called on a moment's notice, and who could just as quickly provide us the answer about DeKalb County we were searching for.

Special and heartfelt thanks go to our sponsors for their willingness to believe in a project that was little more than an idea being published by a company that was still in its infancy. In the same breath, a load of thanks to Barry M. Levin, who convinced the sponsors of the worthiness of the idea and brought organization to a situation just short of chaos. And to John Millsaps of the DeKalb Chamber of Commerce, without whose continued support and endorsement this book would never have seen the light of day.

Lastly, my deepest appreciation to my wife, Rebecca Robinson, who endured (and endured and endured) while a dream took flight and landed in these pages.

Rob Levin
August 1993
Atlanta, Georgia

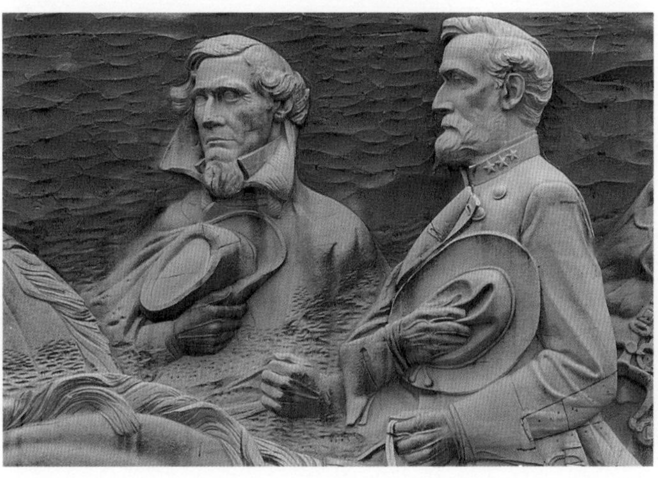

PHOTO BY THOMAS ENGLAND

Foreword

In retrospect, had we known what we were getting into, we might have thought twice. Essentially the plan was to chronicle one week in the life of DeKalb County. Simple enough.

Then the work began. And the deeper we got, well, the deeper we got. It appeared as if every detail spawned more details. Logistics became a nightmare. Phone calls by the hundreds were made. Faxes flew.

By Sunday afternoon, Senior Photographer Scott Robinson, Senior Writer Margaret Kirk and Office Manager Leahbeth Yap had constructed a makeshift news center — complete with computers, phone lines, coffee and snack trays and fax forms — in the conference room of the Perimeter North Inn at I-285 and Buford Highway.

The out-of-town photographers were already camped out at the Inn. The hotel's front desk grew immediately weary of the sudden influx of phone calls that at times virtually jammed their switchboard. Sunday night everybody grew nervous.

The first person out the door Monday morning was Michael Schwarz, who had a 3:30 A.M. assignment at the DeKalb distribution center of the *Atlanta Journal and Constitution*, the paper where he was formerly employed as a staff photographer.

The next seven days were a blur of activity as more than thirty people — writers, photographers, editors, marketing staff, support staff, etc. — rushed in and out, night and day. Everybody did what they were supposed to. Better yet, everybody did more than was required. Time and again, photographers would put forth the extra effort to capture the right image, the perfect exposure. Three times Ken Hawkins (photo editor at *Georgia Trend*) coaxed pilot John Matthews up in his open-cockpit biplane to get the image he was looking for over Stone Mountain. One morning at 3 A.M., after Scott Robinson, from Los Angeles, had finished shooting at Mama's Country Showcase, he decided this would be the perfect time to shoot the I-285 and I-85 interchange. When Gordon Joffrion tired of the angles he was shooting of the caretakers of the historic Decatur Cemetery, it dawned on him to photograph the crew from a perspective most people never see — from inside an open grave.

After Chuck Young, one of Atlanta's leading corporate shooters, finished some work on the ground at the construction site of the new DeKalb jail, he slung cameras over his shoulders, checked his insurance papers and climbed the construction crane to get a bird's-eye view. Alan Weiner of the *New York Times* climbed under a cow for an udderly delightful perspective, and Rob Nelson of *Newsweek* got mooned at an Emory University frat party (sorry, shot not included in this book).

The writers were equally as enterprising. Linda Patillo, a correspondent for ABC News, interviewed a professional tree climber while he hung upside down. Terry Wells spent a day in a police car while Don Winbush, former bureau chief for *Time* magazine, explored the richness of DeKalb's academic community. Cheryl Crockett delivered remarkably sensitive material about the county's medical community (including the tale of a young boy who had endured two liver transplants at Egleston Children's Hospital).

The list goes on and on. Other writers and other photographers, all contributing to the story of a week in DeKalb County.

But as you read, you will also notice sidebars on many of the varied businesses in DeKalb County. Not only are they are our sponsors, but their first-person narratives reveal much about themselves, and oftentimes the county, that is unique and refreshing. It is for this reason that we opted to make them an integral part of the book, instead of lumping them together in the back. The sponsor photos were taken by Alan Weiner, Scott Robinson, Michael Schwarz and Ken Hawkins, and Margaret Kirk conducted the interviews from which the narratives were culled.

But the question may linger in many minds — why DeKalb? The short answer is *why not?* The more thoughtful response is that it is without a doubt the most unique county in Georgia. It is the richest in international culture (over a hundred nationalities in the county schools), economically diverse, one of the most efficiently run counties on cost of services provided and laden with colleges and other other academic concerns. It has Stone Mountain and the second busiest airport in Georgia, one of the last working dairies in the area, the U.S. Centers for Disease Control and Prevention (one of our sponsors, and one of the few times the CDC has ever attached its name to a commercial undertaking of this nature), Mama's Country Biscuit in Lithonia and the bucolic town of Pine Lake. Never heard of it? Neither had we until we stumbled across it.

Is this a tribute to DeKalb? Sort of. But then again, the county has its problems, and big ones at that. Crime and the concern of some residents that South DeKalb is all but ignored by North DeKalb. The typical urban woes of drugs and gangs. The blight of East Lake Meadows. But the county is working diligently on these issues and that, in essence, is a lot of what DeKalb County is about. A county of the working class, people who create things for a living.

And what we hope we have created is a book that tells part of their story. There is much left to be told and a whole volume of books could never do justice to the more than 500,000 people who call DeKalb home. But this is a start.

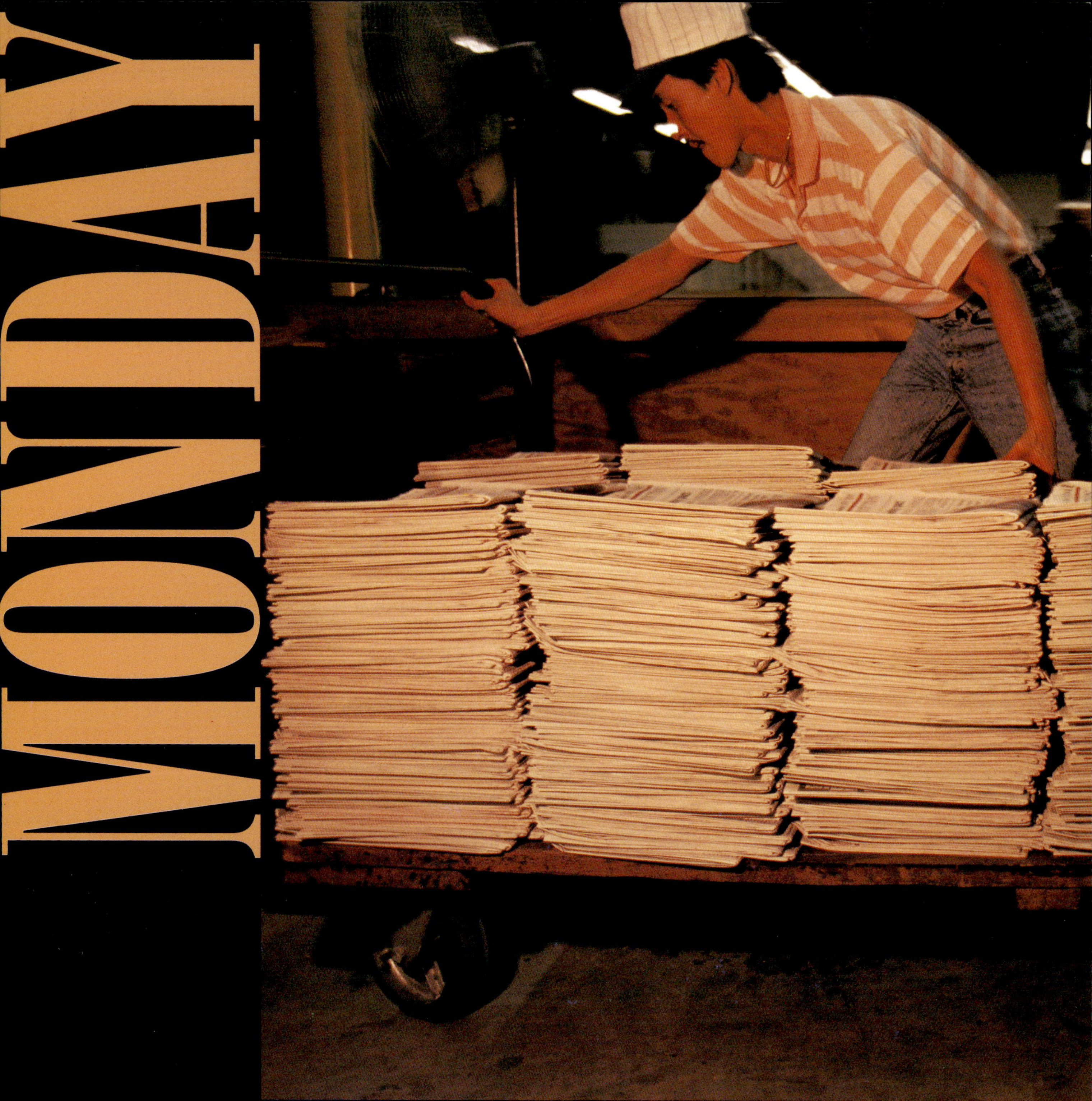
MONDAY

3:45 AM *The day starts very early when you deliver the morning paper. More than thirty Atlanta Constitution carriers picked up their bundles from this Northeast Expressway warehouse and were on their way before 4 A.M. on Monday, delivering about 80,000 papers in DeKalb.* Photo by Michael Schwarz.

Today is Monday, September 21—a new day, a new week, in DeKalb County, Georgia.

Under the colorless, still-nighttime sky, Albert Davis leaves his home in Stone Mountain to go to work at 1:30 A.M., to help assemble and distribute the early editions of the *Atlanta Constitution*. Several hours later, Judy Boone checks to make sure that each breakfast tray at the Holiday Inn Crowne Plaza Ravinia has, among other items, two pats of butter and a long-stemmed red rose. Just outside Lithonia, seventeen-year-old Britt Phillips slowly wakes up, already thinking about the Big One, Friday night's high-school football game between his own Lithonia Bulldogs and the archrival Lakeside Vikings.

In downtown Decatur, Mayor Michael Mears slides behind his place setting at the Square Table restaurant to read the newspaper and dine on his traditional 7 A.M. breakfast (two fried eggs, sliced tomatoes, two buttered biscuits) delivered by waitress Gladys Hill. At a nearby table, six women from Decatur First United Methodist Church's book group sit together after coffee and ponder the meaning of life's choices (appropriately, one group member wears a "No Lottery" button).

And in the kitchen of their two-story brick home on Decatur's Clairemont Avenue, Ben Turner serves cereal and milk to his four blond-haired daughters (Sarah gets the red cup), while discussing who does what for Mom's birthday tomorrow.

A handful of MARTA's North-South line riders huddle at the Chamblee Station for a rapid rail commute into downtown Atlanta. In Tucker, the cooks at Matthews Cafeteria have already finished baking from scratch all of today's desserts—lemon and chocolate and sweet potato pies, peach and cherry and blackberry cobblers. On a day when the Olympic Banner is hoisted over Atlanta's City Hall, Lisa Hanson quickly arranges her week to concentrate on DeKalb County's role in the 1996 Olympic Games. And at Dunwoody High School, 1,100 students meander to class inside the two-story, yellow-orange brick building, including junior Sonya Michele Gomez. She loves Spanish. She studies a lot. "My life," she says, "is just a big book."

On this rainy Monday, a day when cloud clusters barely give the sun a fighting chance, 545,837 citizens in DeKalb County start a new day.

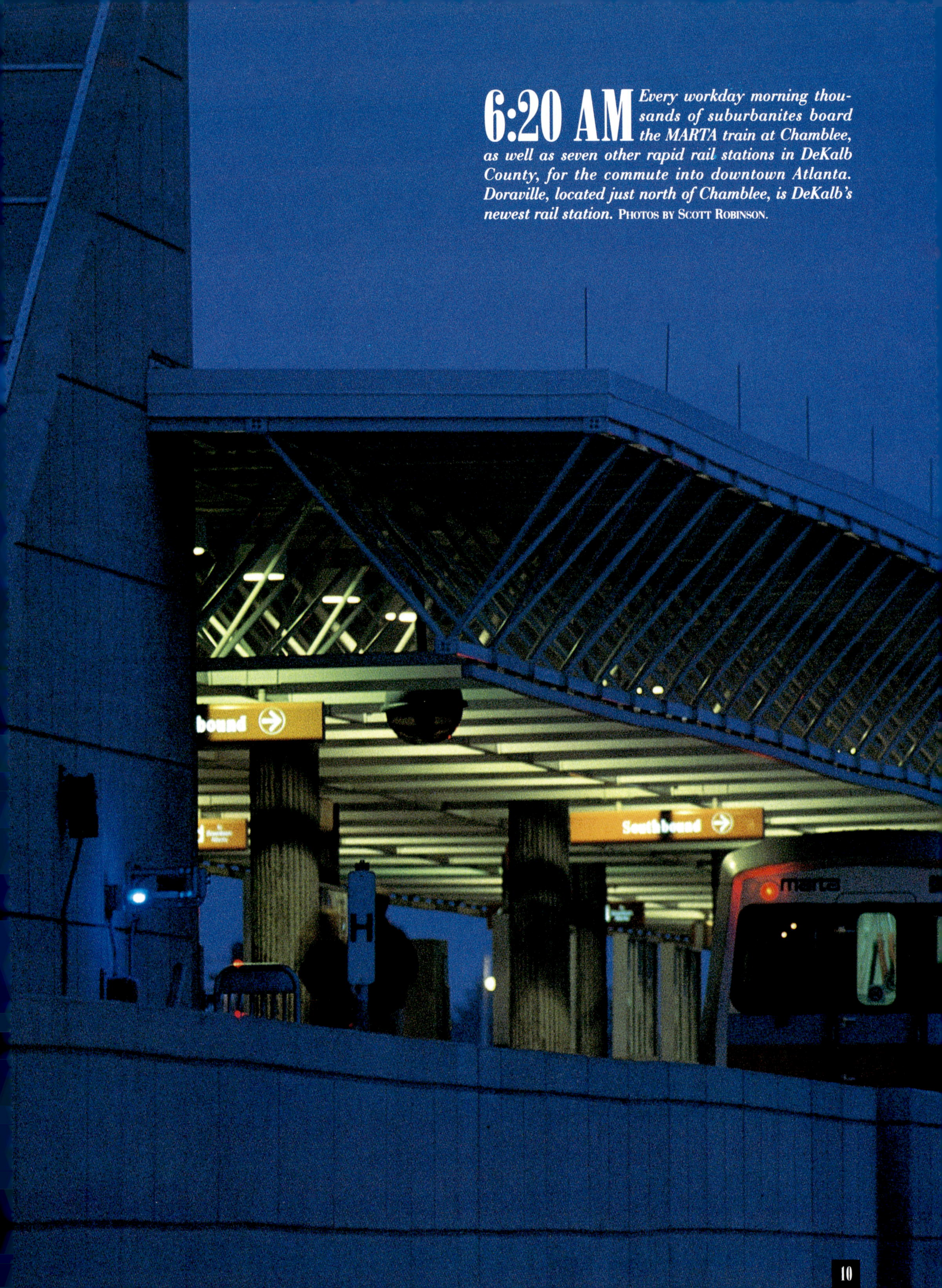

6:20 AM *Every workday morning thousands of suburbanites board the MARTA train at Chamblee, as well as seven other rapid rail stations in DeKalb County, for the commute into downtown Atlanta. Doraville, located just north of Chamblee, is DeKalb's newest rail station.* PHOTOS BY SCOTT ROBINSON.

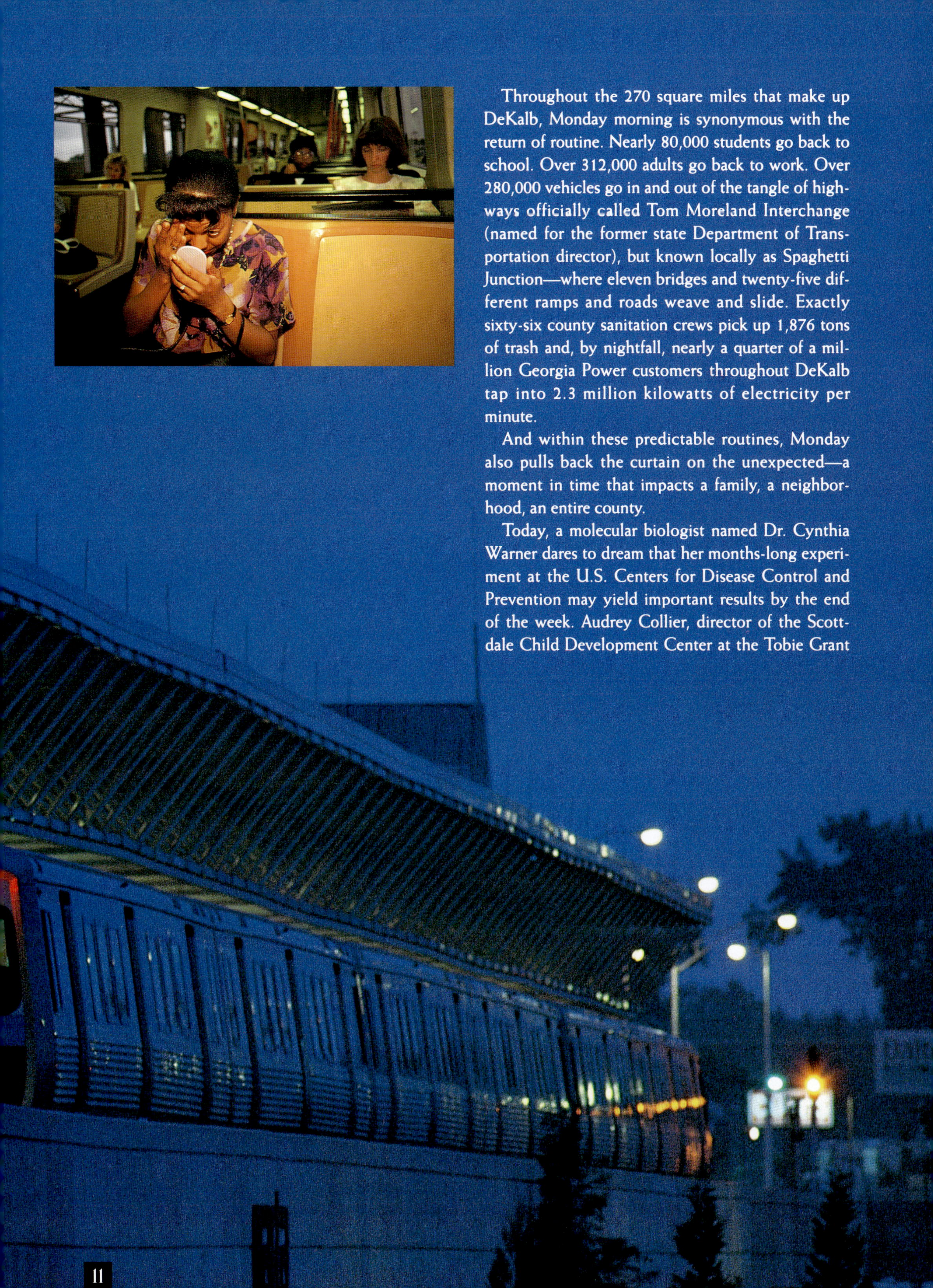

Throughout the 270 square miles that make up DeKalb, Monday morning is synonymous with the return of routine. Nearly 80,000 students go back to school. Over 312,000 adults go back to work. Over 280,000 vehicles go in and out of the tangle of highways officially called Tom Moreland Interchange (named for the former state Department of Transportation director), but known locally as Spaghetti Junction—where eleven bridges and twenty-five different ramps and roads weave and slide. Exactly sixty-six county sanitation crews pick up 1,876 tons of trash and, by nightfall, nearly a quarter of a million Georgia Power customers throughout DeKalb tap into 2.3 million kilowatts of electricity per minute.

And within these predictable routines, Monday also pulls back the curtain on the unexpected—a moment in time that impacts a family, a neighborhood, an entire county.

Today, a molecular biologist named Dr. Cynthia Warner dares to dream that her months-long experiment at the U.S. Centers for Disease Control and Prevention may yield important results by the end of the week. Audrey Collier, director of the Scottdale Child Development Center at the Tobie Grant

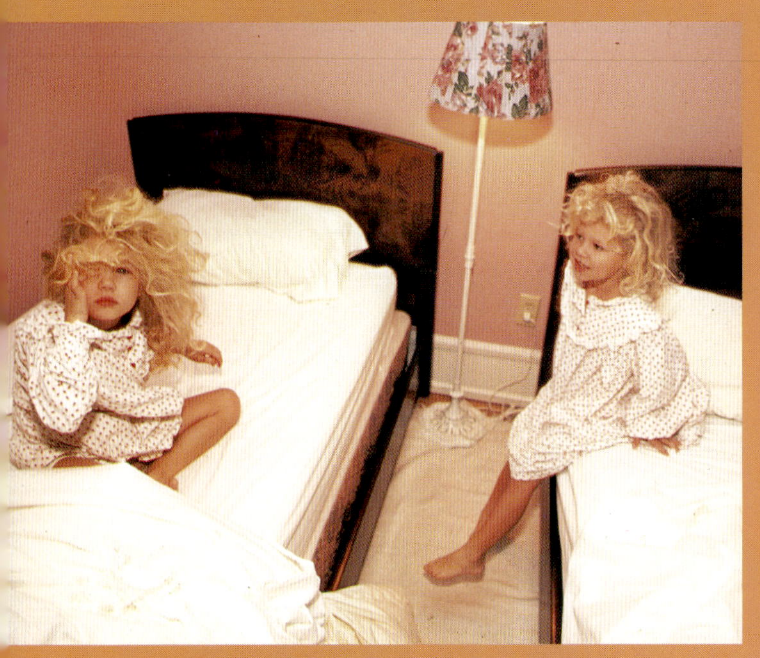

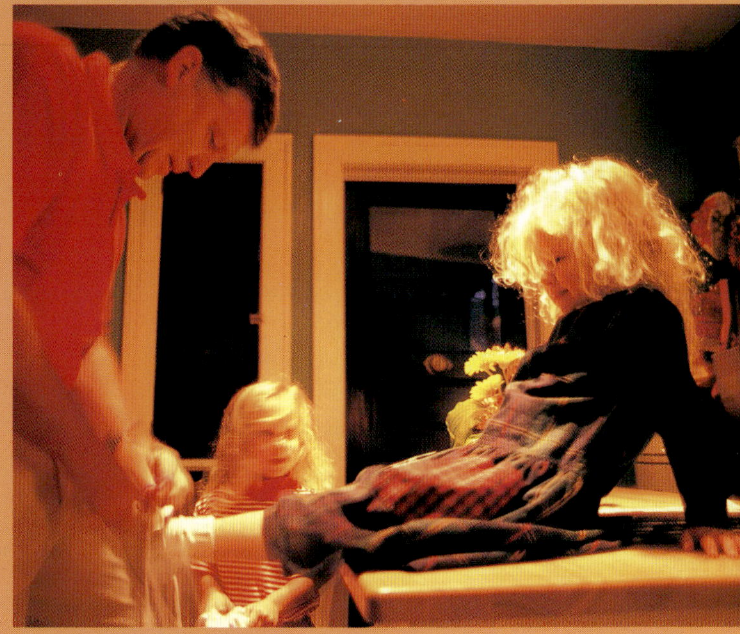

Housing Development, tearfully tells her board that a $10,000 grant just didn't come through for the center that cares for fifty-seven low-income children with working parents. "We just have to work that much harder," she says. Nearly 1,000 unemployed people stand in line at the Georgia Department of Labor DeKalb Field Service Office directly behind Avondale Mall; according to Unit Supervisor Sheila Yarn, this is the busiest day of the week. And today, beautiful Sarah Ann Leoni is born at the DeKalb Medical Center, the same day a tragic, accidental explosion at DeKalb-Peachtree Airport takes the life of a worker.

6:45 AM *The secret to avoiding morning stress, say Ben and Lisa Turner, parents of four blond daughters, all in single digits, is being prepared. Lisa recommends doing as many jobs as possible the night before: choosing four sets of clothes, giving four baths, making sure everyone has what she needs for the following day. Catherine and Sarah are good about getting themselves dressed, while mom fixes breakfast and feeds Rebecca and Elizabeth. After hairbrushing, Ben is off to work at Reebok, Lisa to Decatur's popular Hawthorne Cottage Tea Room and the kids to school. All the planning in the world, Lisa says, doesn't preclude one of the girls announcing at breakfast: "Oh, I forgot, I'm supposed to bring one hundred macaroons to school today."* PHOTOS BY GREG FOSTER.

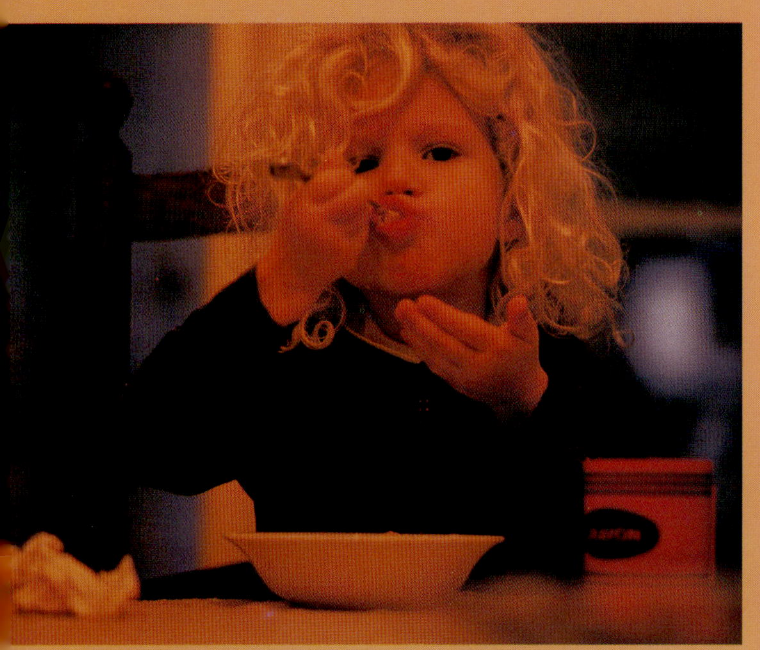

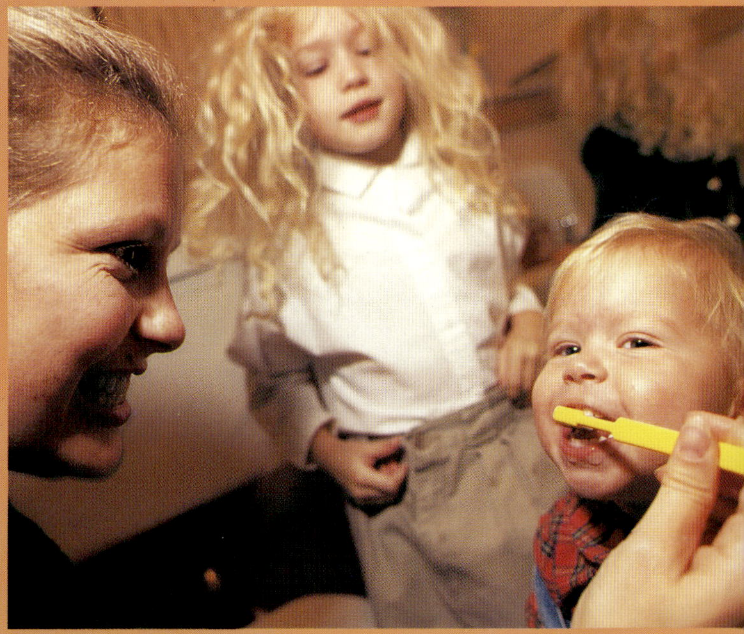

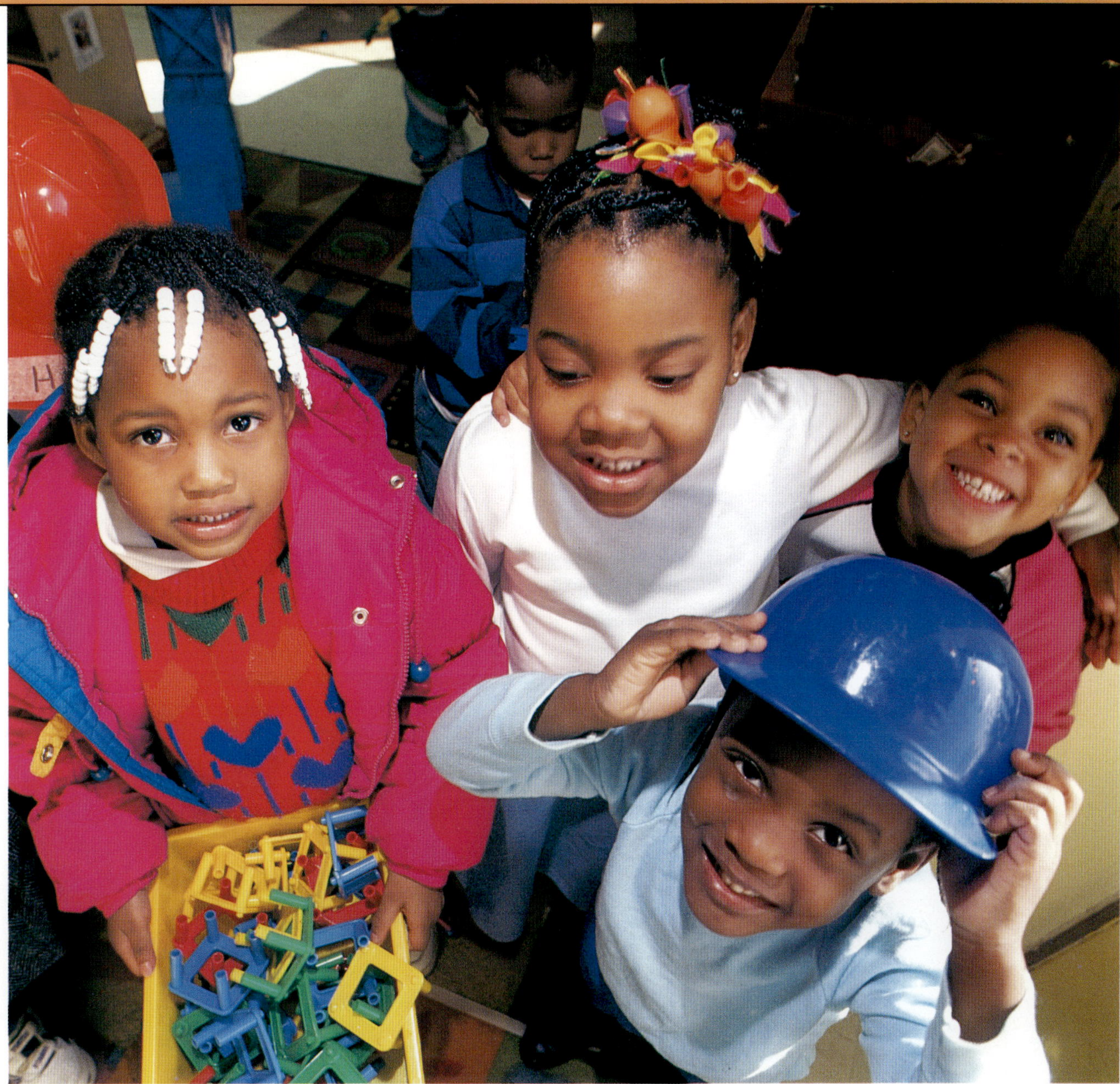

ALAN WEINER

DEKALB ECONOMIC OPPORTUNITY AUTHORITY, INC.

Helping Needy Citizens Help Themselves For Over 25 Years

Since May 1966, when the DeKalb Economic Opportunity Authority came into existence, our overall mission has been the same — to help the county's most needy citizens achieve self-sufficiency. ◆ "Over the years we've looked at different ways to do this, particularly since the funding is not as plentiful today as it was in the earlier days. We do more collaboration efforts with other agencies, in an effort to pool our resources as well as build partnerships. And one thing we do differently is to look at the community's capacity to build on its strengths, to help reduce the need for services to the community. ◆ "One of our major programs involving the community is the DeKalb Neighborhood Leadership Institute. Here, the DeKalb EOA works with potential leaders of low-income communities to help them develop skills and techniques for making a difference in their own neighborhoods. Graduates of the Institute actually manage and run the program through their volunteer efforts. ◆ "I don't think people feel good about themselves if they are just on the receiving end all the time. And that's why the Leadership Institute works. We are building self-esteem when people are able to see themselves as contributing members of society. And in nine years, we have trained over 200 citizens to help lead their communities. ◆ "Our largest program, monetarily, is Head Start. Last year, we served 515 children, ages three and four, from poverty backgrounds. What we try to do is remove any barriers to learning for these children, so that they are ready to take advantage of school. And we now see a much larger percentage of Head Start children actually graduating from high school and experiencing fewer teenage pregnancies and other social problems than is the norm outside of Head Start participants. Too, more of our graduates are going to college, or into employment after graduating from high school. I can think of no better investment. ◆ "Annually, the DeKalb EOA helps over 4,500 low-income citizens of all ages, with an annual budget of $6.2 milllion. And through programs that target homelessness, employment and job readiness, home weatherization and home repair, as well as crisis intervention services such as food, rent, clothing and temporary shelter, we touch the hearts and souls and faces of poverty in DeKalb County."

— Lois J. Burns, Executive Director

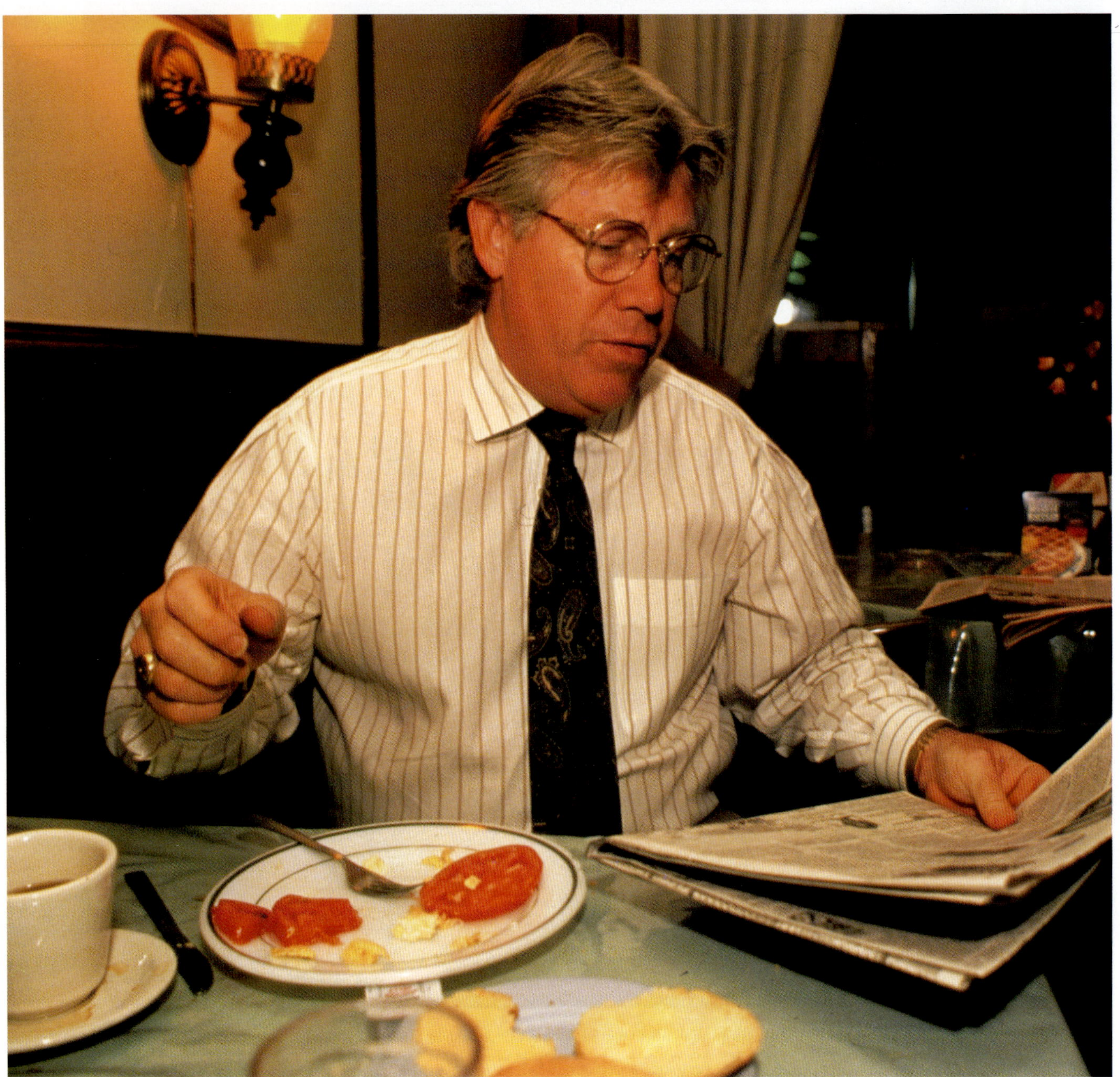

"I thank God every day I have," says Liane Levetan, two months away from being elected the first female chief executive officer of DeKalb County, a distinction she will have earned nearly seven years after life-saving surgery for breast cancer. "What I've always wanted to do is work for my county and see it come to the forefront. I love that."

Levetan, who began this day at 6 A.M. when WSB Radio sounded from her radio alarm clock, will

7:00 AM *Mike Mears starts every Monday at the Square Table restaurant in downtown Decatur. Breakfast is a rare quiet moment in a day of dual roles for Mears who is both mayor of the city of Decatur and the state's public defender of death penalty cases. Mears has made a reputation for himself on both fronts. For ten years he has been at the helm in DeKalb's county seat, promoting a liberal agenda. He makes no apologies. "I don't like the term liberal. I've always considered myself a radical; that's a little to the left of liberal."* PHOTO BY DAVID MURRAY.

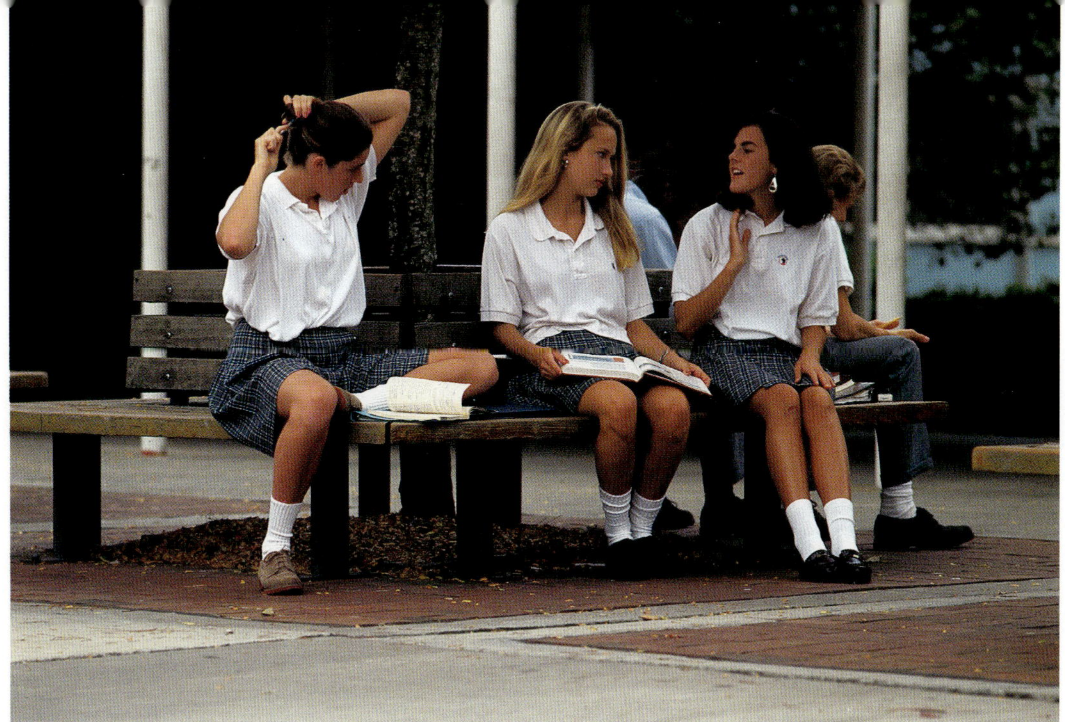

7:50 AM *The difference in students at St. Pius X Catholic High School is more than just a style of dress. Atlanta's only Catholic high school emphasizes community service, as well as quality education. St. Pius students participate in Campus Ministry outreach projects. They build houses with Habitat for Humanity, volunteer in soup kitchens and homeless shelters and work with the elderly. "We aim at producing educated, mature, involved, Christian students who can go out into the world and be leaders," says Principal Donald Sasso.* PHOTO BY MICHAEL SCHWARZ.

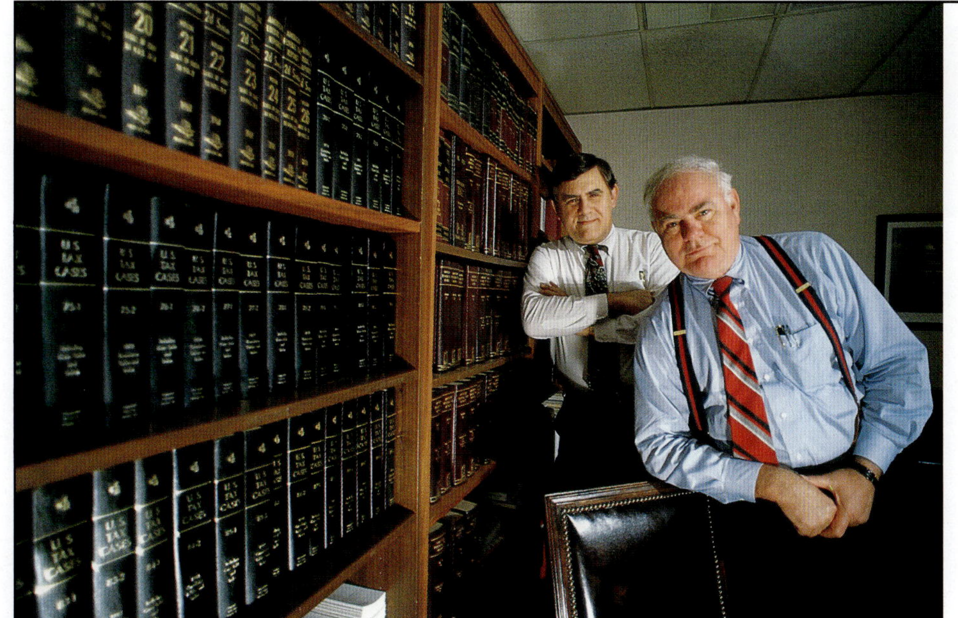

ALAN WEINER

GLADNEY & HEMRICK, P.C.

Certified Public Accountants

since 1971

The professional services we perform center primarily on the financial aspects of our clients' affairs. We place significant emphasis on the basic business facts and consider marketing as well as operational factors in developing professional advice that is individualized to each client's requirements. ◆ "Our belief is that through partnering with small business clients we can assist in the successful growth of each client's business, by providing out-sourcing of business functions to more effectively achieve business objectives, which is a front-burner business necessity. Our goal is accomplishing successful results in a quality, cost-effective and timely manner. ◆ "The professional services we offer fall into five general categories: accounting and auditing, tax services, monthly client services, management advisory services, and financial planning. ◆ "Small business financial consulting and personal income tax management represent over half of our business. The balance of our business is represented by estate tax administration and planning, employee benefit plan administration and annual audits and reporting. We have never tried to specialize in a specific industry, and I think we have been able to manage the economic downturn because we are not overly focused in any particular industry. Which doesn't mean we haven't had to quickly react to the economy, though. ◆ "In 1979, our firm merged with the practice of David C. Hemrick, Jr. It was then that we at Gladney & Hemrick increased our accounting and auditing for local government cities, counties, and school districts. Mr. Hemrick retired nearly eight years ago. And while most of our audit work is done from our DeKalb office, we also have a full-service office in Athens."

— William D. Gladney, C.P.A., Founder of Gladney & Hemrick

Pictured are William D. Gladney, founder, and Ernest R. Barefield, partner

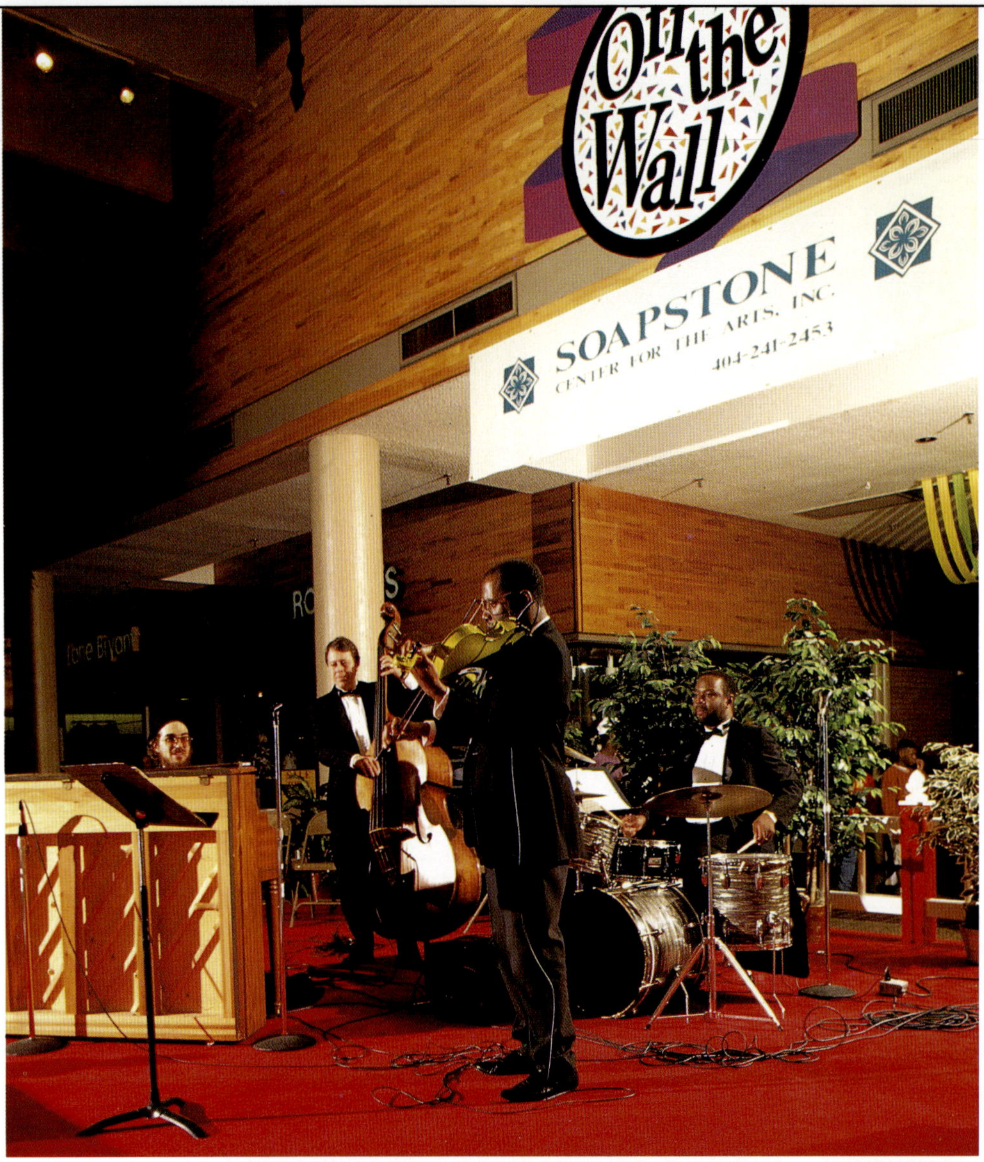

SCOTT ROBINSON

At South DeKalb Mall, we consider ourselves a community. Just like the town squares were in the fifties and sixties, and the fast food restaurants were in the seventies, the shopping center is very much the center of a lot of different towns. Without question, South DeKalb Mall is the town center of South DeKalb. ◆ "Here, you see anything from voter registration drives to jazz concerts, to modern dance to visual arts festivals. Our smorgasbord of activities directly relates to the customers we serve. ◆ "We have actively positioned ourselves as a shopping center that serves Atlanta's African-American community. And given that shopping center management is always evolutionary, we are not yet where we should be — but we are presently doing it better than anyone else. ◆ "South DeKalb Mall appeals to Atlanta's African-American consumer, made up predominantly of South DeKalb residents. Our customers are very much middle-class, educated, up-and-coming customers with an average yearly income in excess of $46,000. ◆ "South DeKalb is a relatively young, vibrant, emerging community, with arguably the most affluent, middle to upper middle-class African-Americans in the country. Too, we have a lower income African-American shopping base, as well as a retired, Caucasian American shopping center base. And we do have a strong customer contingency from the southwest and southeast Atlanta city areas. ◆ "Another important component of this shopping center strategy is our commitment to developing minority-owned businesses. In only three years our entrepreneurial marketplace, such as our cart vendors, has grown to average twenty carts weekly, of which 95 percent are African-American owned. Led by Mall Manager, Robert Grahamslaw, and myself, we have to ensure that the merchants reflect the community as well as the customer base. ◆ "The African-American shopper is no different from any other shopper. They expect excellent products, competitive pricing, quality service, safety and a wonderful, fun environment. And we stand committed to ensuring that our business standards continue to grow, and that South DeKalb Mall has the stores that our customers want. ◆ "We won't rest on our laurels."

— Wendell Kimbrough, Marketing Director

SOUTH DEKALB MALL

More than 100 stores and over 20 cart vendors

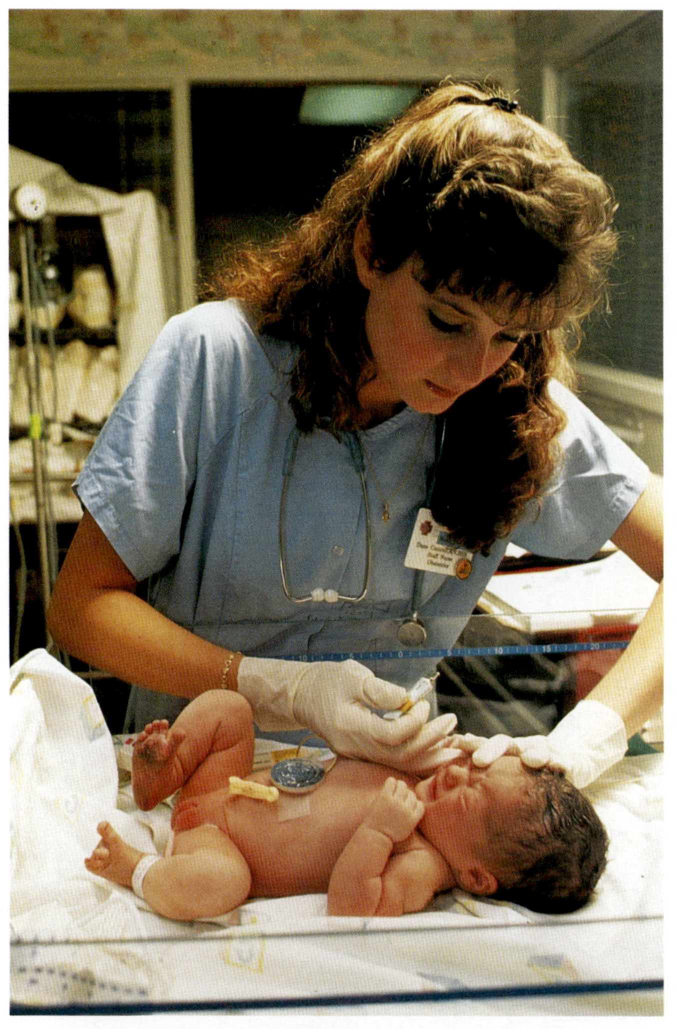

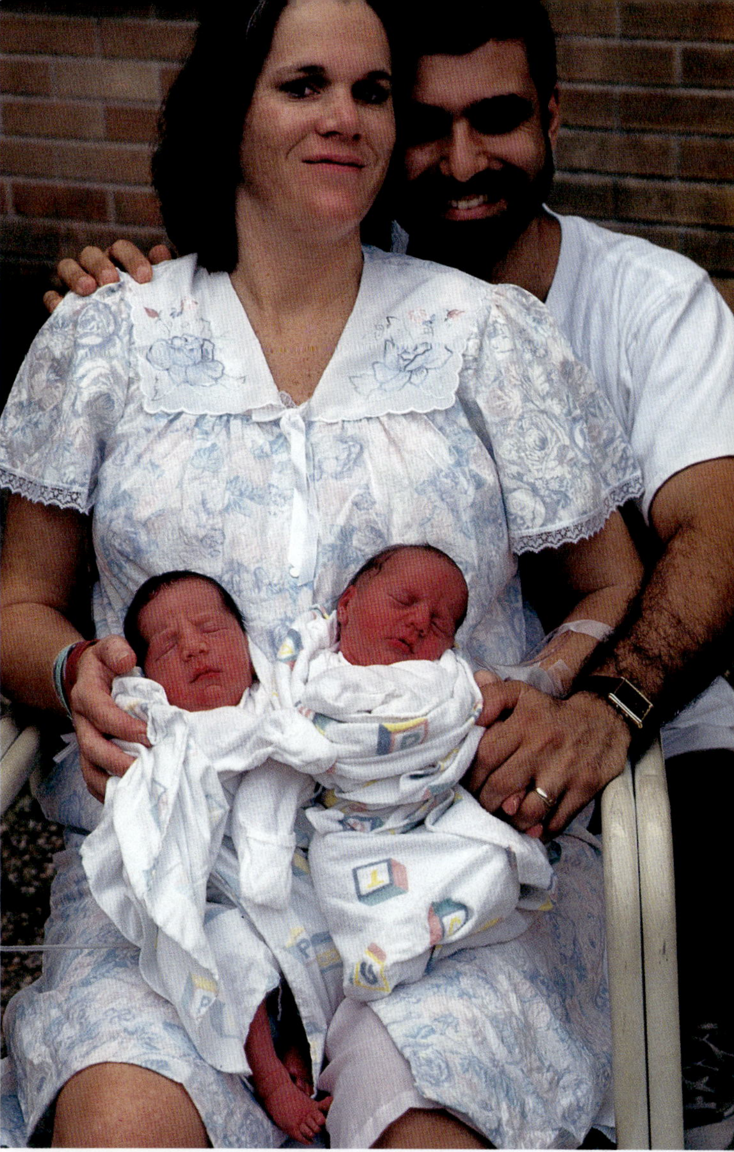

10:02 AM *The month of September saw 249 babies—including three sets of twins—born at DeKalb Medical Center. What began as a 200-bed community hospital in 1961 has more than doubled in size, and is now the fifth largest medical center in Georgia. Summer of 1993 saw the opening of a $15.3 million surgery and maternity center. The center will provide a homelike setting where mothers can labor, deliver and recover. Babies can remain with their mothers, and fathers can stay overnight. Here, Mr. and Mrs. Kenneth Boccaccio shows off their new twins, Dominic Evan (left) and Dana Lynne Boccaccio, and obstetrics nurse Dana Cantrell takes a newborn's footprint for its first official ID.*

PHOTOS BY TOM ENGLAND.

replace Manuel Maloof as DeKalb CEO, a job Maloof claimed for eight years. She will preside over a county that *Time* magazine picked as one of five "bellwether" suburban counties during the 1992 presidential election, on the theory that as DeKalb voters go, so goes the nation. And, indeed, it did. President Bill Clinton received 59 percent of the votes cast by DeKalb County's eclectic population—a mix of rich and poor, black and white, rural and urban, longtime residents and ethnically diverse newcomers.

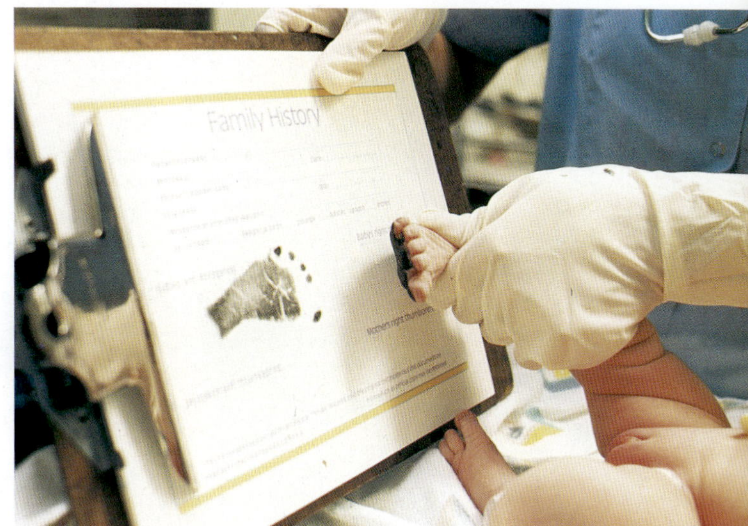

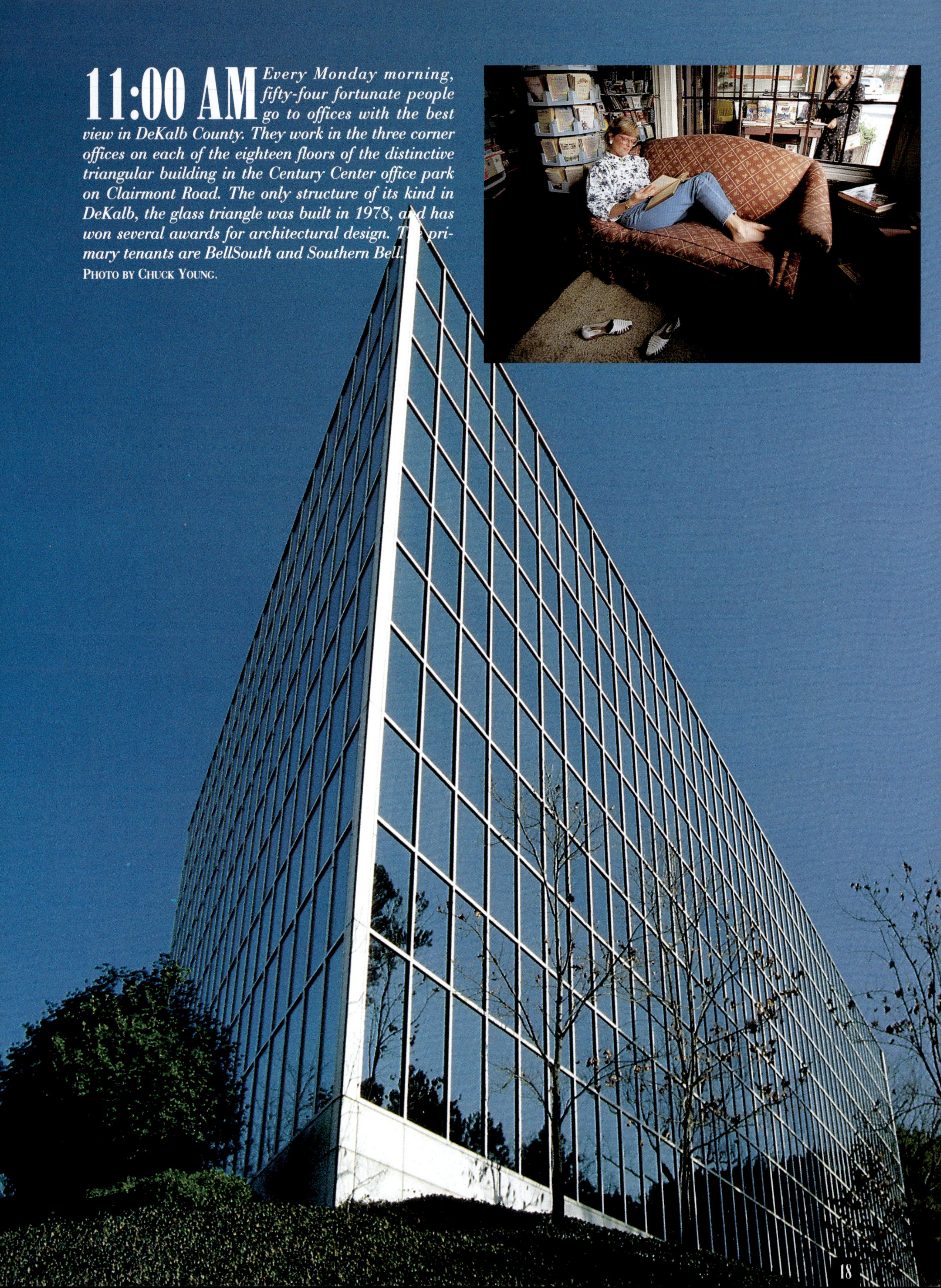

11:00 AM *Every Monday morning, fifty-four fortunate people go to offices with the best view in DeKalb County. They work in the three corner offices on each of the eighteen floors of the distinctive triangular building in the Century Center office park on Clairmont Road. The only structure of its kind in DeKalb, the glass triangle was built in 1978, and has won several awards for architectural design. The primary tenants are BellSouth and Southern Bell.*

PHOTO BY CHUCK YOUNG.

2:05 PM *A sofa by a sunny window entices many a customer at Shakespeare & Company bookstore, such as accountant Kimberley Colvard, to take time out of a Monday with a good book. Outside, Beatrice Nardone of Avondale Estates reviews some of the day's sampling. Unlike its chain-store counterparts, Shakespeare & Company encourages patrons to browse through and even read selections from its eclectic collection of volumes. Says the store manager: "I look at it as a haven for people to come relax and enter another world—the world of books."*

PHOTO BY KEN HAWKINS.

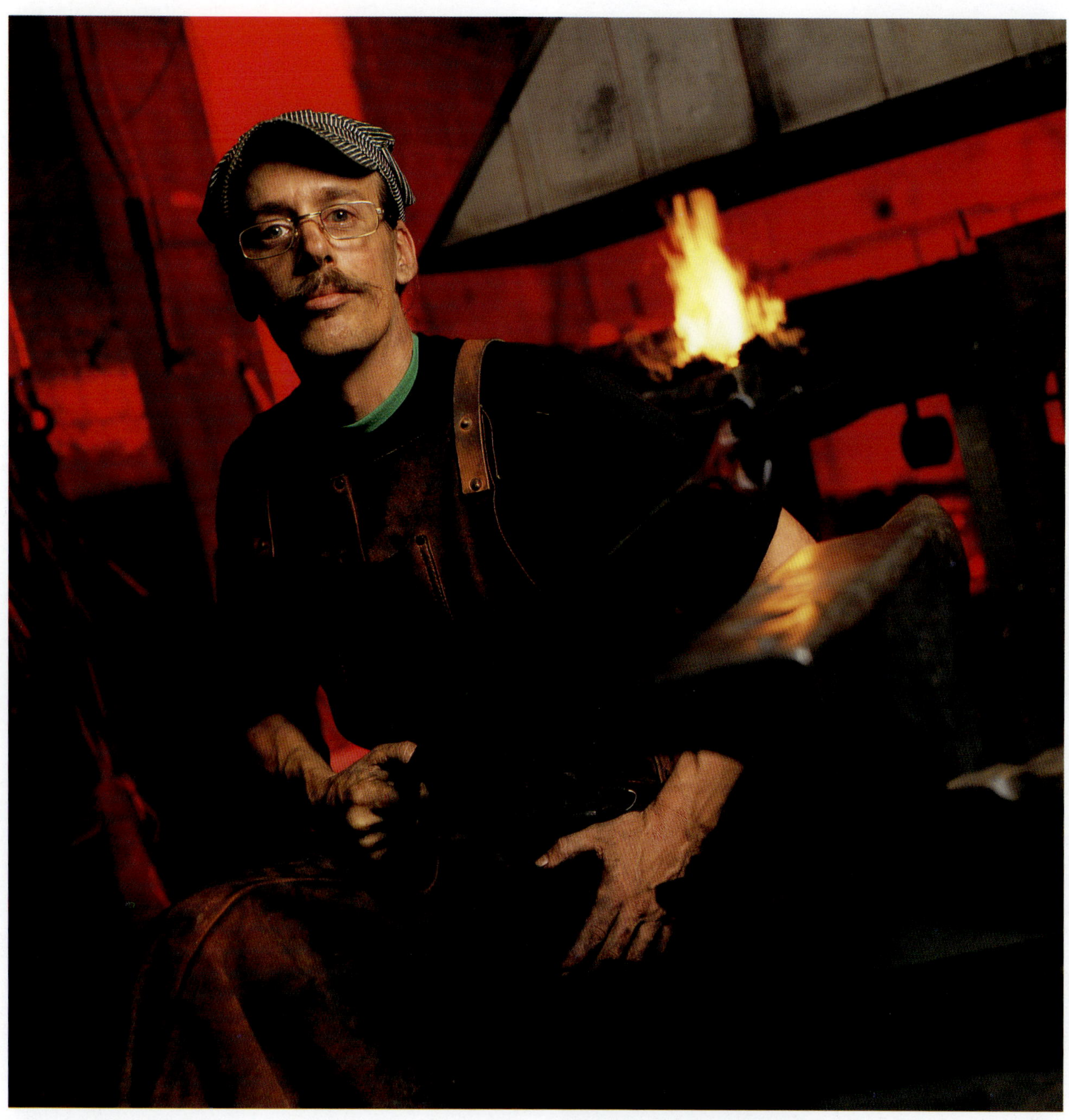

2:40 PM *As a "traditional modern smithy," Bo Weaver does everything—"from fixing lawn furniture to making trees that look like they're alive." Weaver is one of only four blacksmiths in Atlanta, preserving a craft that dates back centuries. The half-Cherokee, half-Scottish Tennessee native plies his trade in what once was a gasoline station in Chamblee's Antique Row. Weaver says Chamblee's small town atmosphere provides a wholesome place to teach his young son about blacksmithing.*

PHOTO BY ANN STATES.

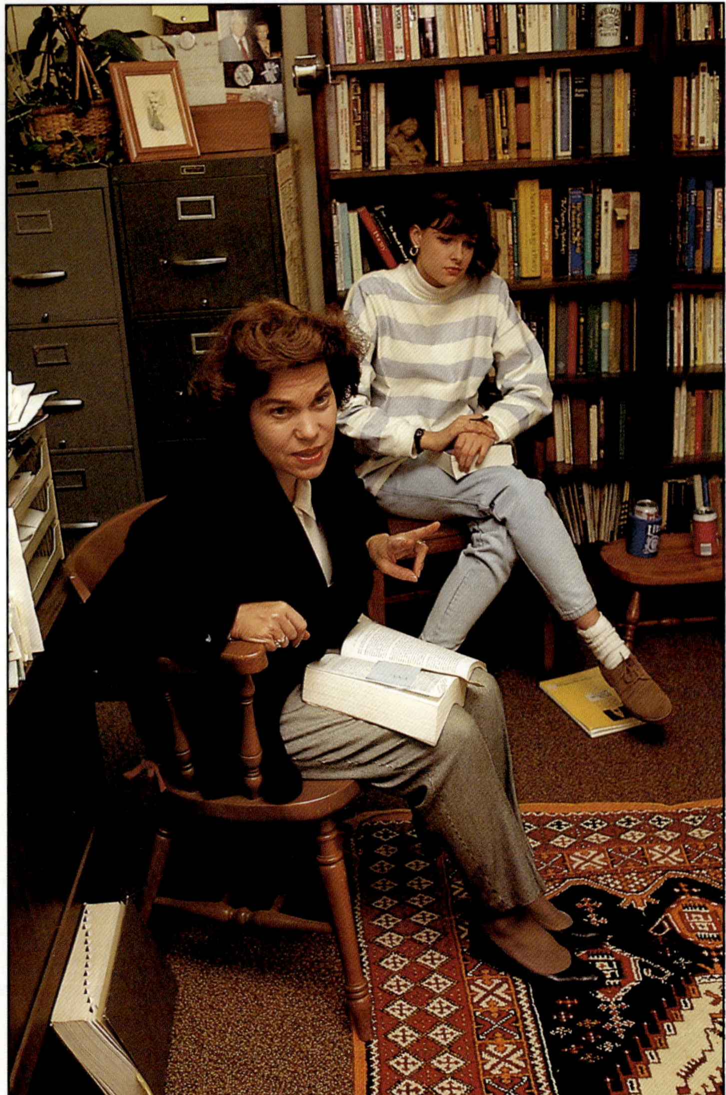
ALAN WEINER

Since Agnes Scott's founding in 1889, the institution has filled an important place in the life of the community. ◆ "Today, we serve many women from the local area who see a women's college as understanding their life's situation. Since we began our Return to College program in the early seventies, it has grown considerably. Nearly one hundred of our 600 women students are more than twenty-five years old. ◆ "I consider these women a real resource. They attend college part-time or full-time, and they may take college in stages, instead of four years straight. Most are between their late twenties and fifties, and the cross-generational friendships that form are enriching for both returning and traditional-age students. ◆ "Of course, students also come to Agnes Scott from many other states and countries and make this their home. They love the Atlanta area, and many of them choose to stay. ◆ "Agnes Scott is a fairly important employer in the county, with 300 full and part-time employees. The combination of the payroll and our demand for goods and services necessary to operate the college results in a significant economic impact. ◆ "Also, as a cultural resource for the community, we've always presented quality music, dance and art on our stages and in Dalton Gallery. We are trying to open up our outdoor track an hour more a day for the community's use for walking and jogging. ◆ "Agnes Scott College's door is open to the community and from all indications, the community knows that."

— Ruth A. Schmidt,

AGNES SCOTT COLLEGE

One of the nation's top ten women's colleges, ranked third among all U.S. colleges and universities in resources per student.

The county that threw its support behind the new president runs on a $270 million yearly budget, two dozen departments and over 6,000 employees. In addition to the CEO, seven elected officials make up the County Commission, with commissioners from five regular and two "super" districts that overlap the five smaller ones. An independent chunk of Atlanta pokes into the west side of DeKalb, and each of the county's eight municipalities—Doraville, Chamblee, Clarkston, Decatur, Stone Mountain, Pine Lake, Avondale Estates and Lithonia—is governed by its own mayor and city council.

As CEO of DeKalb County, Levetan knows she must grapple with a county that is, at times, a pure study in contrasts.

In the last forty years, DeKalb has changed from a largely rural area to a county wrestling with urban versus suburban growth. While pockets of the county are still racially segregated, today's DeKalb is today widely touted as Georgia's most ethnically diverse county, faced with the growing business, housing and literacy needs of its Asian and Hispanic populations. Levetan knows that transients in the county have been blamed for recent crime waves in Clarkston, while John Lawson, the mayor of tranquil Avondale Estates, claims they've had no violent crime in over fifty years. Homelessness and a 6.3 percent unemployment rate trouble DeKalb, which also boasts 425 internationally based companies, representation by 375 of the Fortune 500 companies and an anticipated job growth of 5 percent by 1994. And while stately neighborhoods like Dunwoody and Druid Hills will forever be associated with wealth and money, Levetan is aware that community leaders are working to change the image of a relatively impoverished South DeKalb to progressive DeKalb South.

3:15 PM *In the Village of Stone Mountain, "old" not only is revered, it is incorporated into the everyday life of people who live and work in "The Village." City Hall is housed in an old railroad depot which is a regular stop on the run of the New Georgia Railroad's excursion train. The Village Visitors Center is a bright red caboose, and the visual and performing arts center is housed in a building once used to store and repair trolleys. Nowhere else in DeKalb can you find such novelties as handmade dulcimers, Civil War relics, mason jars and porch rockers. Here, Jeannie Stewart of Stone Mountain is making an afternoon of the village's delights.* PHOTO BY DAVID MURRAY.

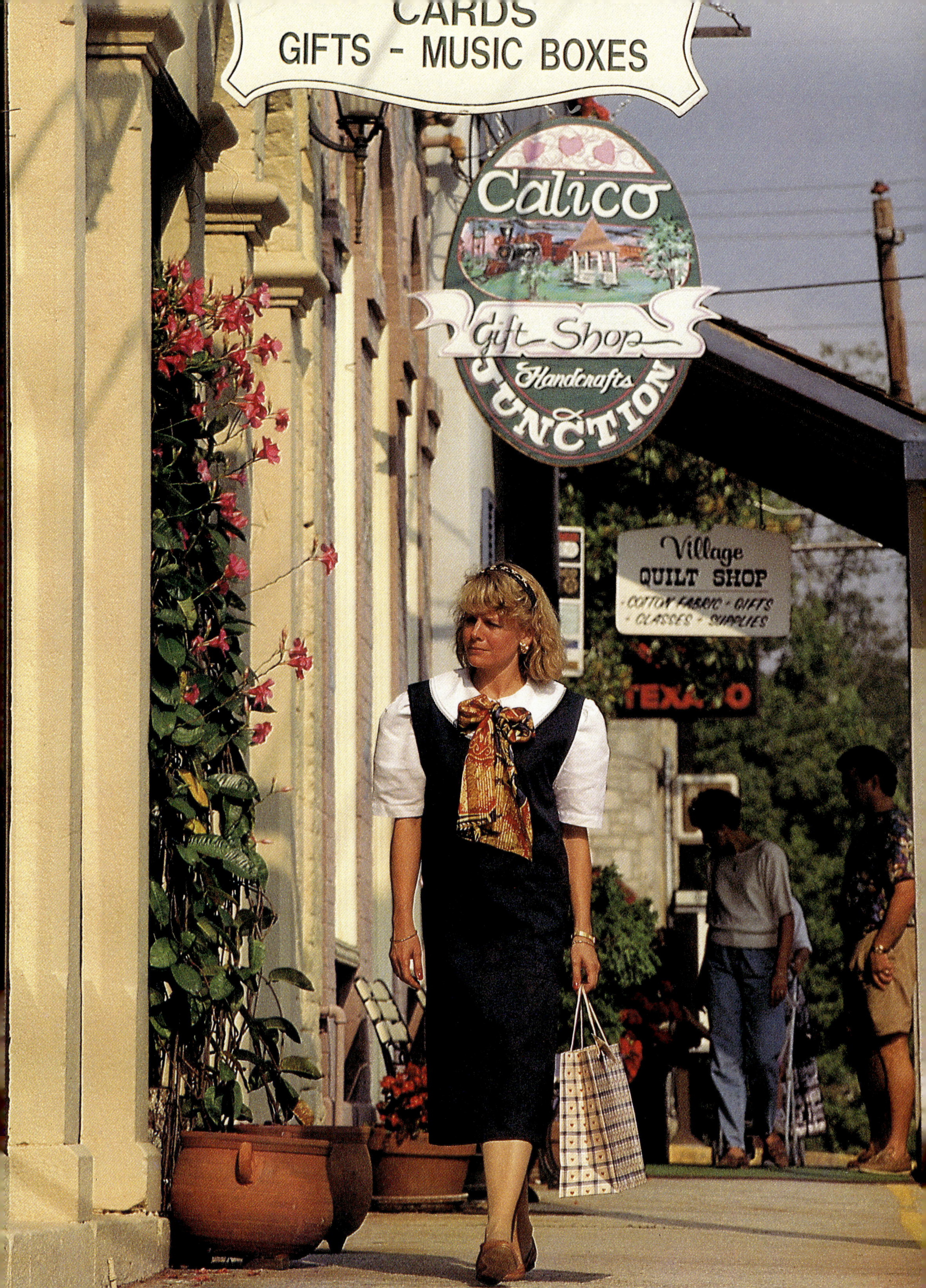
CARDS
GIFTS - MUSIC BOXES
Calico
Gift Shop
Handcrafts
JUNCTION
Village
QUILT SHOP
COTTON FABRIC - GIFTS
CLASSES - SUPPLIES

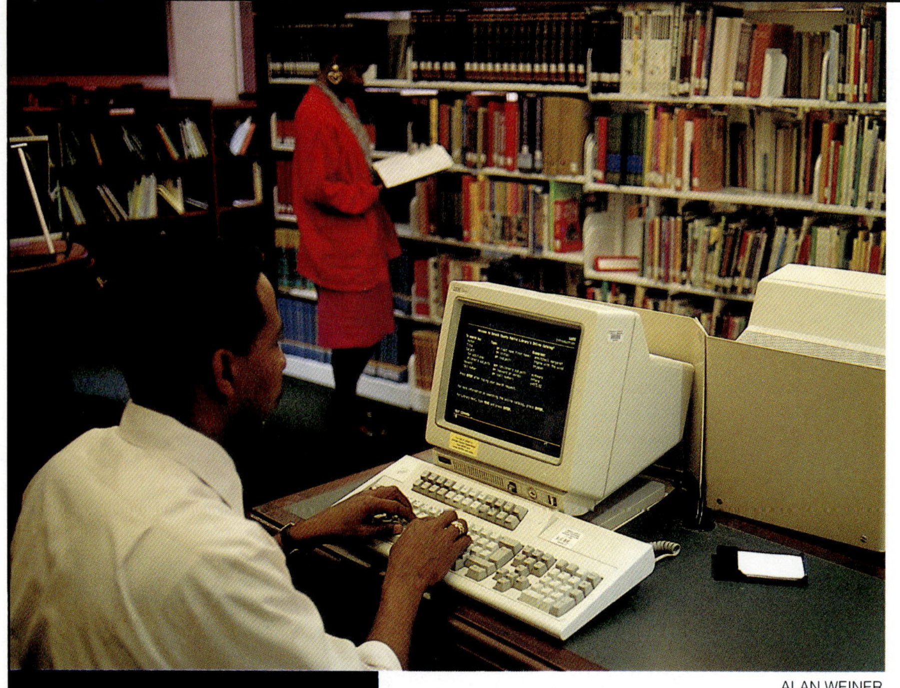

ALAN WEINER

The public library system plays a vital role in this community. The first thing you notice is our beautiful new buildings — but look inside. We are active and involved. We have a dedicated, highly skilled staff, unlimited access to materials from any branch, and we are dedicated to providing information through the latest technology available. ◆ "This is the one place the general public can come for their informational needs. Library patrons can come in and, with little or no technical knowledge, find their way through our user-friendly computer system to find books, access information through CD ROM, or link into a nation-wide or local network to achieve almost unlimited access to information. ◆ "Our libraries are community places, strongly supported by Friends of the Library. We provide specialized services based on branch location, and meeting rooms for town meetings and other gatherings. We want everyone to feel they are a part of the library. ◆ "Our libraries are also family places, where families can visit together to expand their knowledge, and where federally funded literacy services are provided. ◆ "Thanks to our five-year, $29 million expansion program, we've grown from twelve branches to twenty-six, and we've been able to locate libraries in communities previously lacking one. We now circulate more than 2.7 million books and other materials per year. ◆ "If there is a bottom line, perhaps it is that no one should think of DeKalb County Public Library as a place to come and 'be quiet.' This is a place to come and get involved."

— Donna D. Mancini, Library Director

THE DEKALB COUNTY PUBLIC LIBRARY

26 branches; 1 million books; 3 million users annually

On this Monday morning, Levetan acknowledges none of these issues as problems. "The word is *challenges*. I don't have the word *problems* in my vernacular. Sure we've got challenges. The number one issue is jobs and economic development at a time when—let's call it the way it is—we don't have a booming economy throughout the nation. But DeKalb is very unique. It's extremely strategically located, and has a good infrastructure in place. And while we're a mature county, we still have room to grow."

In DeKalb County, growth is evident. On Monday afternoon, engineers and road crews are literally pounding the pavement on $52 million of road-construction projects. Officials at Fernbank's fabulous $42.8 million Museum of Natural History are besieged by last-minute details and a massive clean-up effort before the October 5 grand opening. Along Memorial Drive at Camp Circle, the first skyline silhouettes of four towers appear at the site of the new 1,974-cell county jail, the largest public building project ever in DeKalb and one of the largest jails in the United States. Black tar paper covers the new building facade at DeKalb Medical Center, where workers are also building a new surgery and obstetrics pavilion scheduled to open in mid-1993. And in Lithonia, the management of the first minority-founded and controlled bank in Georgia in sixty years, has all but announced that First Southern Bank will open its first branch office.

The county, however, does not measure its success by bricks and mortar alone.

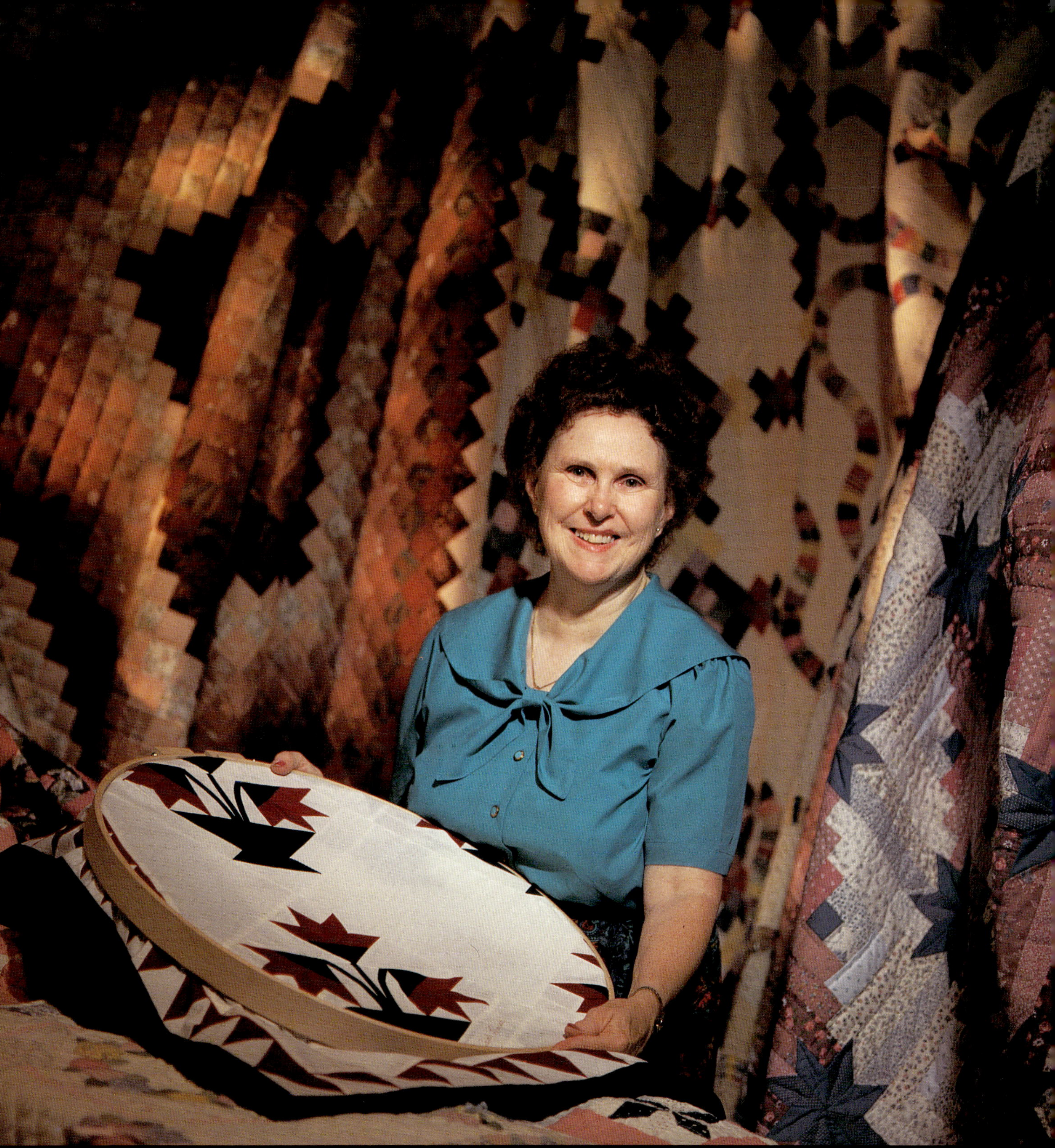

4:00 PM *The Village Quilt Shop in the Village of Stone Mountain specializes in preserving the genteel art of quilting. But, don't expect quilters to be gentle when it comes to fighting what they consider to be unfair. Quilts in traditional American patterns are being manufactured overseas and sold in the United States at prices below those of American handmade quilts. Village Quilt Shop customers recently participated in a nationwide petition drive which resulted in concessions from the Smithsonian Institute, one of the importers of foreign quilts. Says quilt-shop owner Joyce Selin, "That's our heritage. We're trying to protect what's ours."* Photo by Ann States

Today, the latest issue of *U.S. News & World Report* announces that Emory University, the 156-year-old "Harvard of the South," is one of the top twenty-five universities in the nation. Hall's Flower Shop and Garden Center, located for a quarter of a century on the same fourteen acres outside Stone Mountain, is among the top hundred FTD florists nationwide; plugs for spring and summertime perennials went into the ground today. DeKalb-Peachtree Airport is Georgia's second busiest airport, yet so conveniently located to downtown Atlanta that airport directors claim passengers can land and be at a business meeting in Buckhead in twelve minutes. From all over the world, collectors of Native American artifacts make their way to a nondescript building in a strip of junk stores, garages and launderettes on Avondale Road; outside, the sign says "Ray's TVs," but inside, "Ray's Indian Originals" is a veritable paradise of baskets, kachina dolls, jewelry, pottery and a rare beaded bag so precious to its owners that even $20,000 from Whoopi Goldberg couldn't buy it. "Every piece," says owner Ray Belcher, "has a story."

And like every good story, Monday in DeKalb comes to a close, ending in rush hour traffic, dinner, family and meetings.

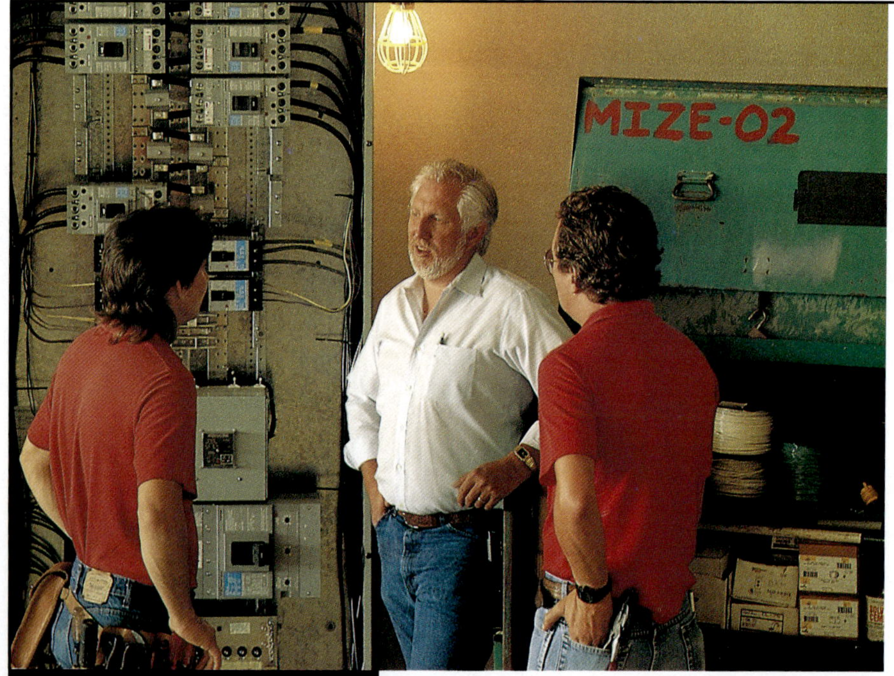

SCOTT ROBINSON

T. H. MIZE ELECTRIC COMPANY

Nine employees,
Twenty-four hour emergency service

I began working in the electrical industry in 1971, after graduating from Clarkston High School, as an electrician's helper. My father was an electrician and helped me get started in the electrical industry. ◆ "I chose the electrical industry mainly to provide a living, but then founded T. H. Mize Electric Company in 1984. I enjoy being an electrician and take pride in doing a good job, a quality job, satisfying our customers. I like the challenge of wiring different types of equipment and then watching the equipment operate properly. ◆ "We specialize in commercial and industrial accounts, working with customers in the design and building phases of retail strip centers, hospitals, restaurants, and other industries. I especially enjoy meeting customers and solving their electrical problems and needs. ◆ "I'm proud that while electricians tend to move around a lot, ours don't. My lead electricians have been with me six and seven years. My wife, Bobi, and my brother, Linley, work with me in the office. My brother, Timothy, works with me in the field as an electrician. ◆ "I have lived in DeKalb County most of my life, and I enjoy working in DeKalb County. While there is almost always someone out there who will do the job cheaper, customer satisfaction may not always be achieved. At T. H. Mize Electric Company, we strive for quality more than quantity. Most of all, we are committed to total customer satisfaction."

— Thomas Hudson Mize, Owner

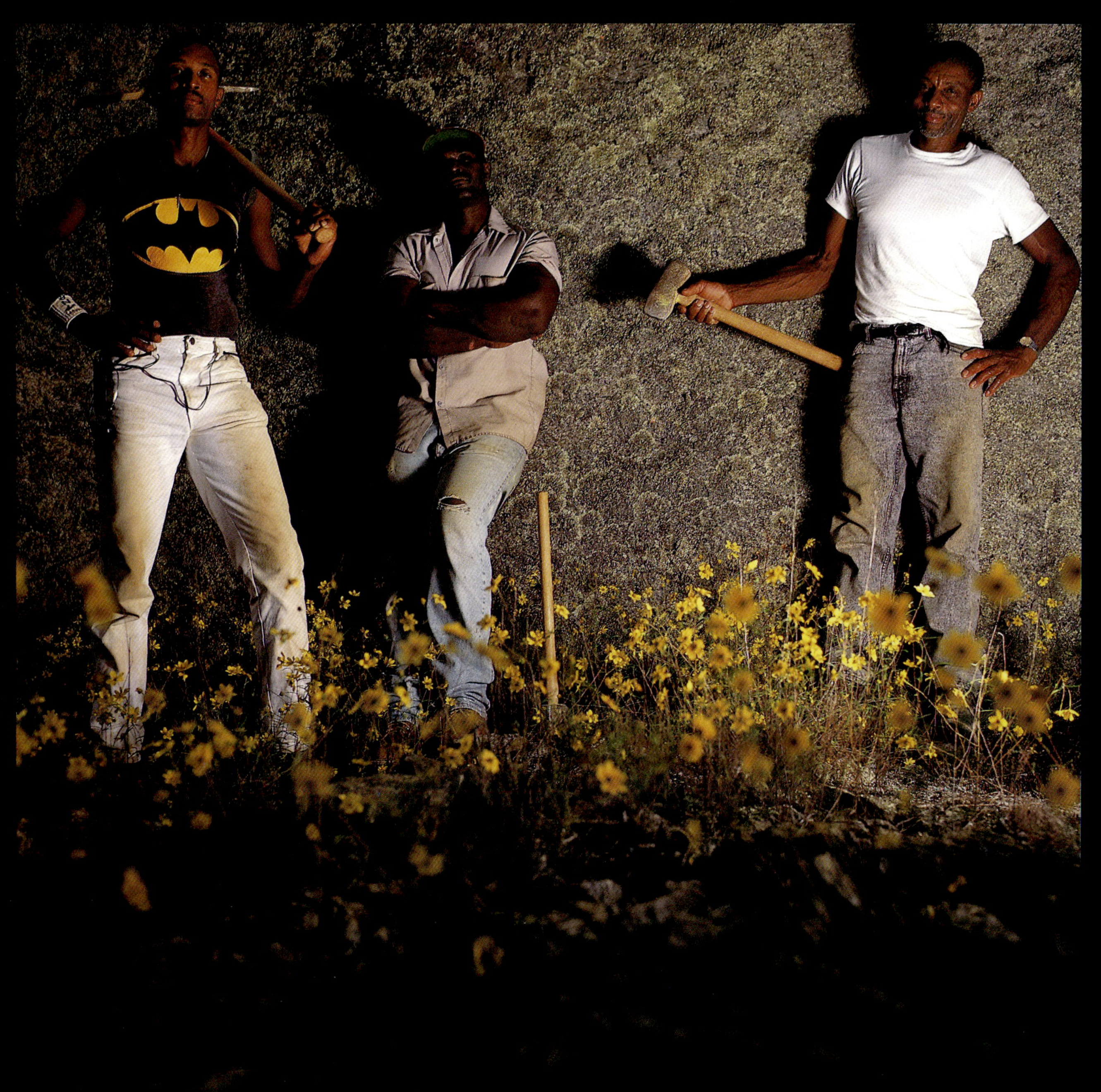

5:48 PM *Stonemasons Reggie Kilgore, his father, cousins and two uncles still work the granite of Stone Mountain the way it's always been done—with sledgehammers and a knowledge of the stone passed down through generations. Reggie and his brother Phillip Kilgore, pictured here, are third generation Lithonia stonecutters, having learned the trade from their father Judge Kilgore (also pictured) who was taught by his father Gus Kilgore. It takes four to five years to master stonecutting, Reggie says, but the rewards are many, including pride in workmanship that can be seen, literally, around the world.*

PHOTO BY ANN STATES.

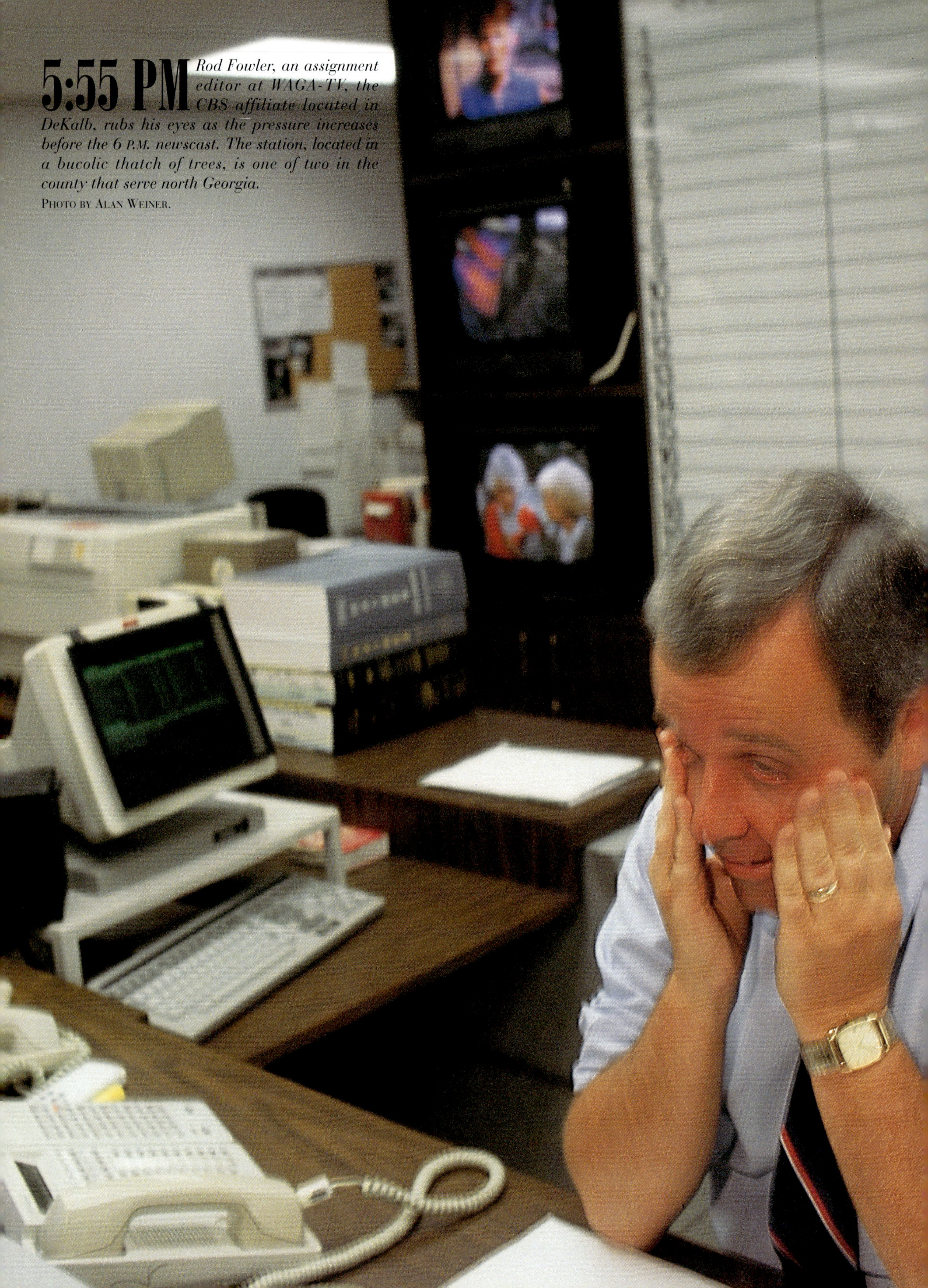

5:55 PM *Rod Fowler, an assignment editor at WAGA-TV, the CBS affiliate located in DeKalb, rubs his eyes as the pressure increases before the 6 P.M. newscast. The station, located in a bucolic thatch of trees, is one of two in the county that serve north Georgia.*

Photo by Alan Weiner.

Around 6 P.M., Liane Levetan fairly bursts off the elevator and into a roomful of doctors gathered for a political forum at the DeKalb County Medical Society, interrupting their happy hour with her firm handshakes and convincing small talk. Judy Boone's fourteen-hour workday finally ends after a party for United Parcel Service at the Holiday Inn Crowne Plaza Ravinia. Michael Pumilia, Georgia's senior obedience judge for the American Kennel Club, barks out commands ("Call 'em and drop 'em. Heel!") to the three dogs and three owners in his class at the Atlanta Obedience Club in Chamblee. "Turn up your hearing aids!" Marge Custance, president of the largest chapter of the American

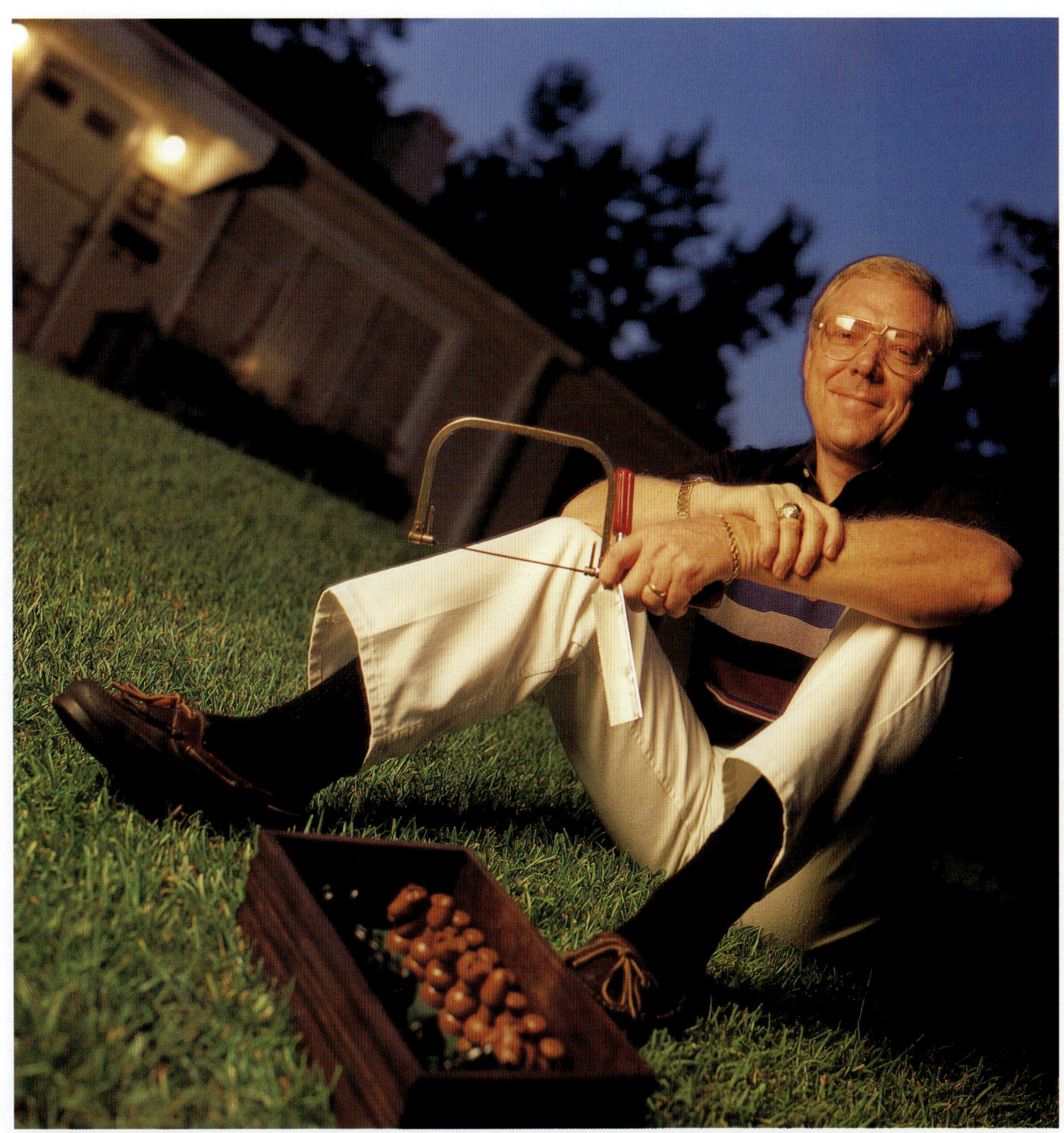

7:35 PM *John Lawson has been carving wood since he was child. His "daddy liked to whittle," and he "just got a knife and started." Lawson carves to relax from the rigors of his dual career as a civil and criminal trial lawyer and part-time mayor of Avondale Estates, an elected post he has held since 1988. The mayor says this chess set, which took a year of carving, is his favorite work. The demand for his work is great, but "if it gets to be a business, it isn't relaxing any more," he says.*

PHOTO BY GREG FOSTER.

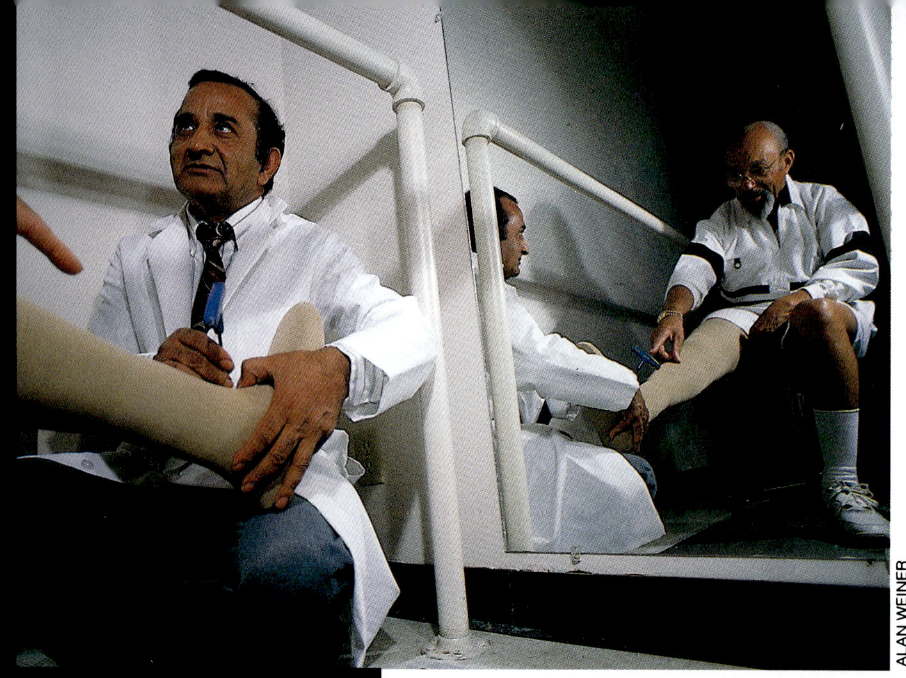

AMERICAN PROSTHETICS, INC.

Founded by Hanif Chaudhary, Certified Prosthetist
Offering high-quality prosthetic and orthotic services

For twenty-five years I have been in the prosthetic and orthotic field. I always wanted to work helping people and felt this field was unique because it gives people a new life. ◆ "While in Pakistan I learned about a new training program in prosthetics and orthotics. I was accepted into the program, and from there I had training in England, Scotland and later at Northwestern University Medical School in Chicago. I decided to come to the United States and establish my profession, and I eventually came to Georgia. In March 1986, I founded American Prosthetics, Inc., in DeKalb County. ◆ "Over the years, the prosthetic technology has changed a lot. Today, there are more hi-tech materials available, which are more functional and attractive. With the new technology we are able to fit amputees with a more functional prosthesis. For instance, here are some comments from one of our patients, Arthur G. Kinnebrew, seventy-four: ◆ 'On December 16, 1985, while standing behind my car, a semi-tractor trailer jackknifed in the road and came straight into my parked car. The truck hit my left leg against the bumper of the car and took the leg off, right then and there. My surgeon thought I would never be able to wear a prosthesis, but after rehabilitation I was able to wear one in 1986. It was painful to wear, and I could only wear the prosthesis to go to church, on crutches. ◆ 'I moved from Detroit to the Atlanta area in 1987 and met with Mr. Chaudhary a couple months later. After patiently listening to me, he surmised my prosthesis could be modified to compensate for the way my stump was projecting. He did that with a new socket that cradled my fatty tissue. It was so much better! Since that time, we have perfected my prosthesis with lighter materials and modifications. I can now wear my prosthesis all day. Mr. Chaudhary helped me get my life back.' ◆ "Like Mr. Kinnebrew, 99 percent of the people who come into my office are successful in wearing a prosthesis. The joy in their faces when they realize that is quite special."

— Hanif Chaudhary, President

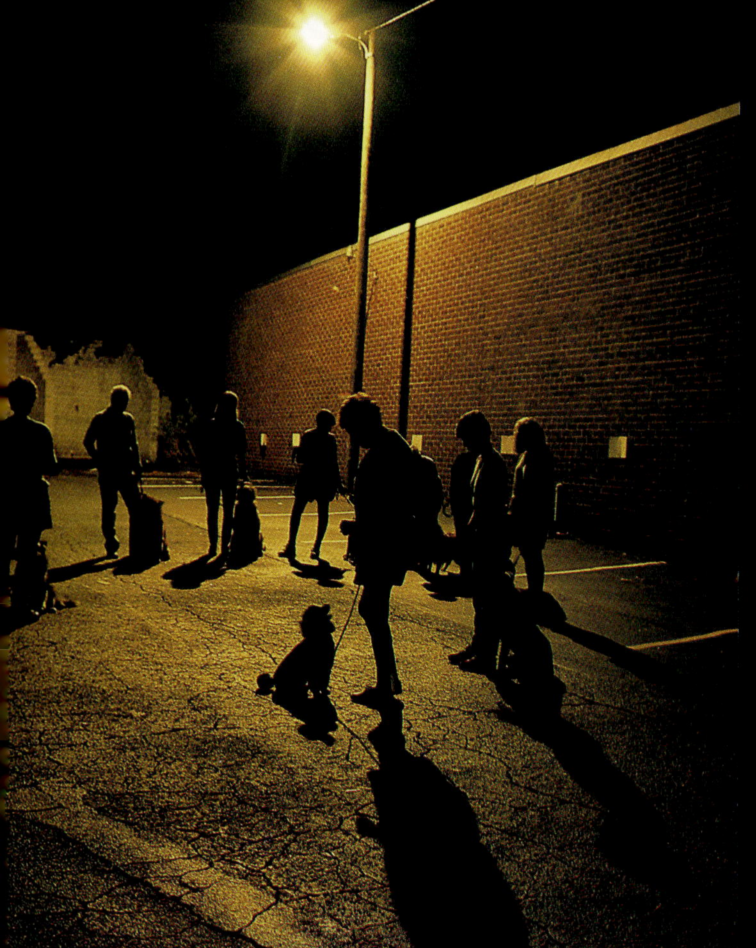

8:40 PM *Monday night is beginners night at the Atlanta Obedience Club where patient instructors work at turning a roomful of excitable pets and their doting owners into models of canine conduct and puppy parenting. The 100-member club, which holds classes in a Chamblee warehouse, has been in business since 1950. Owners can be more reluctant than pets to give up their bad habits, according to training director Kathy Kilgallon. "It's hard to tell an owner he can't baby his dog. Raising a dog is like raising a child. Sometimes you have to be firm."*

PHOTO BY KEN HAWKINS.

Association of Retired Persons in the Southeast, jokes playfully with 140 AARP members in the Oak Grove Church Fellowship Hall, a captive audience for guest speaker Georgia Attorney General Michael Bowers.

Doraville Mayor Gene Lively wears a blue plaid shirt, boots, jeans and a gold Atlanta Falcons emblem around his neck as he calls the Doraville City Council meeting to order, just as the clock strikes eight. Tonight's agenda? Street hockey, billboard advertisements, the high cost of computer equipment and a proposed law designed to prohibit something everyone in DeKalb has an opinion about: nude dancing. This particular ordinance defines lewdness in great detail. "Everyone says we don't want any nude dancing in Doraville," says city attorney Ed Carter.

And in Decatur, the four Turner girls are tucked in bed about the same time that Mayor Michael Mears presides over a twelve-item City Commission agenda that includes honoring the Decatur Teacher of the Year (Clairemont Elementary School Teacher Vivian M. Stephens); a new development plan at 917 Scott Boulevard (tabled); safety in and around Decatur's MARTA station; designation of Decatur as a sister city with Trujillo, Peru (passed); and an ordinance that sets the property assessment ratio at 40 percent (passed).

In due course, the first city government to put its commission meetings on television calls it a night. After all, everyone wants to get home in time to see Murphy Brown admonish Dan Quayle on the CBS season opener.

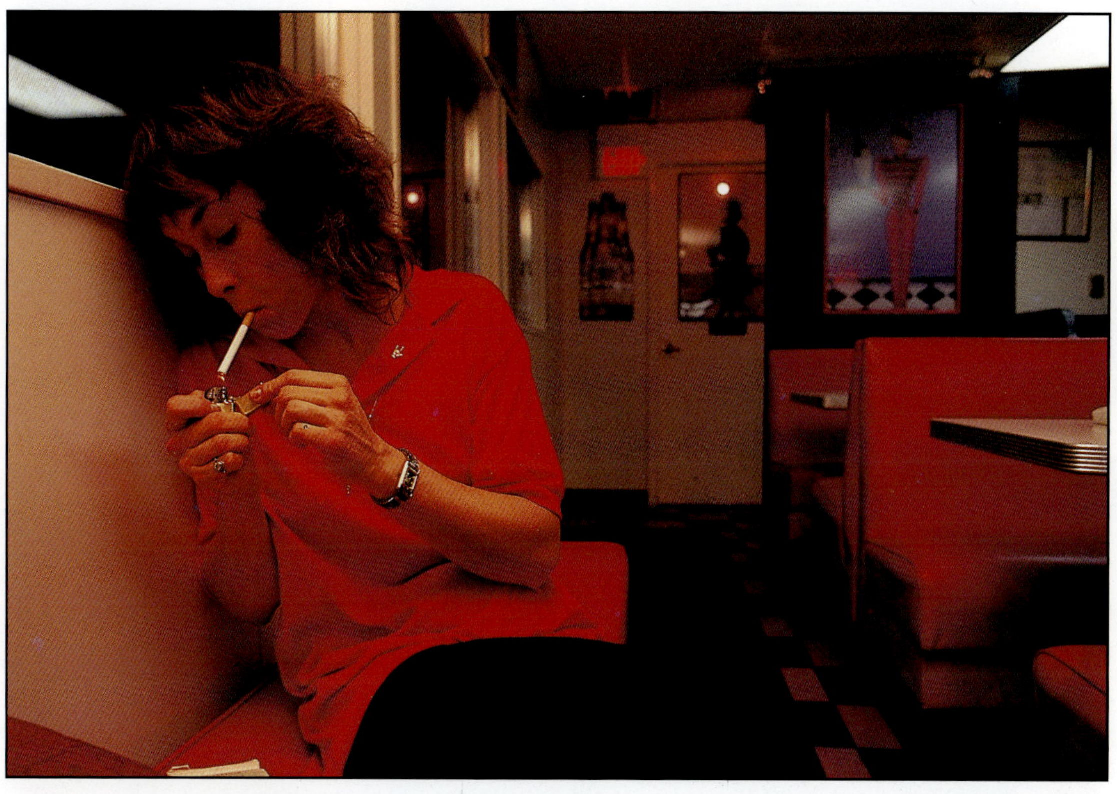

11:10 PM *The more things change the more things seem to stay the same in the small North DeKalb community of Brookhaven. MARTA's earthmovers may have swept away the dilapidated old Barbecue Kitchen. But as soon as the dust settled, Topper's appeared. A chrome-and-neon burger-and-shake place, it was far removed in appearance and cuisine from the site's previous occupant. Unfortunately, it, too, died a few months after this photo was taken and the waitress, who has just ended her shift at 11 P.M., was out of a job.*

Photo by David Murray.

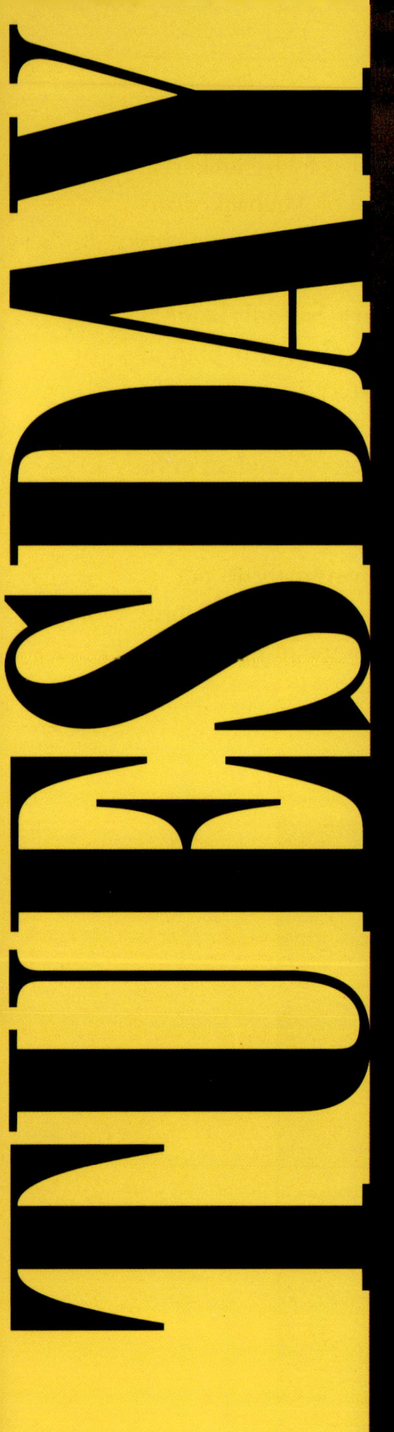

Autumn arrives in DeKalb County today at precisely 2:43 P.M., ending the coolest summer in sixteen years.

At first glance, what happens throughout the county on this bi-seasonal Tuesday paints a simple picture—young and old, work and play, home and business. Take a closer look, however, and Tuesday's people and places color DeKalb with all the dimensions the county possesses, at times as much in contrast as the seasons of the year.

Tuesday begins with Bob "Yankee" Reinig, a thirty-year veteran with Mathis Dairy, as he heads out in the early morning hours along Milk Route 266-D in North DeKalb, his truck loaded with yogurt, milk, numerous cheeses and butter for such familiar customers as the Andersons, Mrs. Leonard, the Reynolds, Mrs. Cleveland and the Weavers. "We specialize in home delivery," says Reinig, "and we try to be done before the kids go to school."

Reinig, truth to tell, is a throwback to a time when agriculture and dairy farms were major factors in the county's economy. Before the 1950s, DeKalb was primarily a rural area. Today, it is the second largest county in the state in terms of population, businesses and jobs. Agriculture is virtually non-existent in DeKalb's economic base, which depends on industrial and office parks, hotels, shopping centers, universities and health-care-related industries. DeKalb citizens find employment in the county's service-based industry, retail and wholesale businesses,

4:50 AM *While most of DeKalb sleeps, Robert "Yankee" Reinig of Mathis Dairy is delivering fresh dairy products, eggs and orange juice to front porches in DeKalb's neighborhoods. The dairy's radius stretches sixty miles, including Reinig's home delivery in Druid Hills. Mathis is one of the last home-delivery dairy companies in America, tenaciously surviving in an age of convenience stores. All but one of the Mathis cows have been moved to farms outside of the Mathis Rainbow Drive headquarters, where only the popular Mathis mascot, Rosebud, awaits children who tour the dairy and pet her.* PHOTO BY ALAN WEINER.

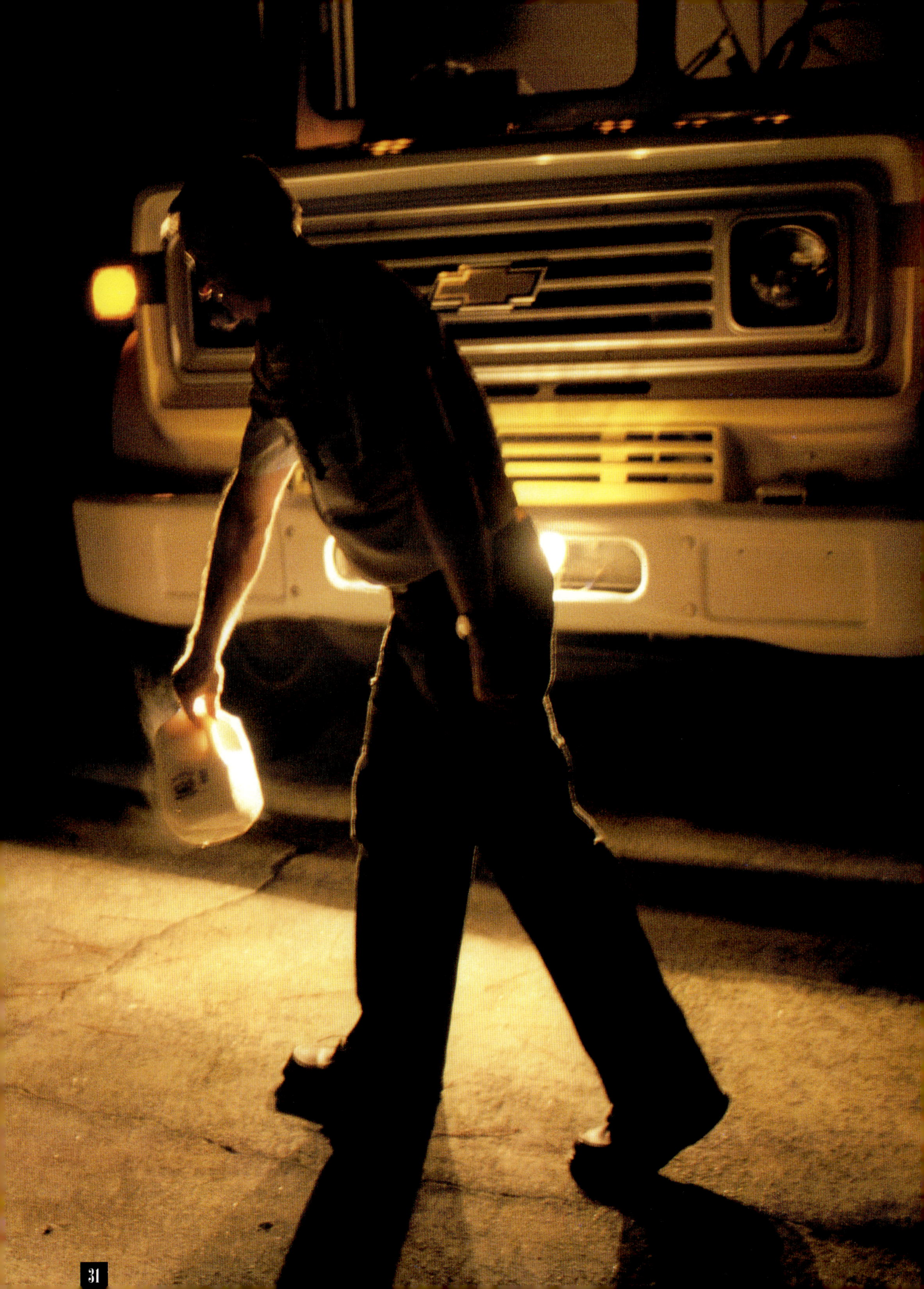

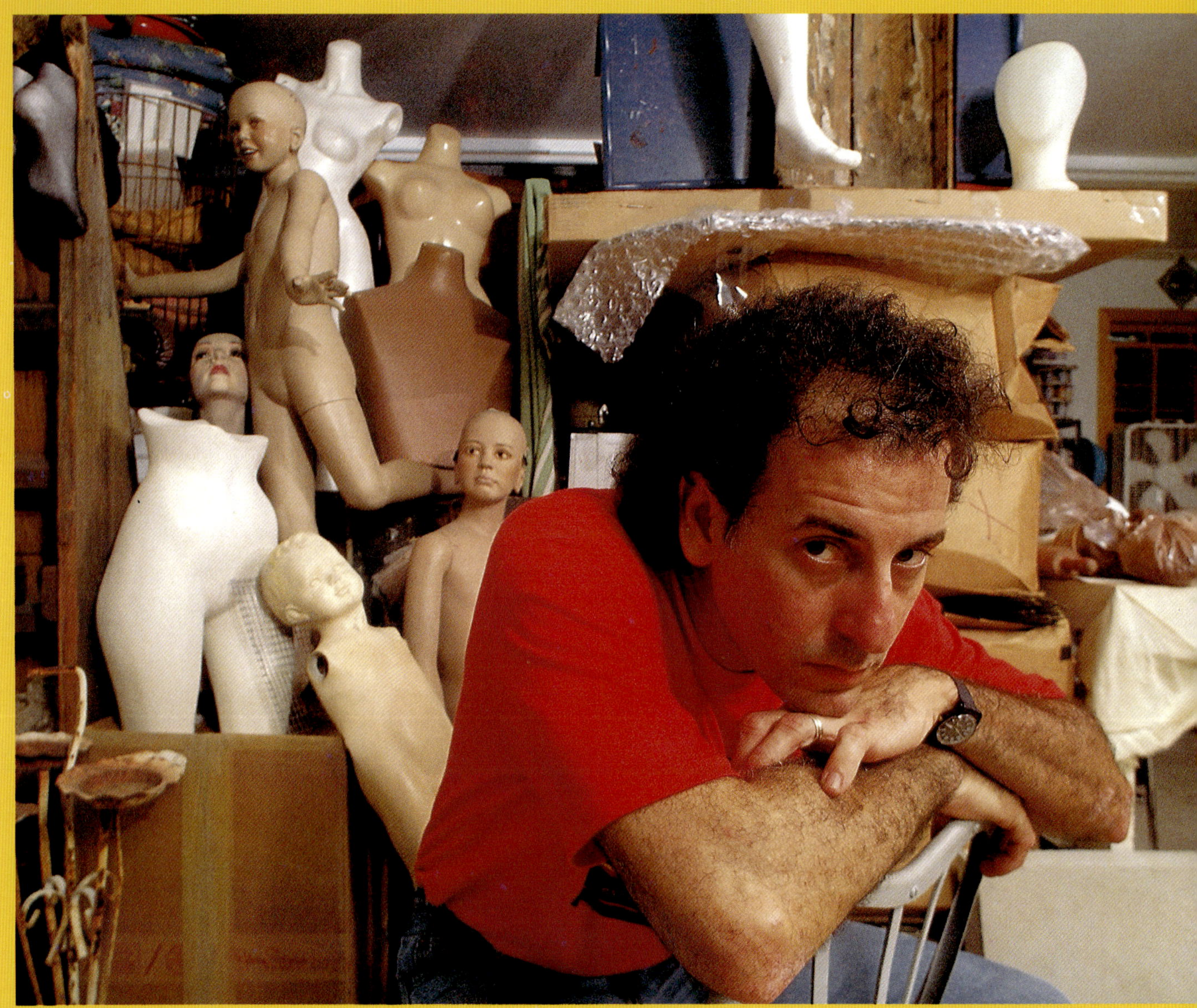

8:00 AM *Winnona Park's Mario Petrirena was one of many Cuban children who were sent to America alone in the early 1960s by parents who sought freedom from Fidel Castro's oppressive regime. Today, Mario is a successful artist (primarily clay) who says his works express his personal experiences and feelings. He recently participated in Cuba, U.S.A., a nationwide showing of works by Cuban-Americans whom he describes as "artists caught between two cultures."* PHOTO BY ALAN WEINER.

government, manufacturing, medical and teaching professions. So diverse is the county's employment base that one out of four workers in the metropolitan Atlanta area works in DeKalb.

The second day of classes gets underway at the Central Campus of DeKalb College with a VIP visit from Georgia Gov. Zell Miller, amid the sights and sounds of construction for a new four-story library and media center. DeKalb College, with 15,500 students on three campuses, is the largest feeder school of any two-year college in Georgia. And the unfamiliar sight on campus this Tuesday is not necessarily Governor Miller, who was a part-time history instructor at DeKalb in the late sixties. Rather, the Jim Cherry Learning Research Center is the first construction on campus in nearly twenty years and the first building on this Clarkston campus to rise more than two stories.

Ariela Abramowsky, two, and Max Kampf, three, attend the Zaban Preschool Full-Day Program on the beautiful grounds of Zaban Park in Dunwoody. Ariela's mother, Dr. Diane Farhi, is a pathologist; Max's mother, Carol Kampf, coordinates staffing, job search and outplacement services. They both work full-time. Says Kampf: "I feel guilty since I would love to spend more time with my son. Sometimes I have a sick feeling in the pit of my stomach and I feel uncomfortable reading negative articles about working moms. But I feel good about the Zaban program."

8:10 AM *A native of India, Lobsang Tenzin Negi begins every morning with meditation. A Tibetan monk, Lobsang came to Emory University in 1991 to study psychology and philosophy. Wearing his monk's robes, Lobsang practices Guru Yoga, a Buddhist visualization technique designed to "transform one's negative emotions and energies into positive energies and to strengthen the sense of goodness within oneself." Lobsang's text is the Yamantaka Sadhana, which contains the teachings of Yamantaka, who is said to be the embodiment of wisdom.* PHOTO BY TOM ENGLAND.

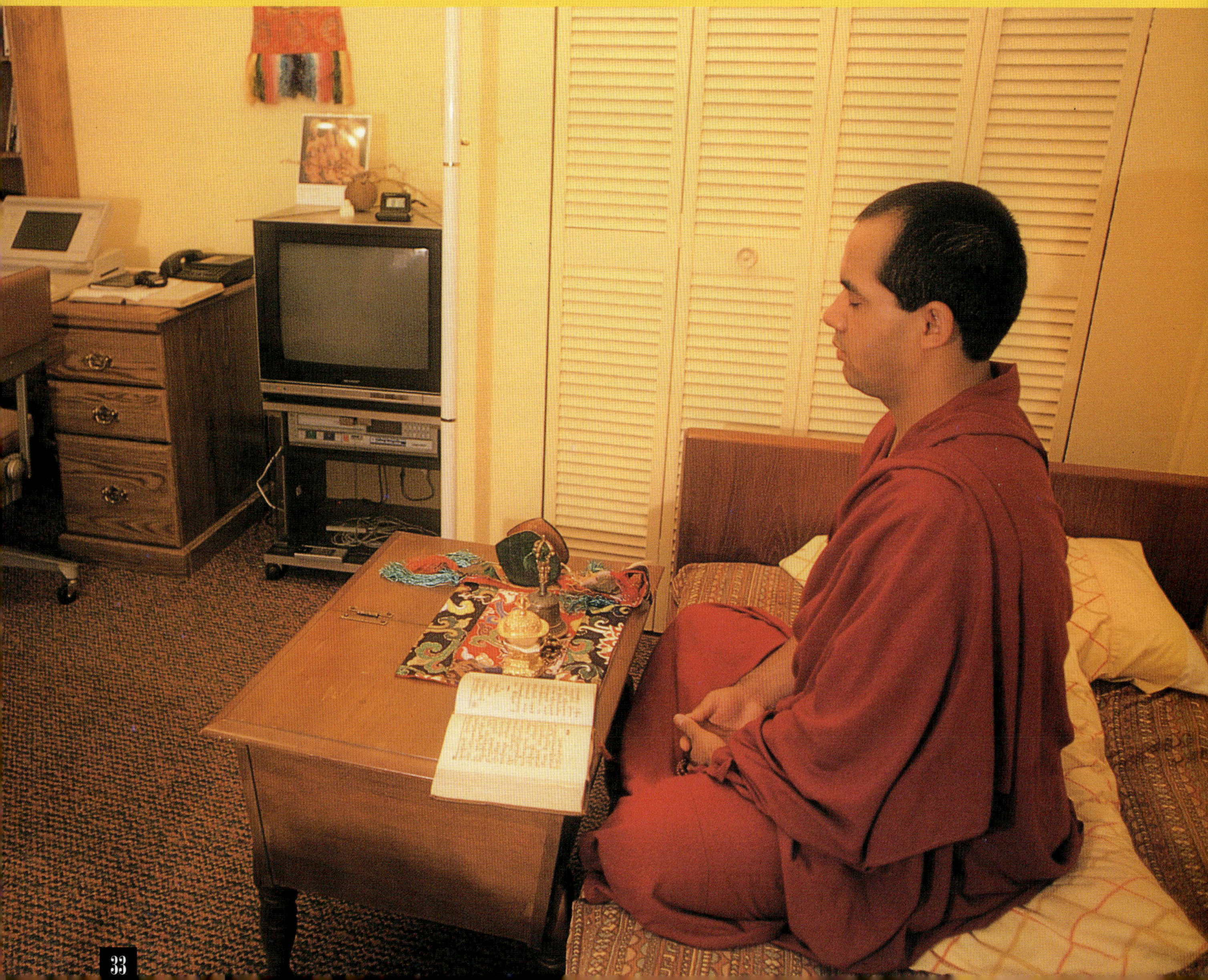

Agnes Spivey, eighty-seven, and Caroline Avera, eighty-five, live at Wesley Woods, one of the first retirement facilities of its kind when built twenty-seven years ago. Their day—filled with walks, shopping, rest, and tea with gingerbread—begins when they change their "stat" report. Every resident's door has a minuscule sign that flips from white to red. When they go to bed at night, it's white. As soon as they wake up, they change the sign to red, indicating everything's fine. If a sign isn't changed, there's a knock on the door to make sure everyone's all right. Concedes Mrs. Spivey: "It's independent living, but we're not quite as independent as we used to be."

9:46 AM *Georgia Gov. Zell Miller chose the Central Campus of DeKalb College as the site of a morning press conference during which he announced his plan to use proceeds from the new state lottery to provide free college tuition to Georgia high-school students who maintain a B average.* Photo by Ken Hawkins.

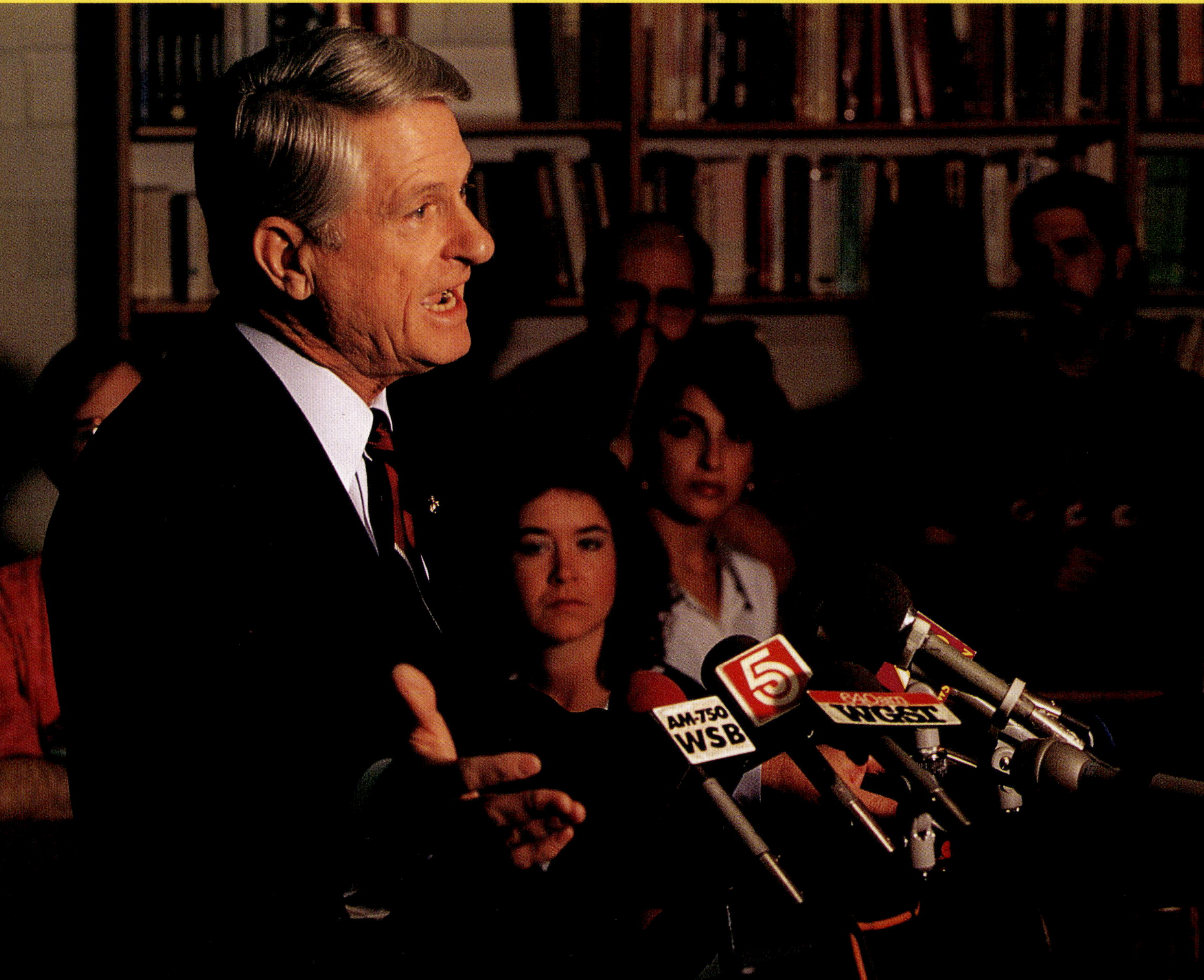

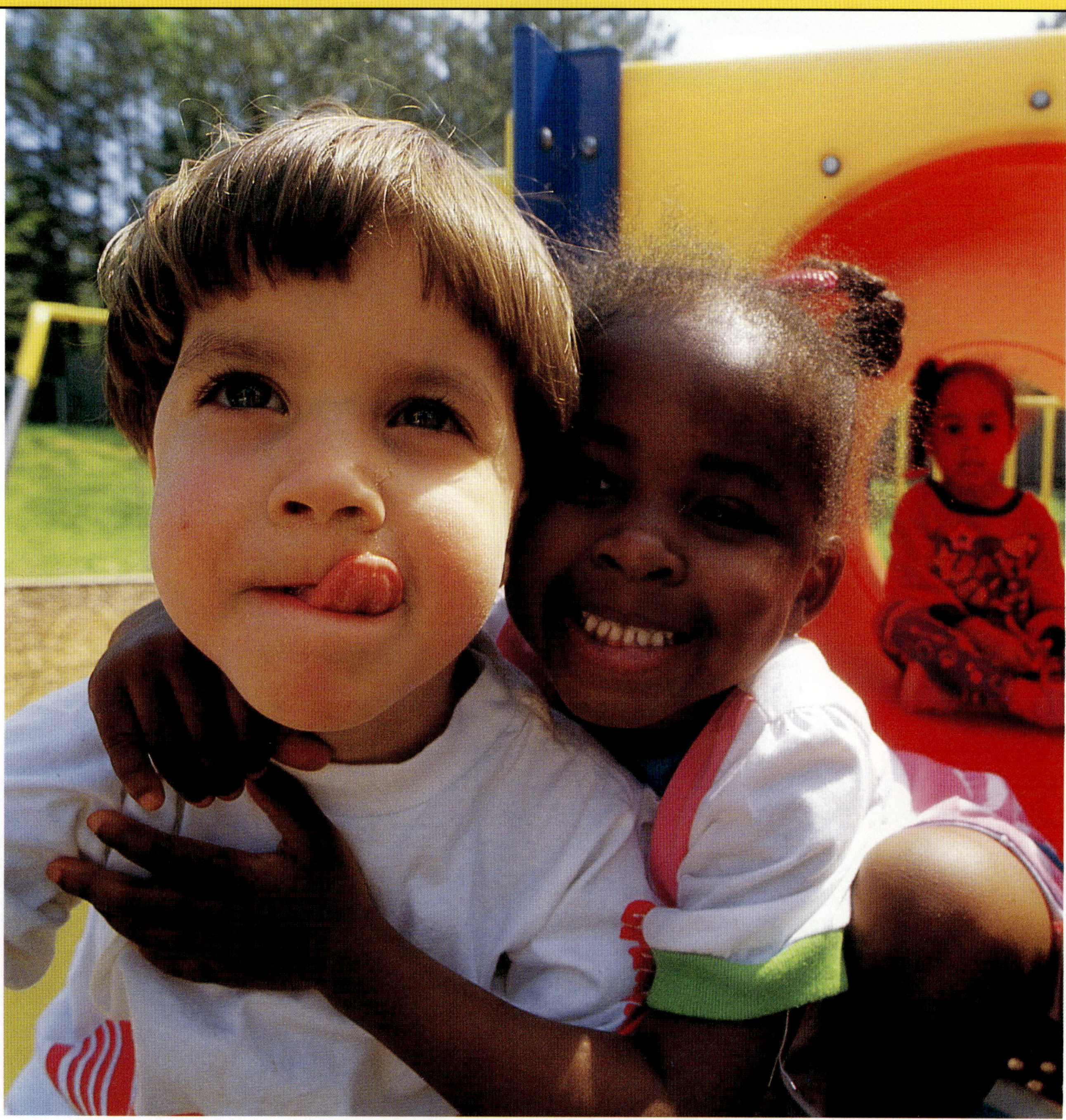

ALAN WEINER

SmithKline didn't want to be in the child care business. The liability and the upfront costs were prohibitive. But our work force is 70 percent female, and with the increasing number of two-income families and single parents, we just knew that the need was there. ◆ "AmeriCare removed all obstacles to us providing child care for our employees. The uniqueness of AmeriCare is that they would run, finance and operate a center as a separate entity. We sold them the land for the facility, but to the outside eye it appears to be on our land. They designed the architecture to blend in with our new facility here, and our parking lot runs into theirs. ◆ "We opened Christmas week, 1991. We are open from 6:00 A.M. to midnight, five days a week, with room for 150 children. And our experience has been, once an employee brings a child here, they stay. ◆ "This is a true early learning center. There's everything from arts and crafts and dance to computer learning and gymnastics. There is an entire learning atmosphere devoted to building and enhancing a child's strengths and his or her self-esteem. Our employees say it's the best child care they have ever participated in. ◆ "Our parents like the idea of the personal attention they know their child is receiving. They like the quality of the staff, the fact that if there's a problem they can be there in two or three minutes, the idea that they can have lunch with their children. And the center offers a get-well room, where a child may stay if he isn't feeling well. If the child takes a turn for the worse, the parent is right here. But otherwise they can work and not take a sick day that they may need later on. ◆ "The parents feel connected to their children all day. They can visit, and through a video monitoring system, they can watch them play and learn. One parent wrote that SmithKline and AmeriCare had relieved the 'day care stress syndrome' that she was going through when she dropped her child off at day care and then drove away to work. Now, they come together—to work and the early learning center. ◆ "Our parents are our best salespeople. Parents will stop you in the hall and just say, 'Thank you. This is the best.' "

— Paul B. Ethridge
Director of Human Resources, SmithKline Beecham,
a client of AmeriCare Early Learning Centers

AmeriCare Early Learning Centers

A Turn-Key Employer Based Child Care Solution

John Whorton, Chief Financial Officer

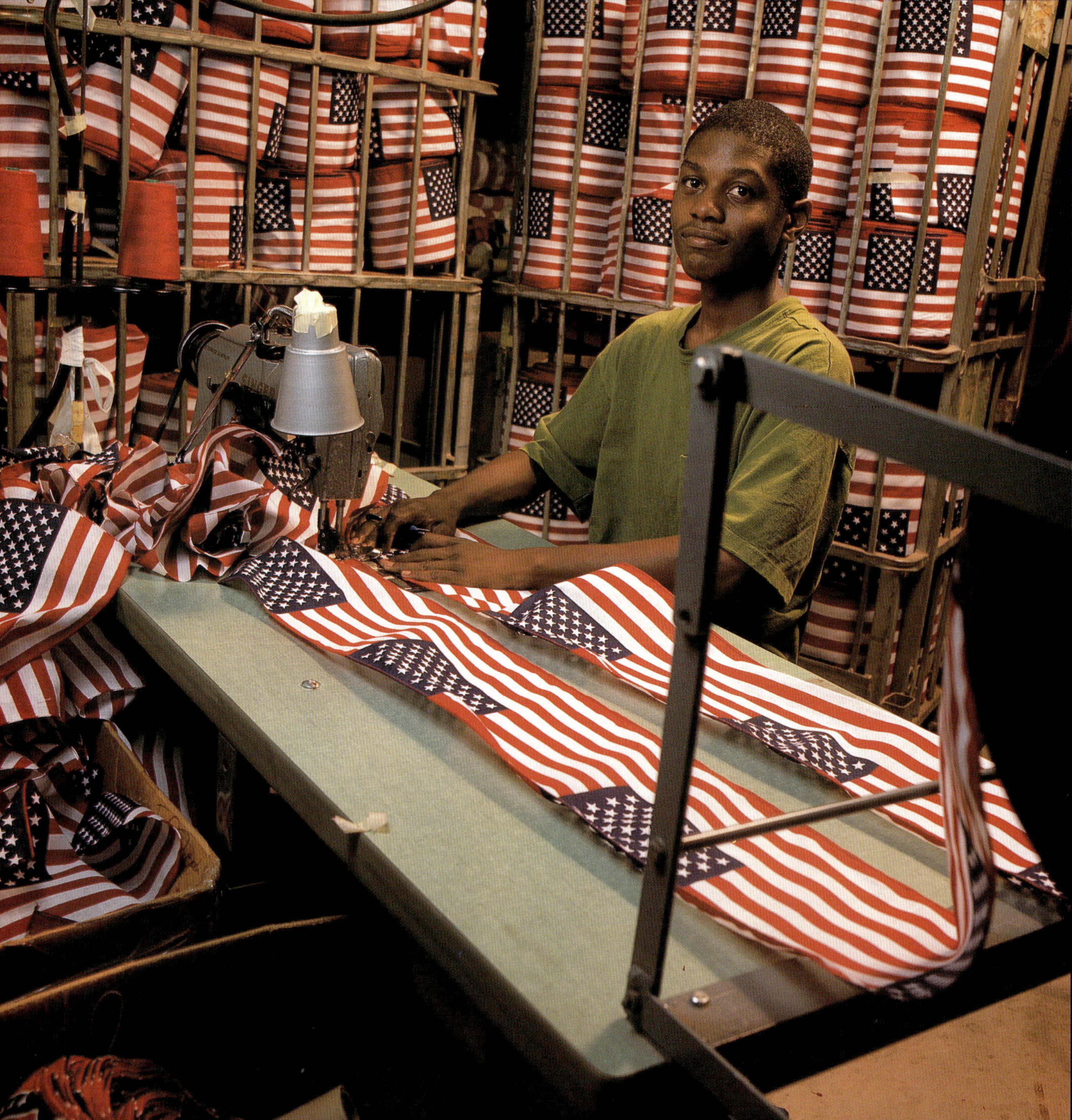

10:10 AM *Even with the on-going controversy over Georgia's state flag and the fast-approaching Olympics, this morning at Atlas Flags—where Kerry Akies is at work in a sea of red, white and blue—is calm compared to when Desert Storm translated into "Flag Storm" for the Tucker company. There was a run on American flags, says co-owner Robert Rosenthal, who recalls "people ten deep in here all day long and phones ringing off the hook. We did a year's worth of business in two mornings." Atlas hand-makes millions of American flags every year, with the handheld 4x6-inch Old Glory-on-a-stick accounting for the majority of the business (including 120,000 for the Clinton inauguration).*
PHOTO BY ANN STATES.

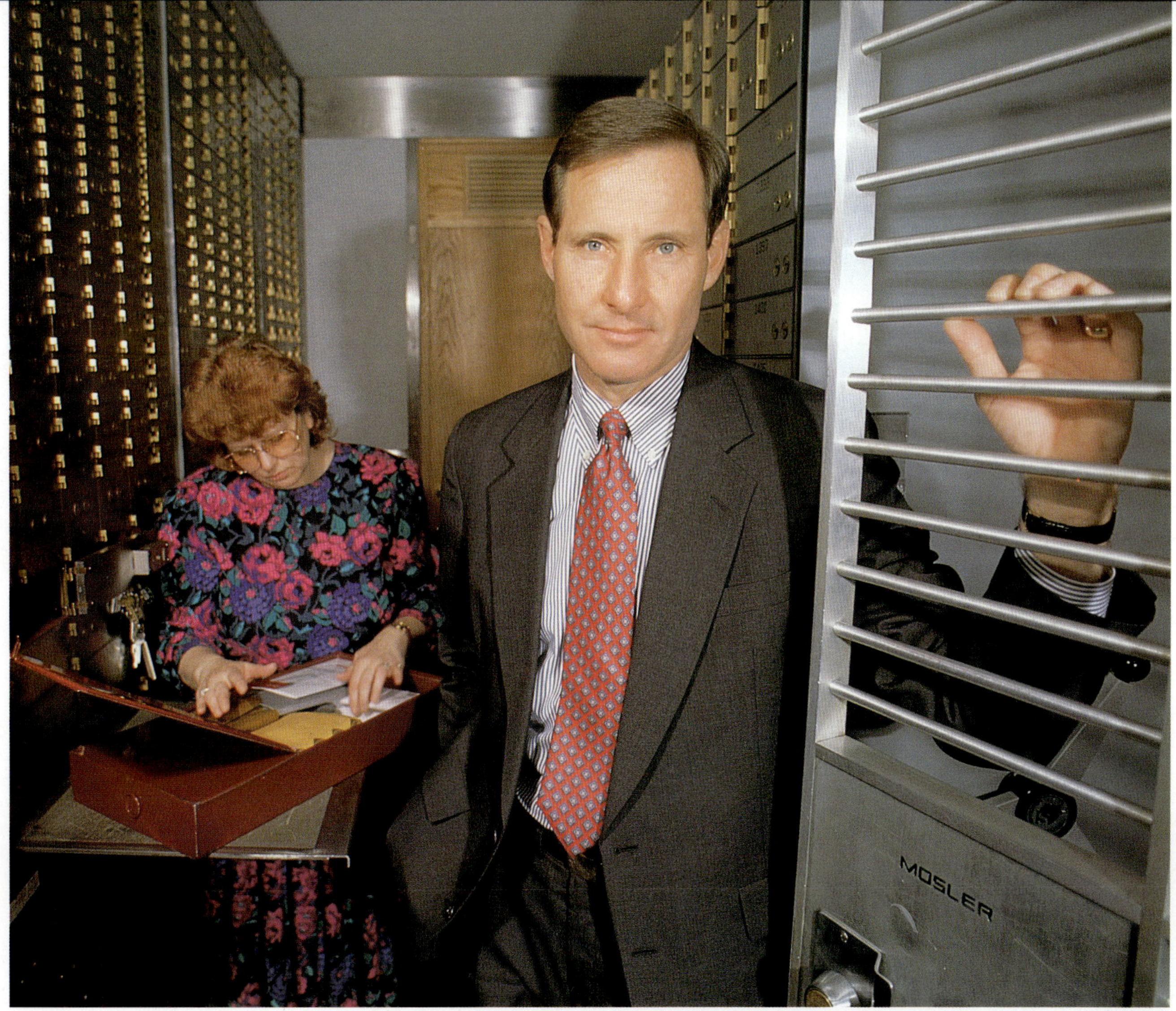

ALAN WEINER

When individuals and consumers say they want a community bank, we at NationsBank don't think that necessarily means small. ◆ "Rather, we think of a community bank as a bank committed to the customers and to the community it serves, and that describes NationsBank. We try to provide good, hands-on personal service, with a full range of services to meet the needs of our customers. We have a particular slogan: NationsBank has the power to make the difference. And we really believe that. ◆ "DeKalb County means so much to us. We have 20 banking centers in the county, and that represents about twenty percent of our metro-Atlanta market. ◆ "It's important to us to try to be a part of the community and put something back into the community. We are represented on the boards of a number of different organizations throughout the county. And we are playing a major role in the DeKalb Initiative, raising funds for economic development from 1993 through 1996. The money will be used to attract new businesses, as well as retain business and improve transportation, which is especially important with the Olympics on the horizon. We're proud that NationsBank is already one of the major sponsors for the 1996 Olympics. ◆ "In DeKalb, we certainly plan to expand as the population does, and as the needs of the community demand it. We have opened three banking centers in the past four years alone. We see the Southeastern part of the county as a prime area for expansion. There is a good bit of vacant land south of I-20, where there is good access to transportation and a major airport, as well as a good work force. ◆ "In addition to the 250 people employed at the NationsBank banking centers throughout the county, we have several hundred associates in our NationsBank Northeast Center located in DeKalb, just off I-285. Some of our major departments are headquartered there, including our commercial finance division and our real estate corporation. ◆ "And one thing that really comes to mind when I think about DeKalb and NationsBank is how the county has changed, and how we have recognized and embraced the diversity. We have a lot of international and racial diversity in DeKalb. We do our best to hire bilingual people for offices where we have a lot of bilingual customers. And while we do not have someone in every office who speaks a foreign language, we circulate a list of people within NationsBank who speak every foreign language we can find. ◆ "We do this for one reason only. To serve the DeKalb community."

— **David H. Gould, Jr., District Manager**

NATIONSBANK

With twenty banking centers and The Northeast Center serving DeKalb County. Full-service banking for a full range of customers.

By mid-morning, Clarkston Mayor Ernest Carroll reviews a schedule that reflects the changing needs of this "Small Town With the Big Heart" and 5,500 people—a meeting with DeKalb County Health Department officials to try and hire a multilingual physician for Clarkston, another meeting to coordinate special programs to keep young people off the streets. Clearly, Clarkston is a mix of old and new, home to the state's second oldest woman's club facility and the largest Hindu temple in the Southeast.

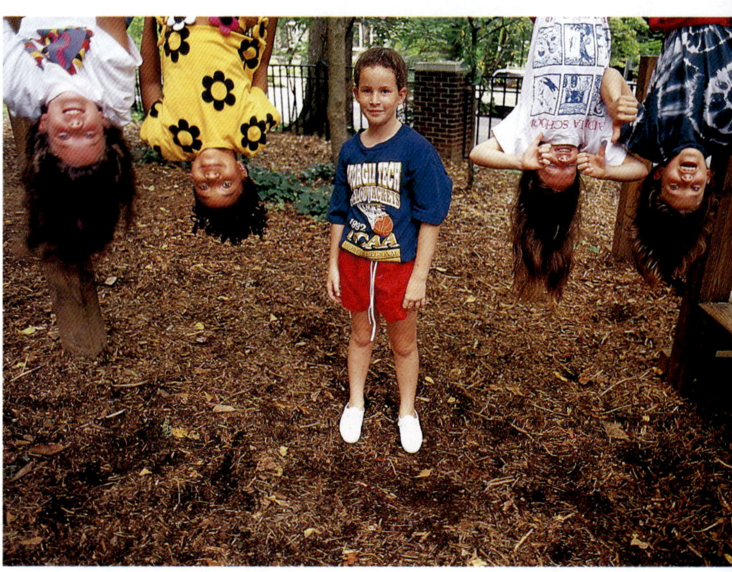

According to Police Chief Roger L. Larm, "Clarkston may still be the small town with the big heart, but it's trying to survive a big city rush." From his office just outside the courtroom in Clarkston's City Hall, Larm cites these statistics: over the most recent five year period, Clarkston has witnessed a 360 percent rise in calls for police service and a 632 percent increase in violent crimes committed by juveniles. "I want to do some real old-fashioned policing," says Larm, who has pursued grants and

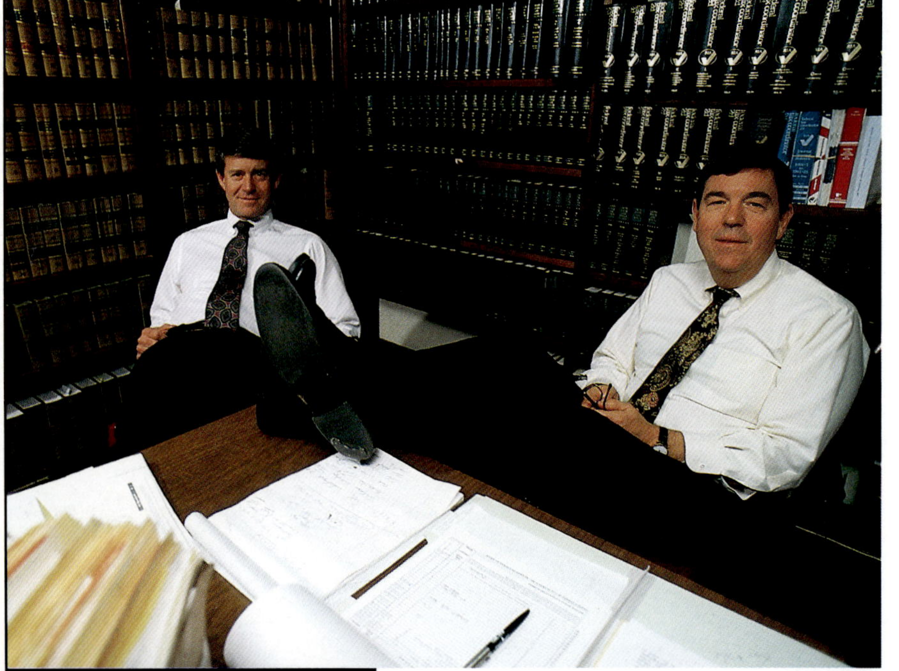

ALAN WEINER

ZACHARY & SEGRAVES

Founded in 1946, its eight attorneys serve clients throughout the Southeastern United States.

At Zachary & Segraves, we have a business outlook toward the law. William E. Zachary, Sr. was a local businessman and began practicing law on the Square in Decatur, Georgia, in 1946. Mr. Zachary formed a partnership with John Hunter during the 1950s and the firm and its successors have had the same Decatur address since 1961. The current DeKalb State Court Solicitor, Ralph Bowden, was a member of the firm during the 1960s, and J. Ed Segraves and I joined the firm in the late 1960s. William E. Zachary, Sr. served on the Board of Governors of the State Bar of Georgia for twenty-six years, longer than any other Georgia lawyer has ever served. Two firm members have served as President of the Decatur-DeKalb Bar Association and one member served on the Executive Committee of the Atlanta Lawyers Club. Firm members have been active in local civic and charitable groups and in Alumni Organizations, particularly at Emory University. ◆ "The firm has always had a business trial practice representing local and national companies in the southeastern United States. The firm has developed expertise in the construction, development, condemnation, surety, and banking fields and has represented local automobile dealerships throughout the county for over twenty-five years. The firm currently handles surety litigation for several national insurance companies as well as handling surety and lien work for national construction supply houses. Zachary & Segraves has represented clients from the local trial level to the Supreme Court of the United States. ◆ "The eight lawyers of Zachary & Segraves were educated and received degrees from Emory University, the University of Georgia, the University of North Carolina, Vanderbilt and American University. These lawyers want to deliver a quality product to their clients in a timely and efficient manner. Zachary & Segraves' philosophy is to help our clients do business within the framework of the law rather than to treat the law as an obstacle to the efficient management of their businesses."

— William E. Zachary, Jr., Partner

10:22 AM *You won't find students sitting in front-facing rows of traditional desks at Paideia School. What you will find at the private school are students pursuing creative and academic excellence through a teaching philosophy that is quite old but quite at home in a modern setting. Paideia, while not literally translatable, generally means educating the whole person in the context of the whole community. The approach apparently is successful. Fully 100 percent of Paideia graduates go to college. Founded by parents twenty-two years ago in the Druid Hills neighborhood, Paideia today has 600 students, from pre-kindergarten through high school. Here, Michael Yin takes a short break from his peanut butter and jelly sandwich, and Caroline Schatten stands amid her upside-down classmates on the playground. Meanwhile, in more serious pursuits, teacher Peter Richards leads his class in a discussion. His students are, left to right, Ben Ku, Molly Gunn, Lindsay Harper, Leigh Stapleton, Anna Schwartz and Laura Bassett. On the top row, left to right, are Tony Carter and Harding Royster.* PHOTOS BY MICHAEL SCHWARZ.

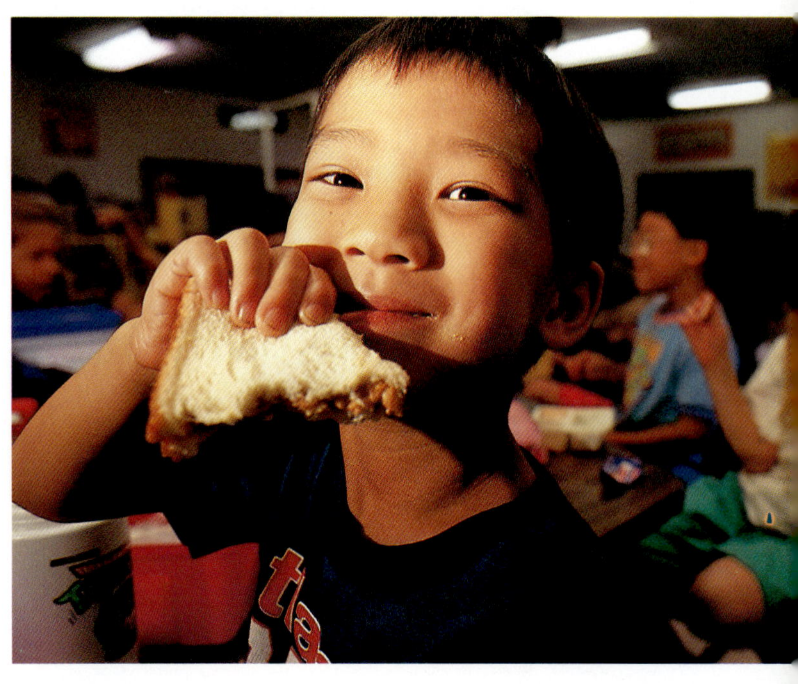

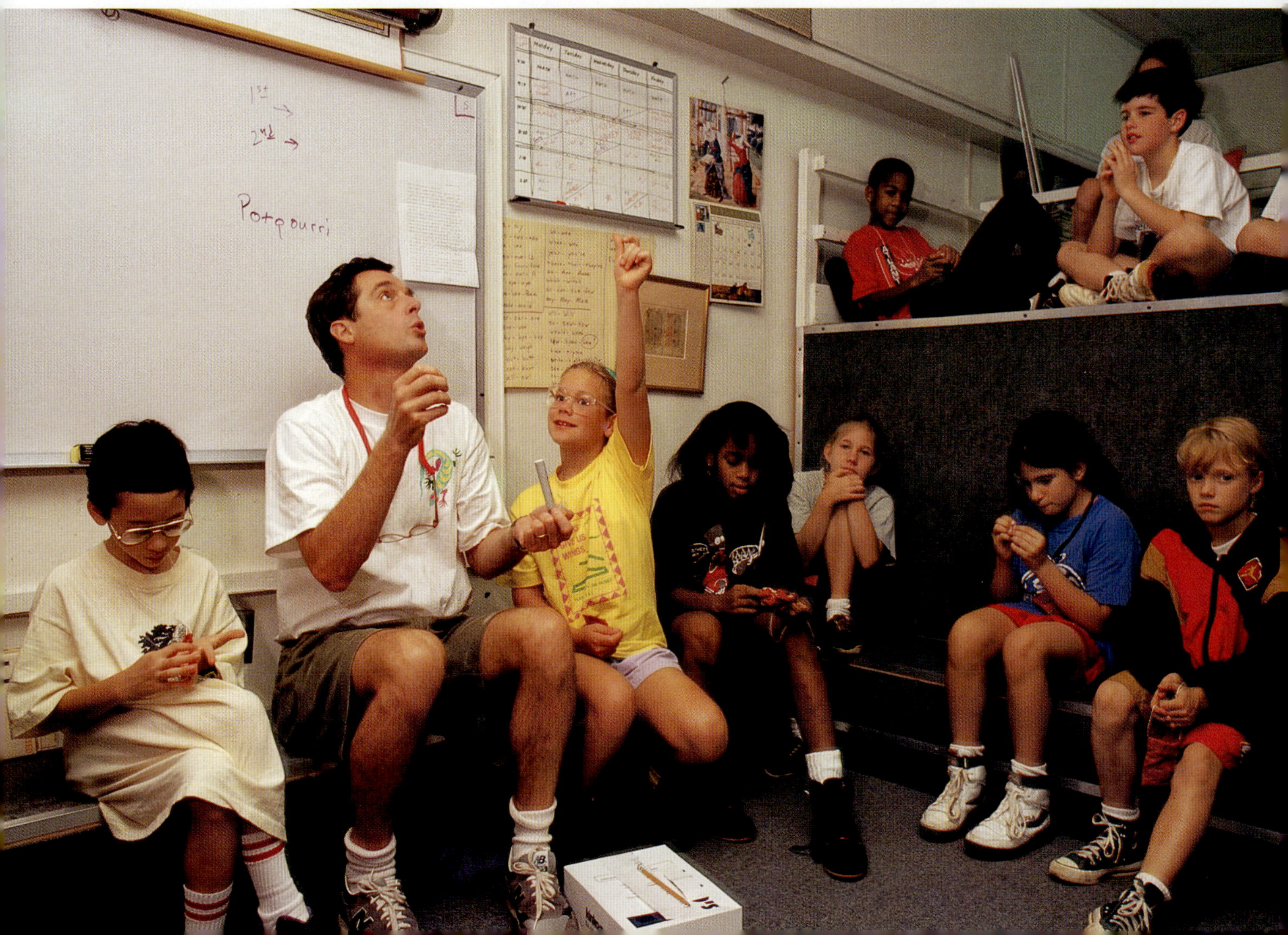

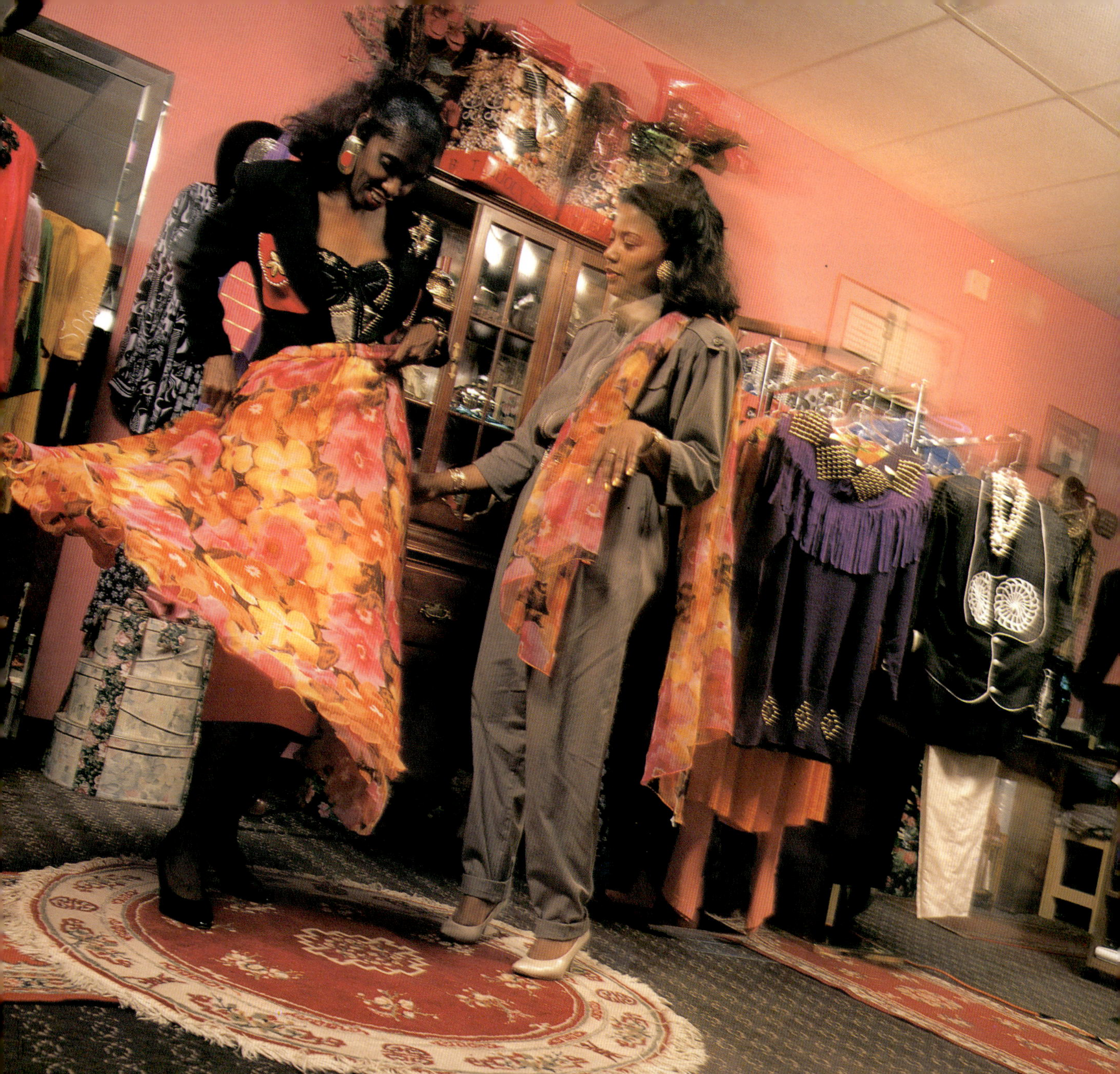

10:50 AM *Don't let the ordinary exterior of Phoebie's Boutique fool you. Over the eight years that Marcia Watson-Lopez has been in business, her elegant couture clothing has been seen on some of the most prominent women in Georgia, as well as across the nation. Phoebie's customers are primarily black and well-to-do and include recognizable names from local business leaders to international show-business greats. She insists that her shop carry "nothing risque, nothing trashy," and a little conservative, to suit her local clientele. "I like for a woman to be noticeable when she walks in the door." Judging by the outfit being previewed by customer Anna Naugles, that shouldn't be any problem.* Photo by Ann States

11:15 AM *Internationally known gardener and showman Ryan Gainey is arguably the most written-about man in DeKalb County. His home, gardens and incomparable personal style have been the subject of features in such major magazines as House and Garden and National Geographic. September found him in the midst of filming a special for the Public Broadcasting System. His Decatur home has been on every area garden tour, and his imaginative designs are a much-anticipated highlight of the annual Atlanta Flower Show. But beautiful gardens take planning—the side of Gainey's work most people never see—such as he does here in the study of his home.* Photo by Tom England

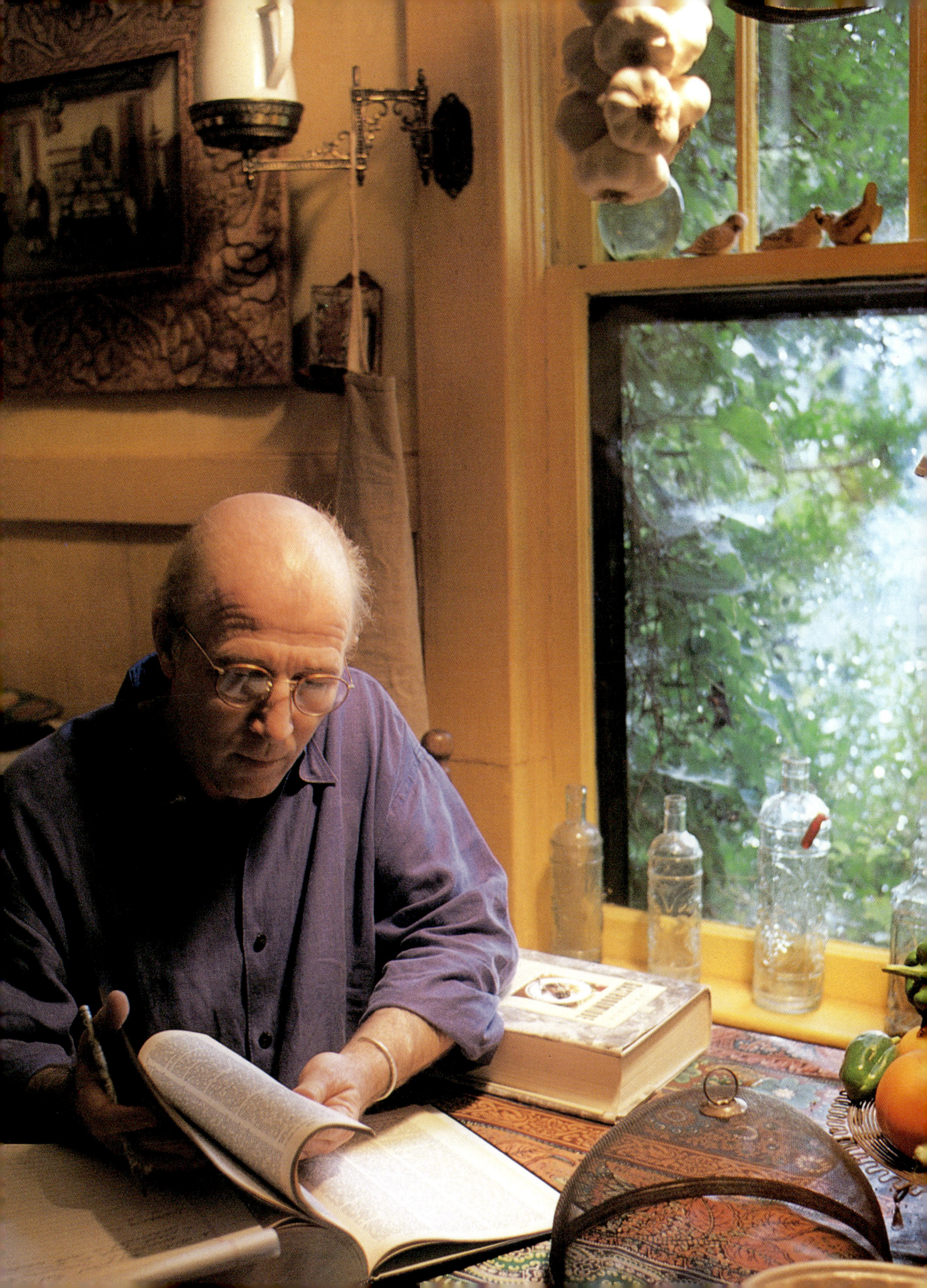

11:15 AM *A new DS-130/W scanning electron microscope, being operated here by technical director of the Yerkes SEM, Robert Apkarian, is giving scientists around the world even more reason to come to the Yerkes Primate Research Center at Emory University. The powerful tool magnifies specimens—ranging from heart tissues to drill bits—ten to one million times their original size with precision and detail, utilizing facilities and personnel said to be the best in the world. It has proven to be a valuable resource for scientists in fields ranging from cardiovascular medicine to polymer chemistry, geology to forensic medicine. The Yerkes Integrated Scanning Electron Microscopy (SEM) Microanalytical Facility is one of several educational and research institutions located in the Emory University area of DeKalb County.* PHOTO BY MARILYN FUTTERMAN.

prayers to hire more than his staff of twelve police officers, especially officers who speak Vietnamese, Spanish or Arabic. "I want to put some bilingual police officers out on foot in those areas where the crime is, to work with the people and the juveniles. I'm a big student of Wyatt Earp, the way he used to do his marshaling by going out and getting involved in the community."

At noon in Druid Hills, the neighborhood that gave the cinematic world *Driving Miss Daisy* is so quiet that even the katydids strum along with the crickets.

In a county that's changed rapidly in the last several decades, the neighborhood of Druid Hills practically places a premium on staying the same. At Oakdale and Ponce de Leon, Blane Peacock of

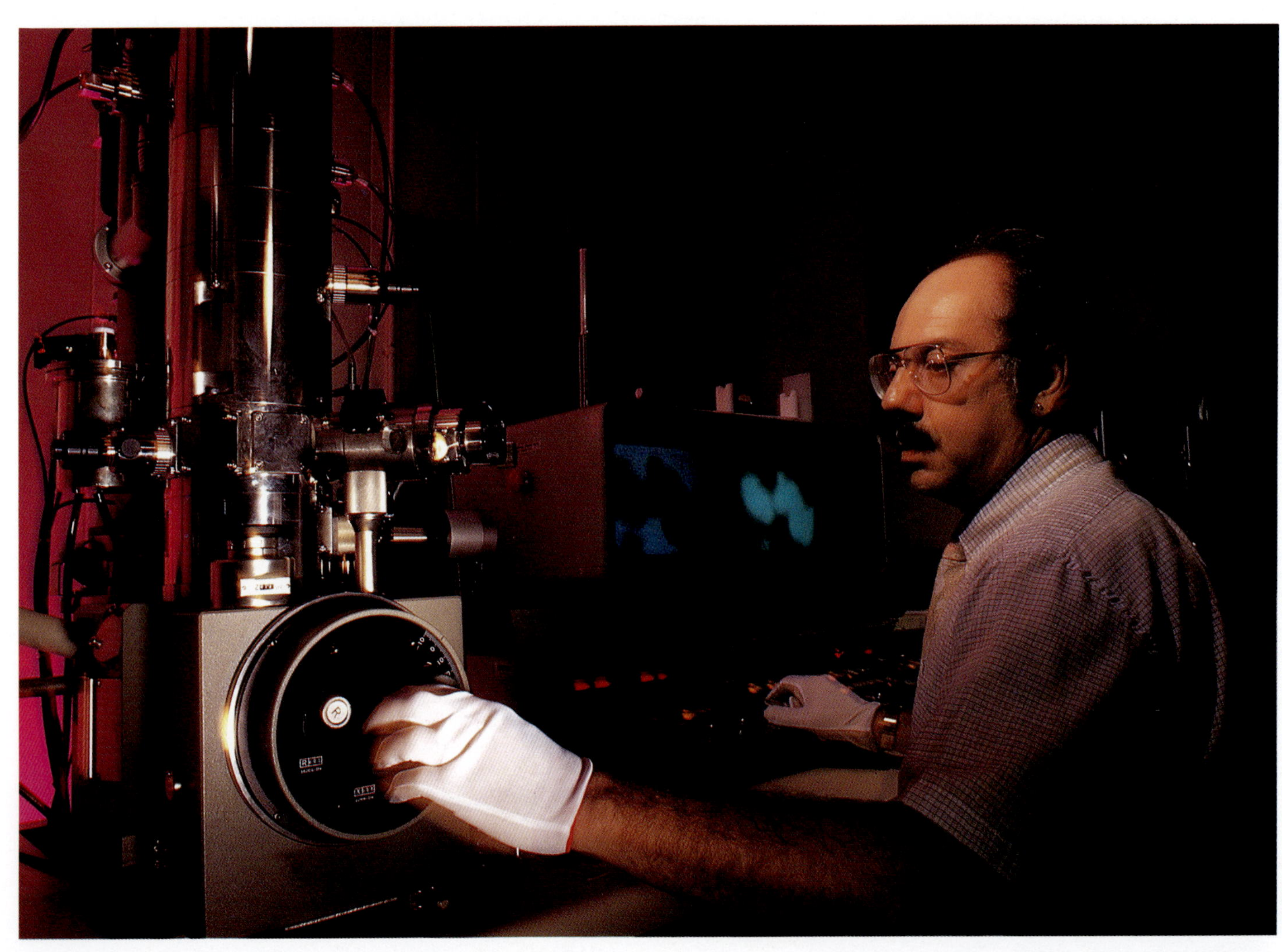

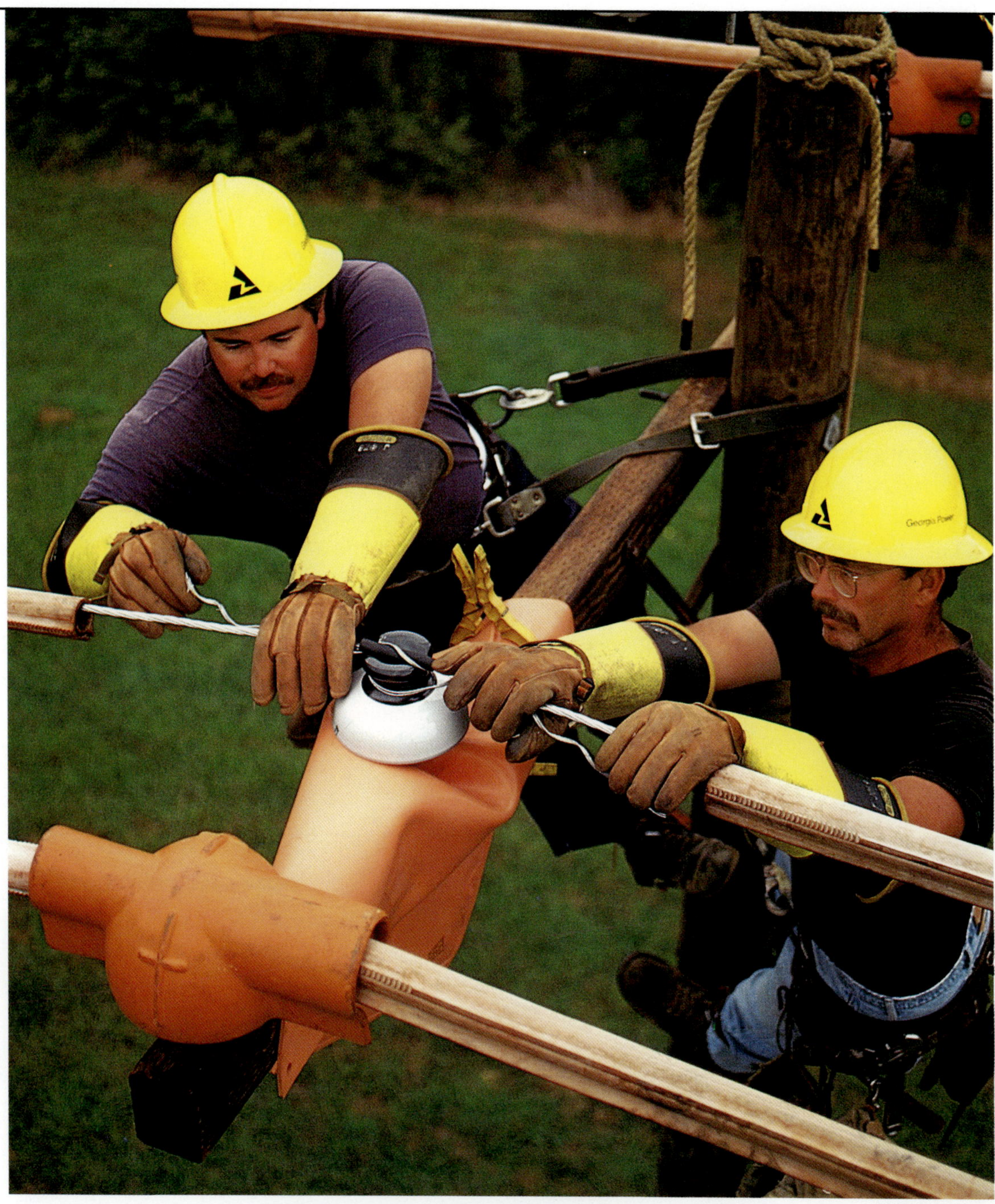

SCOTT ROBINSON

At Georgia Power Company, all of our customers are right here. In DeKalb County, we have close to a quarter of a million customers. And while other businesses can go out and find customers in California or Montana, our customers are our next-door neighbors. ◆ "Call it enlightened self-interest or just being a good citizen, our long-term commitment is to the success of the communities we serve as well as to ourselves. We strengthen the community and our markets when we positively address issues that affect growth and development, infrastructure, education and the general quality of life and well being of our customers. ◆ "What we try to do at Georgia Power is work with the cancer societies, the heart funds, the chambers, the art societies, the development authorities and the educational institutions to make the area that we are in a much more attractive place for people to work and live. ◆ "At Georgia Power, being a 'citizen wherever we serve' is more than a motto, it's a way of life. I think one of our biggest achievements is that we have employees at every level involved in the community. We've got folks working at little leagues, charity fund-raisers, on local boards and in the classrooms. And not because we forced them or because it's part of their jobs—but because they believe in it. ◆ "The bottom line is this, we want to be a team member—a member of a total community team. We'll take leadership roles or subordinates, it really doesn't matter as long as we can play a positive role in a total community effort. We believe that is the best strategy for long-term success."

— E. Lamont Houston
Metro East District Manager

GEORGIA POWER COMPANY

240,000 customers in DeKalb County

Construction Mode, Inc., and two other carpenters are renovating a house, and their main job is to create a new facade so that the Italian Renaissance style complements others in the neighborhood. The original houses here, built from the teens through the 1930s when tuberculosis was prevalent, often included porches as a preventive measure; folks back then believed that if they slept outdoors, they could avoid catching TB.

On the campus of Agnes Scott College, freshman Brandi Thomas, eighteen, smiles broadly and accepts the bulging package from the campus post office clerk, her second parcel in three weeks. Contents? Several CDs, a high-school yearbook she worked on but hasn't seen, and a pair of suede shorts ordered from Chadwick's of Boston.

Twenty-four years older than her fellow freshman, Rochelle Kreahe is one of Agnes Scott's Return-to-College (RTC) students who now make up 20 percent of the 600-member student body. While sitting in a class called "Introduction to Literature and Composition," she jokes that RTC is a euphemism for "old" but allows that, "I don't think I have an advantage over the young students—well, maybe in political science, where I've actually lived through some of the things we are discussing."

In any one of DeKalb County's 138 regional and strip malls, afternoon bookstore customers reflect the county's diverse demographics. At Northlake Mall, the top seller of the week at B. Dalton Book Seller is *The Ways Things Ought to Be*, by conservative radio commentator Rush Limbaugh. At Tall Tales Bookshop in Toco Hills Promenade on North Druid Hills Road, customers are reading Susan Sontag and Susan Faludi and a new book about violence in modern relationships called *Trauma and Recovery*. And in the First World Bookstore in South DeKalb Mall, books by Malcolm X, Angela Davis, Alice Walker, Maya Angelou, Terry McMillan and Toni Morrison are prominently displayed.

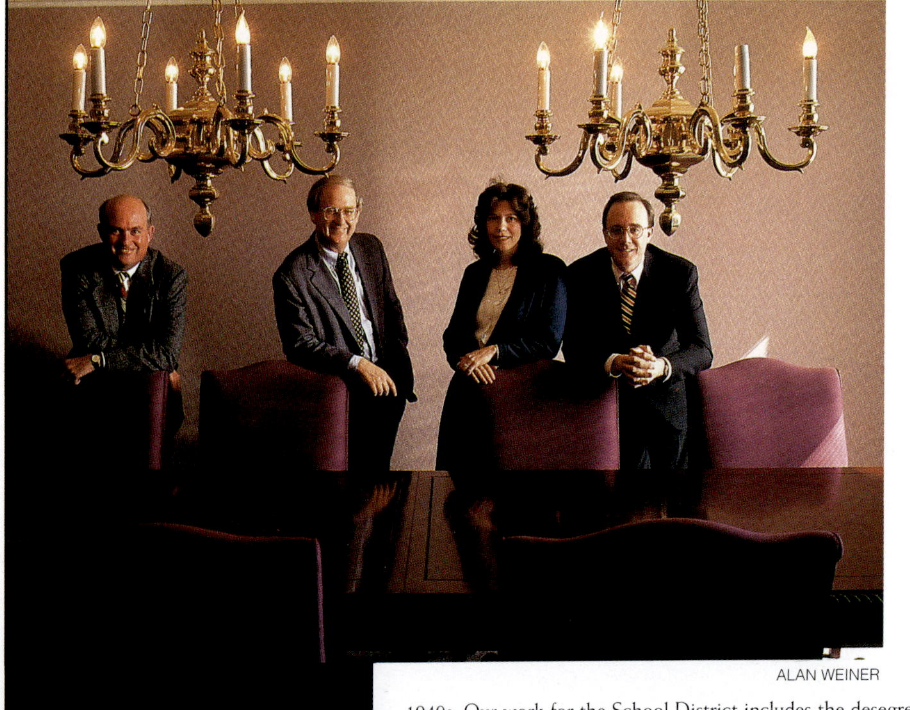

ALAN WEINER

WEEKES & CANDLER, LAW OFFICES

A professional corporation

The law firm of Weekes & Candler has been in existence in DeKalb County since 1927. ◆ "The founders, Mr. John Wesley Weekes and Mr. Murphey Candler, were born and raised in DeKalb County and were active in local politics. They both were elected to the Georgia Legislature, Mr. Weekes when he was only twenty-one years old. He also served as mayor pro tem of Decatur. ◆ "Mr. Weekes and Mr. Candler were outstanding individuals and excellent attorneys. Mr. Weekes served as county administrator beginning in 1927 and continuing for fifty years. I took over for him when he retired, handling estate administrations and guardianships when the county has to appoint someone to do so. Since 1927, this firm must have handled 2,000 to 3,000 cases in that capacity. ◆ "Mr. Candler was judge of the DeKalb Juvenile Court for many years as well as having a large private practice. He began representing the DeKalb County School District in the 1940s. Our work for the School District includes the desegregation case filed in 1968 on which I began working when Mr. Candler died in 1972. In 1991, it reached the United States Supreme Court, which ruled that the DeKalb School District's system of neighborhood schools was constitutional. ◆ "Today, the eight lawyers of our firm continue to handle different aspects of law such as litigation, estate planning and administration, corporate and education law. Jack Rhodes represents the cities of Stone Mountain and Clarkston, and Terri Candler, Murphey Candler's great-niece, specializes in family law. ◆ "And we've been in Decatur over sixty-five years."

— Gary Sams, Attorney-at-Law

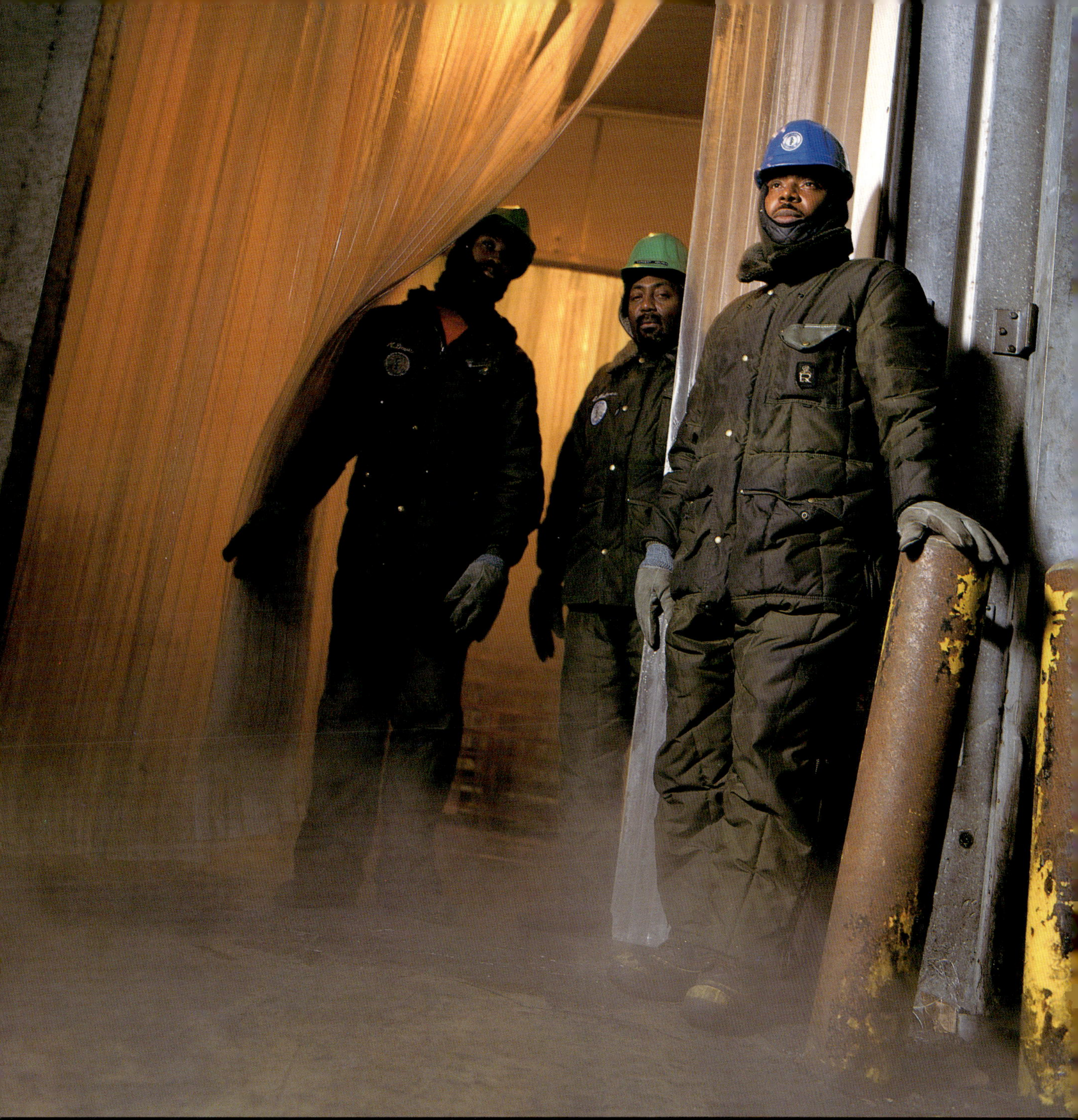

11:39 AM *If you're looking for a vacation from the heat of an Indian Summer, you might consider Commercial Cold Storage. The Pleasantdale Road facility is the largest above-ground cold-storage warehouse in the world—twenty-one acres, more than 15 million cubic feet, under one roof. Much of it is cooled to fifteen degrees below zero, requiring*

photo of workers Earnest Holmes, Michael R. Jolly and Michael G. Davis, taken at the entrance to an ice-cream storage room. Commercial stores and distributes frozen and refrigerated food for major grocery chains, restaurants, hospitals, prisons, fast-food chains and school systems in the southeastern United States. There are an estimated two million pounds of french fries in stock at all times.

12:05 PM *Students come from all over the world to attend Cross Keys High School in North DeKalb where more than half of the students are foreign-born. A student body that represents forty-seven nationalities and speaks forty-three languages presents special challenges and opportunities, according to Principal Pete Spencer. The school frequently finds itself fulfilling the role of helper to entire families, as well as educator to students. The school houses a "survival skills" program that is the first stop for foreign-born high-school students who will attend schools throughout the county. Nevertheless, the students assimilate into their new culture easily, especially in academics. Last year the top 10 percent of the student body consisted entirely of international students. The valedictorian was Hispanic, the co-salutatorians were Oriental and black. "I could write a book," Spencer says. "It's wonderful." Pictured here, with flags of their native countries, are students from Guatemala, Afghanistan, America, the Dominican Republic, Cambodia, Peru, Thailand, Ghana, Mexico, Eritrea, Venezuela, El Salvador, Laos, the Philippines, Spain and other countries.*

PHOTO BY GORDON JOFFRION.

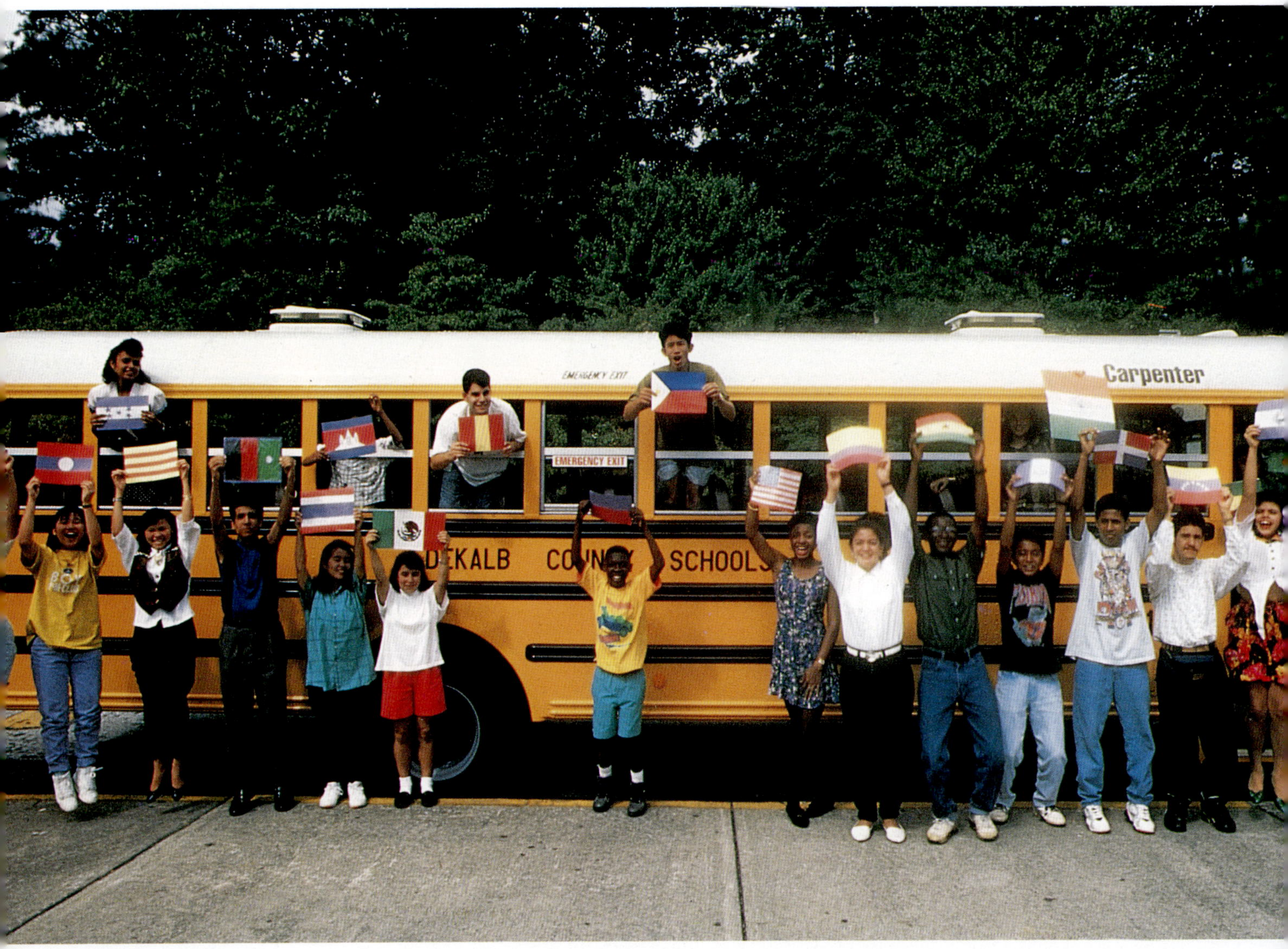

Gospel singer Anna Naugles spends the afternoon at Phoebie's, a chic, exclusive dress shop in a strip mall along Wesley-Chapel Road where owner Marcia Watson-Lopez (known far and wide as "Phoebie") makes everyone feel at home. "A lot of my customers stop by because they're friends," says Phoebie, whose racks are filled with dresses made of sequins, satin and silk in an $80 to $400 price range. "I give them the run of the store."

Mark Allen, an animal control officer with Trapper John Animal Control, buys a tear-gas mask and attachable canteen at Old Sarge Army-Navy Surplus on Buford Highway, a warehouse-like store adorned with hundreds of military uniforms, ever-popular camouflage clothing and dozens of parachutes hanging from the ceiling. What does he think of Old Sarge? Says Allen, "Not a lot of Gucci here. There's more substance than style."

The Tuesday Night Strikers show up around 6 P.M. for their regular bowling league night at the Stone Mountain Fair Lanes bowling alley, just about the time a strike in lane number twenty brings a round of "high fives" from a group of young bowlers.

At 7:14 P.M., conductor Tom Anderson explains this evening's rehearsal to members of the DeKalb Symphony Orchestra. "Things are a little chaotic tonight because we've got two different groups of musicians rehearsing for two different performances." But it's not long before Anderson is leading the eighty-five orchestra members through a number of Broadway tunes, a Strauss waltz and a Rossini overture from *The Barber of Seville*. There are no "high fives" here; an open downward palm means gentle, an open upward palm means louder, cupped hands mean fuller. The orchestra, a mix of amateurs, college students and paid professionals, responds beautifully to Anderson's signals.

As night returns and the rain falls, eighteen-year-old Thomas Hays Guthrie of Decatur, son of Dr. and Mrs. Shirley Guthrie, becomes an Eagle Scout in Eagle Court of Honor ceremonies at Holy Trinity Episcopal Church. Scoutmaster Greg Catledge presents the award, and Tom's mother pins it to his uniform. After the ceremony, Tom proudly shows visitors his Eagle Scout project, a painted mural of Noah's Ark at the Holy Trinity Episcopal Shelter for Women and Children.

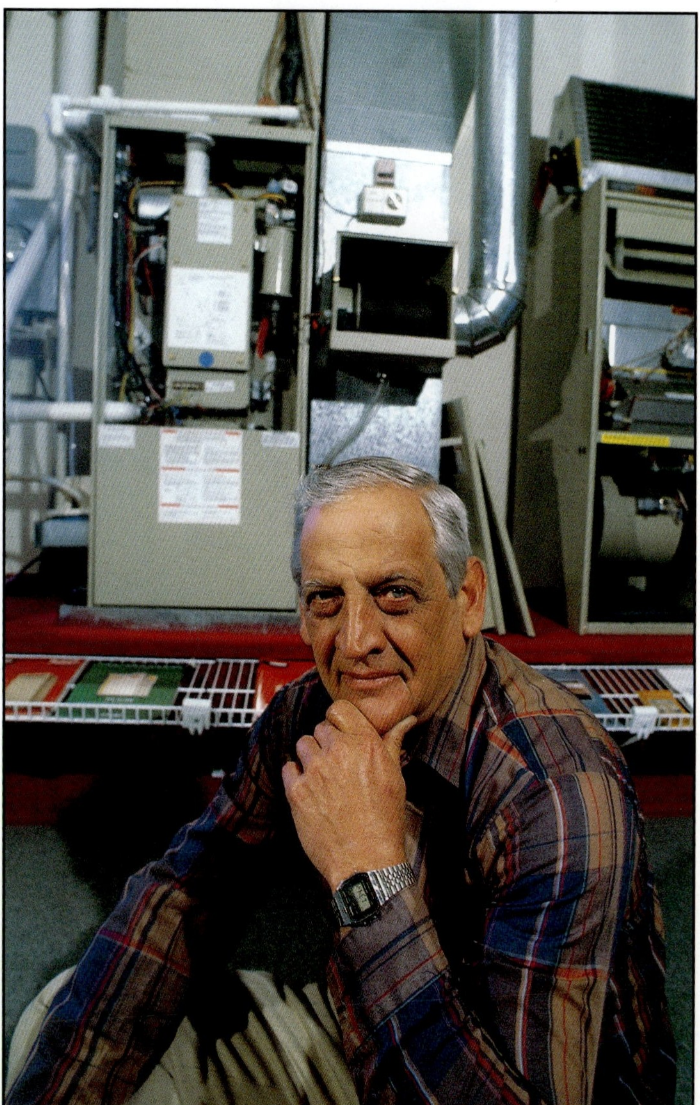

ALAN WEINER

I founded A.C.S.S. (Air Conditioning Systems Service) Company in 1970, though I began my career in 1953 when I joined the Plumbers and Pipe Fitters Union. We have worked closely in building this business and it's not unusual for us to work nights and weekends throughout the year—whatever it takes to get the job done. Hard work has kept this company growing for the past twenty-two years. ◆ "Our main line of business is service and installation of heating and air conditioning equipment for residential customers and commercial businesses. We have the largest window unit repair shop in Atlanta. Customers can bring their window units to A.C.S.S. for a free estimate. Our company offers customers free second opinions on equipment that has been condemned and free estimates on replacement equipment. We offer a wide variety of brand-name equipment. A.C.S.S. features a showroom where customers can physically touch the equipment and also, a parts department where you can purchase parts for home repairs. ◆ "Over the last twenty years, the industry has changed with the new EPA regulations and government standards. You can be assured A.C.S.S. is following these guidelines as they affect the consumer."

— **Johnnie Stephens, Owner**

A.C.S.S. COMPANY

An air conditioning system service company, serving the greater Atlanta area for over twenty years

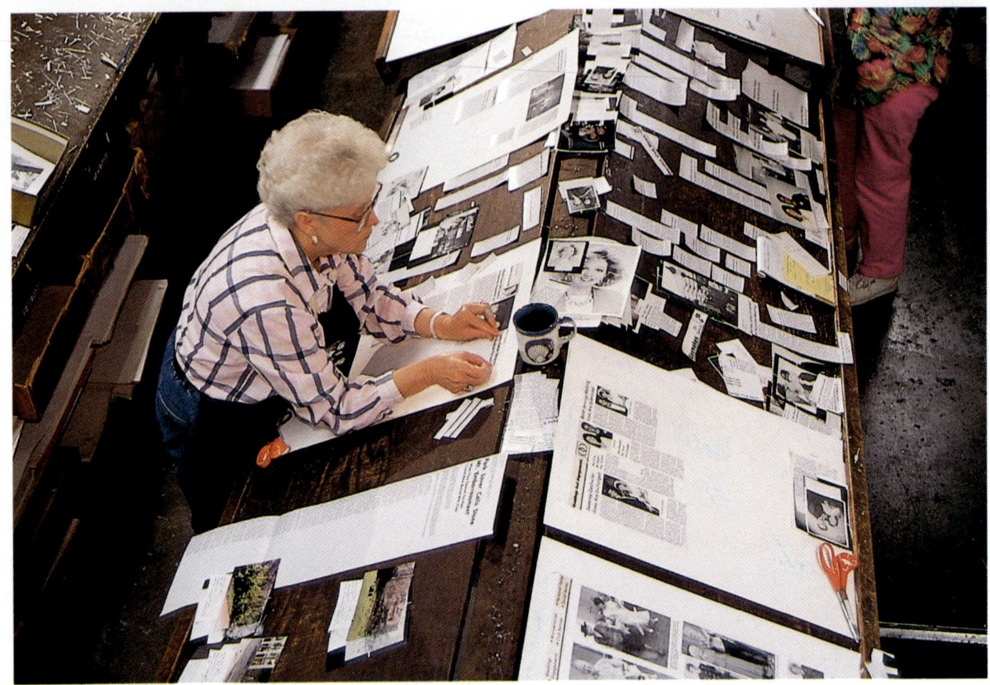

12:30 PM *Tuesday found news editors and graphic artists laying out pages of the* DeKalb News/Sun, *the county's home-delivered weekly newspaper. The forty-five-year-old newspaper was to cease publication unexpectedly shortly after the Christmas holidays, throwing more than one hundred employees, including Editor Helen Ordner (shown here) out of work. The* News/Sun *had been the county's main source of news about local government, school and community news. The company would continue to publish an expanded version of the county legal organ, the* Decatur-DeKalb News/Era.
PHOTO BY CHUCK YOUNG.

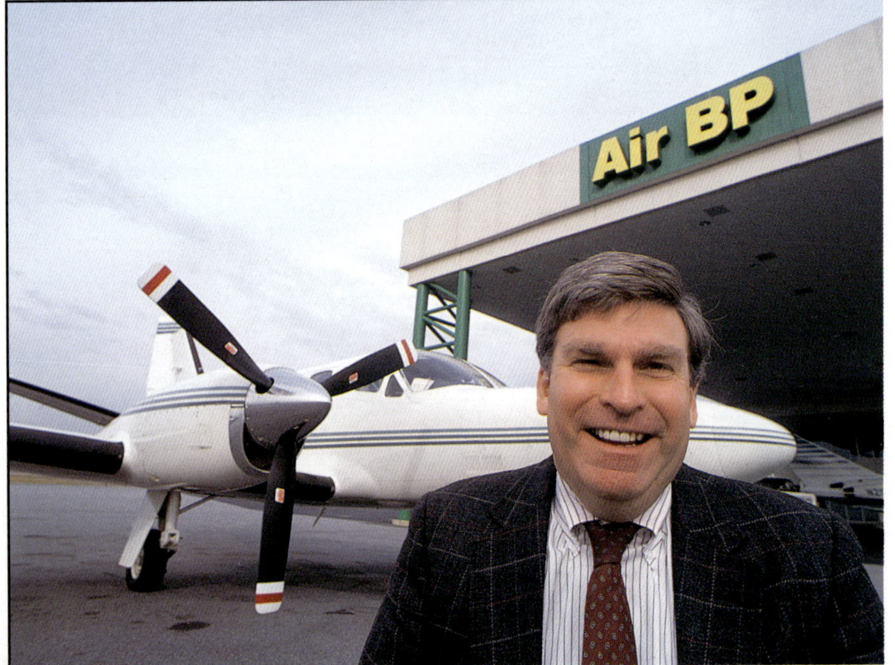

ALAN WEINER

AIR BP ATLANTA

DeKalb-Peachtree Airport

A full-service FBO featuring an Airside Canopy and award-winning services for pilots and passengers

At Air BP Atlanta, we like to say that 'You never have to ask twice.' That's how committed we are to meeting our customers' needs through quality service, courtesy and consistency. ◆ "Air BP Atlanta is a full-service, fixed-based operation located at the DeKalb-Peachtree Airport, ready to serve pilots and their passengers. Our trademark green and yellow logo is displayed on our distinctive 8,000 square-foot Airside Canopy, where passengers and planes stay dry and comfortable, no matter what the weather is like outside. ◆ "Once you've landed, our services are designed to meet the needs of pilots and passengers alike. Through Air BP's complete line service and state-of-the-art facilities, we offer everything from overnight hangar storage to fuel to rental cars for pilots — as well as limousine service, steak and lobster dinners and executive conference facilities for passengers. ◆ "We are available twenty-four hours, seven days a week. Our clients range from an individual owner-pilot to the president of a large Fortune 500 company coming to the Atlanta area for business. ◆ "In 1990, Air BP chose the DeKalb area because of the diversity of the industry in the area, and the number of Fortune 500 companies that do business in the DeKalb County area. ◆ "Each day, those business connections result in over fifty flights in and out of Air BP Atlanta. And we're in a growing stage. We've been at the airport for four years, and owned by Air BP for two years. Our fuel sales for 1992 were up 12 percent over 1991. Our traffic has similarly increased. It's a great location and an excellent facility."

— R. Earl Davis, General Manager

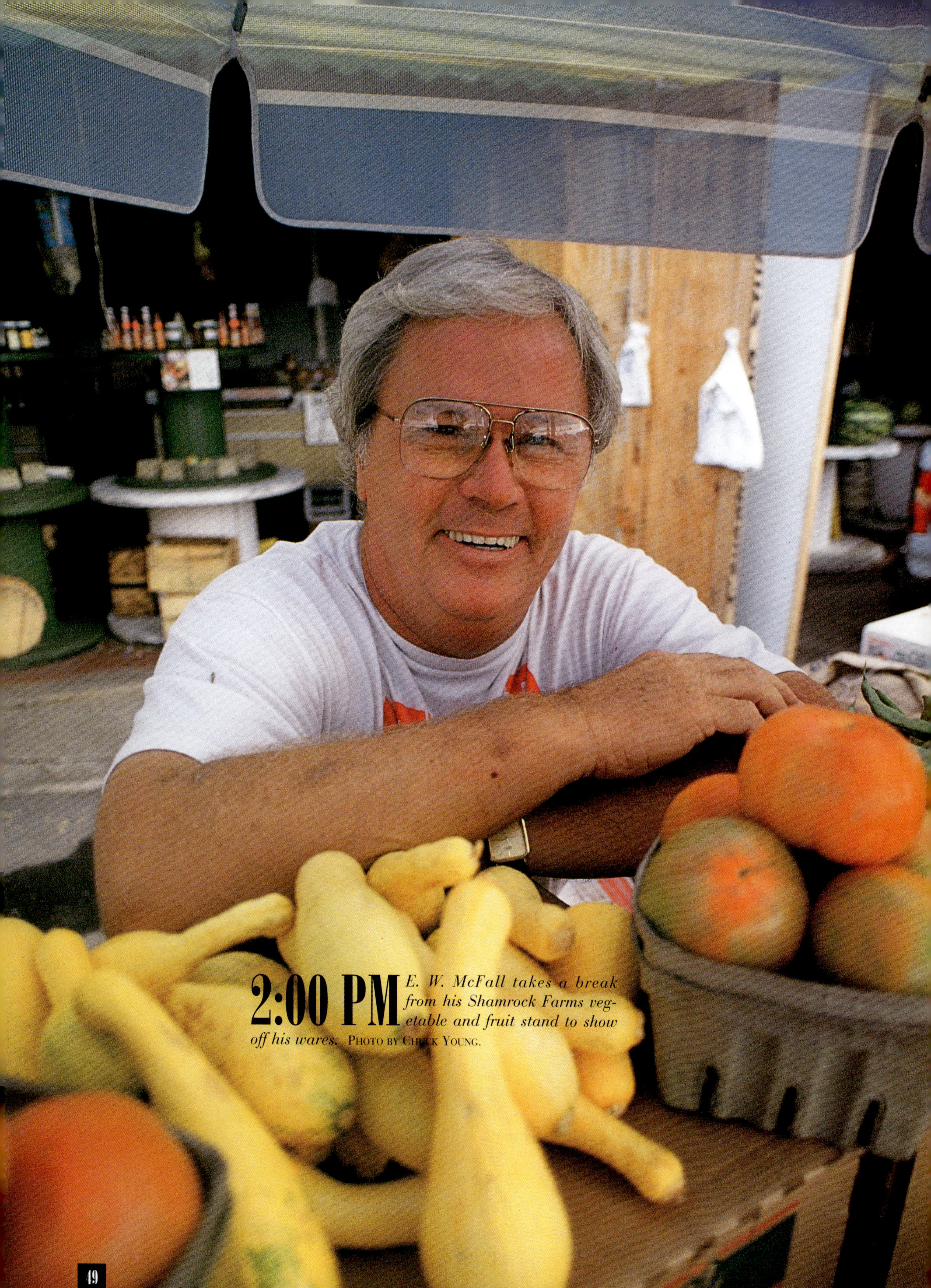

2:00 PM *E. W. McFall takes a break from his Shamrock Farms vegetable and fruit stand to show off his wares.* PHOTO BY CHUCK YOUNG.

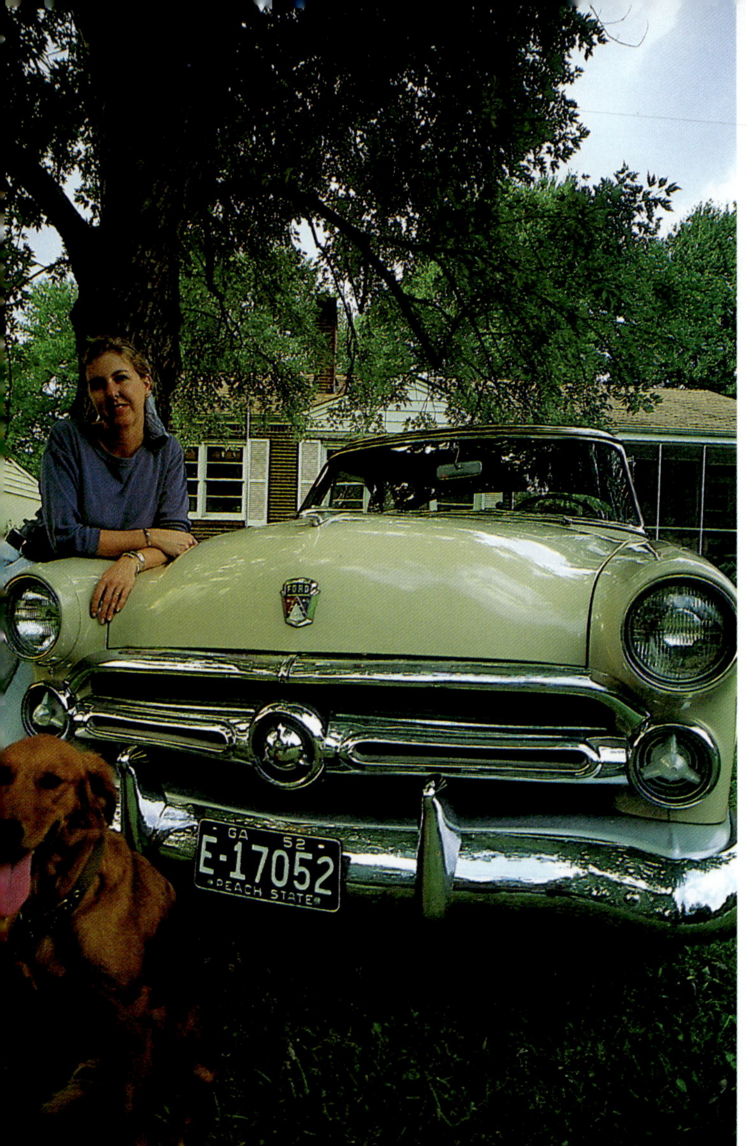

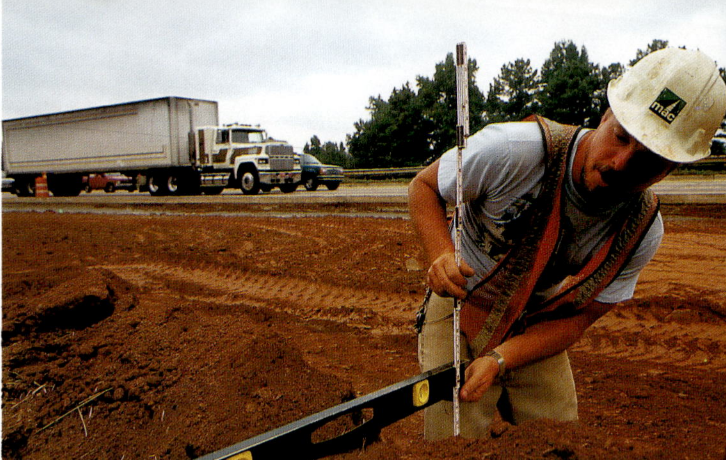

3:30 PM *In a county that is 269 square miles in size, there is highway construction going on somewhere all the time. Motorists can expect the commute between Atlanta and southeast DeKalb to be faster and smoother when extra lanes are opened along a five-mile stretch of I-20 in October 1993. An additional four miles of improvements will be completed by the summer of 1994. DeKalb County's three interstate highways will be the beneficiaries of a revolutionary high-tech traffic-management system expected to be in place by the time millions of visitors flock to Atlanta for the 1994 Super Bowl and the 1996 Olympics.* PHOTO BY SCOTT ROBINSON.

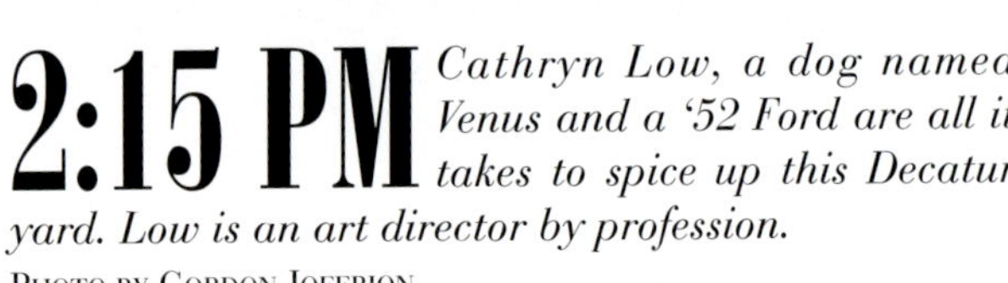

2:15 PM *Cathryn Low, a dog named Venus and a '52 Ford are all it takes to spice up this Decatur yard. Low is an art director by profession.* PHOTO BY GORDON JOFFRION.

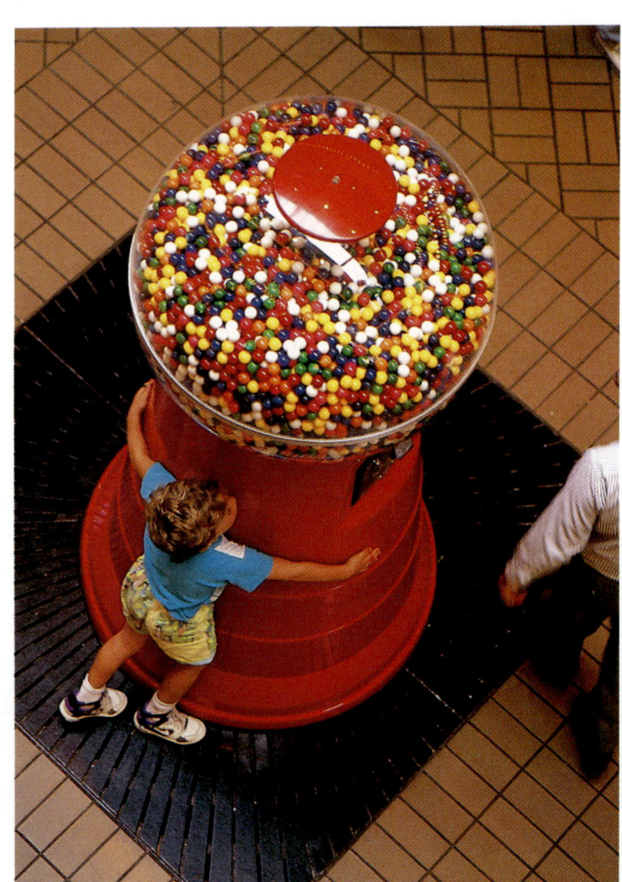

3:30 PM *The oversized scale of this bubble-gum machine is just right to be the centerpiece for Atlanta's largest mall food court. This youngster could have chosen her snack from twenty-one food-court vendors at Perimeter Mall, plus three specialty restaurants. Located in the affluent Dunwoody community, the mall draws its clientele from all over the metropolitan area and beyond, making the centrally located food court an ideal spot for people-watching. Perimeter is DeKalb County's largest mall, with three anchors and 185 specialty stores.* PHOTO BY TOM ENGLAND.

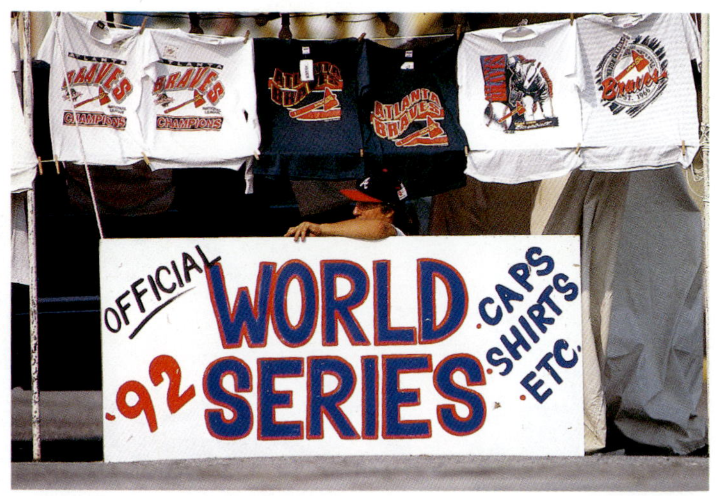

4:00 PM *Braves fever is as rampant in DeKalb as anywhere on this hot Tuesday afternoon, as evidenced by the sea of memorabilia for sale here and elsewhere.* Photo by Scott Robinson.

4:30 PM *Sometimes sports can become a family affair. In the case of the Luckie family, it is an all-consuming affair, as triplets (left to right) Dustin, Michael and Miles all play for the Clarkston High School football team. When football is out of season, they merely turn their interests to other sports, such as baseball and wrestling.* Photo by Jim Cook.

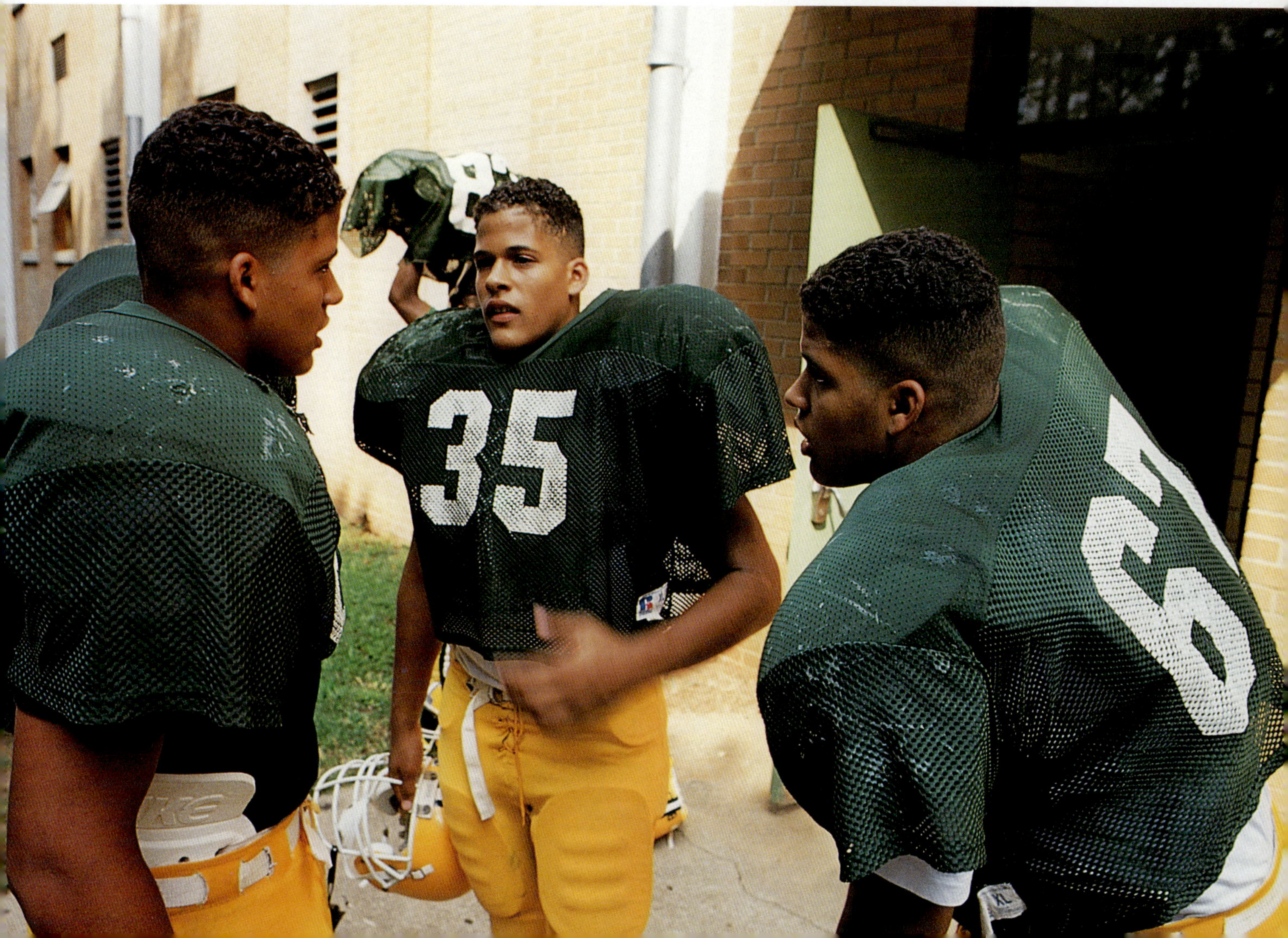

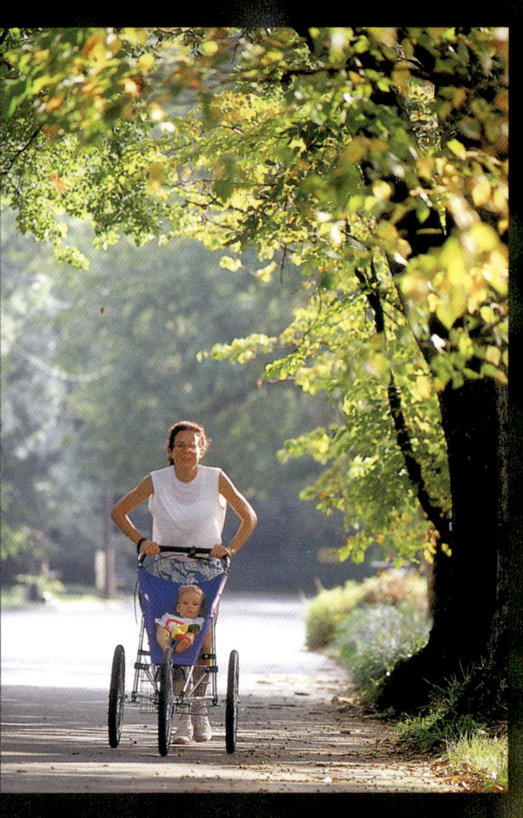

5:02 PM *Susan Pesce jogs with son Matthew, ten months, along tree-shaded Springdale Road in Druid Hills. One of Atlanta's premiere neighborhoods, Druid Hills is known for its fine old homes and the series of linear parks designed by landscape architect Frederick Law Olmsted, creator of Central Park in New York City. Susan and her husband are expecting their second child.* PHOTO BY GREG FOSTER.

6:10 PM *Kim Sheffield, and her four-year-old son, Brett, close the day by testing the waters at the Avondale Estates lake.* PHOTO BY DAVID MURRAY.

5:35 PM *Apartment living holds a particular appeal to many DeKalb residents, who prefer to leave the lawnmowing to someone else. Complexes compete for the attention of apartment-seekers by providing amenities, from pools and clubhouses to services that mimic those found in a small town: voter registration, dry cleaning, recycling and video rentals. The 296-unit Summit Oaks complex in Clarkston has two pools, tennis courts and a new fitness center—and of course, the mailboxes where residents such as Kelly McDonald and Patricia Biethmuller occasionally bump into each other.* PHOTO BY MARILYN FUTTERMAN.

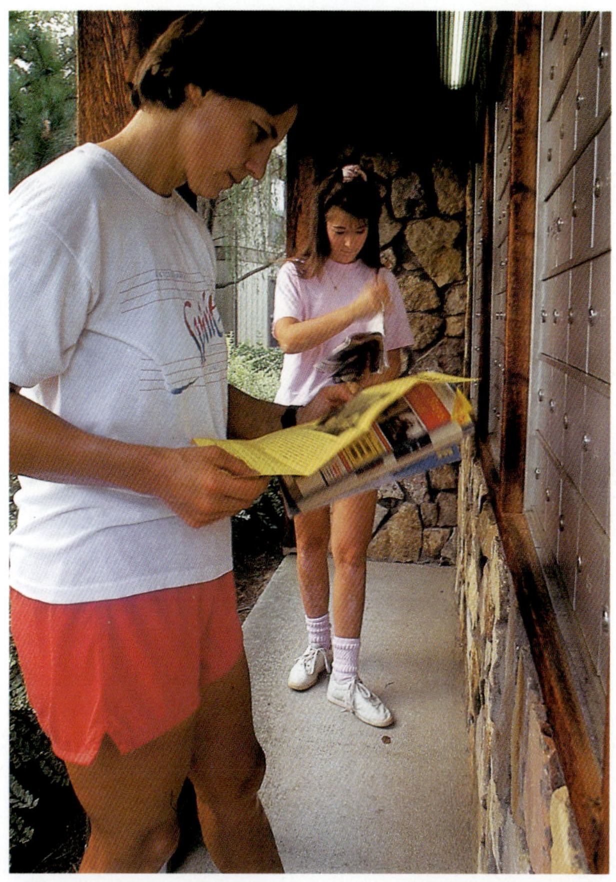

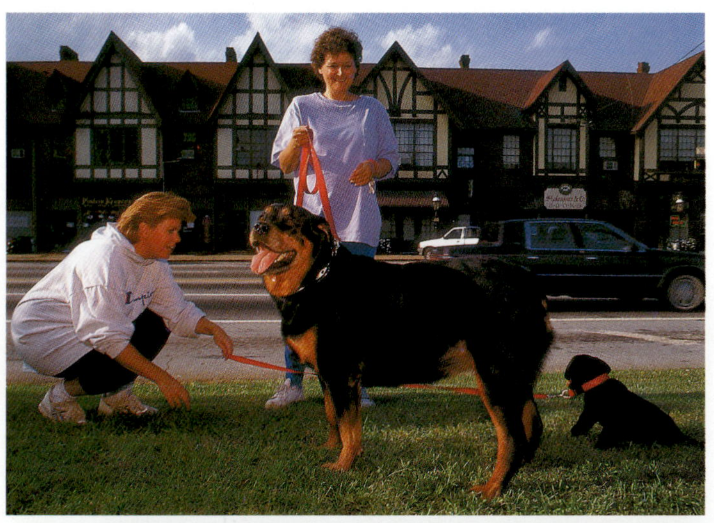

6:30 PM *Susan McGhee Rieker and Sandra Ford spend a few minutes in downtown Avondale Estates and give their friends, Dorsey and Cocoa, a minute to relax.* PHOTO BY DAVID MURRAY.

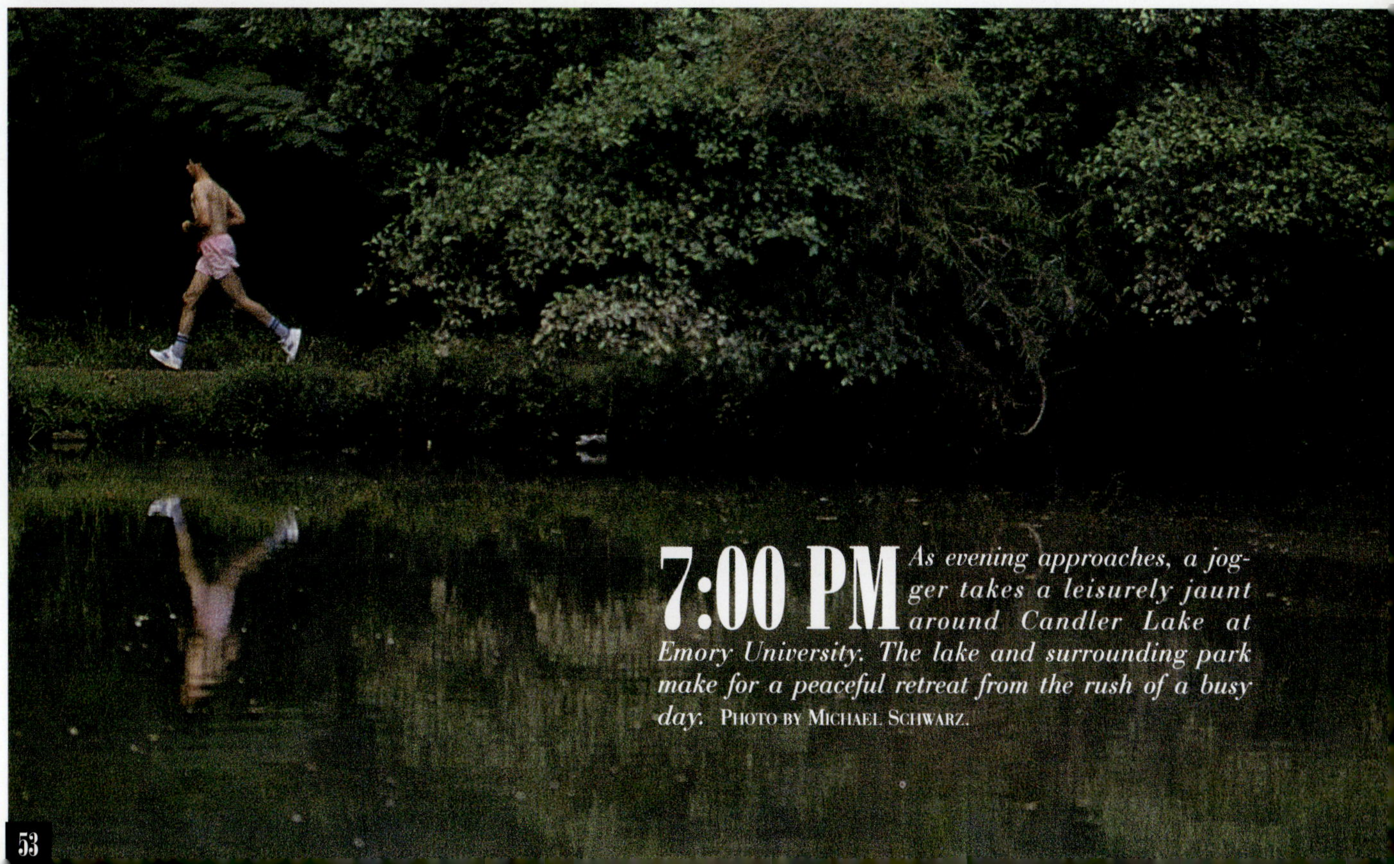

7:00 PM *As evening approaches, a jogger takes a leisurely jaunt around Candler Lake at Emory University. The lake and surrounding park make for a peaceful retreat from the rush of a busy day.* PHOTO BY MICHAEL SCHWARZ.

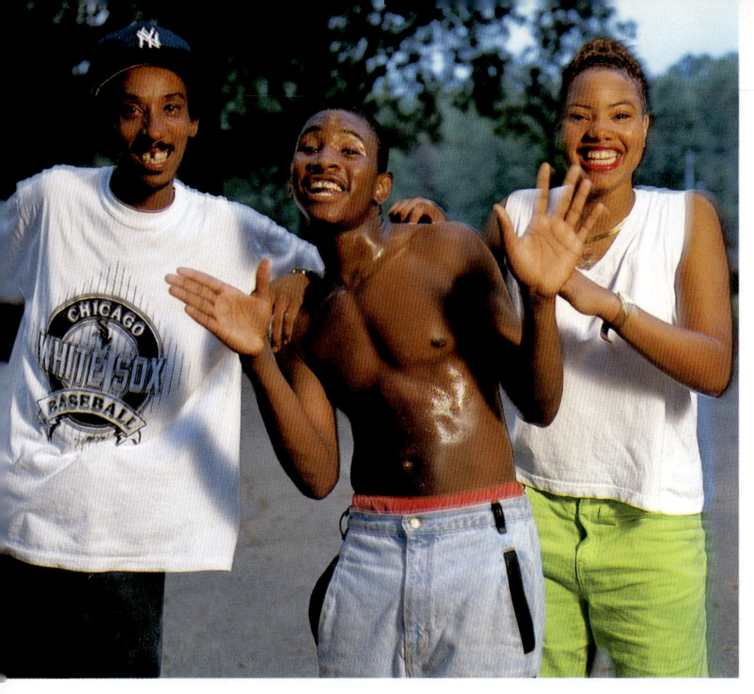

7:39 PM *Anywhere there's a hoop and a ball in DeKalb you're bound to find a pick-up game of roundball or general fun. At Longdale Park on Memorial Drive in Atlanta-in-DeKalb, Pamela Hill, Stacey Knight and Anthony Harkness clown for the photographer before returning to their game. DeKalb's Department of Recreation, Parks and Cultural Affairs operates thirty-six parks with outdoor basketball goals, as well as recreation centers, golf courses, tennis courts, athletic fields, playgrounds and lakes on 3,575 acres throughout the county.* PHOTO BY ANN STATES.

And while Scouting is as American as Mom, Apple Pie and Baseball, the consensus is not as clear on a thirty-three-year-old nude dancer Nova White. "I'm an entertainer," says White, who has firmly grasped the First Amendment issue surrounding her craft. "My dance is about the total woman. I should be able to dance where I want to dance." Community officials and residents disagree and have been pushing hard for ordinances to control the activity.

Four-month-old Kyle Sebring is too young to be an Eagle Scout and his mother Paige is too tired and concerned to worry about nude dancers. It's 9:40 P.M., and they've just arrived at the Emergency Room at Northlake Regional Medical Center. Several hours ago, Kyle started coughing, wouldn't take his bottle and became uncharacteristically fussy. "He's not himself," says Mrs. Sebring, looking down at the twenty-pound bundle whom she tries to comfort in her arms. Dr. Eric Deal, ER director,

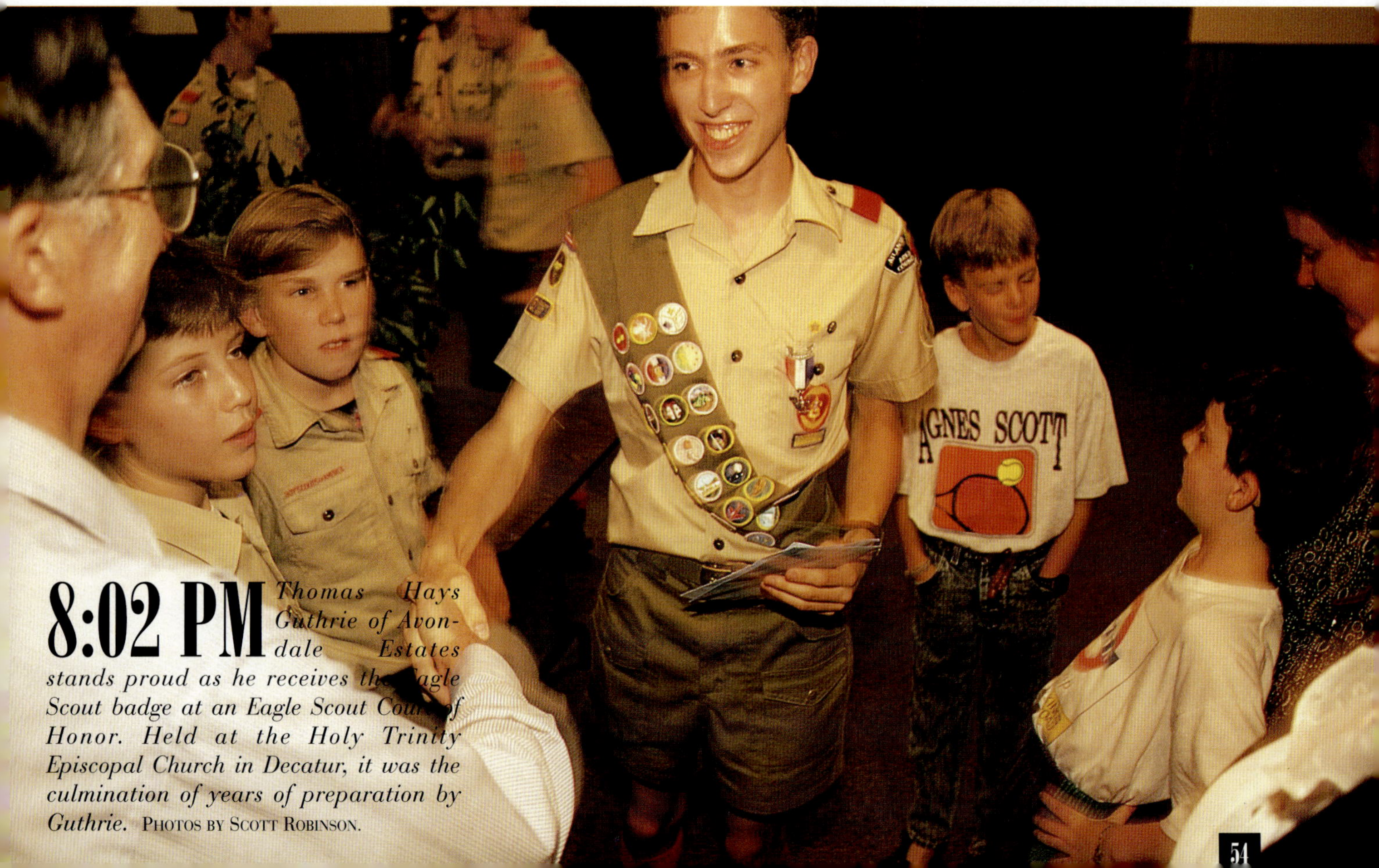

8:02 PM *Thomas Hays Guthrie of Avondale Estates stands proud as he receives the Eagle Scout badge at an Eagle Scout Court of Honor. Held at the Holy Trinity Episcopal Church in Decatur, it was the culmination of years of preparation by Guthrie.* PHOTOS BY SCOTT ROBINSON.

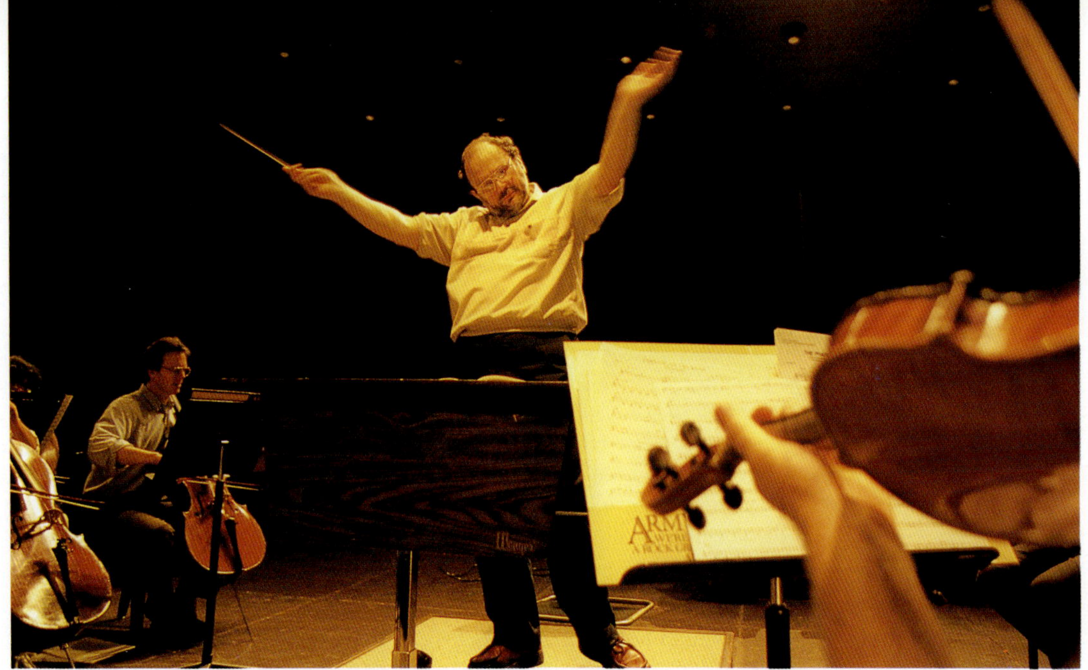

orders tests and eventually rules out anything serious, like pneumonia. Kyle has a slight fever, an ear infection and a cold—a diagnosis that's a welcome relief to tonight's busy ER staff, which has already treated patients suffering from car accident injuries, chest pains and broken bones. Just before midnight, the Sebrings go home to Tucker, where everyone finally goes to sleep.

8:16 PM *Conductor Tom Anderson leads the DeKalb Symphony Orchestra through rehearsal paces at DeKalb College. Founded in 1964, the orchestra is made up of professional and talented amateur musicians, and is supported by DeKalb College, where it holds the majority of its concerts. The orchestra, which includes violinist Lynne Webster (pictured here) presents a fifteen-concert series annually, and frequently is invited to perform in other Georgia cities. Specializing in all varieties of classical music, the orchestra also performs a popular annual children's concert.* Photos by Ken Hawkins.

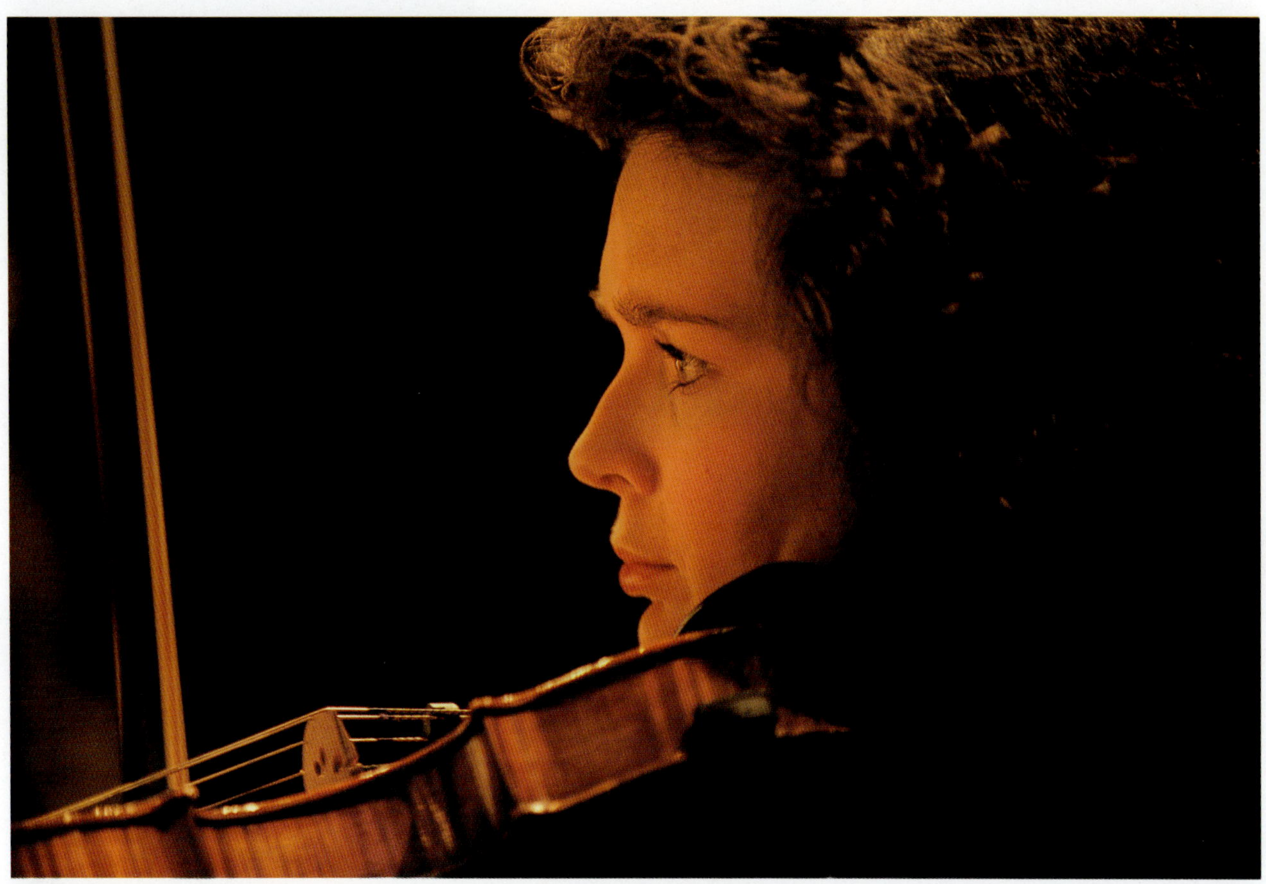

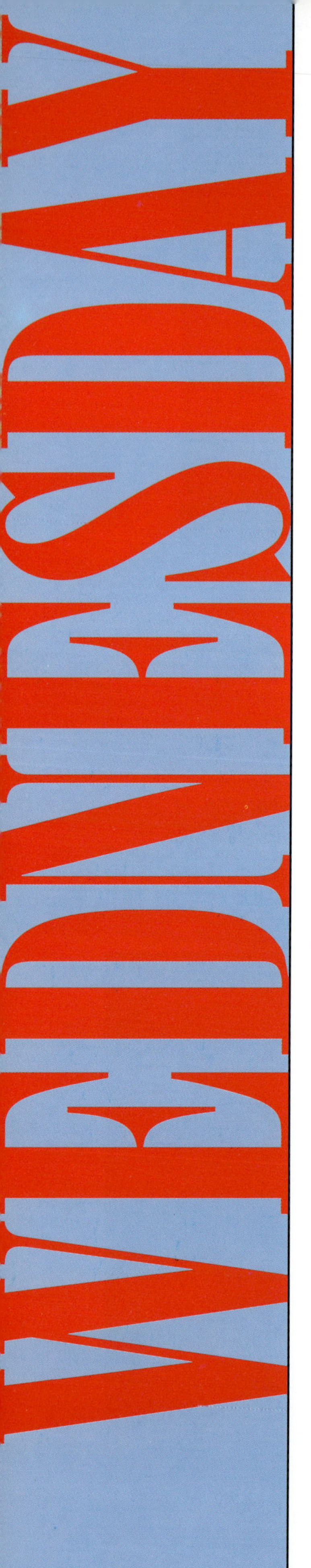

Decatur Hospital is a small private facility. And what that means for each individual patient is more concentrated care. Patients don't get lost. There is a nurse ten steps away from every patient, at all times. Our entire medical staff is attuned to the needs of each individual, to make sure he or she gets the most up-to-date care available. ◆ "One of the things you should look for in a hospital is how much experience the hospital staff has in a particular area of expertise. That will determine how the staff responds to your problems, their degree of medical skill, how well they know the equipment and how advanced the equipment will be. ◆ "Decatur Hospital provides the latest in medical services in several different surgical specialties, and was one of the first hospitals to offer and perfect laparoscopic gall bladder surgery. Other services include ophthalmology; gynecology; orthopedics; oral surgery; urology, including lithotripsy to remove kidney stones; ear, nose and throat surgery; and its nationally recognized 'You're Becoming' plastic surgery program. Our hospital also provides one of the most comprehensive adult substance abuse treatment programs, as well as an eating disorders treatment program that receives referrals from all over the country. ◆ "Decatur Hospital probably performs more eye surgery than any other hospital in the Atlanta area. When a hospital has a large volume of cases in any one area, that helps define that institution as an efficient and highly skilled operation. There are a number of reasons to explain why that's true at Decatur. ◆ "First, the hospital has decided that in terms of equipment, it will always provide the most modern, state of the art equipment available. The administration has made a concerted effort to give the twenty-plus ophthalmologists, as well as the other medical specialists who practice here, the most up-to-date technology for the benefit of our patients. They are extremely responsive to the needs of the doctors, which is not something you find in every hospital. When you are working with a big hospital, they might say, 'Let's put it in next year's budget.' Here, the first question is, 'Is there a need?' And the response is, 'We will get it.' ◆ "And second, the ease with which the doctors work throughout the hospital and with the nursing staff is remarkable. And those combined elements translate into the most advanced, skilled and person-

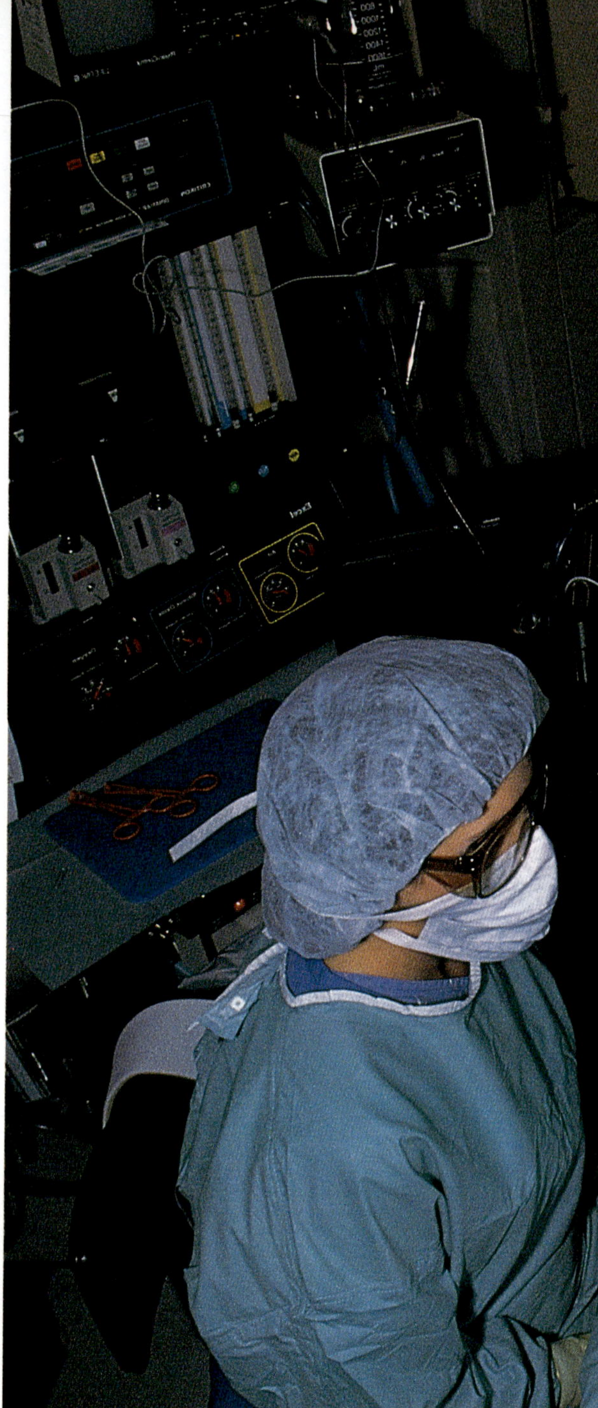

DECATUR HOSPITAL

120 Bed Facility with 225 employees. Opened in 1973.

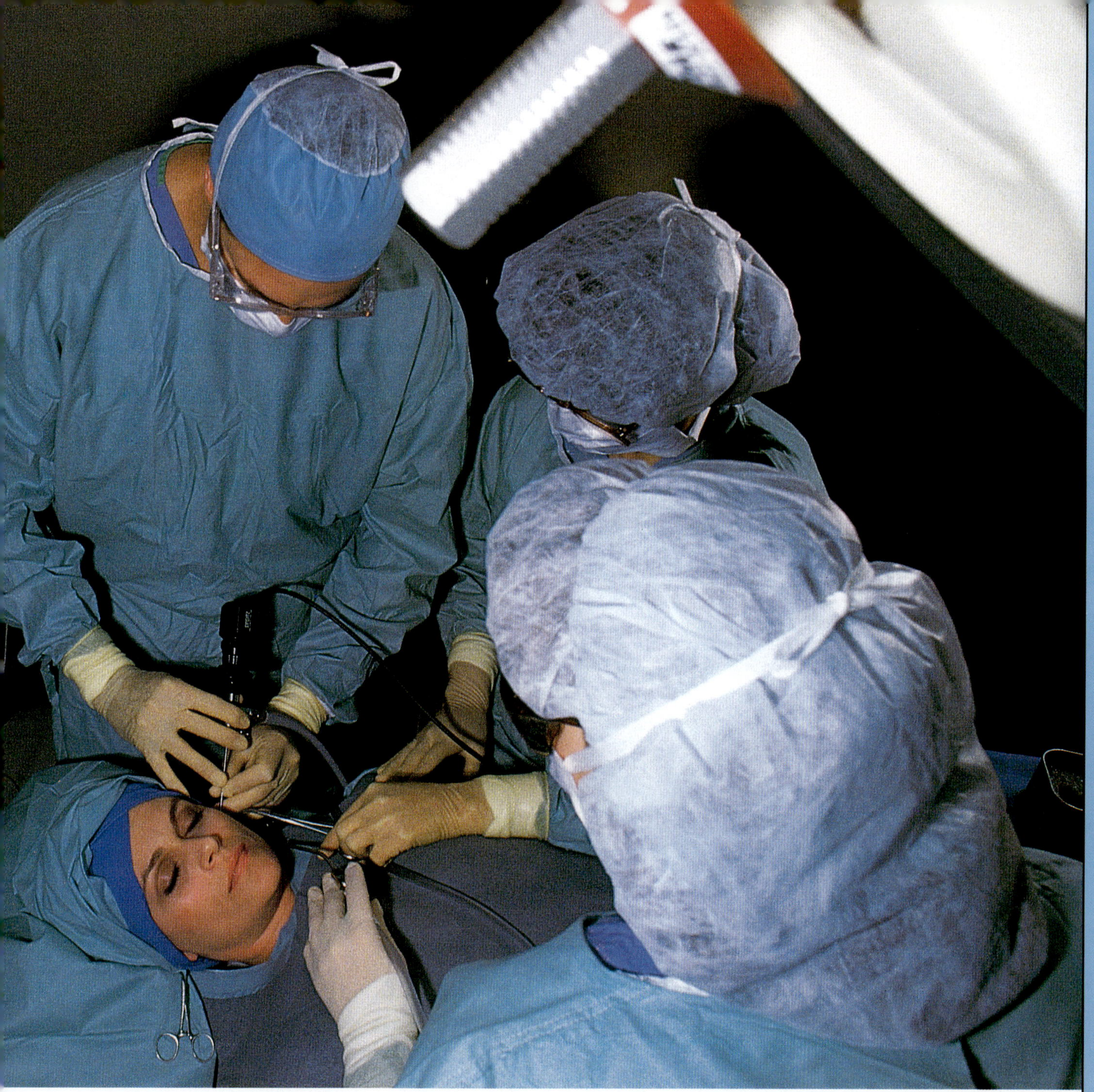

ALAN WEINER

alized patient care available. ◆ "We have a wide range of patients — anywhere from six months to 103 years old. Most of the cataract surgery is for older patients, but even young children may have congenital cataracts or crossed eyes that necessitate surgery. ◆ "And we like to always remember that we are a community hospital. Which means that we provide some extra special services for our patients, like a courtesy van for transportation to and from the hospital. And Decatur's 'Care + Center' is like an after-hours doctor's office for an emergency that isn't quite life threatening but nonetheless needs prompt medical attention. You can have your own doctor meet you here, or arrange for a house physician to see you or a member of your family. ◆ "When people think of Decatur Hospital, I would like for them to think about a small hospital with a caring attitude and the ability to respond quickly to the needs of the patient. That's important to us. That's what we're all about. We are state-of-the-art in every respect. That's why we like to say that we are the hospital where quality care gets personal."

— Dr. Stephen P. Leff, Ophthalmologist, Vice-Chief of Staff

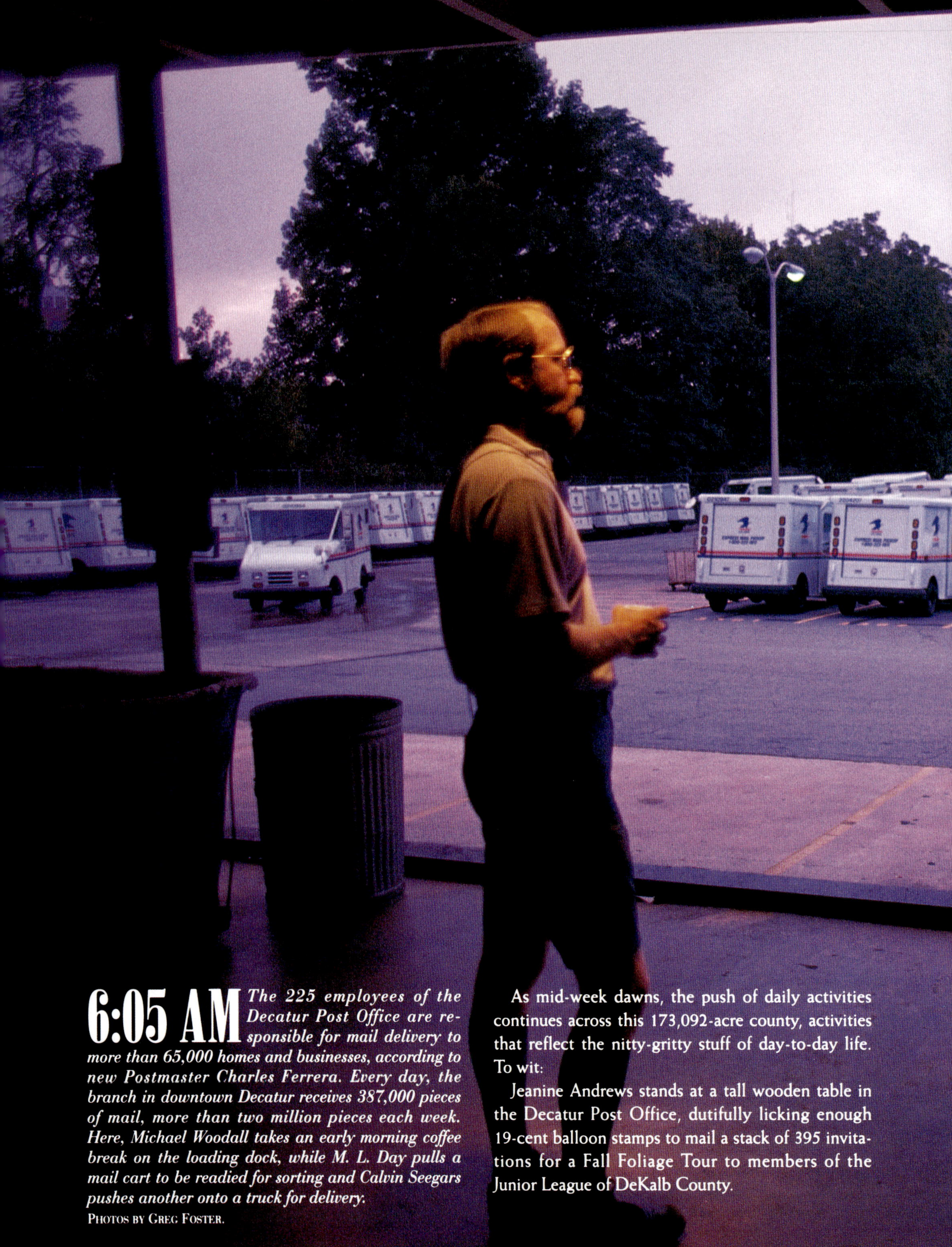

6:05 AM *The 225 employees of the Decatur Post Office are responsible for mail delivery to more than 65,000 homes and businesses, according to new Postmaster Charles Ferrera. Every day, the branch in downtown Decatur receives 387,000 pieces of mail, more than two million pieces each week. Here, Michael Woodall takes an early morning coffee break on the loading dock, while M. L. Day pulls a mail cart to be readied for sorting and Calvin Seegars pushes another onto a truck for delivery.*
PHOTOS BY GREG FOSTER.

As mid-week dawns, the push of daily activities continues across this 173,092-acre county, activities that reflect the nitty-gritty stuff of day-to-day life. To wit:

Jeanine Andrews stands at a tall wooden table in the Decatur Post Office, dutifully licking enough 19-cent balloon stamps to mail a stack of 395 invitations for a Fall Foliage Tour to members of the Junior League of DeKalb County.

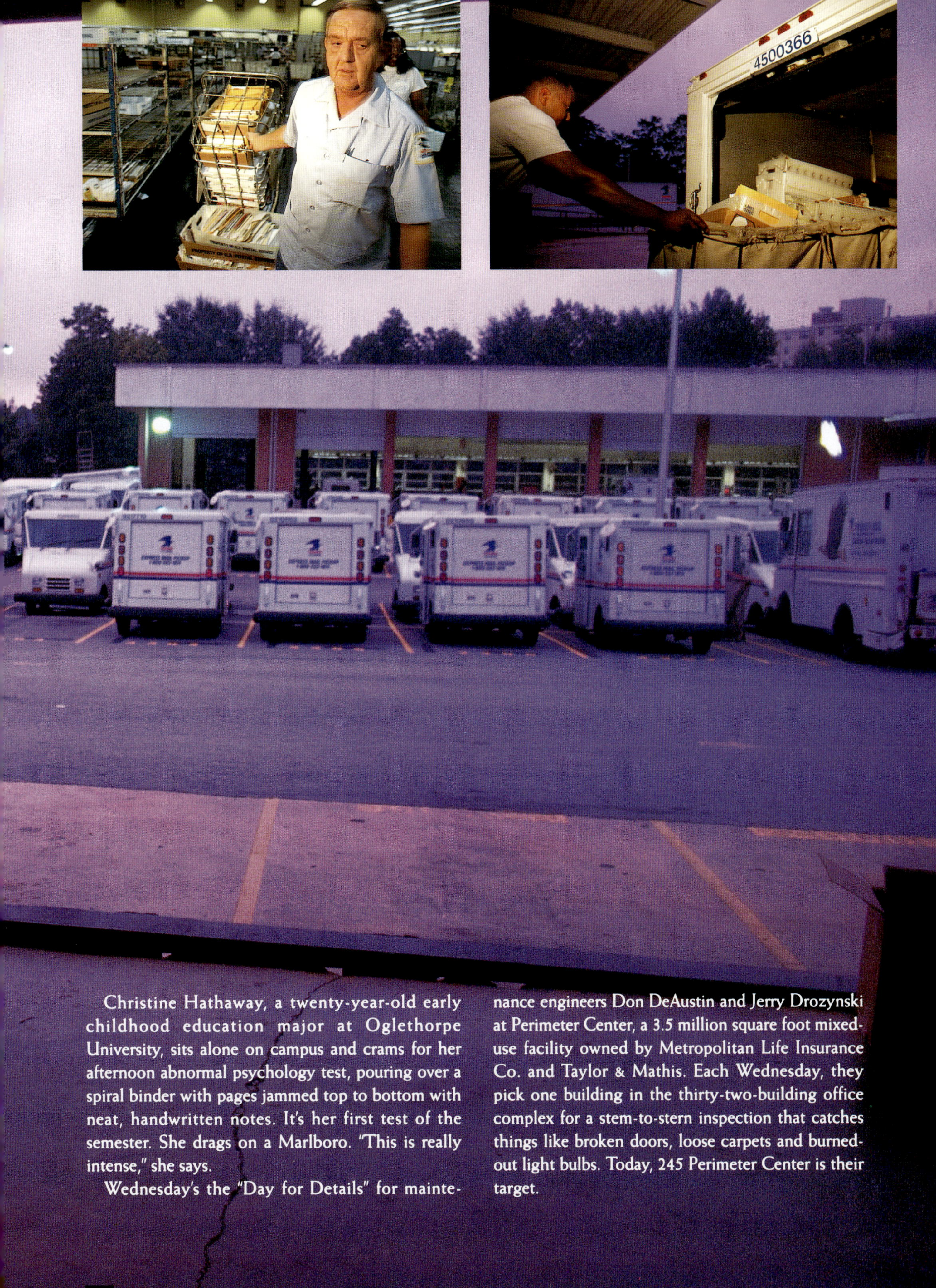

Christine Hathaway, a twenty-year-old early childhood education major at Oglethorpe University, sits alone on campus and crams for her afternoon abnormal psychology test, pouring over a spiral binder with pages jammed top to bottom with neat, handwritten notes. It's her first test of the semester. She drags on a Marlboro. "This is really intense," she says.

Wednesday's the "Day for Details" for maintenance engineers Don DeAustin and Jerry Drozynski at Perimeter Center, a 3.5 million square foot mixed-use facility owned by Metropolitan Life Insurance Co. and Taylor & Mathis. Each Wednesday, they pick one building in the thirty-two-building office complex for a stem-to-stern inspection that catches things like broken doors, loose carpets and burned-out light bulbs. Today, 245 Perimeter Center is their target.

6:20 AM *In the gray dawn, the lights of one of DeKalb's premiere corporate citizens, Holiday Inn, shine out like a beacon. The worldwide hotel chain had only recently moved its international headquarters to DeKalb and adopted the Crowne Plaza Ravinia as its signature hotel for the area.*

PHOTO BY ROB NELSON.

And today bride-to-be Lisa Colesworthy has taken off from work to prepare for her Saturday wedding to Loren Burke at the Houston Mill House near Emory. Crammed into her back pocket is Lisa's "Stuff to Do" list: pick up gown, pick up necklace for Jo (flower girl), pick up Jo's dress and headpiece;

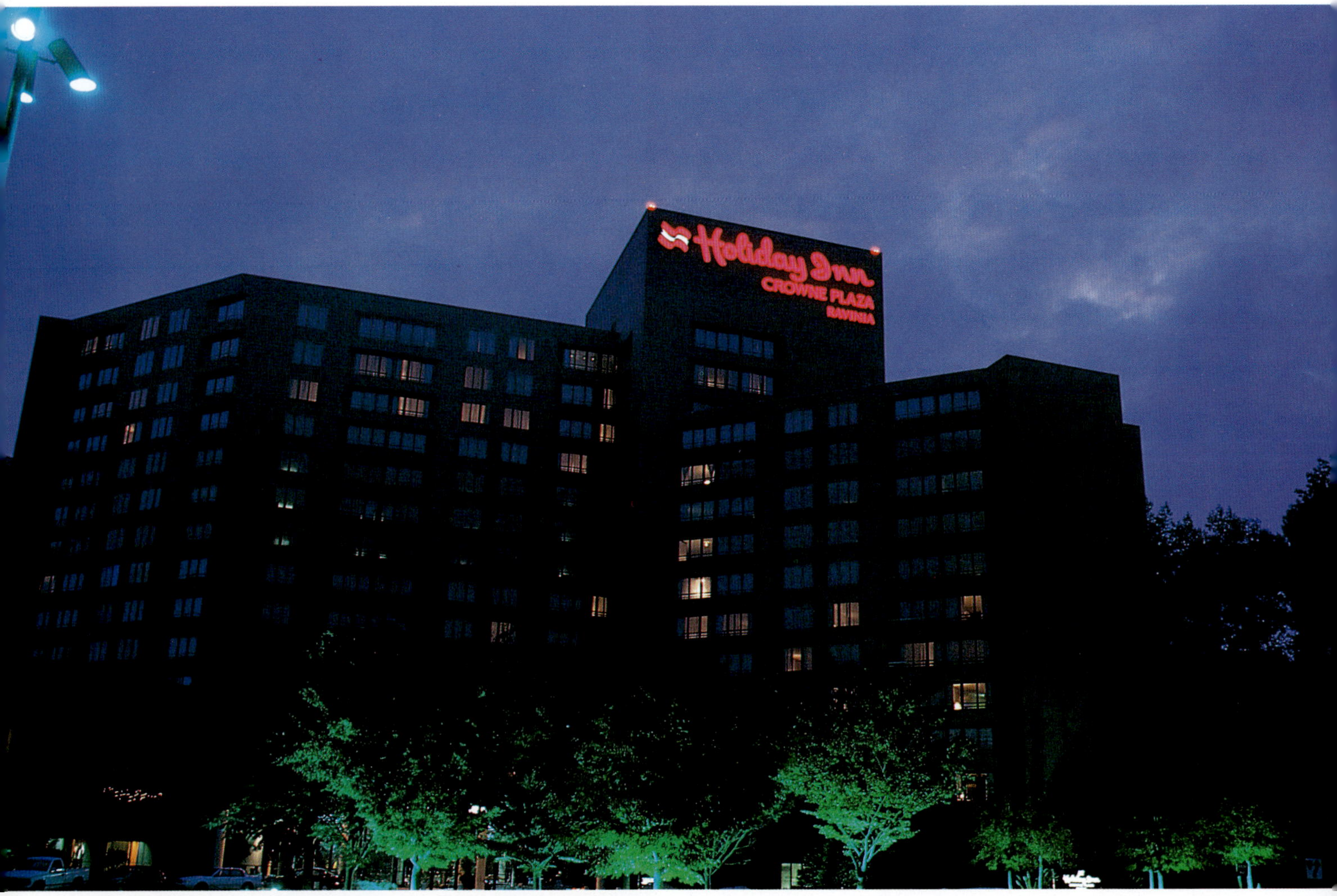

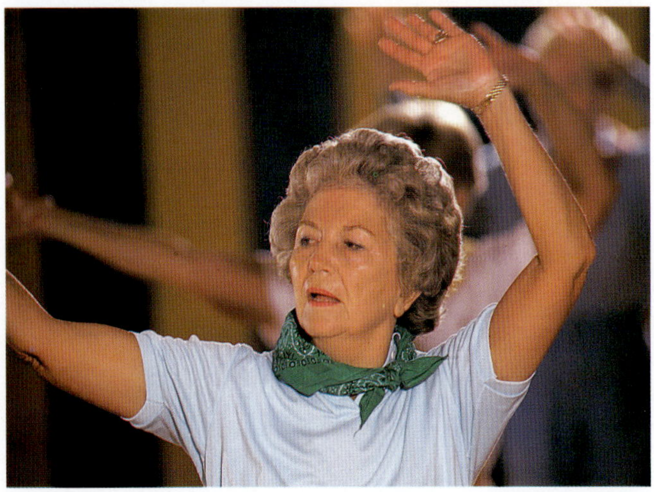

7:50 AM *They're doing the Achy Breaky at Briarlake Baptist Church. Deborah Wingate teaches a light aerobic exercise class for senior citizens at Briarlake. The low-impact, low-intensity workout exercises are done to music which adds to participants' enjoyment, according to spokesperson Bobbie Elzey. Class favorites include country line dances like the Achy Breaky and the Electric Slide. Next on the class agenda, Elzey says, is the Push Tush. The classes are among many activities sponsored by Life Enrichment Services, a privately funded organization operated by and for senior citizens.*

PHOTO BY GORDON JOFFRION.

pick up bridal shoes; go to the grocery store and farmers market; call restaurant to confirm details of rehearsal dinner; pick up rehearsal-dinner dress and shoes; pick up stuff for post-reception party. "I'm tired," she says, "but I'm starting to get excited."

Nearly one hundred people sit in the jury room of the DeKalb County Courthouse, each with a blue stick-on name tag that says "Juror-DeKalb County." John Simmons, who works with the city of Avondale Estates, is seated in the last row, trying to stay awake for a process he considers "part of the American Way." A few seats away, Karen Hand of Tucker, a

8:02 AM *Winnona Park is one of seven elementary schools in the City of Decatur School System. Independent of the DeKalb School System, the city also operates one high school and one middle school, with 2,200 students and 180 teachers. The school system is a source of pride to citizens of the tight-knit municipality. More than 70 percent of Decatur High School's graduating class of 1992 gained acceptance into college, 30 percent of them with scholarships. One quarter of the seniors are members of the National Honor Society.* PHOTO BY TOM ENGLAND.

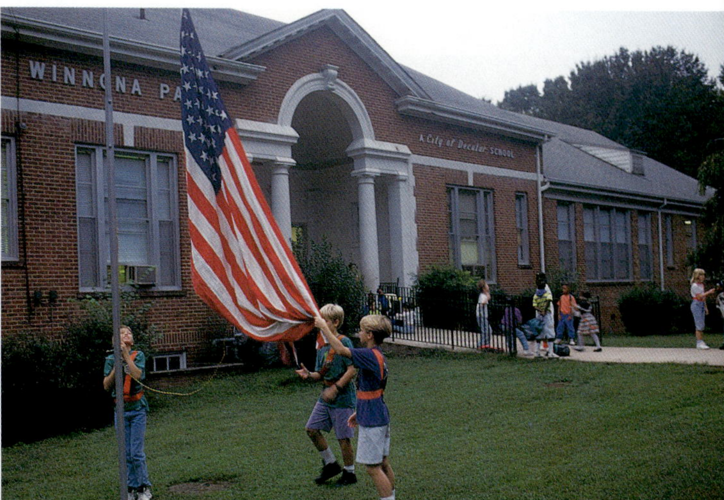

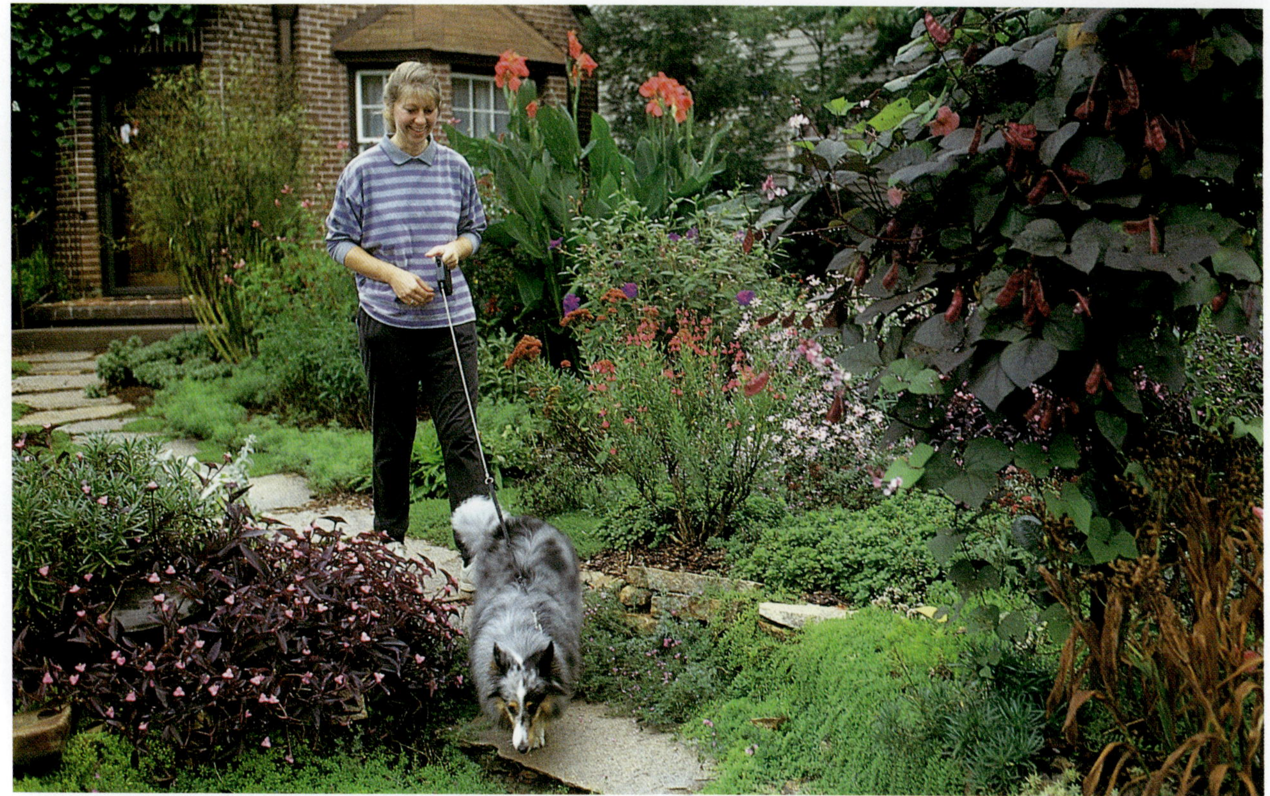

8:15 AM *Among the Purple Hearts flowers and other shrubs of her Winnona Park home, Becky Stewart and her sheltie, named Pepper, find a peaceful place for a morning outing.* PHOTO BY TOM ENGLAND.

8:30 AM *They came from Cincinnati, and they weren't about to let a little rain stop them from enjoying their tour. Rain hats and umbrellas were regulation equipment for this day in September. It may have rained out picnics at Stone Mountain Park, but it was perfect for mall shopping and museum hopping.* PHOTO BY DAVID MURRAY.

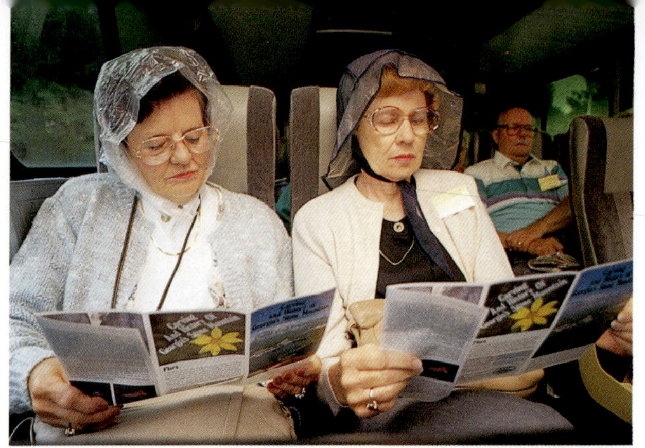

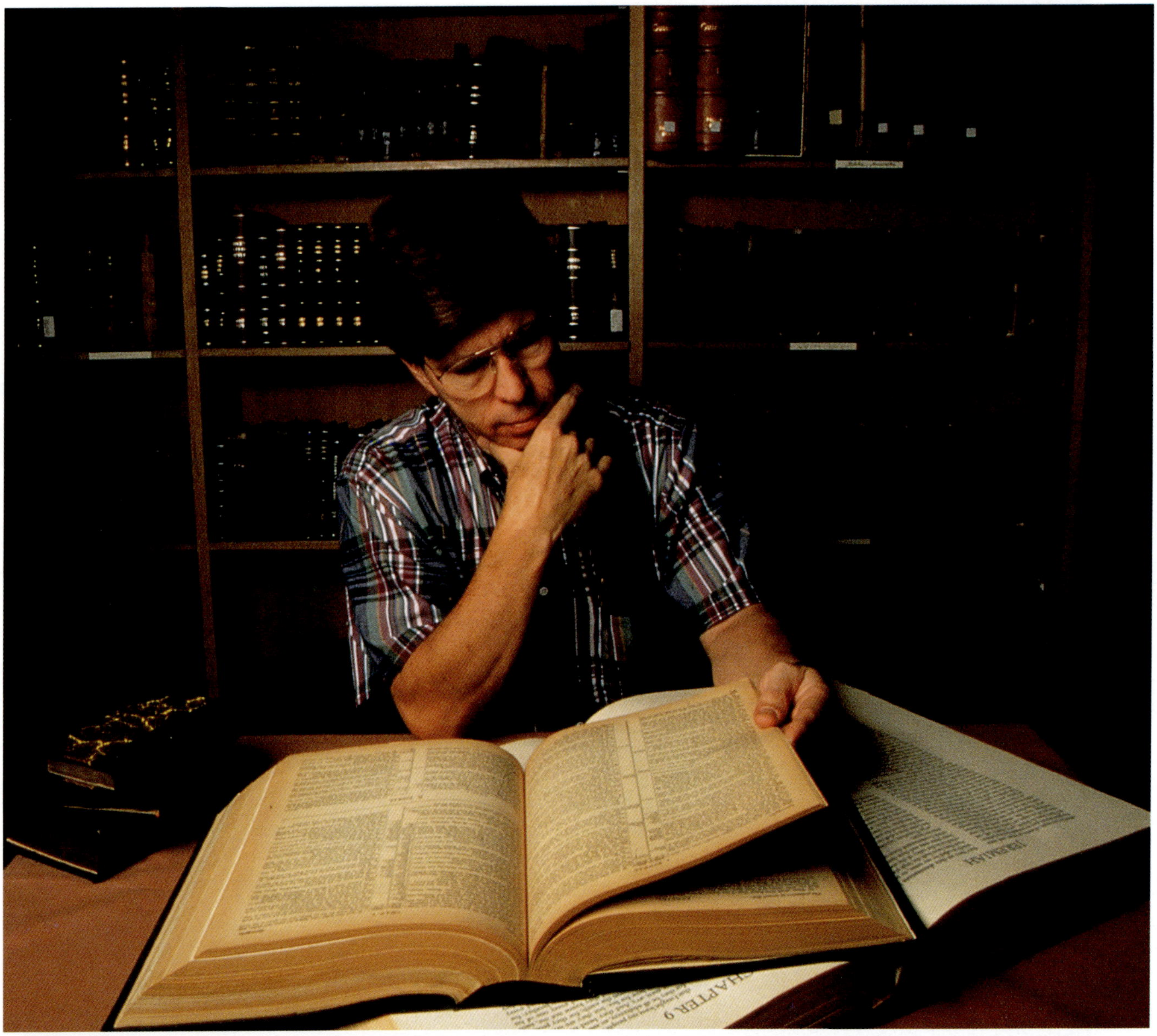

9:00 AM *In a serene setting with huge, old trees on Columbia Drive in Decatur, Columbia Theological Seminary provides both clergy and laity with theological education. Opened in 1828, the school moved to DeKalb County in 1927 from Columbia, South Carolina. More than 600 students—including Christopher J. Bobo, pictured here—are enrolled in five master's and doctoral degree programs. Well-known graduates include Peter Marshall and the late Charles Weltner, who served as chief justice of the Georgia Supreme Court. Of note is the seminary's International Theological Education Program which brings students and scholars from other countries to Decatur and sends local students abroad.*
PHOTO BY CHUCK YOUNG.

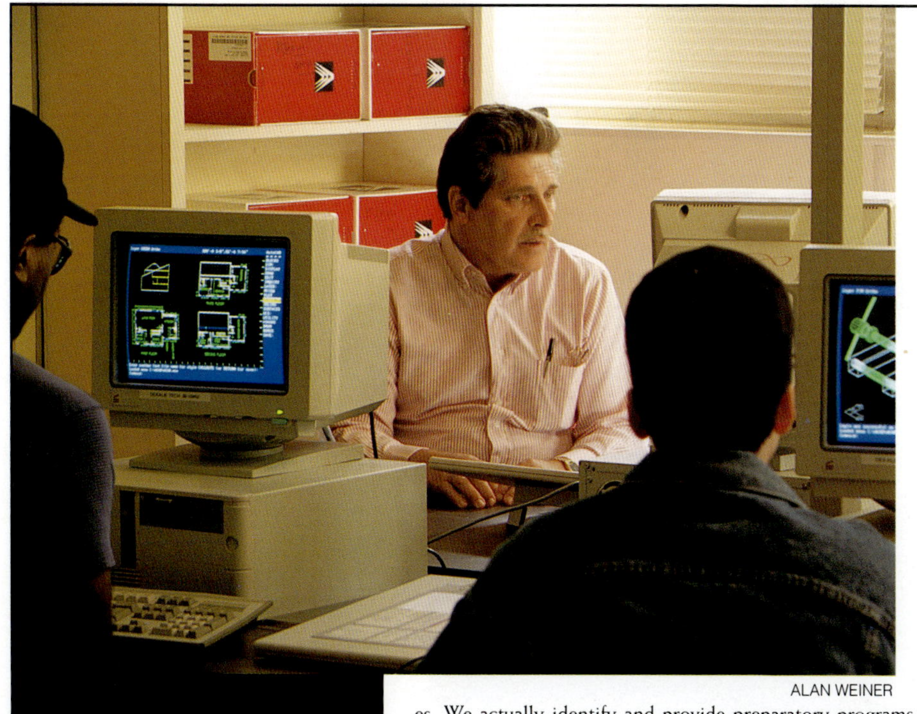

ALAN WEINER

DEKALB TECHNICAL INSTITUTE

The postsecondary unit of DeKalb County School System. Operates year-round at six locations. 565 full- and part-time faculty.

In DeKalb County, there are a growing number of non-English speaking residents. In fact, our latest figures show that 7 percent of DeKalb's population is not native to the United States. ◆ "At DeKalb Tech, nearly 6,800 adults enrolled in our programs each year use English as a second language, which is why teaching English is one of the most important services we perform. ◆ "Our enrollment has grown from eighteen in 1961, to more than 24,000 students in 1992. This makes DeKalb Tech one of the largest public technical institutes in Georgia. ◆ "We are constantly working with businesses and industries throughout the county to help meet their requests for training prospective employees in various occupational skills. These vary from office skills to highly technical computer skills for computer-aided design and manufacturing. ◆ "By serving the needs of DeKalb businesses, we are serving the citizenry who would like to have jobs with those businesses. We actually identify and provide preparatory programs for about fifty-five occupations. ◆ "We are actively involved in serving the underprivileged and the disadvantaged citizenry through federal job training programs. These programs essentially mirror programs that we have — but they are offered at no cost to the eligible individuals. Not only are their studies paid for, they also receive support in terms of cooperation with family services, baby sitting and meal subsidies. ◆ "I see our role at DeKalb Tech as being an agent for change. To change a citizen from being a tax liability to a tax payer is a worthy mission."

— **Dr. Paul M. Starnes, President**

homemaker with three children ages three, five and seven, reads a Harlequin romance novel while retired teacher Delores Henry of Lithonia, sits nearby, quiet and content. "Every citizen," she says, "should participate in the jury system."

And this morning, Virginia Davis awakens at 4:30, and pushes herself through a two-mile exercise walk near her Lithonia home before leaving for work as principal of Woodward Elementary School; the day 709 school buses take thousands of students to DeKalb County schools; the day J. Randall Carroll selects a Christmas card design for Mountain National Bank in Tucker; the day 937 U.S. postal service employees in DeKalb make 245,195 deliveries; the day Junior Troop 3352 in Stone Mountain, one of 400 Girl Scout troops in DeKalb, looks over Indian artifacts and explores Native American culture, while in Decatur the three oldest Turner girls have music lessons at Decatur Church of Christ; the day, like any other day, when money talks within the walls of DeKalb's forty financial institutions, which include seventeen banks with 117 branches, ten savings and loans with fifty-one branches and four international banks; and this is the day eighty children—count 'em!—aged four through twelve and dressed in oversized cowboy hats and blue jeans show up for a Pine Lake Baptist Church Choir Round-up to eat hot dogs and sing "Jesus, Name of All Names."

Throughout the day, throughout the county, the nitty-gritty stuff of life goes on. And yet there are pockets of time and place tucked inside this Wednesday where the hectic elements get pushed to

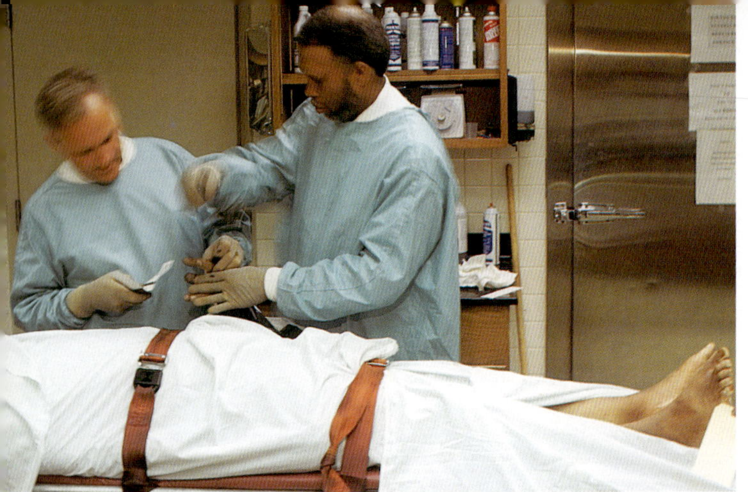

9:40 AM *At the Georgia Bureau of Investigation, the state's premiere criminal investigative arm, Larry Hankerson, a latent print examiner, carefully checks a gun for fingerprints using an alternative light source that detects the flouresence in a fingerprint. Later in the morning, Hankerson and colleague Louis Cuendet take fingerprints of a murder victim.*
PHOTOS BY ALAN WEINER.

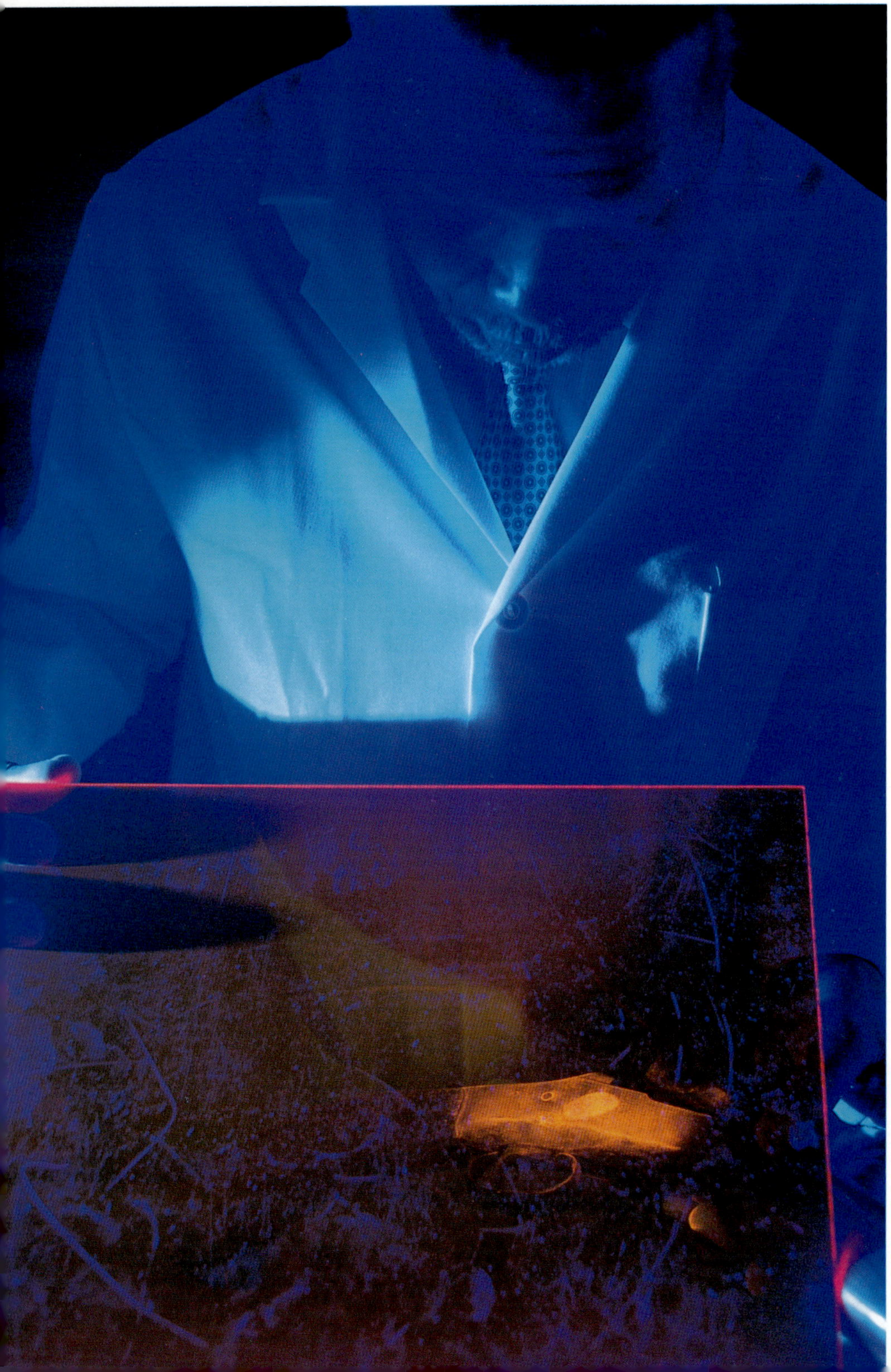

the background, where people actually stop to learn, to remember, to work, to listen, to observe. And within these moments, DeKalb County becomes more than just one of 159 counties in the state of Georgia. It becomes, in a sense, uniquely DeKalb, from morning till night.

It's 8 A.M. The students are American, Mexican, Russian, Chinese, Ethiopian, Nicaraguan, Italian, German, Korean, Turkish, Vietnamese. This is Woodward Elementary School, where nearly one-

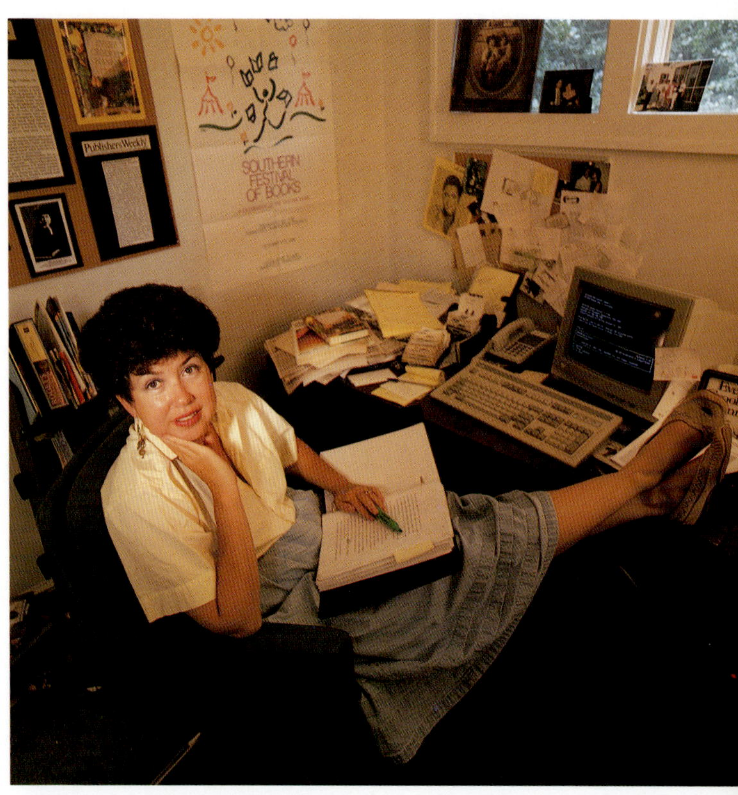

10:17 AM *Kathy Hogan Trocheck's urge to write fiction led her to quit her reporting job at the Atlanta Constitution. The move paid off: her first murder mystery, Every Crooked Nanny, was released to critical acclaim in the New York Times and other publications. Her second novel, To Live and Die in Dixie, is due for release soon. Summing up her lifestyle of late, Trocheck, an Avondale Estates mother of two, noted: "I work at home. I make cupcakes. I plot murder."* PHOTO BY MARILYN FUTTERMAN.

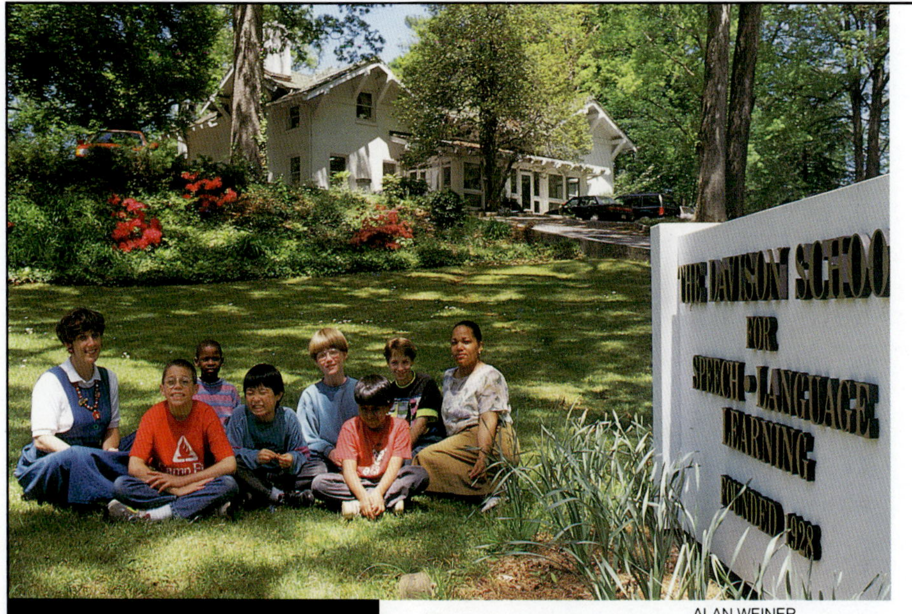

ALAN WEINER

THE DAVISON SCHOOL, INC.

A private, nonprofit facility for language-impaired children. Serving residential and day students, three – eighteen years of age.

When Louise D. Davison founded The Davison School in 1928, she targeted children with speech and language disorders before there was any public law that required such education. And that's what we continue to do—to serve the child who is falling between the cracks in the public system. ◆ "Our signature quote is that 'Language is the door to knowledge.' Children with speech and language disorders are at risk for successful learning because they are not able to compete in an academic environment. Our school is committed to helping these children acquire the communication skills, both spoken and written, that are needed to function in our highly verbal society. ◆ "At Davison, we do language intervention throughout the day—certified special education teachers and communication specialists work in the classroom in small groups, offering them a full range of subjects. Our students are generally one to three years behind their age-appropriate peers in public schools. So what we provide, along with our strong language intervention, is a basic curriculum, reduced to core objectives and presented to them in a way that is slow enough and modified enough to learn. Our small student-teacher ratio permits necessary repetition for learning. And our language-based approach serves as the key that unlocks the student's capacity to learn. ◆ "Our school is unique to all of the Southeast, and probably to any area of the country. And during the nineties, we will continue to modify and carry out Louise Davison's mission to be a strong language school for the children who fall through the cracks."

— Susan P. Smith, Ed.S., Director

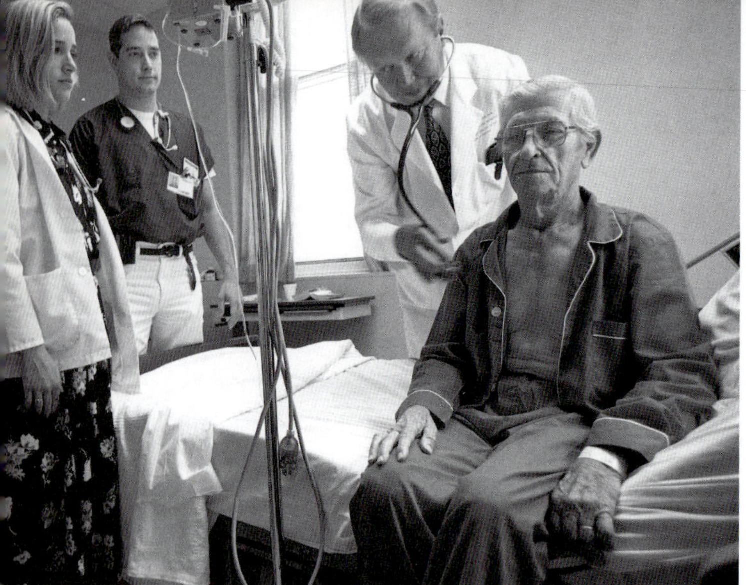

third of the 590 children are foreign born. Where kindergarten through sixth-grade represents thirty-five countries and twenty-four languages, the most diverse student population in the entire county. Where many of the newer students lack basic English language skills and are required to attend DeKalb County's International School for weeks of

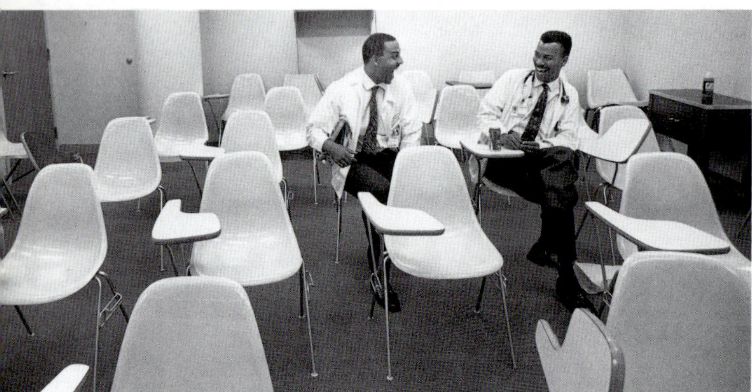

10:45 AM *Emory University Hospital residents are expected to know the situation of each of the hospital's patients and to suggest diagnoses and treatments. Dr. Juha Kokko, the hospital's chief of medicine, examines patient Phaben Waters as residents Carolyn Loscalzo and Allen Garner stand by. Later that day, residents Greg Woolfolk, left, and Robert Hoover relax with a private joke after a class. The 604-bed hospital is best known for its cardiology, oncology and urology programs. All of Emory's staff physicians serve on the faculty of the Emory medical school, the Robert W. Woodruff Health Sciences Center. Emory is a key member of the Georgia Biomedical Partnership which is made up of universities, agencies, hospitals, businesses and other technical and medical organizations located along the Clifton Road corridor.* PHOTOS BY MICHAEL SCHWARZ.

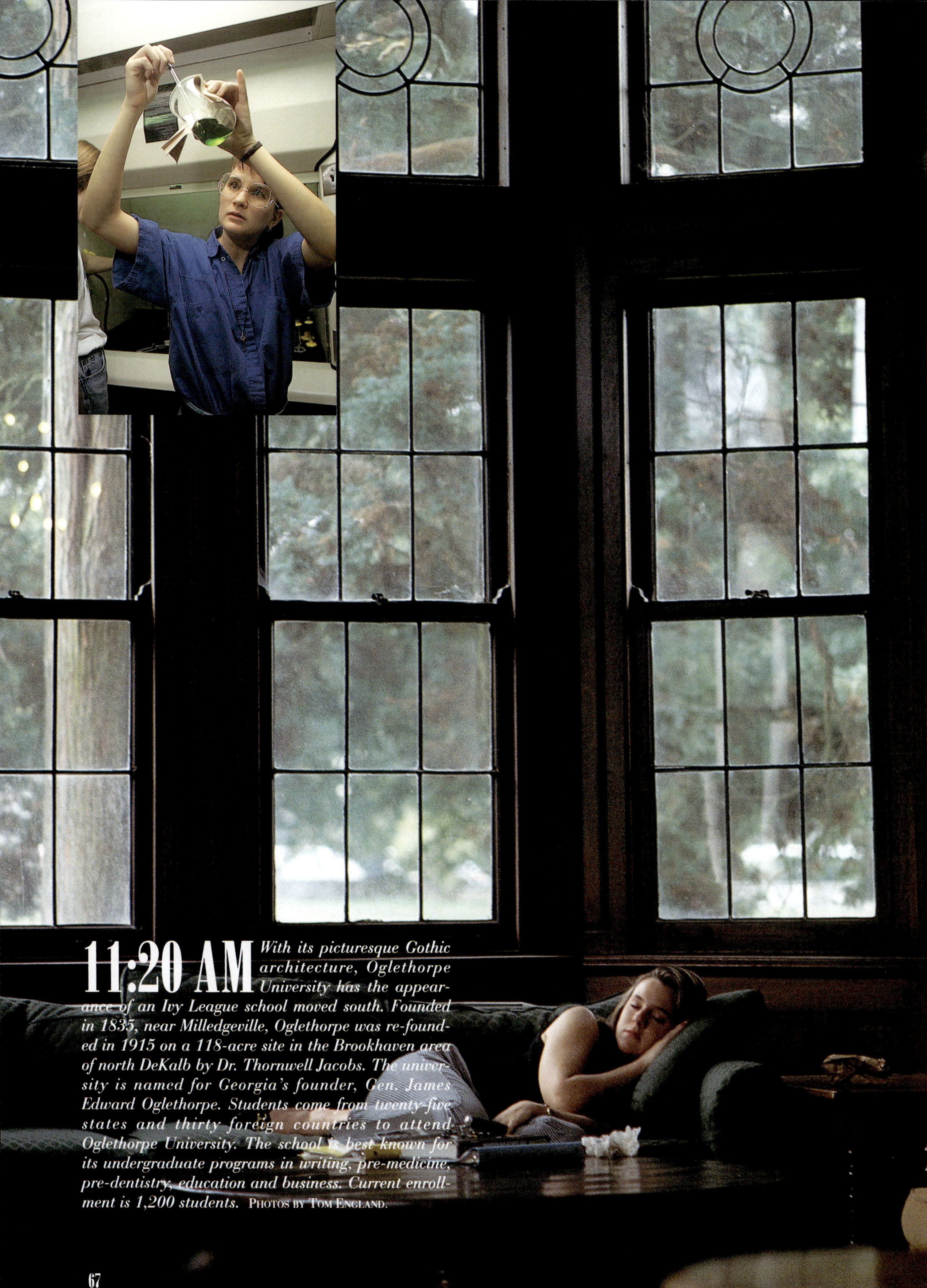

11:20 AM *With its picturesque Gothic architecture, Oglethorpe University has the appearance of an Ivy League school moved south. Founded in 1835, near Milledgeville, Oglethorpe was re-founded in 1915 on a 118-acre site in the Brookhaven area of north DeKalb by Dr. Thornwell Jacobs. The university is named for Georgia's founder, Gen. James Edward Oglethorpe. Students come from twenty-five states and thirty foreign countries to attend Oglethorpe University. The school is best known for its undergraduate programs in writing, pre-medicine, pre-dentistry, education and business. Current enrollment is 1,200 students.* Photos by Tom England.

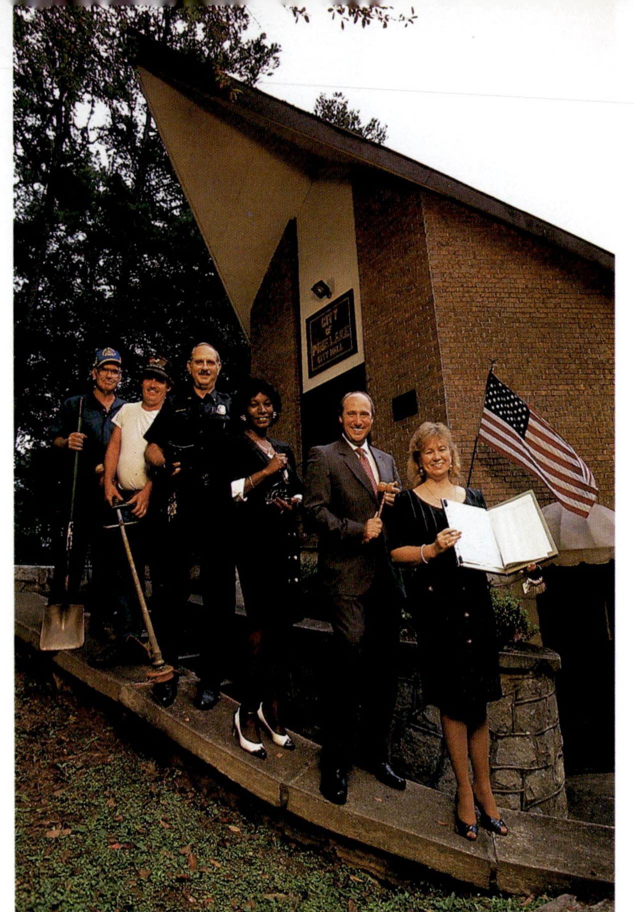

1:30 PM *Pine Lake has only eight employees (six of whom are pictured here) and two police cars. DeKalb's smallest municipality (population: 815) once was a resort community with summer cottages built around a tiny lake. City Manager Judy Griswell recalls coming to Pine Lake to swim when she was a girl and her uncle, Cad Wilkes, was mayor. Pictured outside Town Hall, with the tools of their jobs, are (left to right): Boyd Adams, maintenance; George Etheridge, maintenance; Sam Schlesinger, director of public service; Hazel Baker, city clerk; Neil Copeland, mayor; Judy Griswell, director of administrative services.* PHOTO BY KEN HAWKINS.

intensive English studies. Where Principal Virginia Davis works not only with children and teachers but also with non-English-speaking parents who often don't understand the country's health-care, government and social-welfare systems. "Of all the jobs I've had," she says, "I love this one the best."

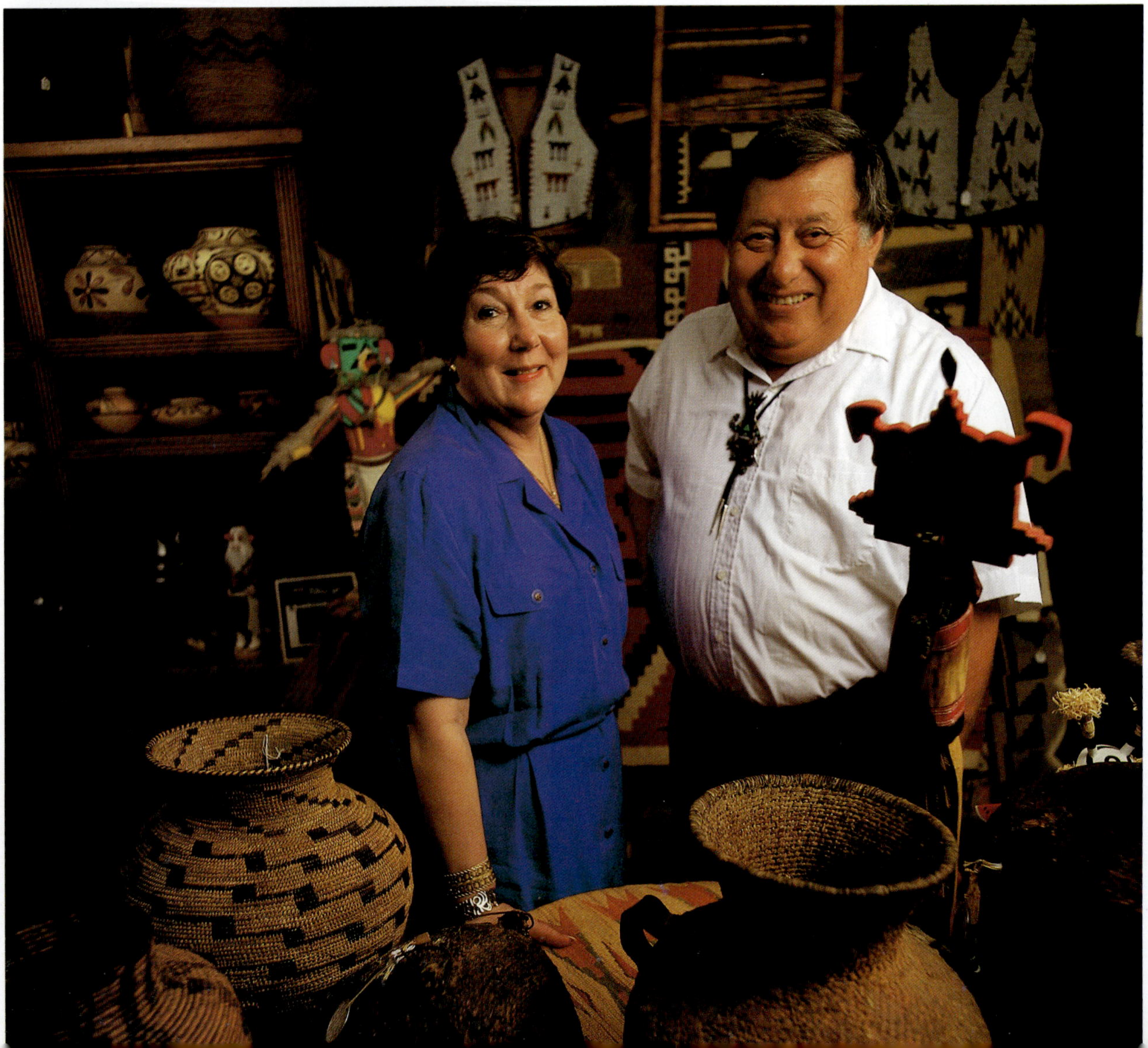

It's 9:15 A.M. at Hunter's Hill, Hunter's Pace, Hunter's Run and Sandstone Shores, South DeKalb developments where homes range from $150,000 to over half a million dollars. . . . In South DeKalb, such relatively new housing developments have created predominantly black neighborhoods for many of the Atlanta area's upper middle-class black families, including Lewis and Linda Vinson and their two children. "This was not designed as a black enclave," says Vinson, an accountant who works out of his home while Linda, an attorney, works in downtown Atlanta for Rogers & Hardin. "The Realtors in other parts of the city simply weren't referring their white clients to these developments. I love it out here. I love the country setting and yet being close to the expressway. It's a great environment for raising kids."

By mid-morning, Crawford Lovett, who has been with the Decatur main post office for thirty-seven years and is retiring in a week, is in a reflective mood. "We touch just about every person in Decatur, every day," he says. "People should take mail service for granted, and they do. Like the sun, rain and weather, it's there. If you look in the mail box and the mail is there, you expect it. If you look and it's not there, you don't feel so good. The only thing we have to offer our customers is service. And it's intangible. As intangible as love."

At noon, Dr. Juha Kokko, chief of medicine at Emory University Hospital, leads a morning report of patient cases submitted by residents. First case: a sixty-six-year-old male with a tennis ball-sized mass under his left arm, an athletic man who's suffering increasing fatigue. For the twenty-seven residents in the classroom, the process of figuring out who the patient is and what has happened to him resembles following clues in a mystery novel. After eliminating other possibilities, the residents at Emory, one of the top medical schools in the country, decide the patient is suffering from lymphoma. Their diagnosis is correct.

3:00 PM *When Peggy Belcher began selling American Indian art from the back of husband Ray's television-repair shop twenty years ago, the couple had no idea that one day they would attract collectors from all over the world. In their Avondale shop, the Belchers have the largest, most representative selection of historical and contemporary collectible art forms in the Southeast. Works cover all authentic Native Peoples, according to Ray who chooses the description over Native Americans, because all Indians address each other as The People, regardless of language or tribe. Ray is half Eastern Cherokee, and Peggy comes from the Sycamore tribe.* PHOTO BY MARILYN FUTTERMAN.

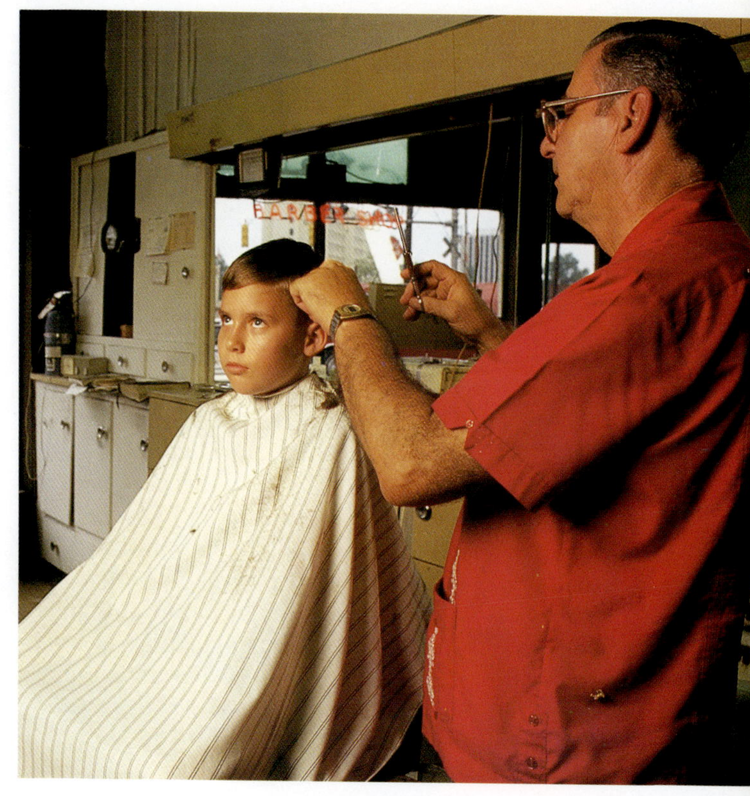

4:02 PM *Customers who patronize the Depot Barber Shop know not to expect much change when they climb up onto David Bennett's chair. And that stuck-in-time ambience, which has changed little in the twenty-four years Bennett has been cutting hair—is exactly as they like it. His customer this afternoon is a patient ten-year-old Keenan Rutledge of Snellville.* PHOTO BY ROB NELSON.

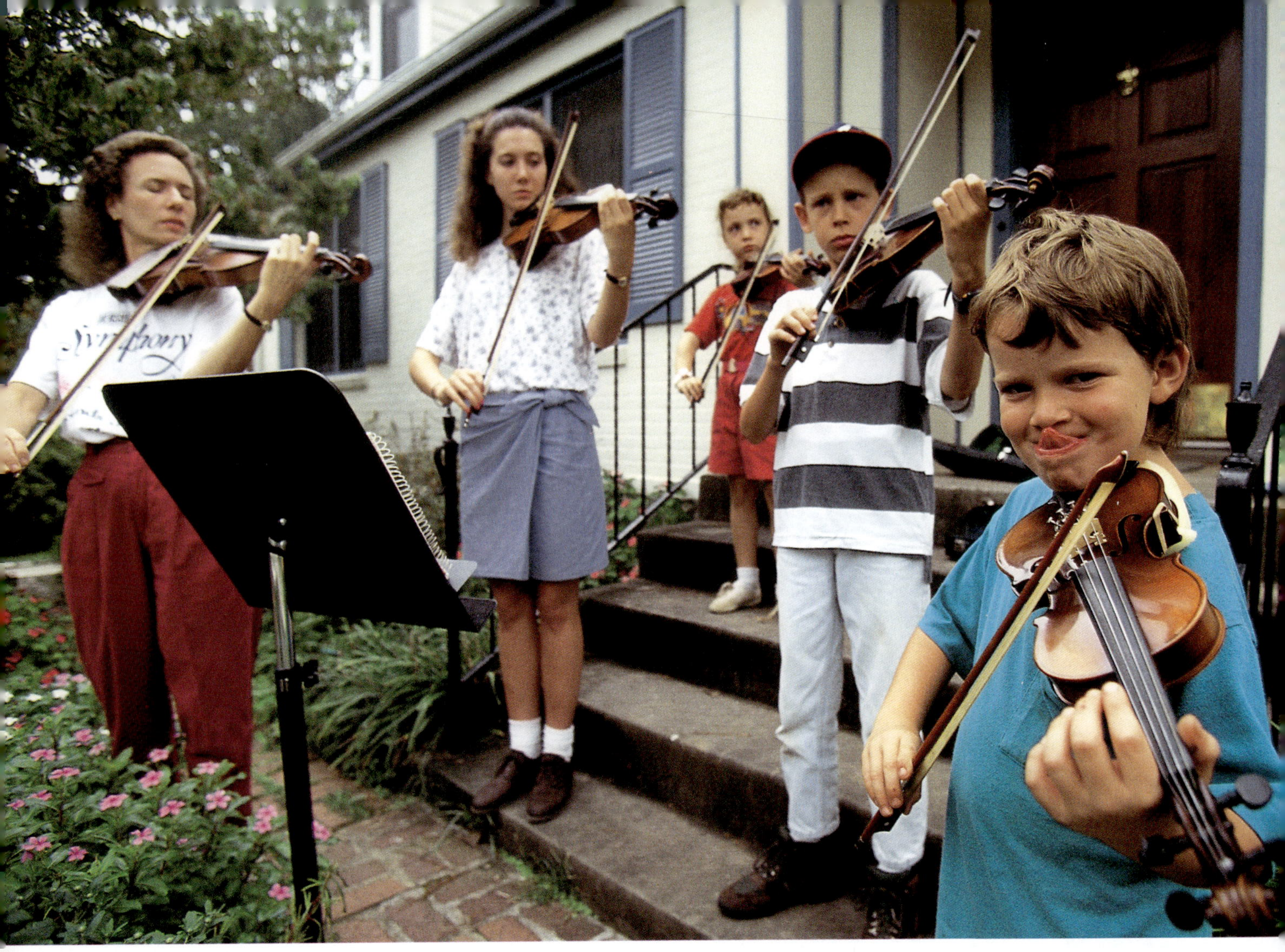

By early afternoon, it's as quiet as always at Pine Lake, a square mile of a town chartered in 1938 after it was developed as a lakeside resort for people in Atlanta. Today, Mayor Milton "Neil" Copeland explains why this residential rectangle can be entered into only from Rockbridge Road; a one-foot boundary around three sides of the city is owned by Pine Lake and prevents any thru traffic. Pine Lake

4:15 PM *Before they know their ABCs, some Decatur children already are accomplished violinists. Gloria Jacobson teaches the Suzuki method in which students learn by imitation. Just as children learn to talk before they learn to read and write, violin students can learn to play before they are able to read musical notes. Jacobson teaches forty students, some as young as three years old.* PHOTO BY KEN HAWKINS.

4:44 PM *DeKalb County established the standard for landfill operation in Georgia when the Seminole Road Sanitary Landfill opened in 1977. The 800-acre facility handles 1,200-1,400 tons of trash a day, five days a week, from all parts of the county. Seminole continues to lead the way as the only landfill its size in Georgia that turns all yard trimmings into mulch and compost that is used on public properties throughout the county. Seminole is expected to reach maximum capacity by the year 2020.*
PHOTO BY MICHAEL SCHWARZ.

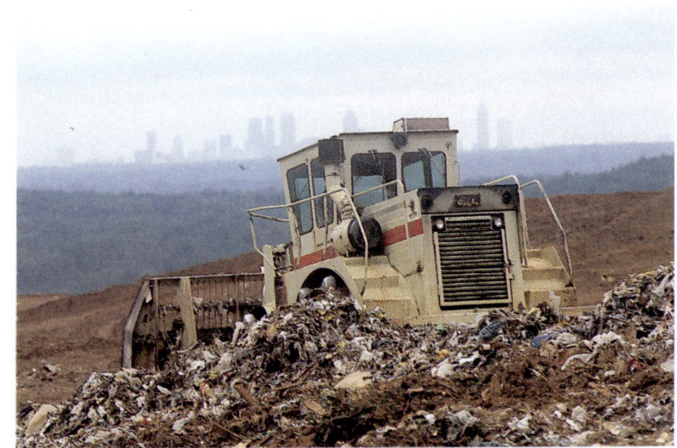

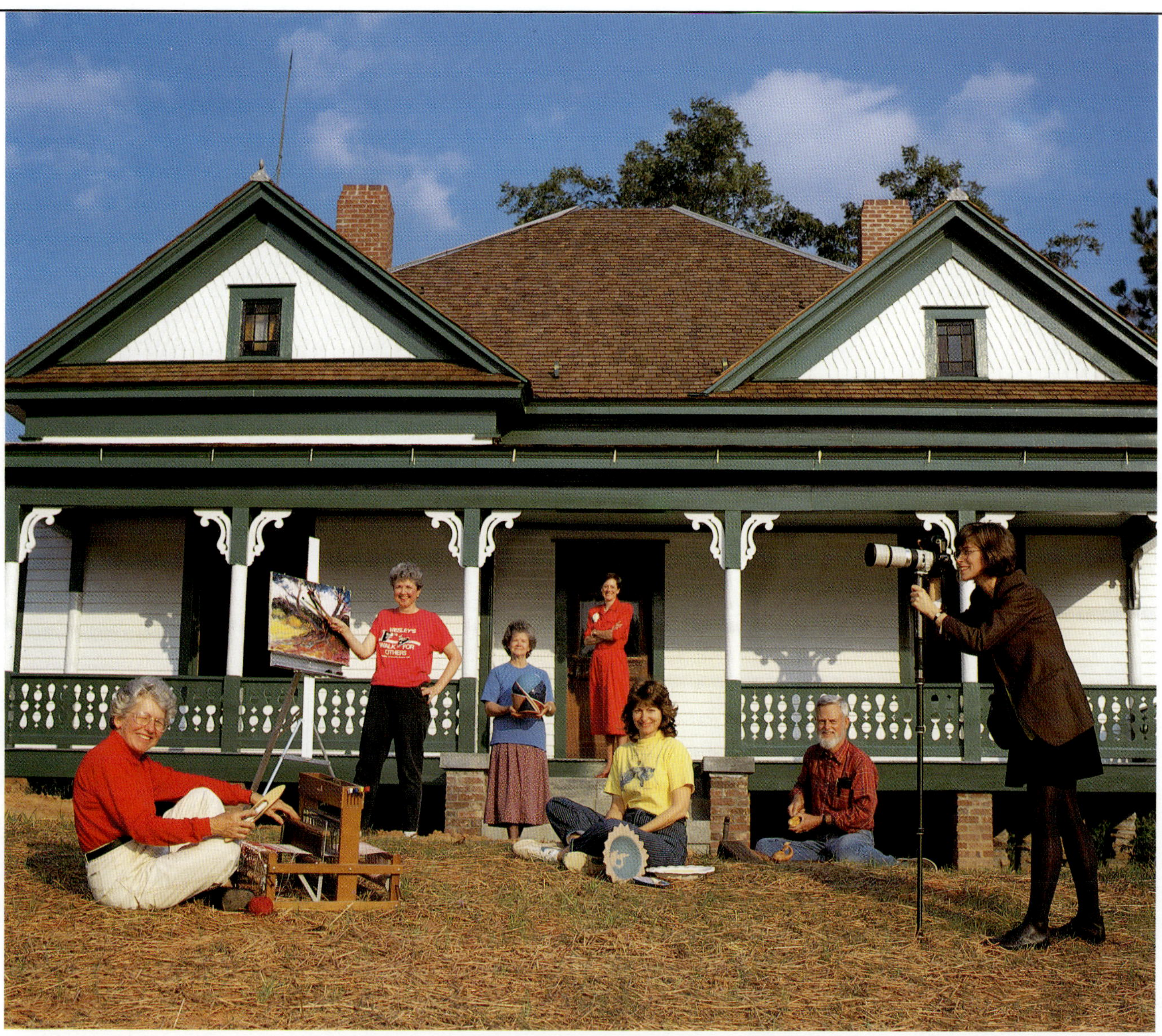

KEN HAWKINS

Since its founding in 1975, the Spruill Center has given tens of thousands of children and adults in north DeKalb County and surrounding communities the opportunity to explore, create, and appreciate art through an extensive program of classes, exhibitions, performances and special events. The growth of the Center's programming—especially the instructional program, the Center's primary enterprise—has been phenomenal. Since the Center moved to facilities in the North DeKalb Cultural Center in 1988, the number of classes offered and people served has nearly doubled to over 600 classes per year for more than 6,000 students. An additional 15,000 people attend the Center's exhibitions, performances, and special events each year. ◆ "But such success has created the Center's greatest problem; we have run out of space! Many popular classes, including summer camp, have waiting lists. Fortunately, just as space has become limiting, the Center received a gift of property—a farmhouse and five acres on Ashford-Dunwoody Road—from Onnie and Ethel Spruill, members of the family that originally settled and farmed much of what is now Dunwoody. The new property will allow the Center to expand and thereby continue to meet the needs of DeKalb County residents for high quality fine arts programming for many years to come. ◆ "Plans for the new property include restoration of the farmhouse—known as the Spruill homeplace—to the era of the 1930s, the heyday of family and community activity, and construction of two new classroom buildings. The homeplace will contain a gallery and small museum of local history, and the new buildings will house classes in fine crafts, such as ceramics, basketry, jewelry, weaving and papermaking. ◆ "As the Center enlarges its facilities, it will continue to expand and improve its programming, offering more music instruction for toddlers and young children and more master classes for advanced art students, launching an outreach program of arts activities for residents of retirement homes and children in after-school programs, and broadening the scope and diversity of its exhibitions and performances. ◆ "Now one of the largest cultural arts facilities in the Southeast, the Spruill Center is a big reason people choose to live in DeKalb County. Through its many classes, exhibitions, performances, and special events, the Spruill Center offers fine arts programming for just about every cultural taste."

— **Marilynn Mallory, Executive Director**

SPRUILL CENTER FOR THE ARTS

with classes, exhibits and performances at The North DeKalb Cultural Center and the Spruill Center Gallery and Historic Home.

has about 900 residents, six full-time and two part-time employees, a City Council, no restaurants, no bars, a few small businesses, the Pine Cone newsletter and a clubhouse. Residents own Pine Lake Park cards, which allows their families and up to six guests to swim in and play around the man-made lake. Mayor Copeland holds Card #001. His house faces the lake, and he jokes that he's in charge of lake maintenance. When the lake gets too high, he simply walks across the street, sticks a board into a flow pipe and diverts excess water into nearby Snap Finger Creek.

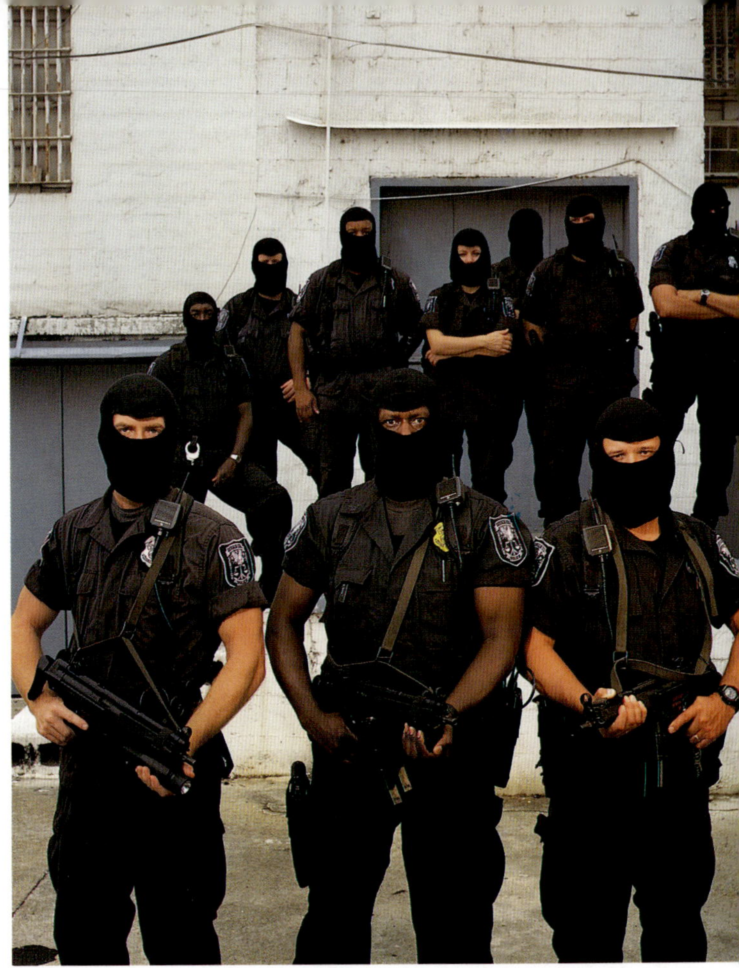

5:10 PM *Drug dealers would be wise to think twice before coming to DeKalb. DeKalb's elite drug strike force is the Black Cats, twelve officers specially trained for the dangerous work of fighting street-level drug traffic. Black Cat Commander Sgt. William Z. Miller, thirty-three, center, describes the team's firepower as "all we'll need," an arsenal topped by 9-mm submachine guns. Since being formed in 1988, the squad has made 5,500 arrests and seized $2 million in cash and hundreds of cars from drug suspects.*

Photo by Scott Robinson.

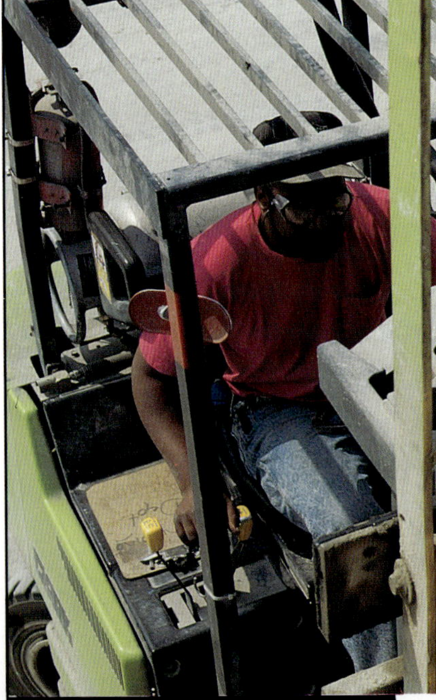

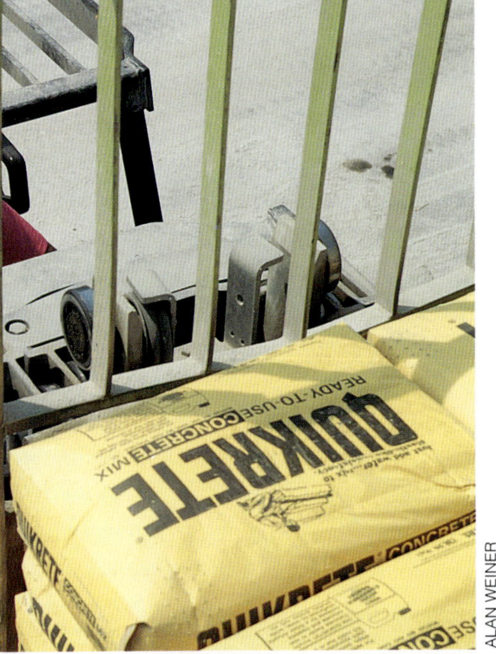

ALAN WEINER

In DeKalb, the more self-reliant the population is, the less strain there is on subsidy programs that the county has to support. That's why we say that our investment is in the people. ◆ "The DeKalb Private Industry Council is definitely a partnership among businesses, government and educators. And basically, we work with two sets of people: those who have never worked, and the long-term unemployed. ◆ "For people who have never held a job, we try to give them the basic skills first, either in literacy skills or work habits, and progress from there to give them job skills towards jobs that are forecast to be available. In some cases, we do design programs specifically for a new business that is coming in, like a hotel or a new company, and we work with companies to custom-design a training program to meet their needs. ◆ "For the other type of client that we have, which is the dislocated workers, we've run programs to give them new skills that they require to find new jobs. We have found that if people are in a job for a long time, they lack the skills to be adaptable for the future. We try to educate them not just to find something like that first job but to have the skills to adapt as the workplace changes. ◆ "One of the criticisms of the program has often been that because the funding is really sufficient to address about 5 percent of the eligible population, that there may be 'creaming' going on. We do not 'cream'—or select the people with the fewest barriers to employment. We've been very, very careful to address the very hardest to serve."

— **Jeffrey Kingdon, Chairman**
Board of Directors

DEKALB PRIVATE INDUSTRY COUNCIL, INC.

A federally financed, private-industry managed program. Designed to provide employment training for the county's jobless and low-income citizens.

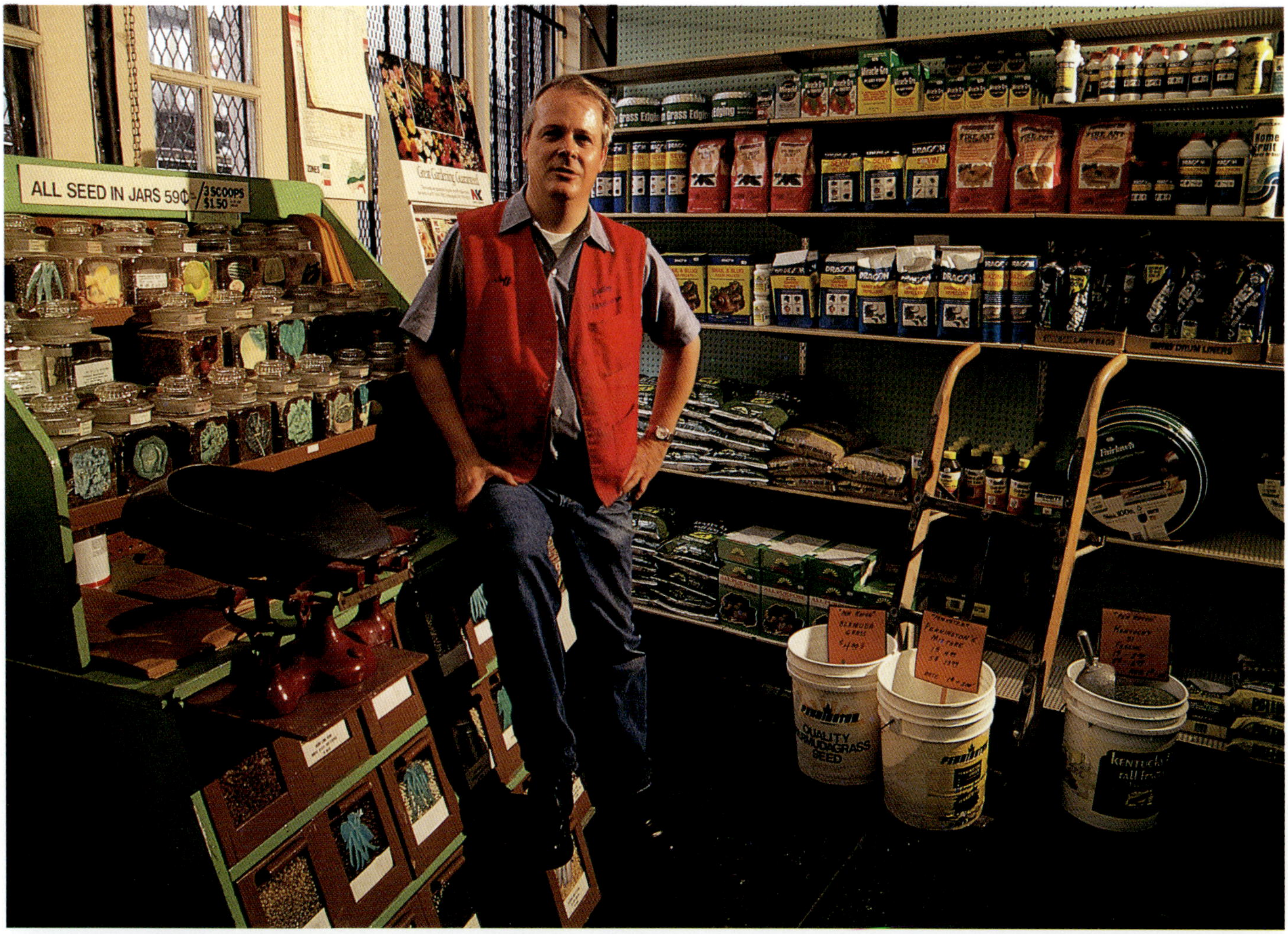

5:15 PM *Jeff (pictured here) and James Bailey like to tell people they were born in the back room of their father's hardware store on College Avenue in Decatur. James A. Bailey opened the store in 1945, and James and Jeff still do business the same way their father taught them. They sell such hard-to-find items as bulk garden seeds, washtubs, meat grinders and kerosene lamps. The customers include the second man ever to step through the door at Bailey's.*
PHOTO BY CHUCK YOUNG.

For dinner tonight, Elizabeth Reed will cook for her husband and three sons in the community kitchen at the Nicholas House, a transitional housing program in Decatur for thirteen homeless families. "I was surprised that I ended up in this situation," says Reed, who graduated from high school and completed one year of college but couldn't find work last year after she and her husband moved from Alabama to Decatur. When her husband then lost his job, they couldn't afford their

5:45 PM *Decatur native David Tatum has been working on and racing cars for twenty-two years. But he's no businessman. That's his wife Rita's job. Make no mistake about it: Rita is the boss at Tatum Auto Service. After eighteen years as a kindergarten teacher followed by a stint at an automobile dealership, Rita bought the auto-repair shop. She said she wanted the best mechanic, so she hired her husband. "There are no arguments," Rita says. "The last say-so is the boss's. And he doesn't care as long as he has money to race." On race days, though, she's on the sideline, "yelling with the other women."*
PHOTO BY CHUCK YOUNG.

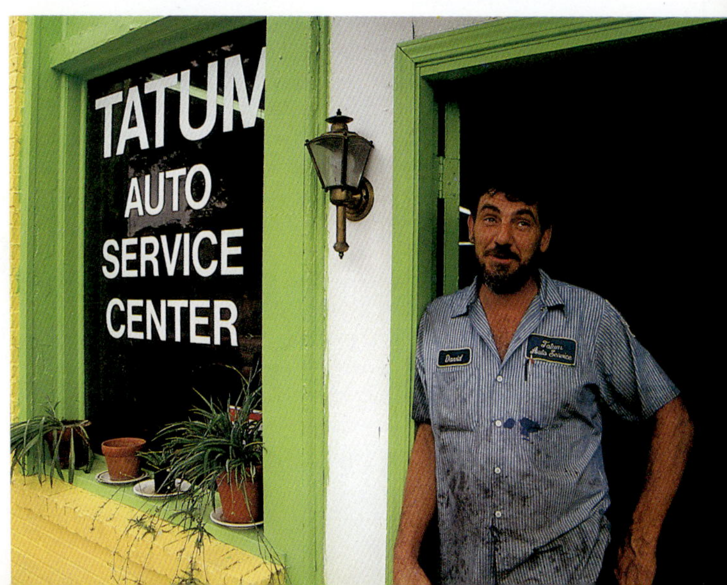

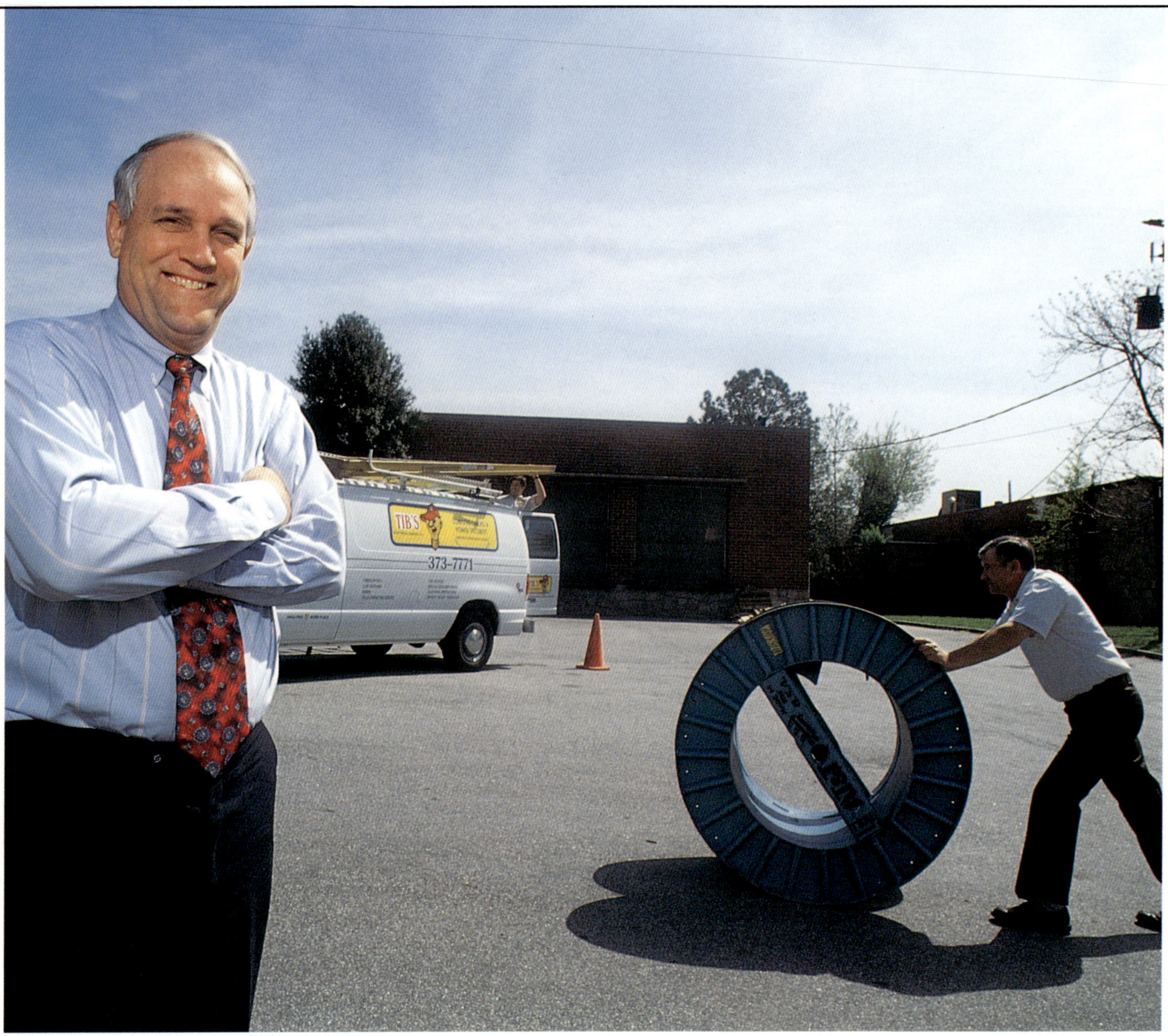

ALAN WEINER

I've been in the electrical service and contracting business since 1971. Tib's can thank DeKalb's commercial and industrial facilities for playing a major role in our success. Today, we are doing much more than just electrical work. As DeKalb's businesses continued to demand quality service and growth in technology, we listened to our customers and geared to meet their needs. ◆ "Today, we've grown into metro Atlanta's industry leader. Over 1,000 companies rely on us to consult and respond to their electrical needs. As a single source contact, we design, install, and maintain computer cabling, fiber optics, video, telecommunications, lightning protection, corrected power, standby power systems, and energy management systems. Another service which has become very popular with our customers has been our preventive maintenance program, no matter what size the facility. Due to changes over time, all wiring needs to be inspected and tested in order to prevent and minimize disruptions and potential losses. ◆ "However, there is no way that Tib's would be the company that it is today without somebody looking out for me. I have been blessed with very good people. We have some long-term employees who have played a major role in positioning the company where it is today. The entire work force has committed to remaining drug-free by agreeing to periodic drug testing. This is a tough commitment from the type of industry where drug and alcohol problems are a major dilemma. ◆ "Tib's also manages through both customer and employee involvement. Total Quality Management (ISO9000) is a management style which has worked very well with our firm. Customers and employees are involved in establishing standards, procedures, training, etc. . . . This quality system has proven very effective in building a team which continues to meet the customers' needs and gives our employees a better place to work. 'Setting the standards in electrical service' is both our mission statement and our commitment to our customers, employees, the general public and the environment in which we live. ◆ "At Tib's, we fix people! That includes going further than just the technical situation at hand and making sure we are easy to deal with, that the customer is completely satisfied and that he or she will rely on us the next time. ◆ "Thank you, DeKalb County, first of all for serving as my nest egg when I first started my business, then for keeping and attracting the right businesses, environment and people for which we could build a successful team."

— **Marvin Tibbetts, President**

TIB'S ELECTRICAL SERVICE CO.

Established in 1971

1991 NFIB

"Georgia's Small Business of the Year"

apartment and moved into Nicholas House, one of three such shelters in DeKalb for the nearly 2,200 homeless people who sought shelter last year. The program helped the Reeds find employment and introduced them to Our House in Decatur, a model program for day care of homeless children. At Our House, Charles Reed, four, began talking and playing with other children and "came out of his shell," says his mom, sitting in Our House before returning to the shelter. "I would love to have the opportunity to volunteer here. It is such a good program."

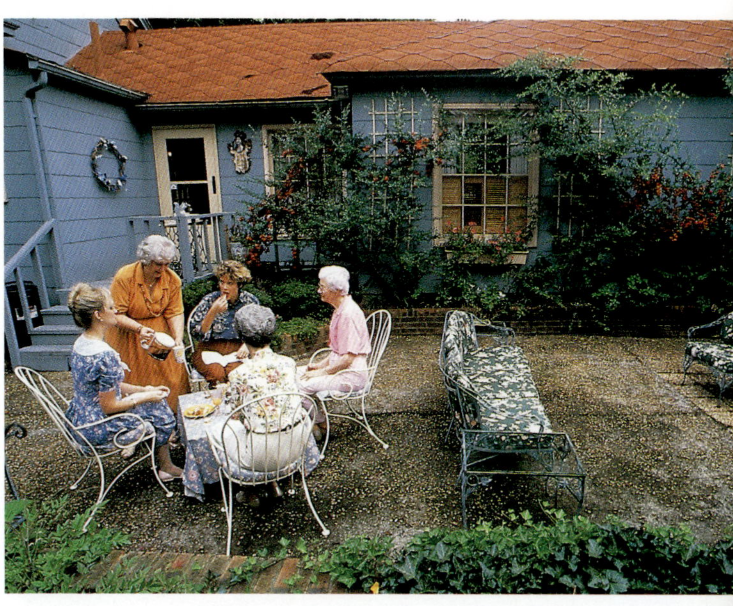

6:00 PM *It's tea and coffee-break time at Rice's Bed & Breakfast in Tucker. Joy Rice opened the inn in 1988, though the five-bedroom plantation farmhouse it's located in dates back to 1833, making it one of the oldest structures in Georgia. No stranger to the world of B&Bs, Joy also operated an upstate-New York inn before locating to DeKalb County. Pictured with Joy (pouring coffee) are Cleo Horne, Betty McElroy, Judi Strickland and Julie King.*
PHOTO BY ALAN WEINER.

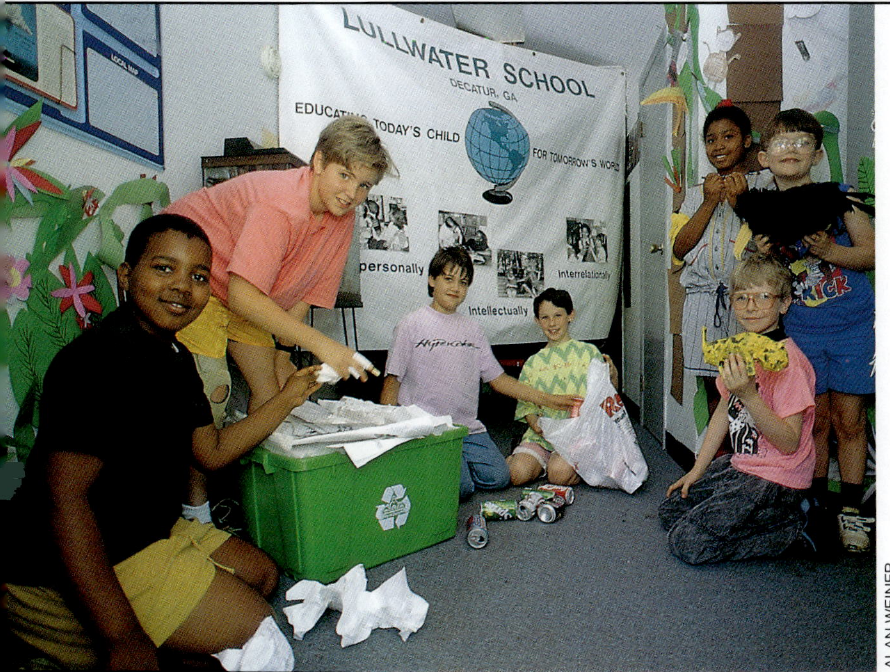

ALAN WEINER

LULLWATER SCHOOL

A private, nonprofit interrelated curriculum Serving Kindergarten – 9th Grades

At Lullwater School, we call it Confluent Education, which focuses on the individuality of the child. Essentially, confluence is the interaction of all the different educational areas as well as the child's social and emotional areas. ◆ "Here, for example, if a child learns about an Indian, they will learn that the Indian came across the Bering Strait. And also that the Native Americans had different living styles, according to geography. So they learn about geography, living quarters and government by learning about an Indian. And as the child develops, this knowledge will transfer to how our government works. ◆ "This type of confluent learning is opposed to a child being isolated and studying the United States government and memorizing the three sections. We prefer to focus on a holistic approach to education, where the child is at the center of the curriculum and studies relate to the real world and make learning and gathering knowledge exciting and meaningful. ◆ "This total-concept approach transfers to other more life-meaning skills where everything around them will make sense. ◆ "Students at Lullwater understand that education spans more than textbook facts, it is a hands-on experience and part of life. Confluence includes living with others and understanding ourselves, all within the atmosphere of small classes. You witness amazing advancement when the interrelationship of self and others takes on meaning. ◆ "We feel it's obviously a program that works, one that builds confidence, self esteem and inner strength. Indeed, on the same tests that the public schools use, we have achievement test scores which increased one and a half grade levels in six months. ◆ "And we are very excited."

— Dr. Joan K. Teach, Director

It's storytelling night at the Callanwolde Fine Arts Center, an evening when a Trio of Tellers — Renee Brachfield and Betty Ann Wylie, professional storytellers; and Sherry DesEnfants, the Youth Services Coordinator with the DeKalb Public Library—perform in the front parlor of the Tudor estate that was once home to Coca-Cola's Woodruff family. For the forty-four people in the audience—who hop, spin and generally delight in the storytellers' craft as they meet Little Red Riding Hood, the Fidget Family, Prindarella and the Pransom Hince—the evening is pure magic. "Storytelling is more than entertainment," says Brachfield. "It's a way to touch people's hearts."

At Fernbank Science Center, the lights dim inside the third largest planetarium in the country as astronomer David Dundee presents a planetarium sky show replete with thousands upon thousands of stars in the autumn night sky. Venus, the brightest object in the sky other than the moon, is prominent in the Southeastern sky.

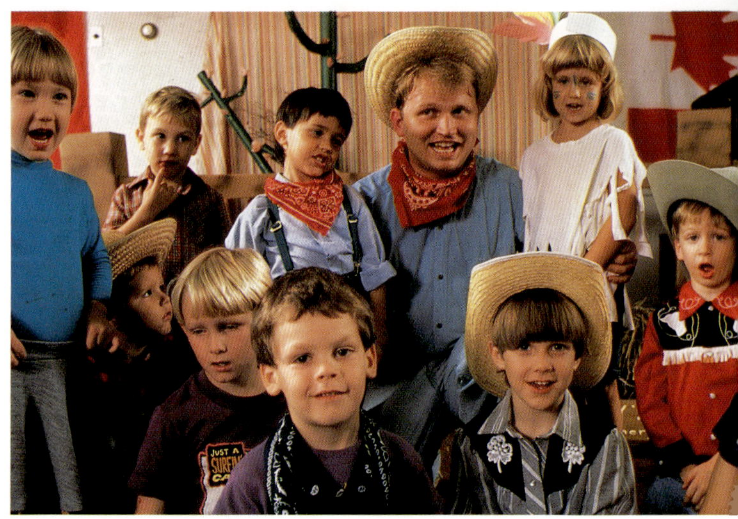

6:45 PM *Participation in the Pine Lake Baptist Church children's choir is increasing, thanks to socials like this hot-dog dinner. Children's pastor David Wylie supervises the dispensing of mustard and ketchup and leads the little cowboys and cowgirls in singing hymns.* Photos by Gordon Joffrion.

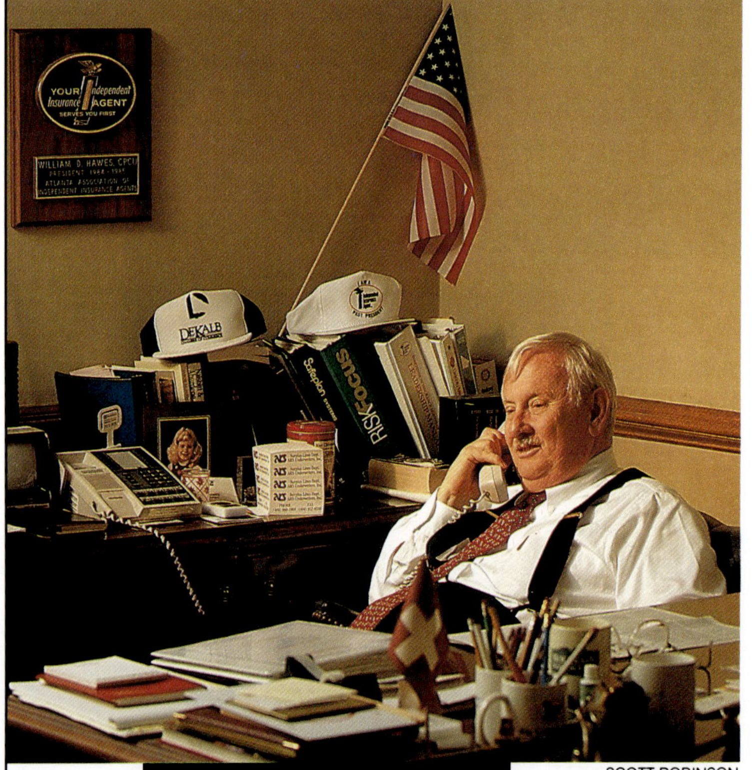

SCOTT ROBINSON

THE HAWES COMPANY

William D. and Kathleen Hawes, owners and employees

We are a very small insurance company, and I do most of my work on the telephone. I try to make myself available to my clients whenever they need anything, which means I'm not usually on the golf course or drinking coffee at the restaurant. And I think that translates into better service for them. ◆ "My wife, Kathleen, and I run the business. I handle the commercial and government entity accounts, like the DeKalb County Board of Commissioners and the DeKalb Board of Education. Kathleen runs the personal accounts, like home and automobile insurance. And because we live and work in Tucker, I like to say that I'm close enough to work that the heater in the car doesn't have time to warm up as I drive in. ◆ "And I have to tell you that I'm quite a community person. My wife says she wishes I would volunteer my insurance efforts and get paid for my civic duties. I have five children, and over time I've started coaching girls soccer, been president of the soccer league and chairman of the Recreation Center here in Tucker, and we're quite involved in the schools and the DeKalb County Partners in Education and the education committee for the DeKalb Chamber. Our education system is second to none. Why, you can go from kindergarten to a Ph.D. and never leave the county. ◆ "I grew up here. I just like the people of DeKalb. And I like their attitude that by being involved, you can make this a better place to live."

— Bill Hawes, President of The Hawes Company

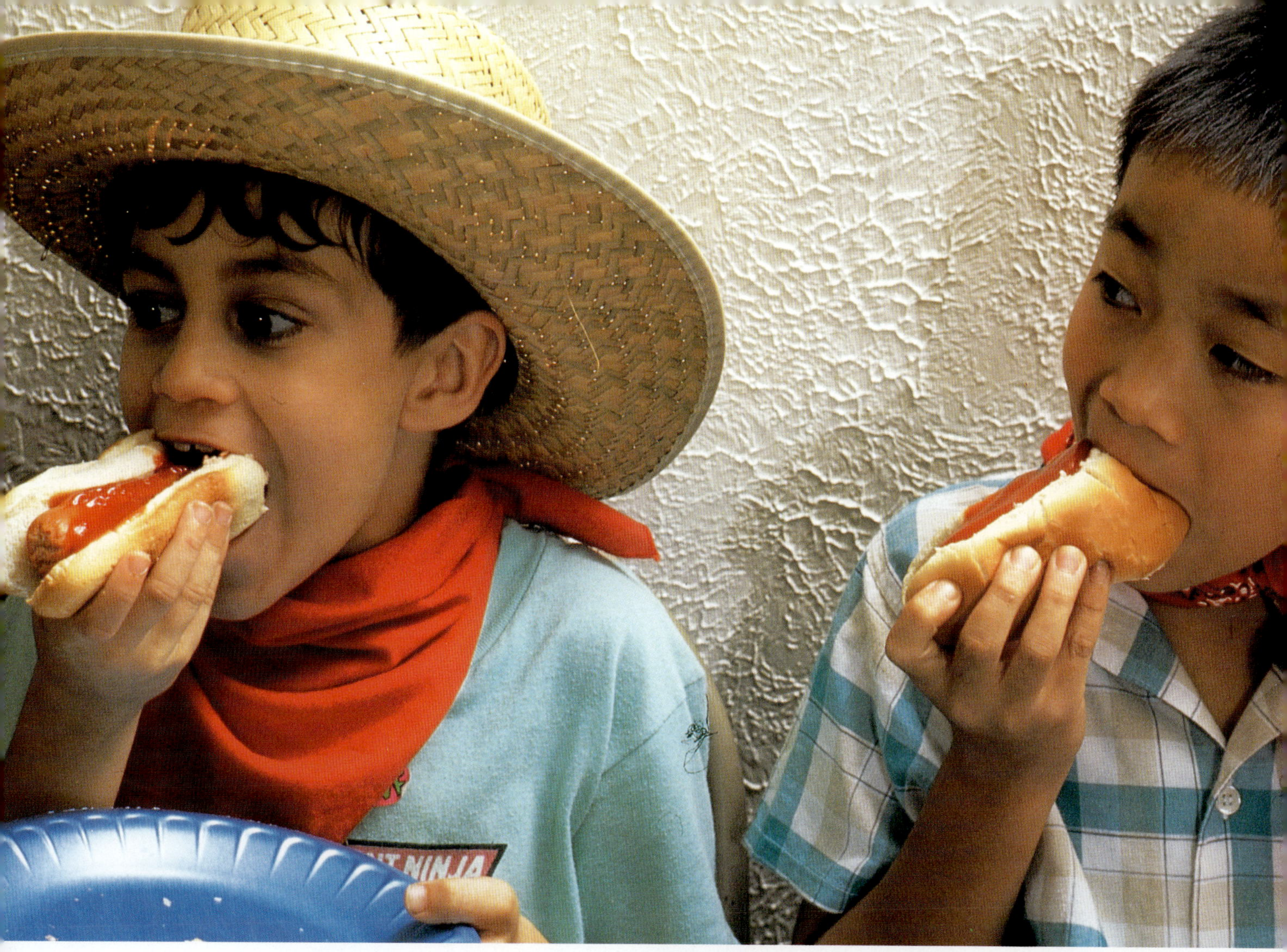

The key constellation is Pegasus, whose main components are four bright stars that form a square resembling a baseball diamond, with some of the dimmer stars of Pegasus placed as the catcher and the batter. Using Pegasus as a guide, Dundee points out other major constellations of fall: Andromeda, Perseus and Capricorn. And no, Dundee protests gently, it's not true that eggs can only be balanced on the first full day of the autumnal equinox, as

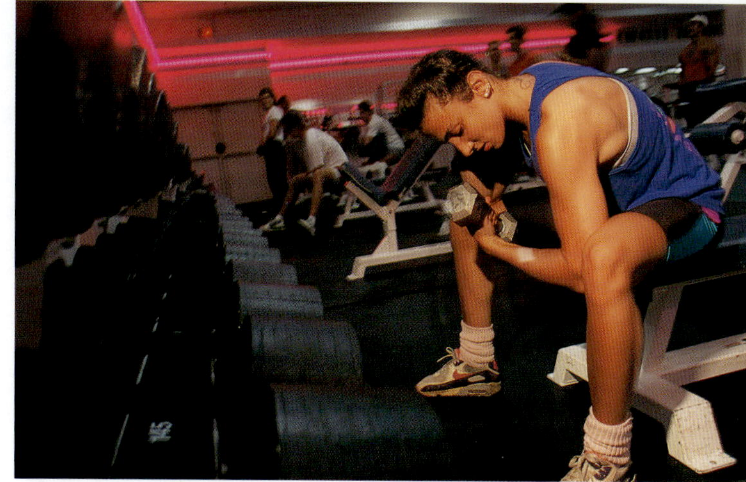

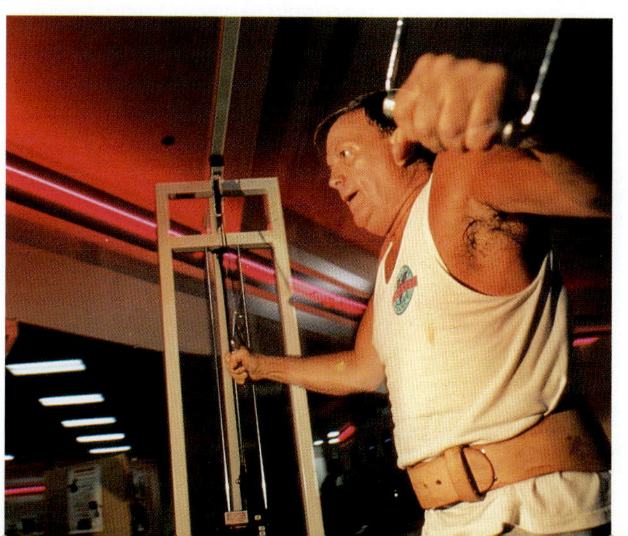

7:30 PM *Even if you don't own a pair of those fashionable Spandex shorts, you can work out at Gold's Gym on Buford Highway. "Who cares? You're just going to sweat in them anyway," says one patron. Here, Tara Goodman pushes herself through some arm curls, while regular Ben Futral sweats through cable crossovers.* PHOTOS BY GREG FOSTER.

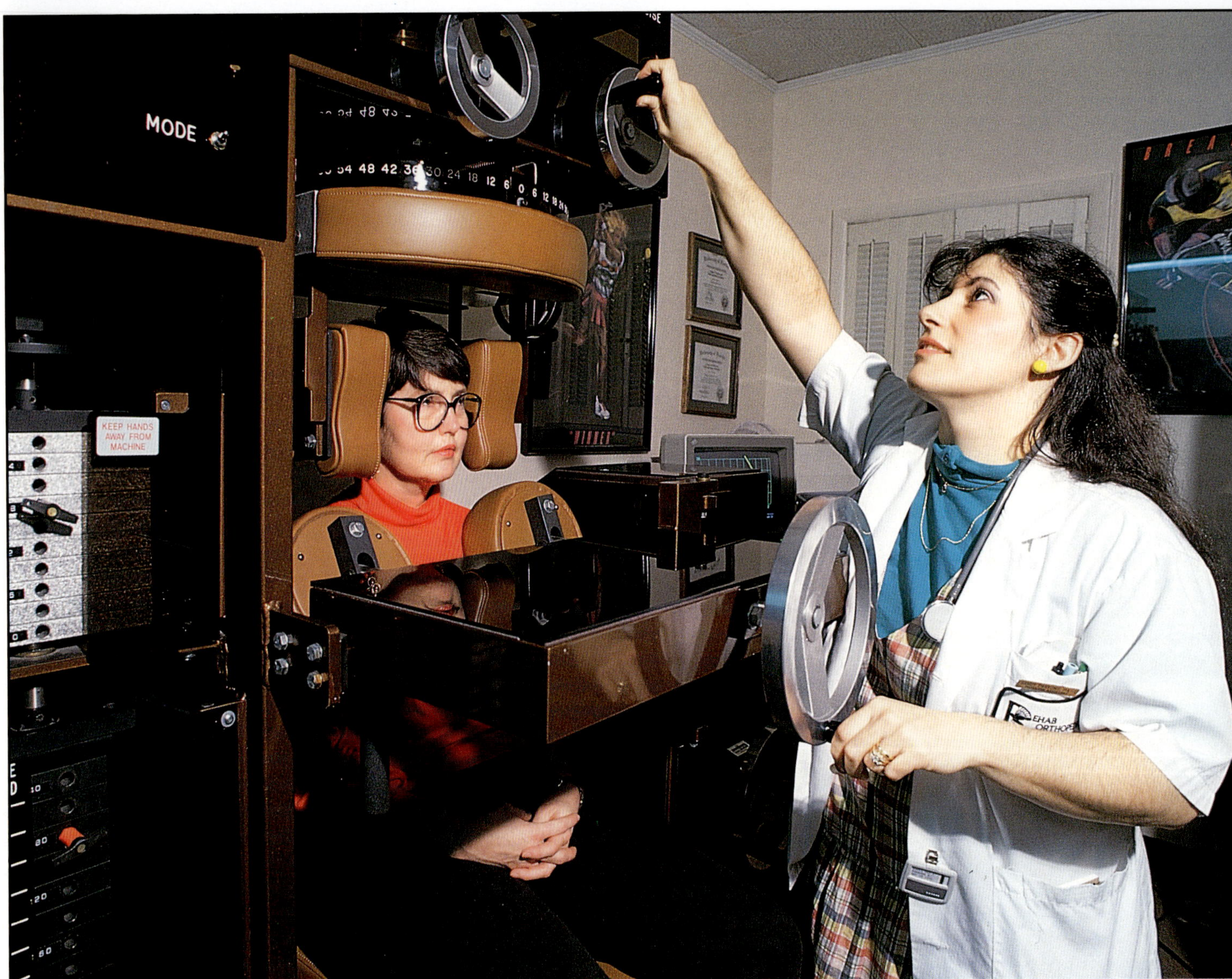

ALAN WEINER

The pain? There are not words to describe it. I was not able to do anything. The most I was able to do was walk around, a little. I was a teacher, at the Atlanta Area School for the Deaf, but I couldn't continue in the classroom. I was in too much pain. And I had to give up tennis. I'm a jock at heart, or I was. ◆ "On a scale of one to one-hundred? When I got to Rehab Orthopedic Medicine (R.O.M.), I was a minus ten. I was in real bad shape. I was in a car accident, and I suffered a severe neck injury. Nearly two weeks after the accident, I was referred to Dr. D'Auria at Rehab Orthopedic. ◆ "I felt very comfortable there. They read my X-rays and concurred that I had ruptured discs in my neck, and soft tissue damage up and down my back. Dr. D'Auria specializes in managing pain without surgery, and I was started on medication, trigger point injections, and physical therapy to help relieve the hard muscle spasms that result from tissue damage. That worked. But at some point, I was not making progress. The pain was still debilitating. Dr. D'Auria recognizes that each case is different, and so he referred me to a hospital for further evaluation. The doctors there recommended surgery. ◆ "After surgery, I began to improve. I continued with intensive therapy at R.O.M., and I knew that I was getting good treatment. I won't go anywhere where I don't like the people. They are very friendly, and in many ways R.O.M. has been like a home away from home. Being injured and trying to get better doesn't give you a lot of time for anything else. This clinic is unique. ◆ "I started to work again. I'm no longer in the classroom, but I'm a computer tech person now. I walk about three to five miles a day. Tennis? A couple of doctors have said no. But I'll be damned if I won't. That's why I keep going to therapy, to R.O.M. I want to get better."

— **Mary Bell, Patient**

REHAB ORTHOPEDIC MEDICINE

Ralph D'Auria, M.D., Owner,
Opened clinic in 1989
Pain management without surgery, for relief and recovery

dozens of people tried to prove early this morning on top of Stone Mountain. If done properly, an egg will stand up any day of the year.

By midnight, in the numbness of late-night hours, the nitty-gritty returns. Inside the Kroger 24-Hour Super Store in Toco Hills Shopping Center, two clerks stack up bags of cat litter as one attempts to break the monotony with an Elvis impersonation of a mock radio announcement: "Live from Kroger 318, it's the John Jackson show!" On Aisle Seven, cases of Chef Boyardee mini ravioli, Dinty Moore beef stew, Prego spaghetti sauce, Mahatma rice and Chicken of the Sea tuna sit on a rolling cart.

Which means only one thing. All through the night, the boys in Aisle Seven will be jamming. Jamming cans.

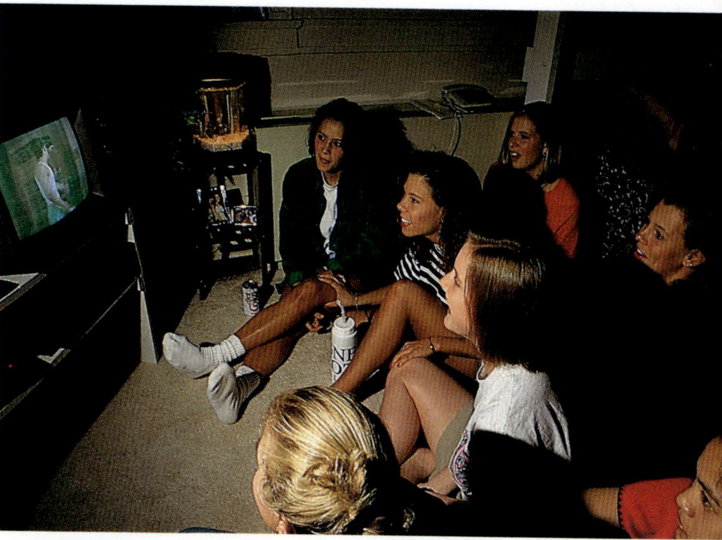

8:50 PM *Parents of Agnes Scott College students 100 years ago would be shocked to learn of the current campus fad, watching the television show, "Beverly Hills, 90210." Parents in 1892 expected the school to see to it that their daughters refrained from "eating imprudently at night" and removing flannel underwear too early in the spring. Students in 1892 were "permitted to correspond only with such gentlemen as were especially named in writing by parents." The name of the Decatur Female Seminary was changed in 1890 in honor of the mother of the school's chief benefactor, George Washington Scott. Glued to the tube for a Wednesday-night ritual are Alana Noble, Mary Snyder, Pam Peel, Merisa Aranas, Christen Drewes, Mary Jordan and Wendy Wheless.* PHOTO BY MARILYN FUTTERMAN.

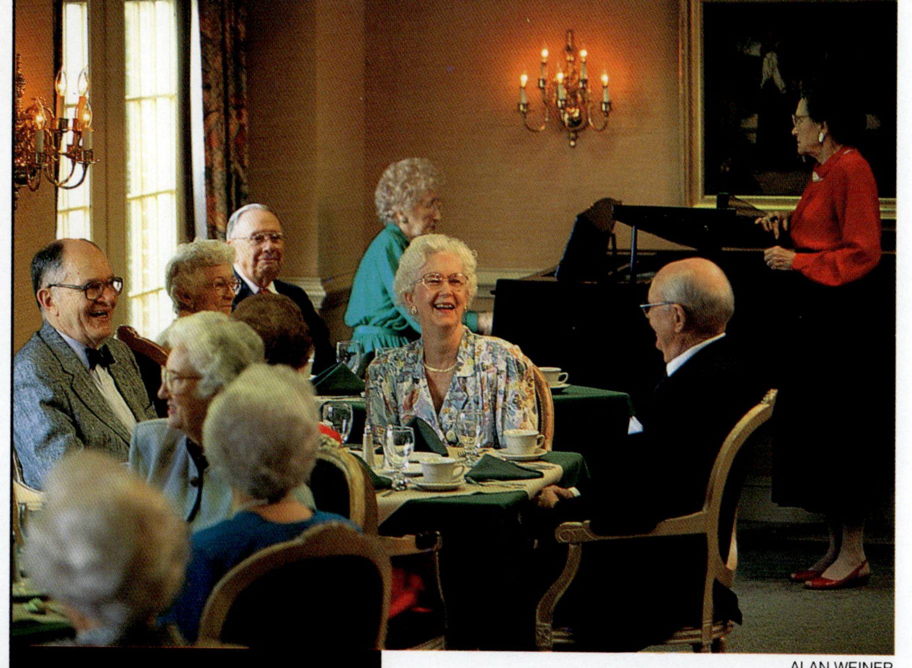

ALAN WEINER

KING'S BRIDGE

A Christian Retirement Community Since 1985

At King's Bridge, 191 apartments are leased for Independent Living and Personal Care. ◆ "We draw most of our residents from a five-mile radius, which indicates an individual has probably lived in the community all their life, and moves here when the house becomes too much responsibility. We're finding, however, that parents are moving here to be near their children, who have transferred to the Atlanta area. ◆ "I feel there are two reasons why King's Bridge provides a pleasurable lifestyle.First, we are a Christian retirement community. Even though King's Bridge is not supported by a church, our Board of Directors has adopted a philosophy of Judeo-Christian principles. Religious activities include a Sunday School class, vesper service with speakers from the community, monthly Communion service and Bible study. ◆ "And second, King's Bridge has a Wellness Clinic providing health maintenance as well as responding to emergencies. Health forums provide an opportunity for healthcare professionals from the community to bring information to residents. Special diets are accommodated and good nutritional habits are encouraged through our food service program. The dining room, which serves all meals, is an important part of life at King's Bridge, as a relaxing opportunity for fellowship."

— **Gayle A. Shaw, Administrator**

THURSDAY

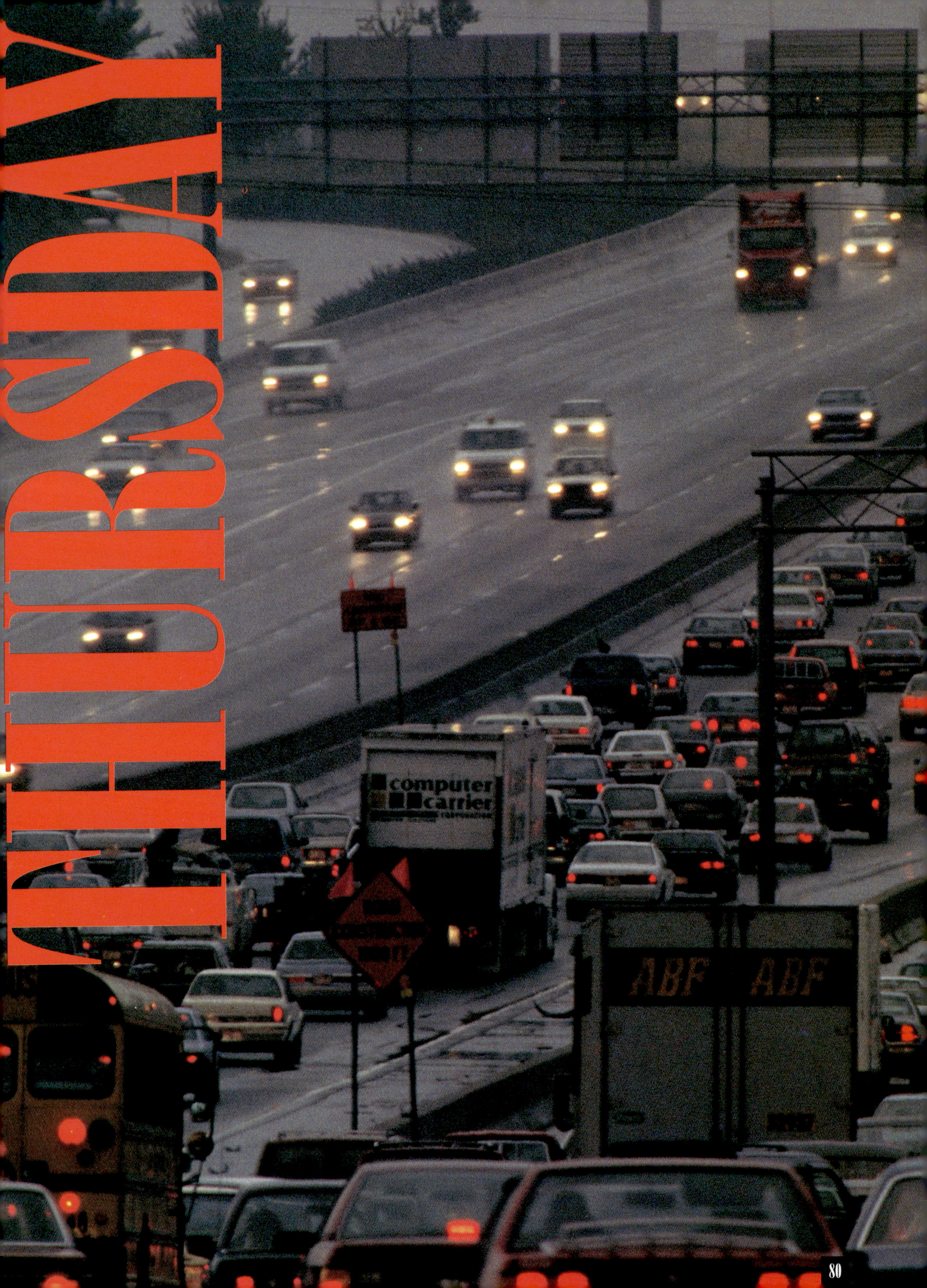

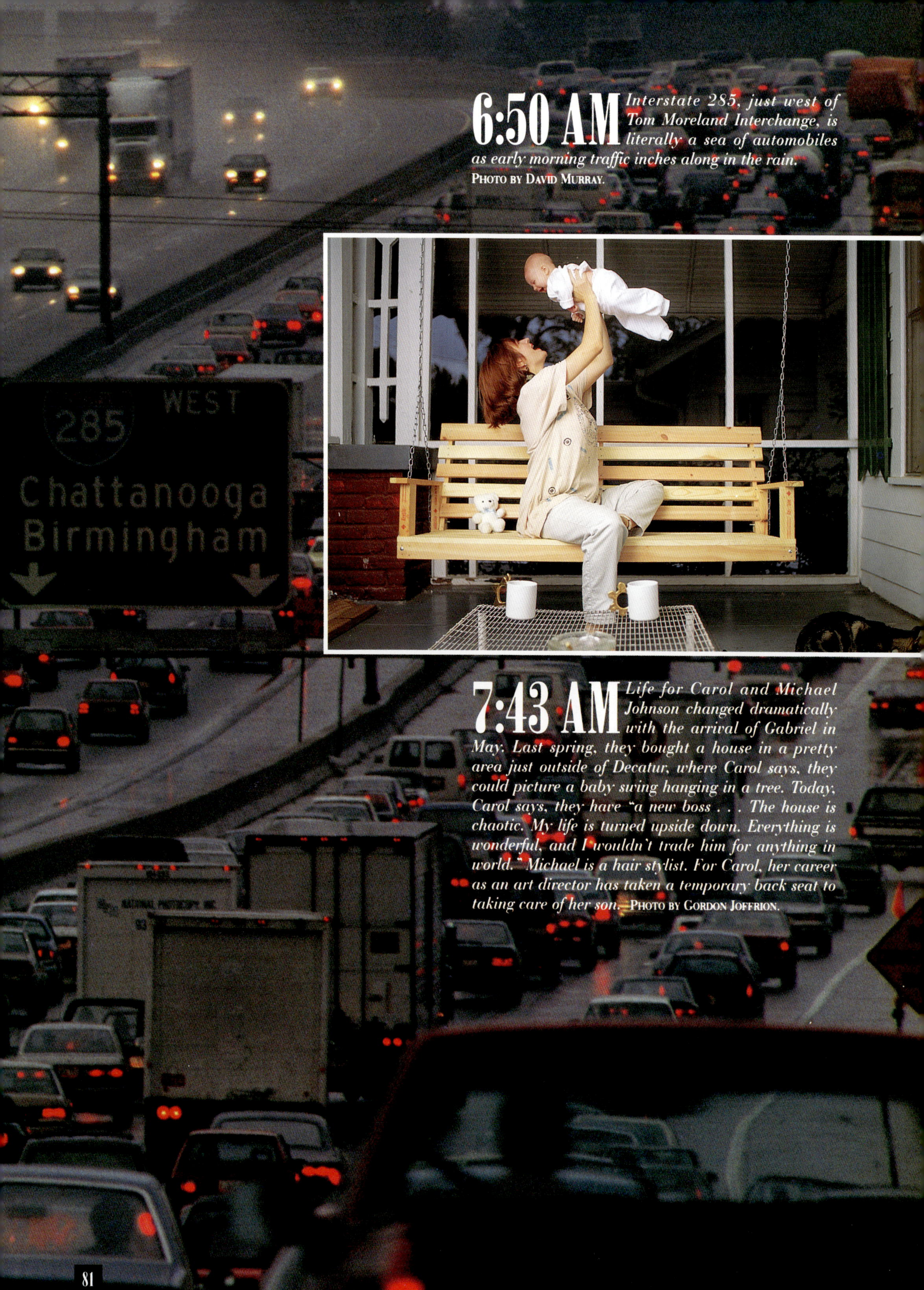

6:50 AM *Interstate 285, just west of Tom Moreland Interchange, is literally a sea of automobiles as early morning traffic inches along in the rain.* PHOTO BY DAVID MURRAY.

7:43 AM *Life for Carol and Michael Johnson changed dramatically with the arrival of Gabriel in May. Last spring, they bought a house in a pretty area just outside of Decatur, where Carol says, they could picture a baby swing hanging in a tree. Today, Carol says, they have "a new boss . . . The house is chaotic. My life is turned upside down. Everything is wonderful, and I wouldn't trade him for anything in world." Michael is a hair stylist. For Carol, her career as an art director has taken a temporary back seat to taking care of her son.* PHOTO BY GORDON JOFFRION.

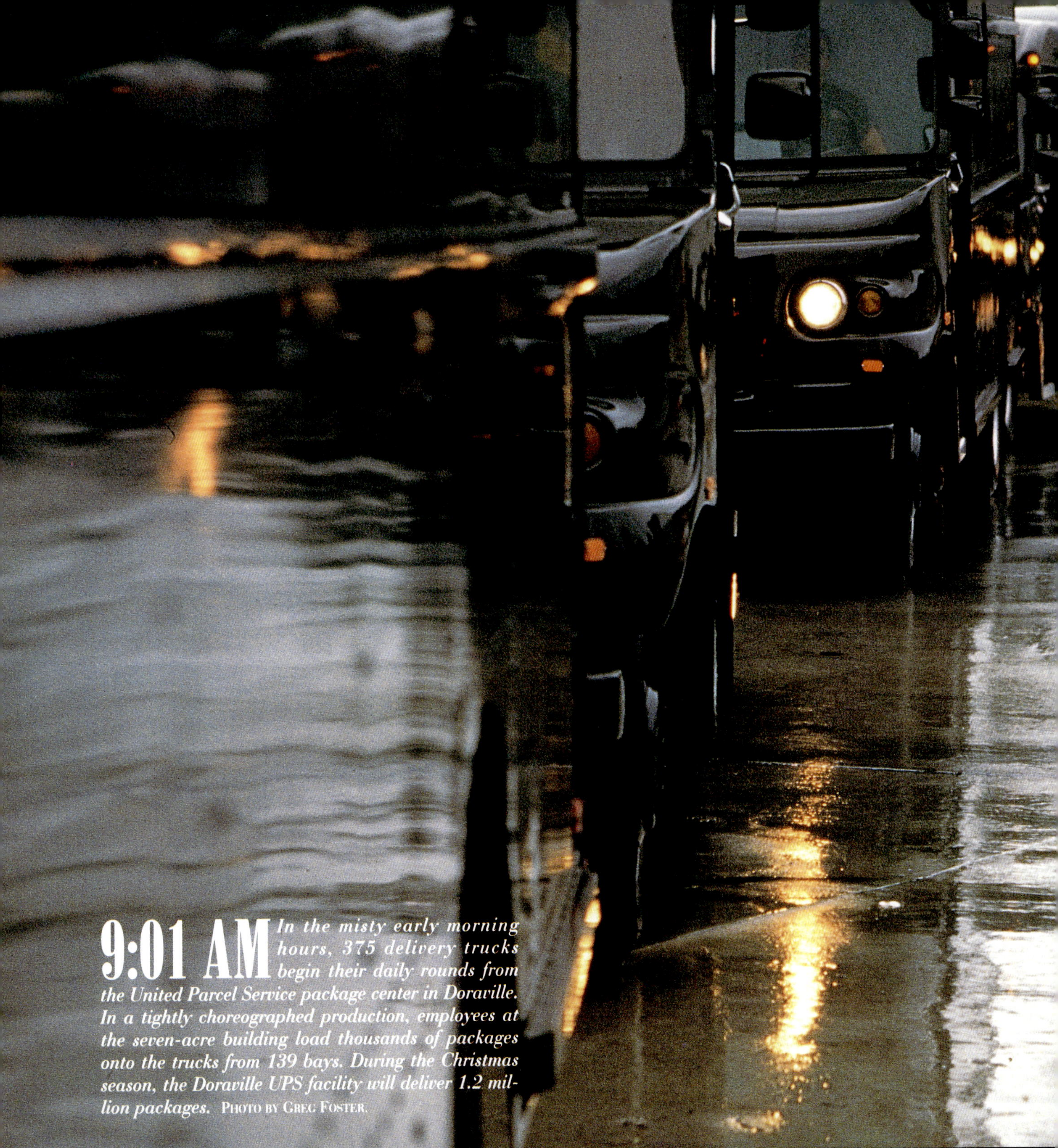

9:01 AM *In the misty early morning hours, 375 delivery trucks begin their daily rounds from the United Parcel Service package center in Doraville. In a tightly choreographed production, employees at the seven-acre building load thousands of packages onto the trucks from 139 bays. During the Christmas season, the Doraville UPS facility will deliver 1.2 million packages.* PHOTO BY GREG FOSTER.

There are any number of things you can bank on today in DeKalb County.

Like roasted turkey and homemade dressing for lunch at Matthews Cafeteria in Tucker . . . 490 professional firefighters in twenty-four fire stations throughout the county, ready . . . the familiar sight of the United Parcel Service truck pulling up to your front door with a package first sorted about 4:30 this morning inside the UPS ground operations facility in the northern reaches of the county . . . fourth-grade teacher Vivian Stephens with a whistle around her neck, rarely used but nonetheless present in case she needs to get everyone's attention at Clairemont Elementary School . . . 38,000 pounds of buffalo-style chicken wings being processed at Suzanna's Kitchen, a frozen-food processor that operates out of Commercial Cold Storage on Pleasantdale Road, the largest above-ground refrigerated warehouse in the world . . . thirty classes and 319 students at the Spruill Center for the Arts.

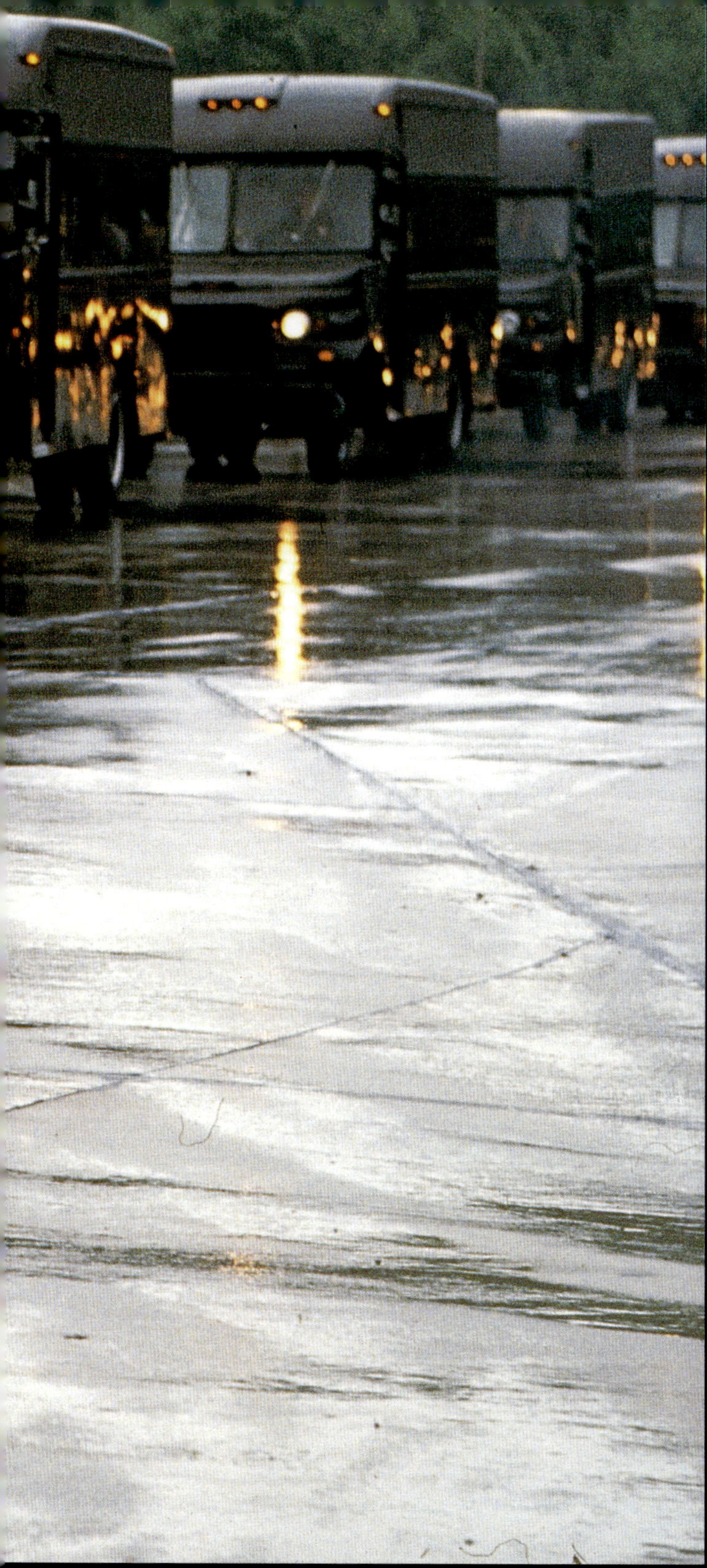

9:05 AM *Granite mining is southeast DeKalb's main industry, although large corporations have replaced most of the small family businesses that encouraged Welsh stonecutters to migrate to the United States many generations ago. W. L. Vaughn (pictured here) and Lauren Coffey work the Coffey quarry with their sons. Stone Mountain granite, distinguished by a swirling pattern and a metallic sparkle, is used in road foundations, buildings, curbing and monuments all over the world. Only a tiny portion of DeKalb's most visible landmark—a mere 7,543,750,950 cubic feet of granite—is above ground; its roots spread for miles around.* PHOTO BY CHUCK YOUNG.

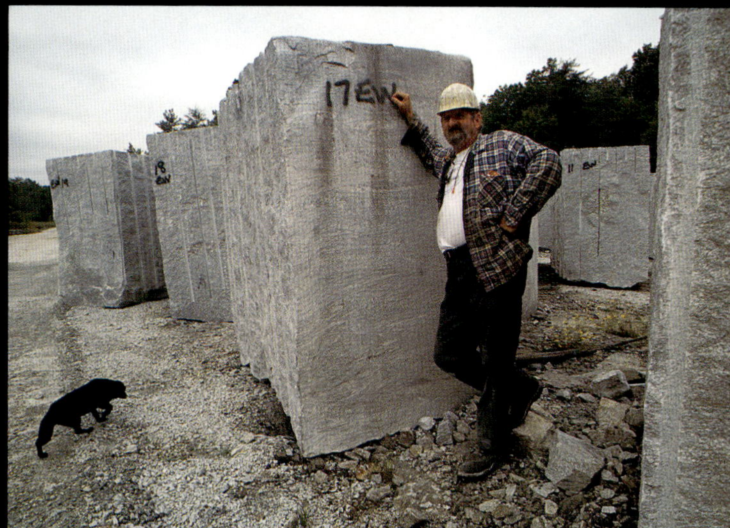

9:39 AM *DeKalb County firefighters have been stopping blazes in the same building for almost twenty years. It's a fire-resistant concrete building in South DeKalb where new recruits train and veterans refresh their firefighting and rescue skills. Also at the DeKalb Fire Department Training Center are a seven-story tower for working on high-rise fire fighting, and a shop where engines, ladders and ladder trucks are tested and repaired.* PHOTO BY SCOTT ROBINSON.

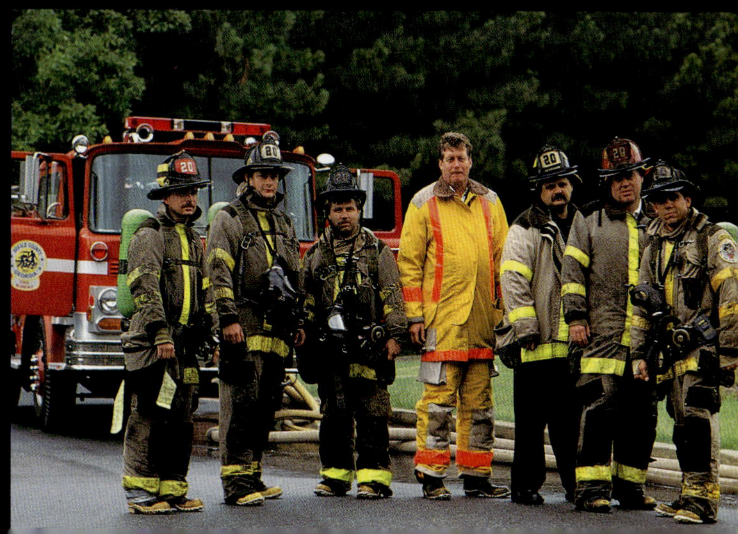

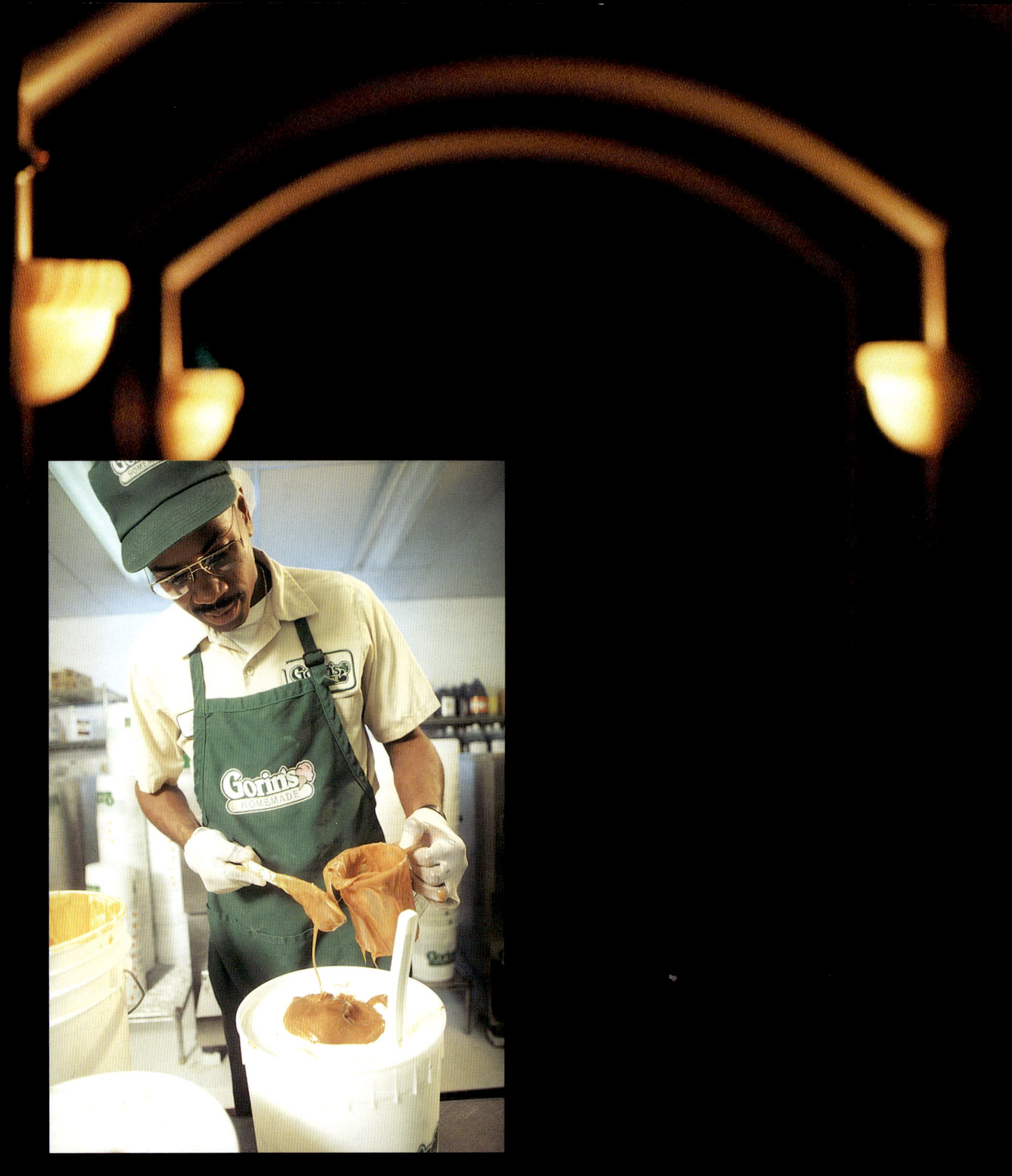

10:30 AM *From a small, unassuming building on a side street in Avondale Estates comes some of Atlanta's best-known confections. Just the names alone are enough to make anyone drool: Oreo Cookie, New York-Style Strawberry Cheesecake, Caramel Craze, Pralines and Cream, and Bittersweet Chocolate. Gorin's Homemade Ice Cream, owned by Bob Solomon and Mark Kaplan, has been voted Atlanta's best ice cream for many years. Here, Jackie McGhee helps make a small batch of ice cream. By keeping the manufactured amounts small, he says, it helps ensure homemade taste.* PHOTO BY TOM ENGLAND.

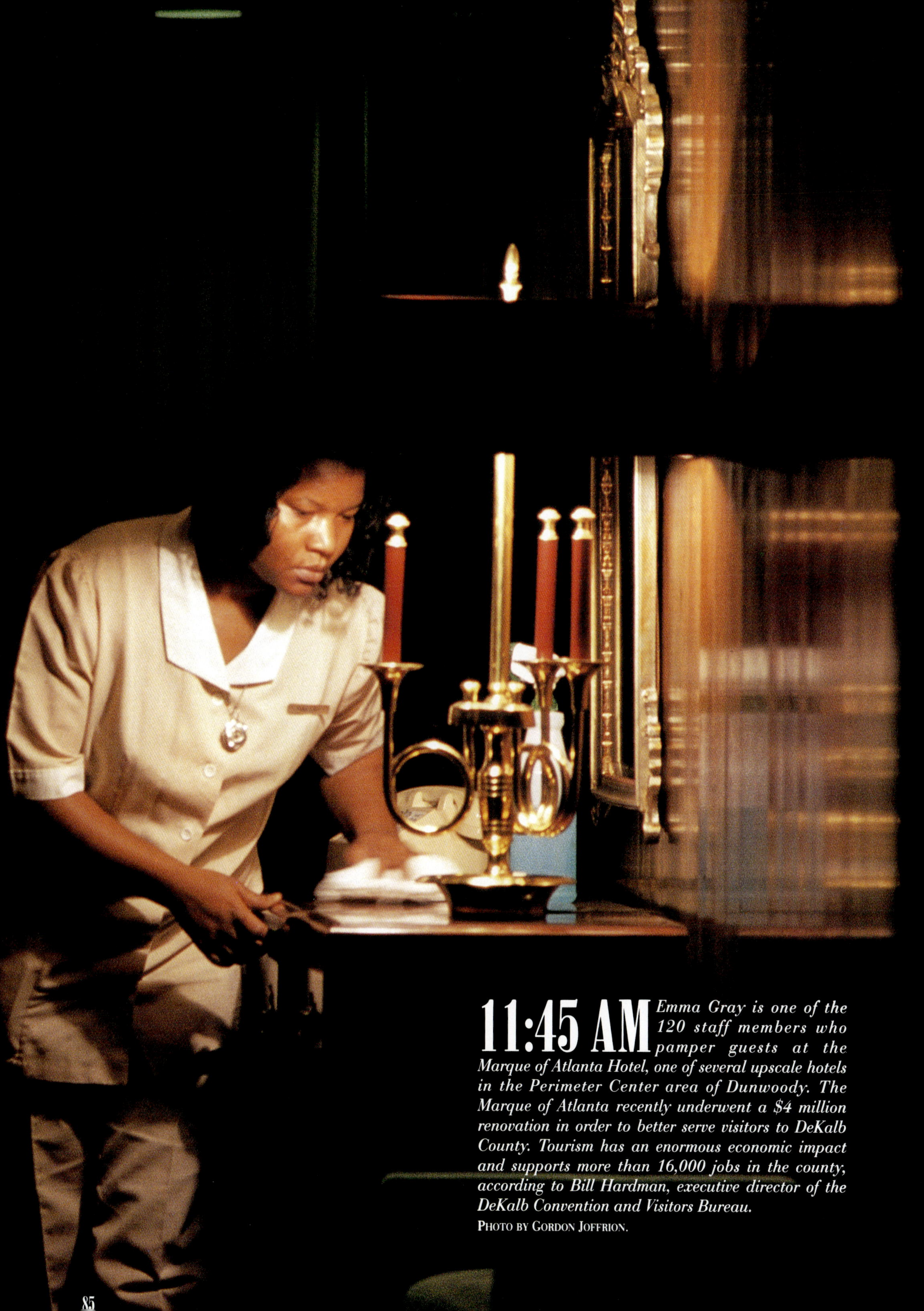

11:45 AM *Emma Gray is one of the 120 staff members who pamper guests at the Marque of Atlanta Hotel, one of several upscale hotels in the Perimeter Center area of Dunwoody. The Marque of Atlanta recently underwent a $4 million renovation in order to better serve visitors to DeKalb County. Tourism has an enormous economic impact and supports more than 16,000 jobs in the county, according to Bill Hardman, executive director of the DeKalb Convention and Visitors Bureau.*

PHOTO BY GORDON JOFFRION.

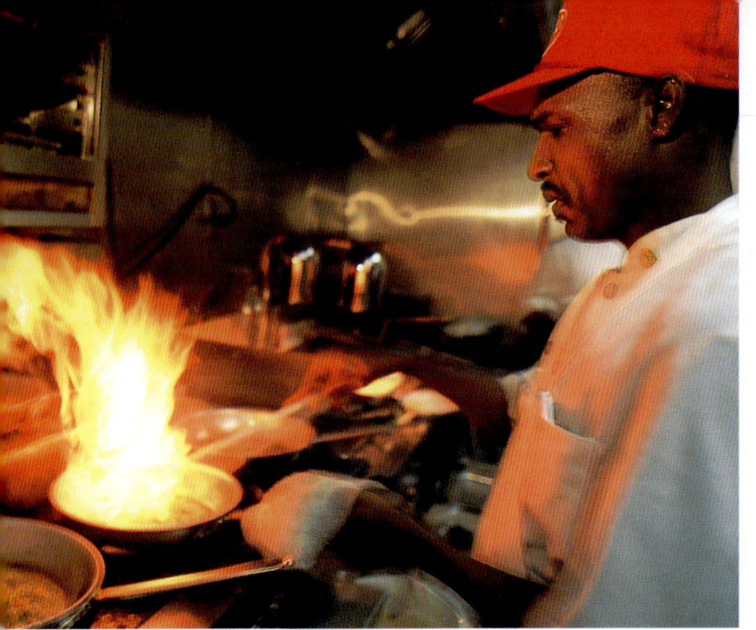

12:15 PM *Lunchtime at Mick's in Decatur is busy both in front of the counter and behind it—where the cook, Nigerian-born Prince Orubo, works.* PHOTO BY GREG FOSTER.

12:30 PM *A trip to Langford's Store on Briarcliff Road is a trip back in time. Pass the old gas pump that still advertises gasoline for thirty-five cents a gallon. Go through the screen door and buy a Coke from Wayne Langford, whose grandfather opened the store in 1939 when the store was surrounded by cotton fields. Today, Langford's is a pleasant anachronism across the street from Briarlake Elementary School. And, while the rest of the world seems to prefer "we never close," Wayne's store hours are "subject to change due to important events like . . . when the fish are bitin'." Of course, you don't have to necessarily shop at Langford's. Gary Ross preferred to take a breather this afternoon by setting up camp in a rocking chair.*

PHOTO BY ALAN WEINER.

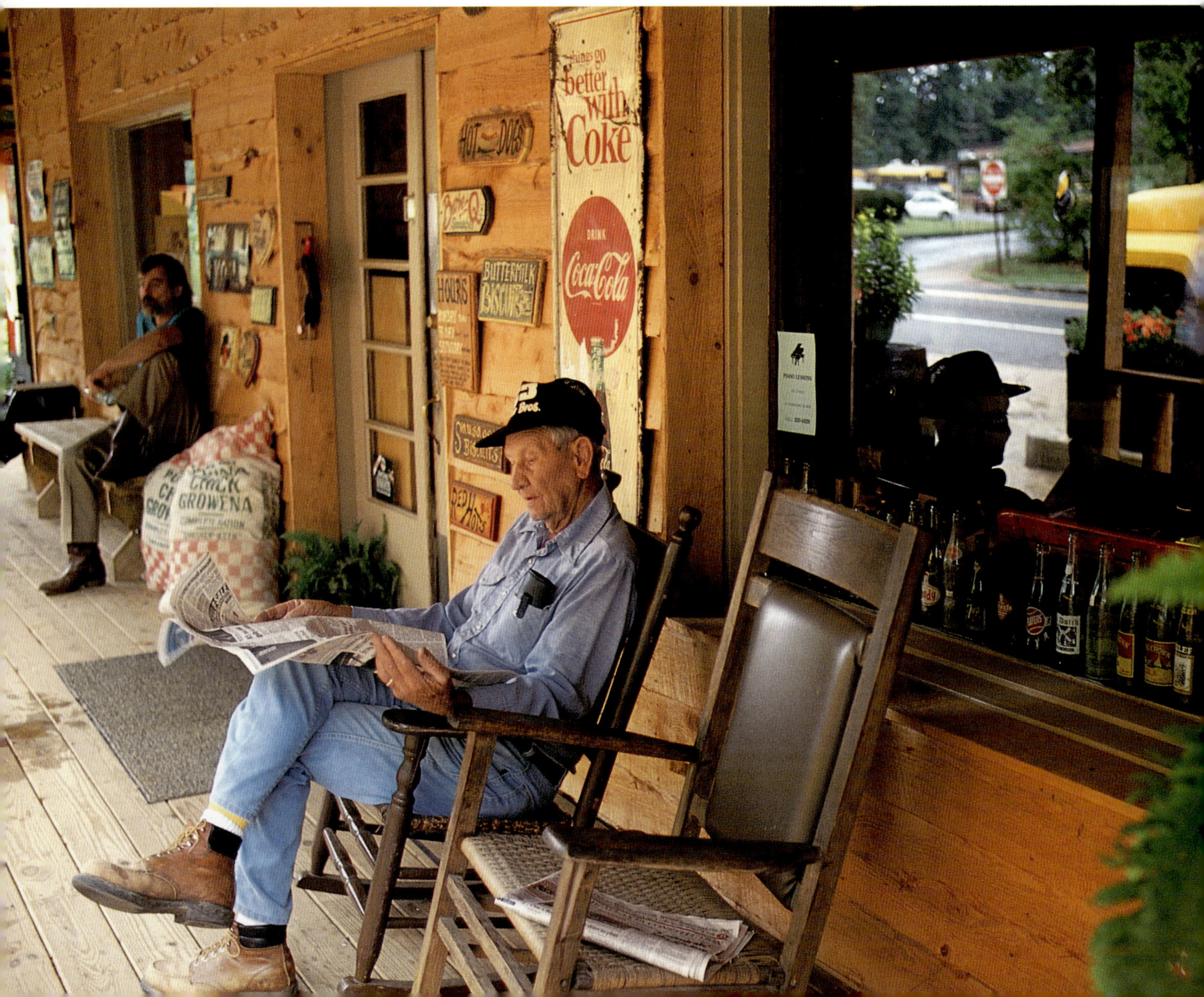

But during these next twenty-four hours in DeKalb County, there are just as many events that can't be banked on, events that would never be considered predictable. For everyone involved, they represent a gamble on the future. And, more often than not, the stakes are high.

In her obstetrician's office, Nancy Lewis, thirty-five, hears her baby's heartbeat for the first time. The baby is due in April. Is it a boy or a girl? She tries to imagine later, her face filled with every bit of joy and wonder the moment deserves.

Yung Lee, twenty-seven, and Li-Chin Wu, twenty-four, sit huddled on a sofa, engaged in casual conversation in the lobby of the Davis Building at Mercer University. They are scared, they are excited and they are friends. They have just registered for their first college undergraduate courses—music appreciation, English 101 and macroeconomics. Lee, from Korea, and Wu, a native of Taiwan, have been in the county for less than two years. They met on campus last quarter when they took an English-as-second-language course. "We studied together," says Wu. "So we decided to do it again."

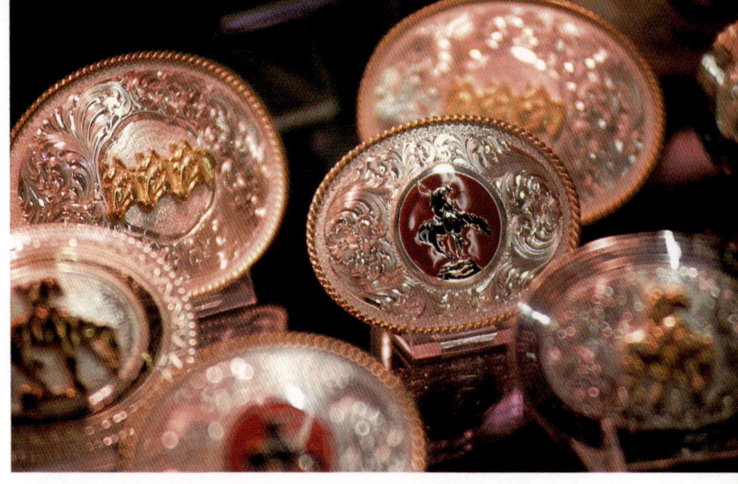

1:30 PM *Though essentially an urban county, DeKalb's country roots are still quite evident at Cowpuncher's Palace on Covington Highway. Cowpuncher's caters to horses and riders and anyone else who prefers jeans, boots, big buckles and Stetsons (all of which are part of Carlos Austin's attire in this photo) to three-piece suits and wingtips. The huge store carries saddles, tack, clothes, hats and, of course, boots—even a size zero cowboy boots for newborn cowboys.* Photos by Chuck Young.

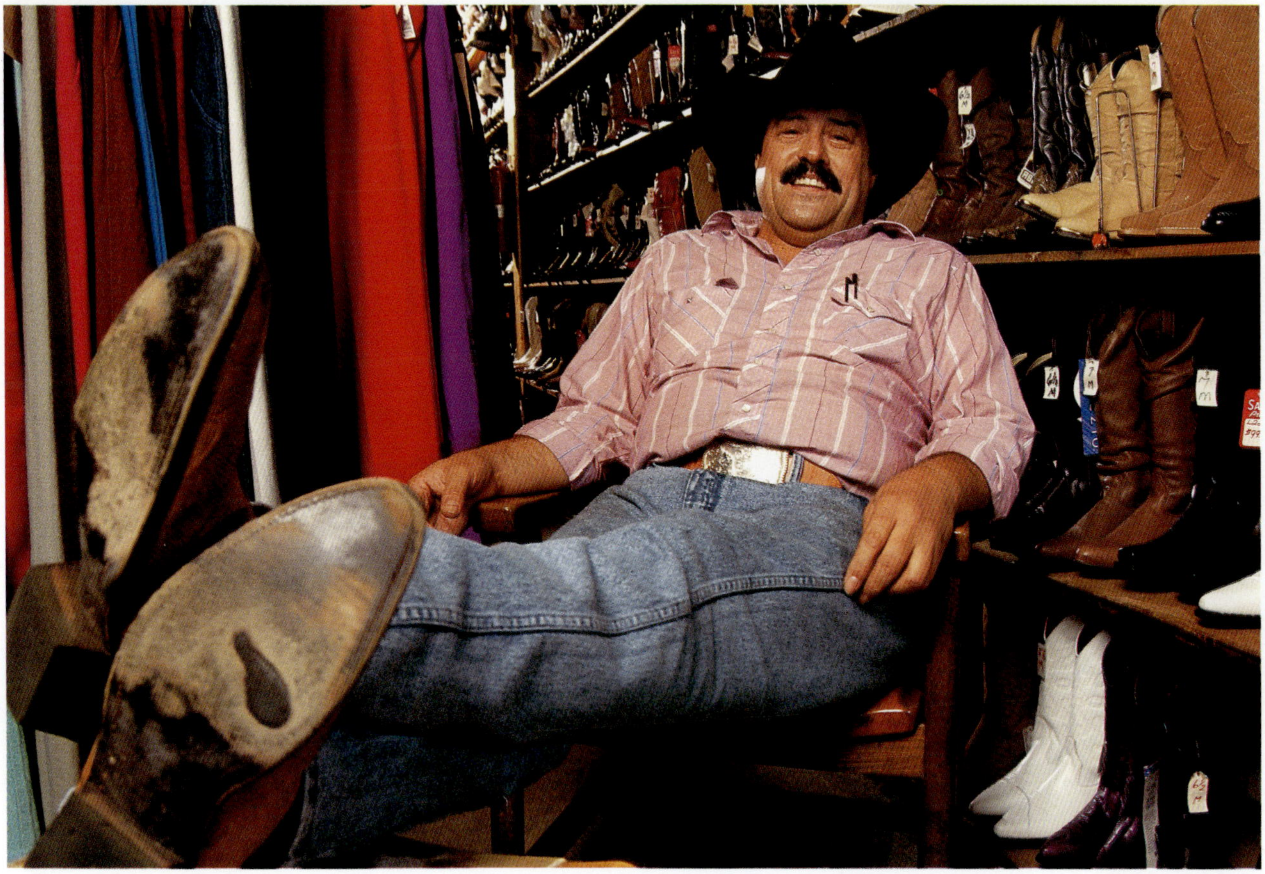

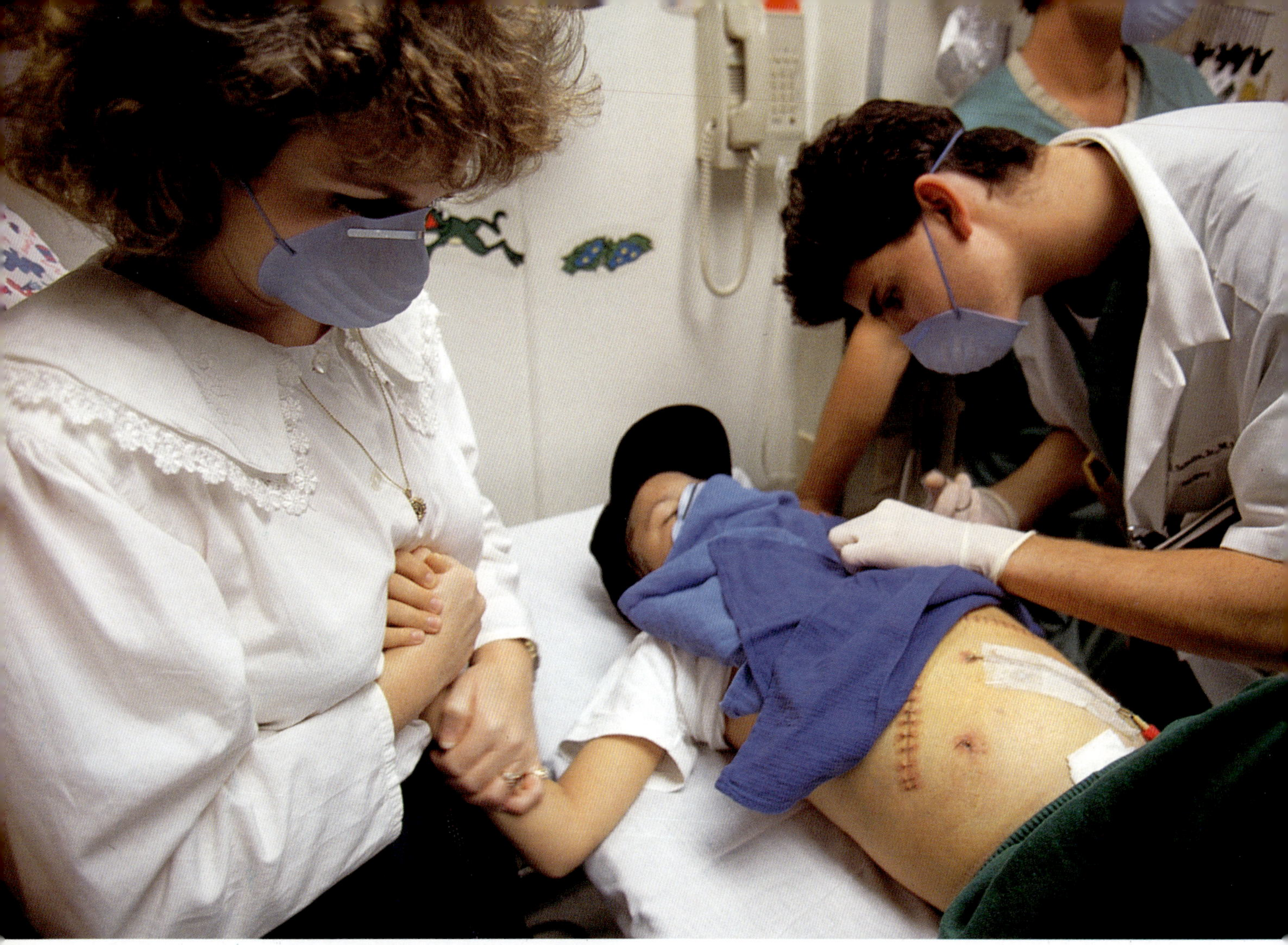

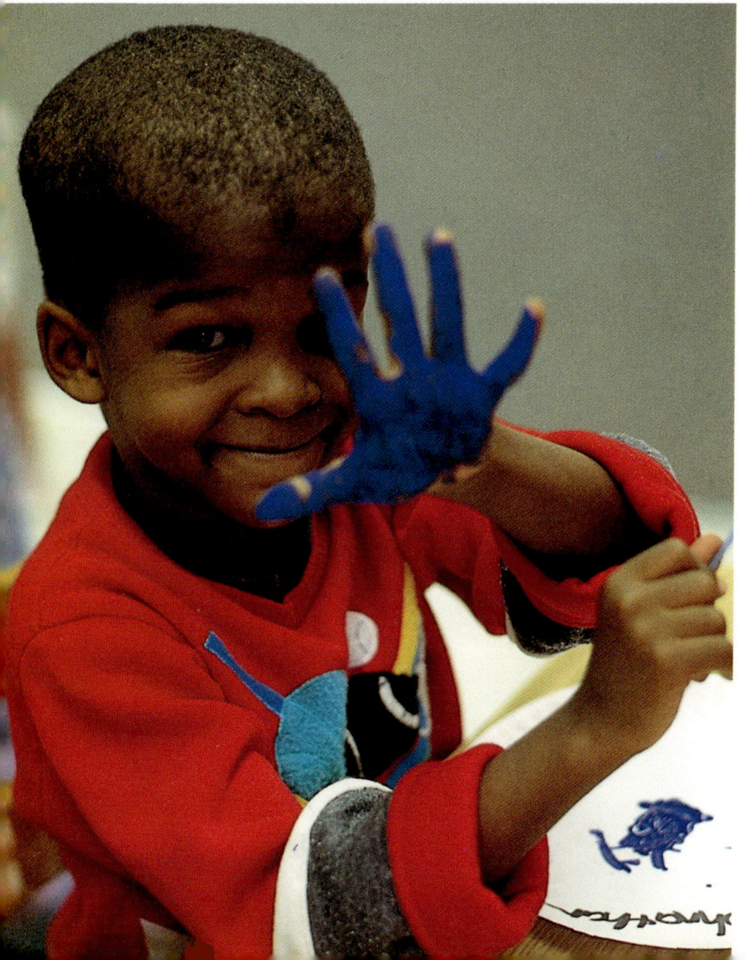

2:33 PM *Vena Grey watches over her son, John, while Dr. Kip Schultz examines the young boy, who has undergone two liver transplants and faces the possibility of a third. Two months ago, John was finishing baseball season and looking forward to playing defensive end for his football team. Today, he is counting on Egleston Children's Hospital at Emory University to restore him to health after a viral infection destroyed his liver. The Griffin youngster spent his tenth birthday in intensive care. The Egleston staff later threw him a surprise birthday party.*

PHOTO BY KEN HAWKINS.

3:30 PM *Our House is DeKalb's only day-care program for homeless children, serving families who live in emergency night shelters they must leave during the day. The Decatur facility provides child care, meals and health care for thirty-six children ages two months to twelve years, with special rooms where parents can take care of sick children and new mothers can recuperate from childbirth. In addition, Our House has a Family Resource Program which helps families with housing, jobs and training.*

PHOTO BY TOM ENGLAND.

Robert W. Campbell is out of sorts. "It's miserable when you're not working," says Campbell, who has worked the assembly line for twenty-eight years at the General Motors plant in Doraville, the only automobile manufacturing plant ever located in DeKalb since it opened in 1947. Today, Campbell and seven other GM employees who live on Reeves Street in Chamblee are out of work because the plant is closed for two weeks—a not all too unfamiliar occurrence to members of Local No. 10 of the United Auto Workers who have witnessed 3,000 layoffs at the plant in the last five years. However, for Campbell and the remaining 2,200 UAW employees at the plant, the future seems a little brighter. General Motors recently announced plans to produce mini-vans in Doraville.

Even with the good news, Campbell can't hide his disappointment that his son won't work for GM. "My son always wanted to work for General Motors, and my wife and I put away $9,000 for him to go

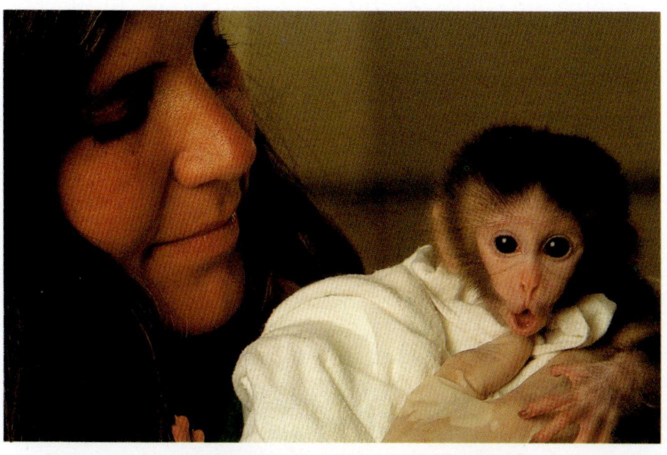

4:15 PM *Wilbur is a rhesus monkey and a "crack baby." In her study of the effects of cocaine on female rhesus monkeys and their offspring at Yerkes Regional Primate Research Center at Emory University, Dr. Jane Ellis has found that a lack of prenatal care and poor diet has greater effect on the baby monkeys than does cocaine. Attending births at all hours has been good practice for Ellis, thirty-six, who is pregnant.*
PHOTO BY MICHAEL SCHWARZ.

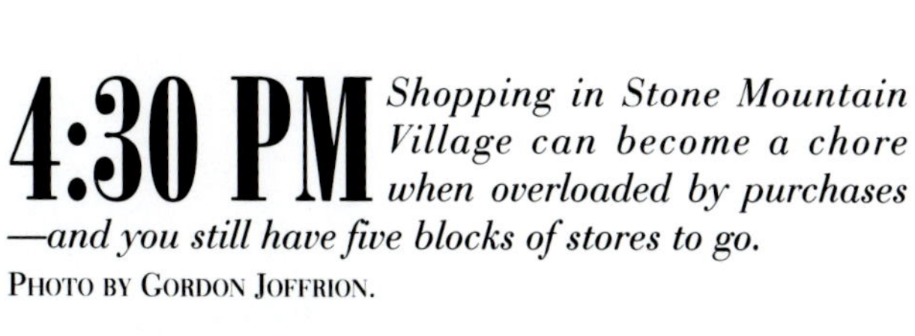

4:30 PM *Shopping in Stone Mountain Village can become a chore when overloaded by purchases —and you still have five blocks of stores to go.*
PHOTO BY GORDON JOFFRION.

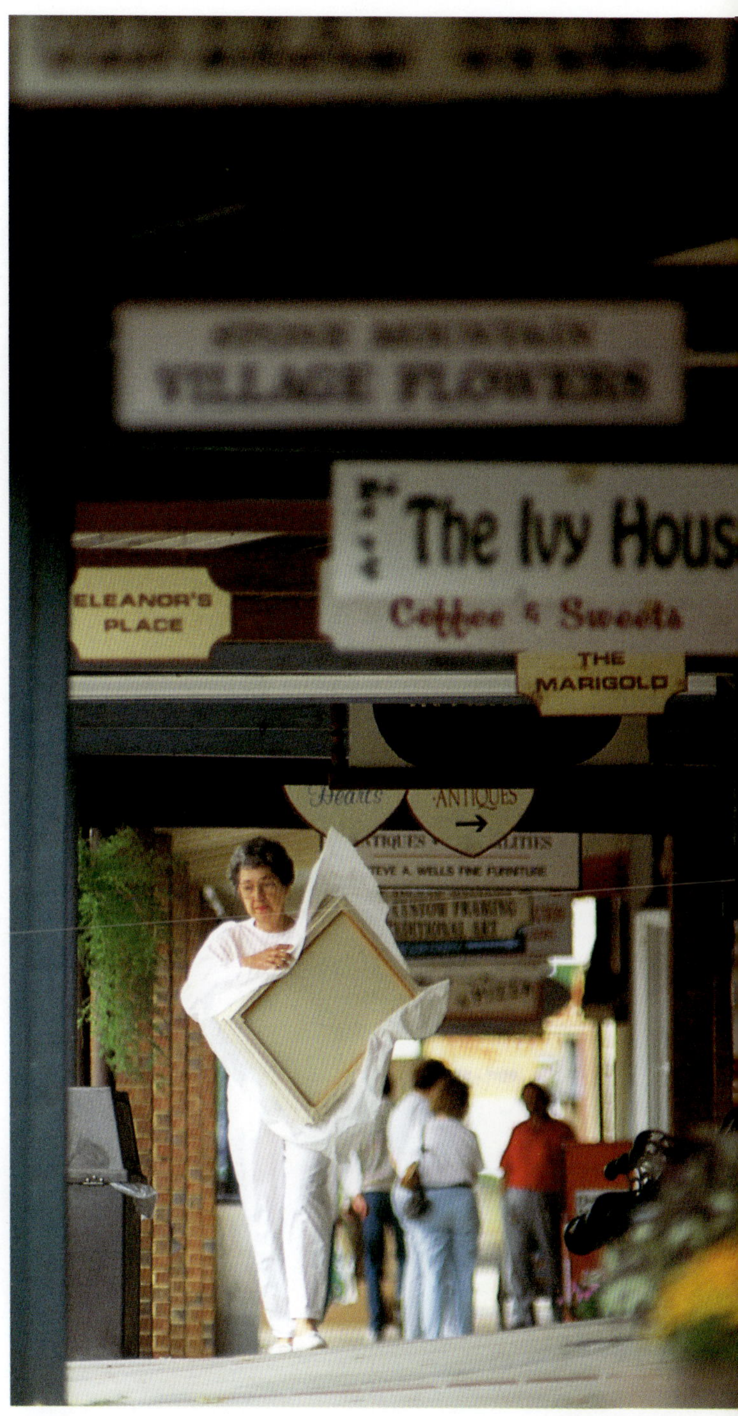

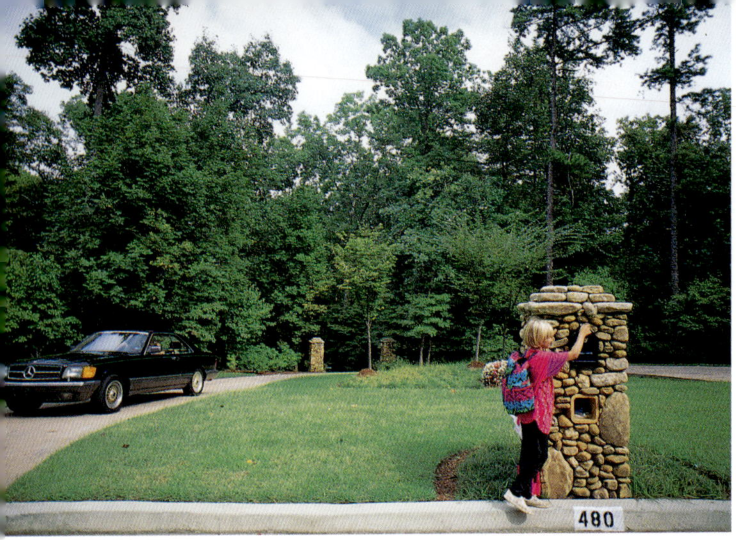

4:42 PM *While Courtney Buchanan retrieves the mail from her family's Stone Mountain mailbox, mom Sally Buchanan waits.*
PHOTO BY GORDON JOFFRION.

away to the General Motors Institute, which is like a college, that would just about guarantee you for supervision if you finished," says Campbell, whose son now works for a steel company in Alabama. "They discontinued that program the year he graduated from high school. It was my ambition for years to prepare the boy for that, and once it went down it took a lot out of him and out of me. We had our hopes up for him having a better position with General Motors than I had. All parents do."

The 1996 Summer Olympic Games may be on the horizon, but DeKalb officials feel the future breathing down their necks.

By 7:30 A.M. Bob Cowig is drinking coffee at the start of a three-hour meeting with the Atlanta Committee for the Olympic Games (ACOG).

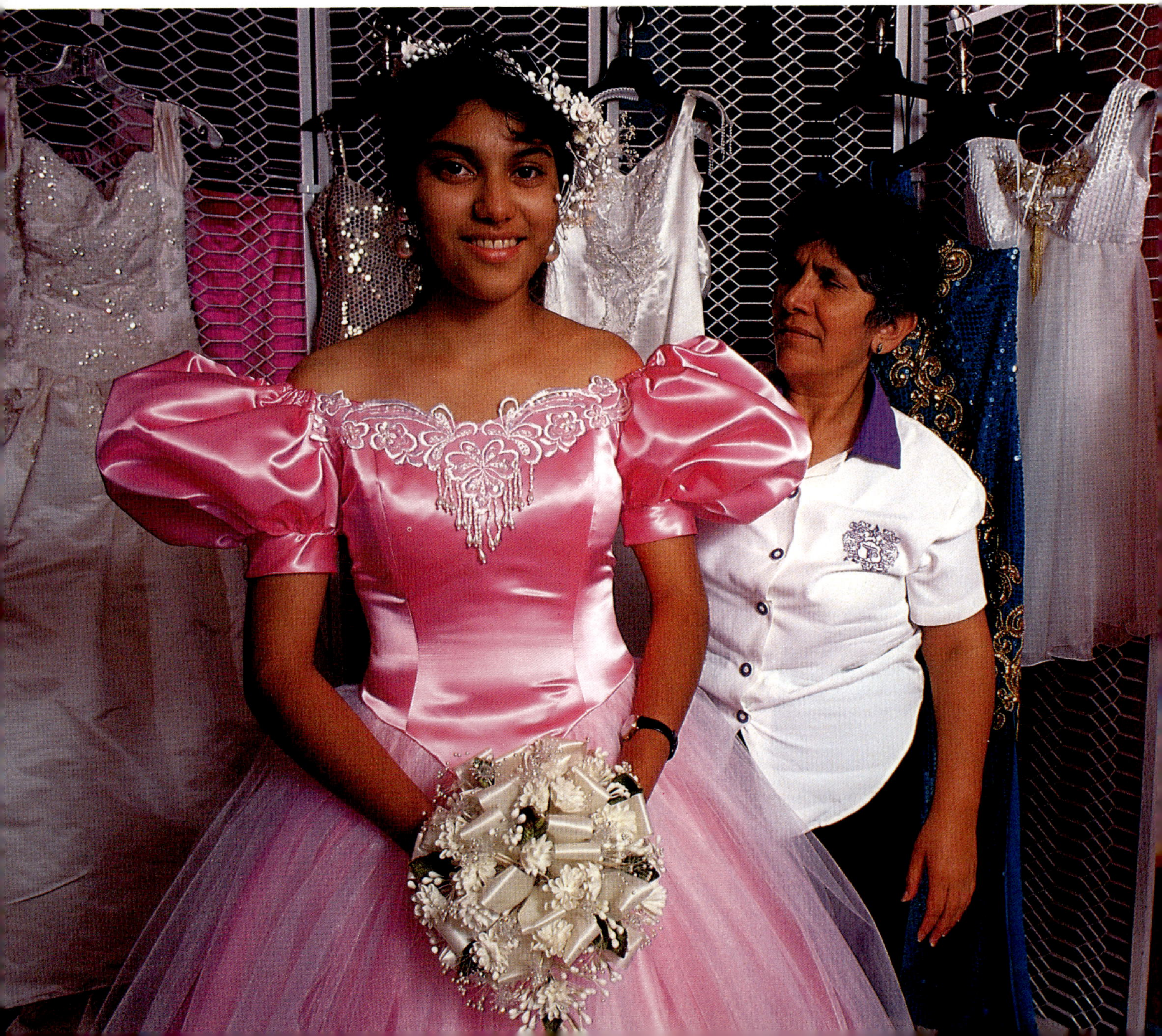

Cowig, director of planning and development for Stone Mountain Park, is assured of six sporting events on the 3,200 acres of Olympic Park—canoeing, rowing, archery, kayaking, cycling, tennis and the cross-country portion of the pentathlon. Today's meeting involves no less than 200 issues concerning planning, design, construction and post-Olympic use and budgets for these events. Back in his office by noon, Cowig is still working on next year's laser show for Stone Mountain, but he admits that nearly 90 percent of his time is now spent on the Olympics.

Between bites of her club sandwich lunch, Lisa Hanson pitches DeKalb County's potential Olympic training sites to Dr. LeRoy Walker, senior vice president of sports for ACOG and incoming

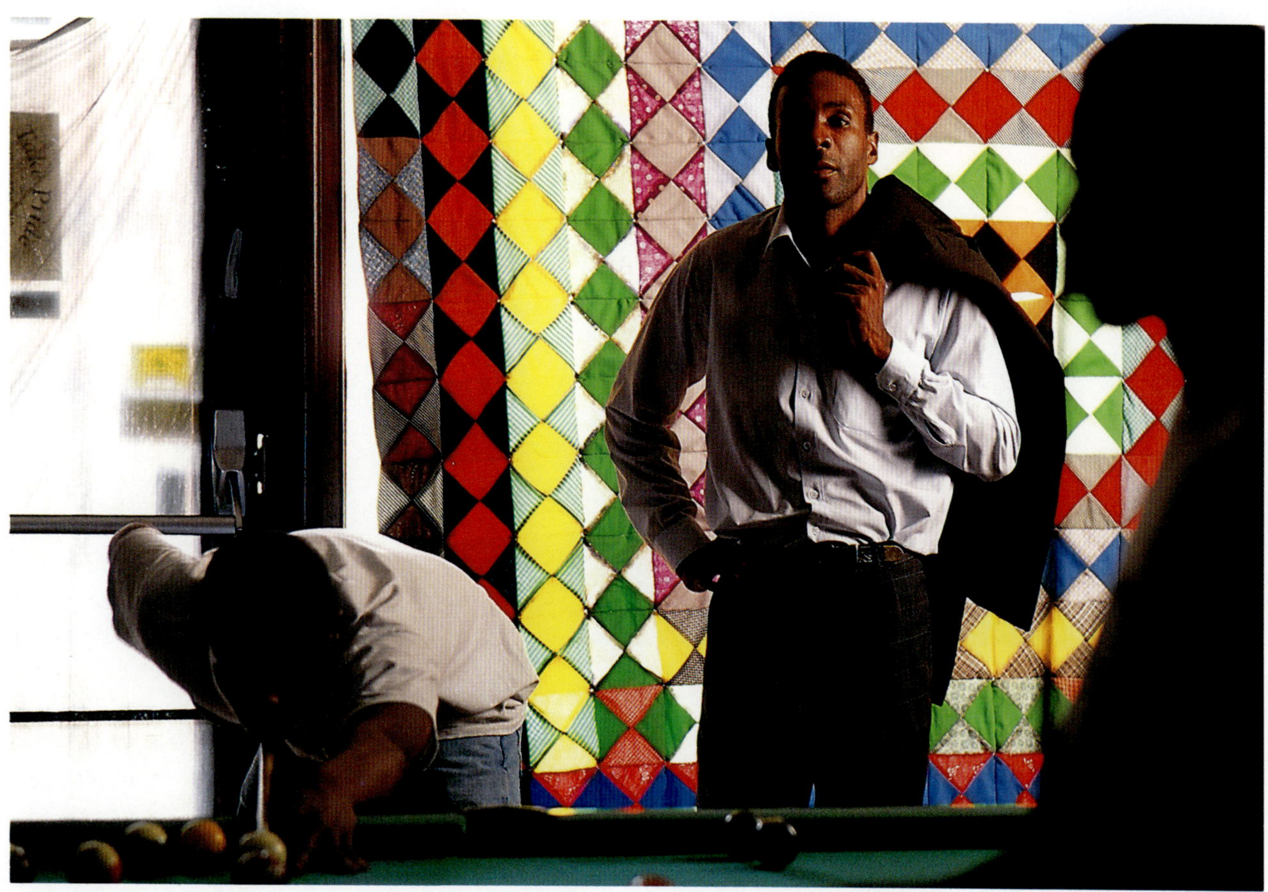

5:00 PM *Maria del Carmen Ortiz stands patiently while being outfitted for a formal gown by Mrs. Barron Martinez in her Tucker shop. In the Mexican culture, when a daughter reaches the age of fifteen, her parents announce with pride that she is no longer a child but a beautiful young woman. Dressed in a gown created just for her, she is presented to the world at a lavish party called a Quincenera. Attended by fourteen girls who form her court, she and her parents accept congratulations from their family and friends. Everything—her gown, the traditional dinner, the dance band—is paid for by a cadre of godfathers and godmothers. For young Mexican-American women, the traditional rite of passage is second in importance only to her wedding day.*

Photo by Marilyn Futterman.

5:30 PM *The Teen Scene gives Lithonia's young people a place of their own for supervised recreation, as well as pursuing their studies and learning leadership skills. The center also secures placement for youths ordered to complete community-service work by the DeKalb Juvenile Court. The center's Student Support Program allows teens suspended from school to continue their class work. Tutoring and a summer recreation program also are provided. Rev. Richard Murphy, pictured here, founded the center, and continues as its director. Murphy also is a Lithonia city councilman.*

Photo by Gordon Joffrion.

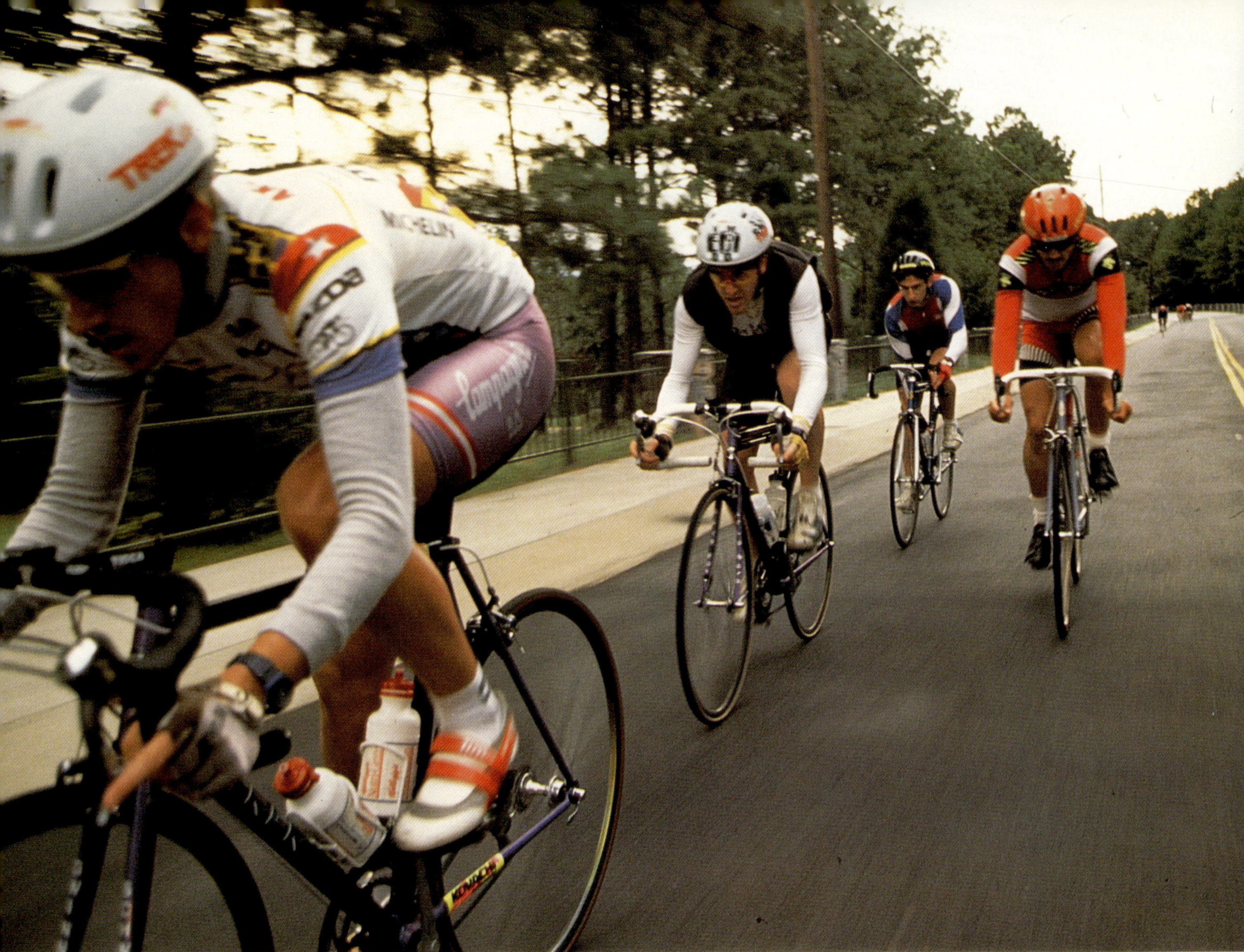

president of the U.S. Olympic Committee. She is competing against every available site in every surrounding county, but Hanson's got an edge that's as good as gold. "DeKalb has the location factor in our pocket," says Hanson, head of Sports DeKalb, who long ago figured that 200 participating countries, fielding a maximum of twenty-six sports each, require a remarkable number of training facilities. With all the educational and recreational facilities in the county, Hanson argues that "we have a heck of a lot to offer. And Dr. Walker recognizes that. The economic impact to DeKalb will be incredible, but we're not in this to make a million dollars. This is part of the whole Olympic effort. Hopefully, everyone will benefit, but we are not going to gouge these people."

While Hanson's job requires her to think four years ahead, John and Vena Grey think about their son's future one day at a time. Only two-and-a-half months ago, John was a healthy ten-year-old, a straight-A student from Griffin, Georgia, who played defensive end for his peewee football team and who played pitcher, shortstop, first base and outfield for his baseball team. On July 20, John experienced heartburn and intense itching, and two days later he was suffering from jaundice. According to doctors, he was attacked by a virus that remains unidentified. Vena says it was "like a hurricane that does damage and is gone."

Today, John is a patient at Egleston Children's Hospital, where he has undergone two liver transplants since September 6. John's body rejected the first liver, and excessive bleeding threatened the second transplant until, John says, he talked to God. He saw a light shining above his head and then God baptized him. John says he now talks with God, every day, about saving his life.

The day has been remarkably free of tests for John, but around 2 P.M. Dr. Kip Schultz arrives to remove the central IV line from his body. Still

6:30 PM *Late every Thursday afternoon, a gang of hardcore bicyclists convene behind an Avondale Estates pizzeria. And then, like a flock of birds launched by an unseen signal, they begin a vigorous ride to Stone Mountain, completely encircling it, and then back to Avondale Estates. It's not a trip for beginners, as stragglers are left behind to find their own way.* PHOTO BY SCOTT ROBINSON.

7:00 PM *If you want something done, ask the Dunwoody Woman's Club. Whether they're staging the Independence Day parade or beautifying the Ashford Dunwoody Road median, these women organize and mobilize to make Dunwoody among the top residential neighborhoods in the nation. One of their newest projects has been transforming the old Dunwoody Park into the new Dunwoody Nature Center. Thanks to assistance from local Eagle Scouts and community groups and cooperation from county government, the nature center—where this photo of the club was taken—has trails, a bird sanctuary, butterfly garden, kiosk and signs labeling natural and historic points of interest. The center also provides a setting for outdoor concerts.* PHOTO BY ROB NELSON.

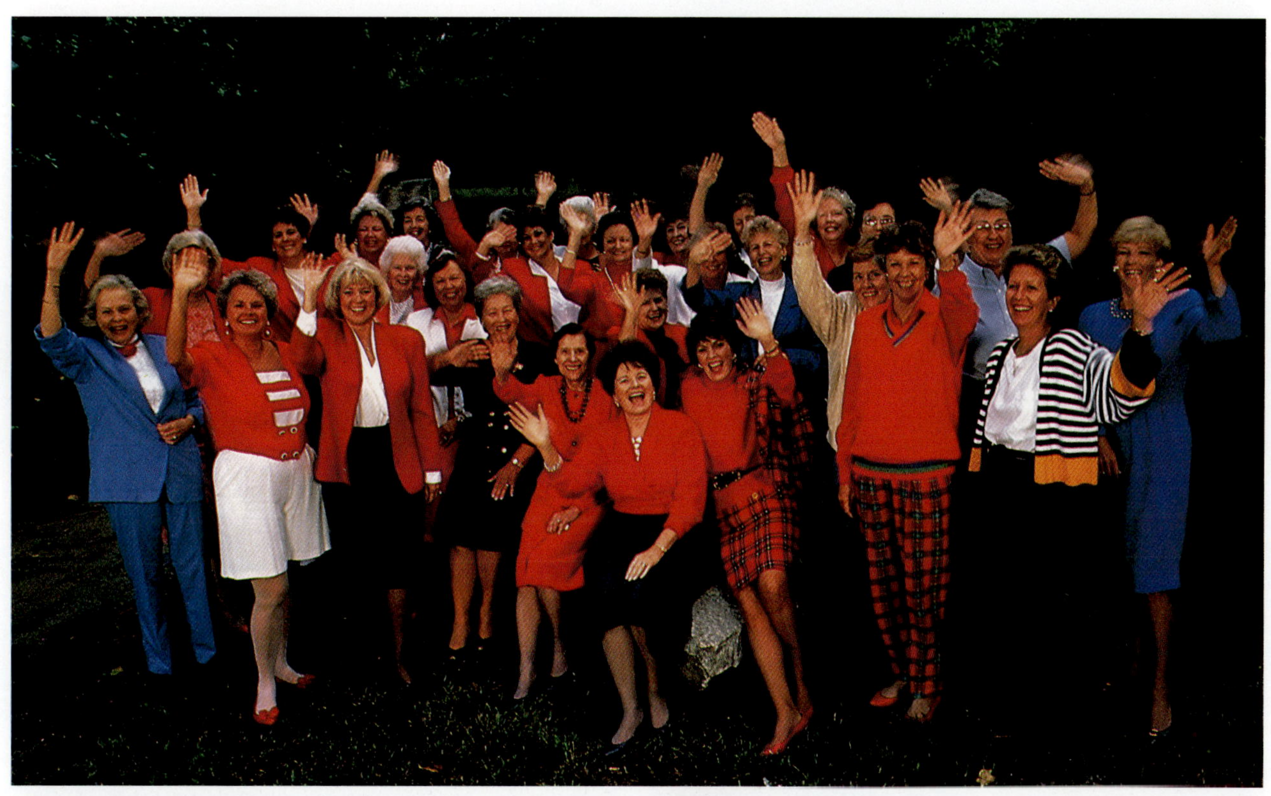

7:20 PM *Even barbecue tastes better when eaten outdoors, as this South DeKalb institution, J&D BBQ and Soul Food, on Memorial Drive offers.* PHOTO BY SCOTT ROBINSON.

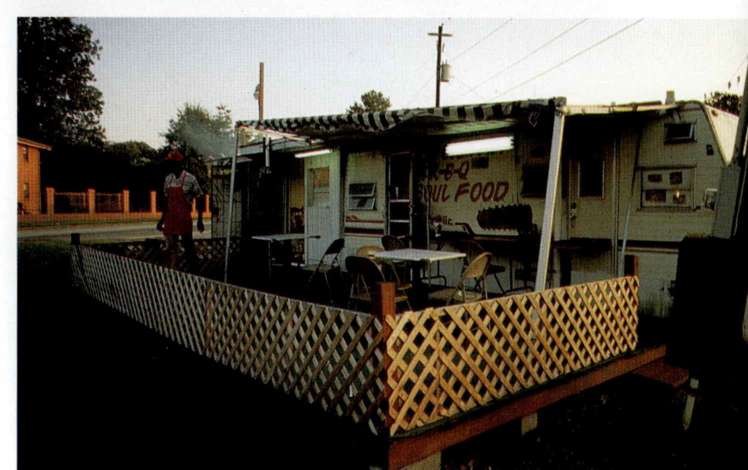

wearing the cap that Atlanta Falcon Scott Case gave him, John walks slowly down the hall to a treatment room, where he's lifted onto an examination table. Dr. Schultz administers a shot to numb the surrounding skin and checks to make sure that John feels no pain before he pulls out a #10 blade and makes a small cut in John's left side. His mother holds his hand. Dr. Schultz decides John feels the blade, although the boy never utters a word, and administers another shot. The room is silent and tense. Nurse Karen Ardell breaks through the stillness and asks John how he likes football. A few seconds later, Dr. Schultz removes the IV line, and holds it up for everyone to see.

By 2:30 P.M., John, who was in intensive care when he turned ten on September 7, is right in the

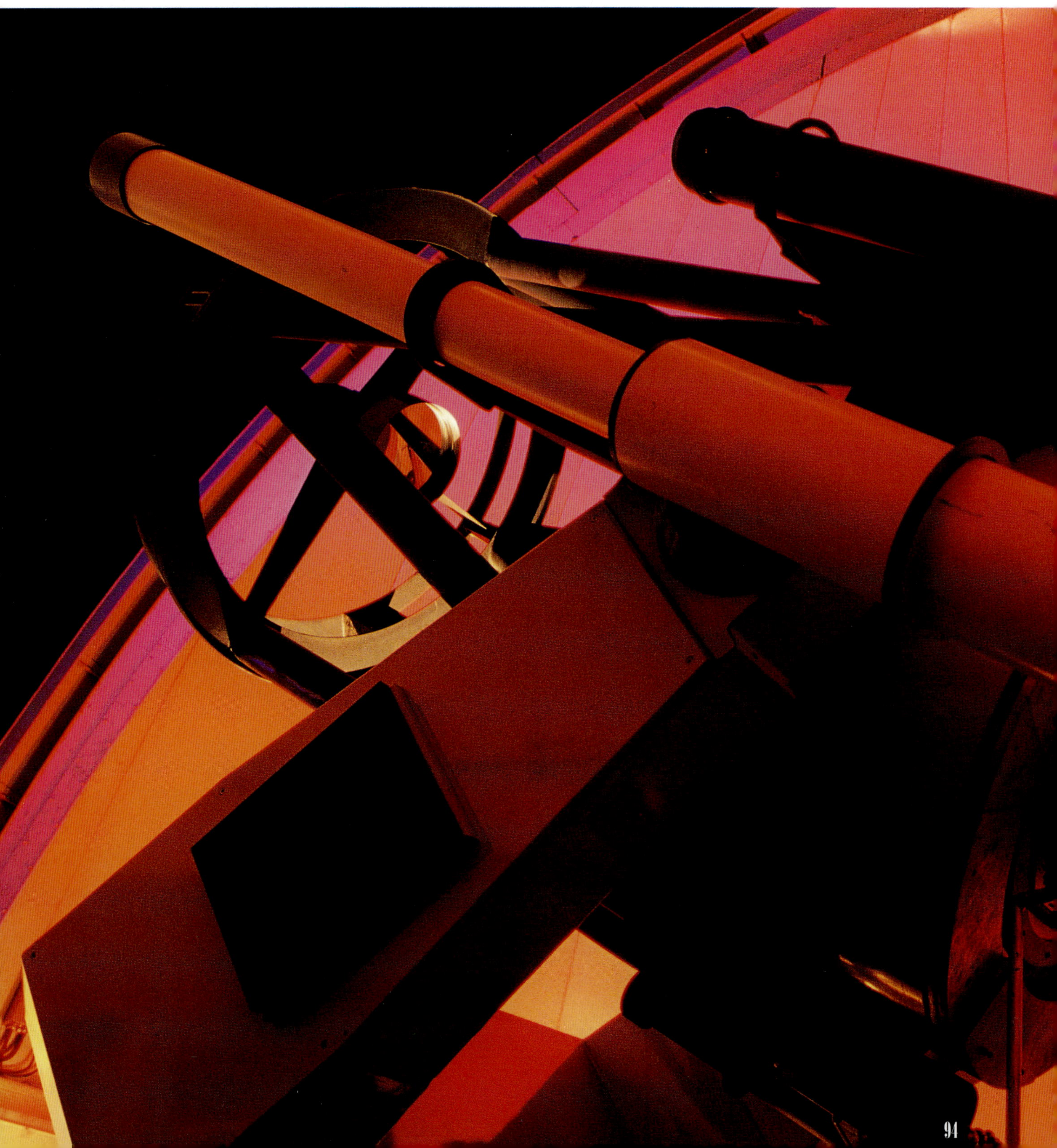

middle of a surprise birthday party thrown for him by the Egleston staff. John Grey watches his son as he celebrates. He marvels at his courage. Last year, he remembers, his son played baseball for two weeks with a broken foot, and never once mentioned any pain.

There is a certain pain that cannot be concealed in the faces at Teen Scene, Inc., a program for poor

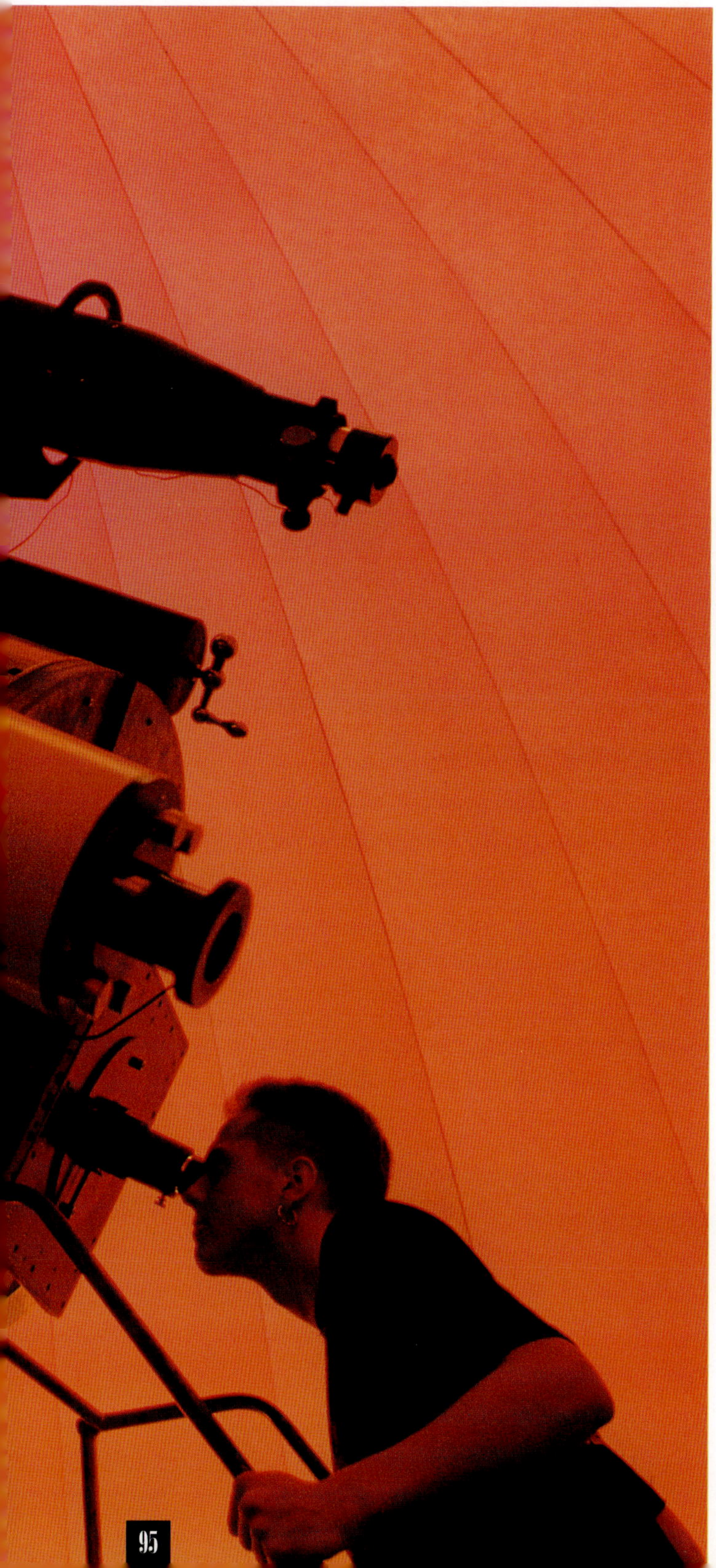

7:30 PM *Educational opportunities in DeKalb are not limited to the young. Nor are they limited to the planet Earth. Schoolchildren, as well as adults, take advantage of Fernbank Science Center, which is operated by the DeKalb School System, but is open to the public. The thirty-six-inch reflecting telescope in the observatory reveals the secrets of the heavens to the public. Fernbank's centerpiece is its planetarium, the third largest in the United States. The facility, which also houses a science museum, is surrounded by an outdoor learning laboratory amid sixty-five acres of old-growth forest.* PHOTO BY KEN HAWKINS.

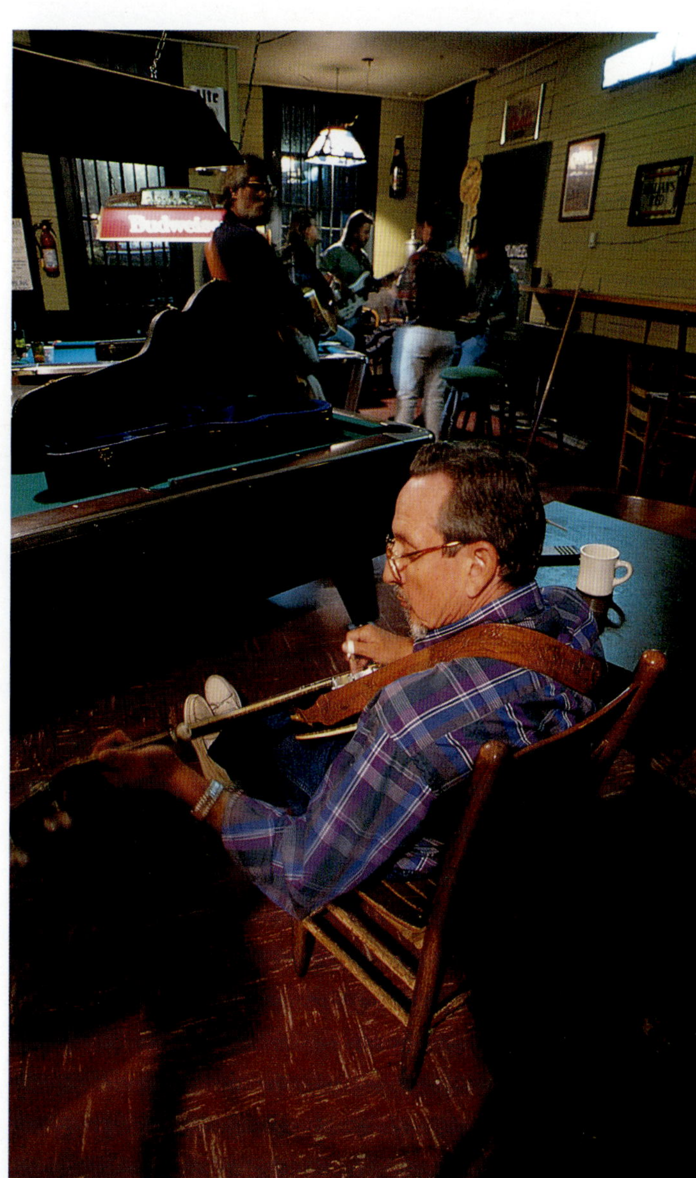

8:49 PM *Thursday evenings in Decatur can sound like a bluegrass festival as pickers and fiddlers from the area gather at The Freight Room on East Howard Avenue to jam deep into the night. Banjo player Al Upshaw tunes his instrument in preparation for the long evening ahead.* PHOTO BY CHUCK YOUNG.

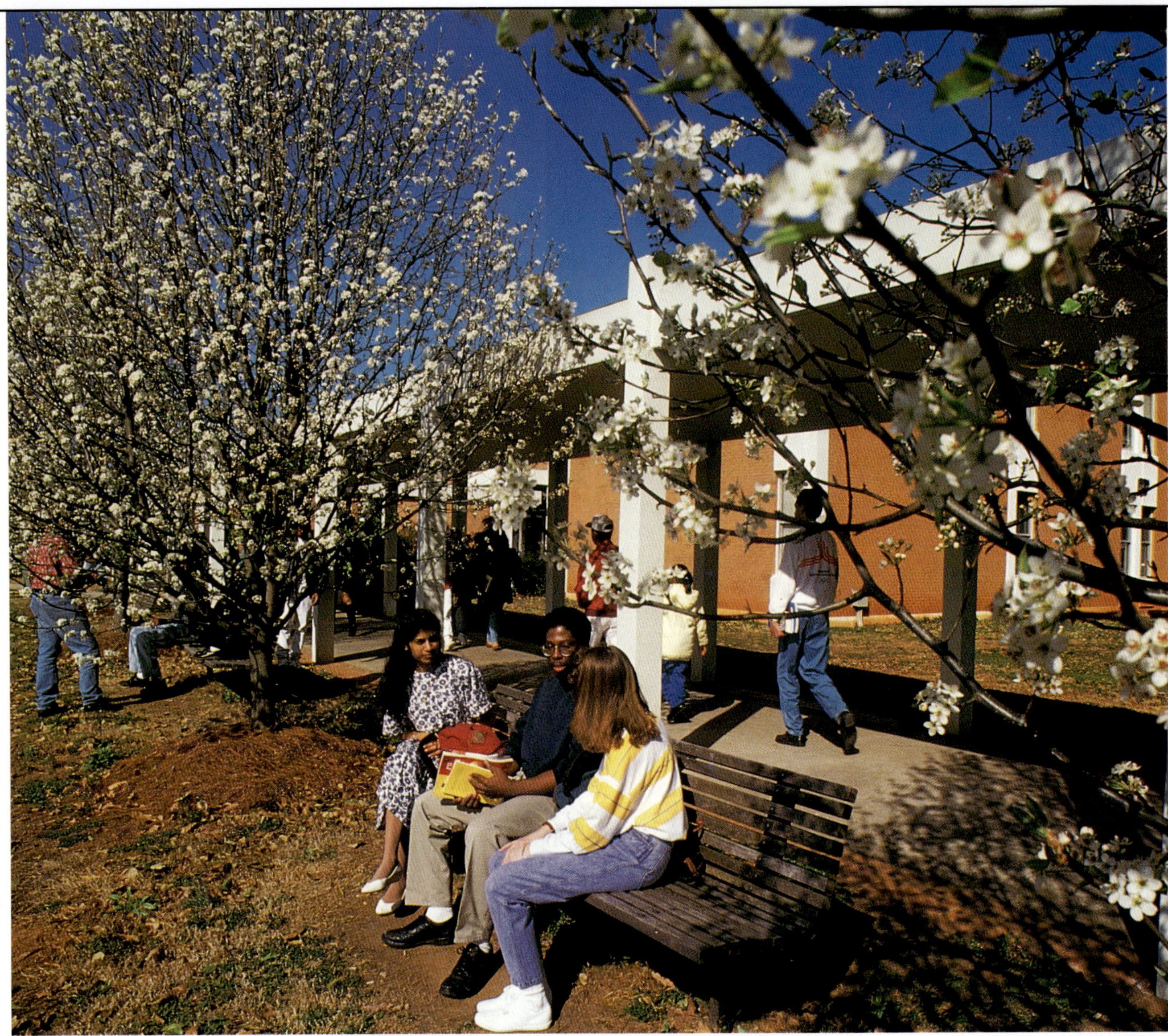

ALAN WEINER

One of our really favorite stories at DeKalb College comes from a student whom we named as our Outstanding Scholar in the University System's Academic Recognition Day — which is really an effort to show that what we are about is academics. ◆ "Having moved here from Pennsylvania and experiencing some personal problems, he had dropped out of high school. Later he obtained his GED, attended auto mechanics school and then applied to DeKalb College. He scored over 1400 on his SAT so we recruited him for our Honors Program. He earned a 4.0 average at DeKalb and is now a student at M.I.T. ◆ "At DeKalb College, we offer that kind of second chance for students. As people think about going back to school or about taking a college course or two, we want them to think of DeKalb as inviting and not intimidating. We also appeal to students who have run into trouble academically at other institutions and are trying to get their academic life back together. We have saved a lot of people through combining a strong academic program with support services and a personal approach which promotes student success. ◆ "Nearly 40 percent of our students are twenty to twenty-one year olds who have not gone to college immediately after high school but who then decide to pursue a degree. And we appeal to people who have started careers and can attend college part time. Only 15 to 20 percent of our students are full time, but over 80 percent come to DeKalb with the idea of pursuing a Baccalaureate degree. ◆ "We also have selected career options which include excellent programs in Nursing and Dental Hygiene. In addition, we offer two programs which no other Georgia college offers: Fire Science Technology and Interpreter Training for the Deaf. Through our continuing education division, we have worked with BellSouth, AT&T, General Motors and others to help retrain employees. And we serve a large and growing population of DeKalb County who use English as a second language. Last year, we had over 1,000 foreign students attending classes at the college. ◆ "DeKalb College enrolls over 16,000 students. And we work with the community to provide programs that these students and the citizens of DeKalb need."

— **Dr. Martha T. Nesbitt,**
Vice-President, Academic Affairs

DEKALB COLLEGE

A part of the University System of Georgia since 1986. Four campuses, with plans for expansion. $10 million Learning Resource Center in Clarkston opened 1993.

or high-risk children in Lithonia that is perilously close to running out of money and shutting its doors. Here, children who have been suspended from school join the Student Support Program every weekday, while others come after school for special tutoring. Today, Alfred Swann, an administrator with the U.S. Department of Housing and Urban Development, tutors one high school and two elementary school students. "We try to help the kids with their homework and we put a lot of focus on discipline," says Swann. "Last year, we had as many as twenty kids who came on a regular basis."

"The center is just about broke," says Rev. Richard Murphy, a Lithonia city councilman and former youth director at the Union Baptist Church who started Teen Scene in 1990. "I've been funding it myself and hoping that one day someone will say, 'Hey, I want to put some money into that.' " The man who's been called the Pied Piper of Teenagers points to a teenager across the room who's interested in the tutoring program. "Peer pressure tells them, 'You're dumb if you go to tutoring,' and I try to tell them they're not. We need to show them love and understanding, because they feel that nobody cares about them."

None of these stories make the News at 10 on Channel 46 tonight, an hour-long broadcast with executive producer Mark Aldren and co-anchors Karyn Greer and Kevin Cokely.

The non-network newscast is well regarded as a thoughtful and often inspired program, but even this talented news team will miss events in DeKalb that change the lives of people in their own focused way. There's a report that Mayor Tom Bradley of Los Angeles is not running for re-election—but no mention that four-day-old Sarah Ann Leoni—the first person born in DeKalb County this week—left DeKalb Medical Center today and went home with her parents.

There's a report of a suspicious car, possibly involved in a murder—but no mention that Sgt. R. L. Wright, a DeKalb County police officer on duty at 7 A.M. investigated his third death by 10:37 A.M.

Karyn Greer reports on the latest Clinton poll—

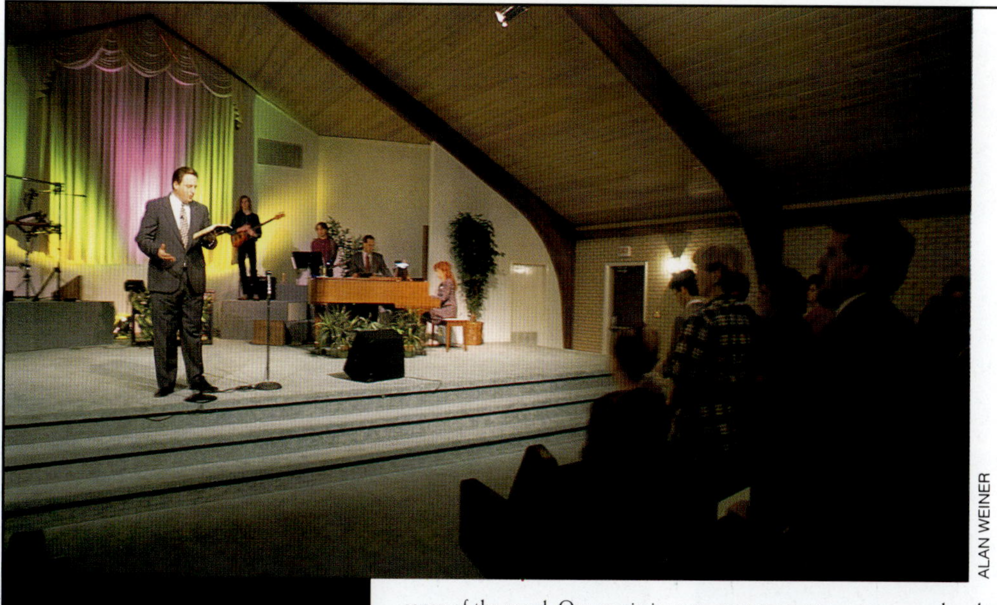

ALAN WEINER

GRACE COMMUNITY CHURCH

Founded in 1988

This is the message we want to tell: that you matter to God and that people matter to God. ◆ "The old concept of religion is that you get into a church and you get busy and you hope that you are accepted by God. Our concept is that you are accepted by God no matter what you have done or what you can do. ◆ "Grace Community Church was begun about five years ago as an inter-denominational community church. Anyone is welcome to worship here. ◆ "We formed out of a basic desire to see a different kind of church for this area. We are not traditional or liturgical in any sense of the word. Our music is more contemporary—we carry a band type of sound rather than a choir. We sing more contemporary music—a lot of choruses rather than hymns. We use different multimedia and dramatic effects to convey the message of the gospel. ◆ "We have 160 members, all different ages, though the congregation definitely has a lot of younger people. We operate on a fifteen-acre campus with a sanctuary, our educational space, offices, a gymnasium and recreation fields. ◆ "We have a fully staffed nursery during services, with the capacity for thirty-five or forty children. For children six to twelve years old, we have K.I.D.S.—Kids in Divine Service, a special worship service where we use puppets, drama and characters. ◆ "Regardless of age, we are really trying to communicate the message that a relationship to the Father through Jesus is still very important to people, even in the nineties. And we try not to use the word 'religion' around here. Instead, we talk about relationships, and a real understanding of God."

— **Phillip A. Underwood, Founder and Pastor**

but there's no mention of the latest findings of Dr. Jane Ellis at the Yerkes Regional Primate Center. Dr. Ellis, in the middle of a three-year study on the effects of cocaine in rhesus monkeys and their offspring, has enough preliminary data to show that lack of prenatal care and a poor diet during pregnancy may have a greater effect than drugs on so-called crack babies. "It's counterintuitive," admits Ellis of her preliminary results, "but maybe cocaine alone isn't the culprit."

Also not making the newscast, despite it being the biggest event of her young life, is Maria del Carmen Ortiz, who stood nervously today inside a Tucker dress store called Barron's Designs and tried on her first full-length formal gown. It will be worn for her quincenera, the traditional Mexican celebration of a young woman's fifteenth birthday.

By three minutes after eleven, director John Dameron shuts down the monitors. Everyone leaves the control room. It's empty. With nearly an hour left in Thursday, the news team is already thinking about tomorrow.

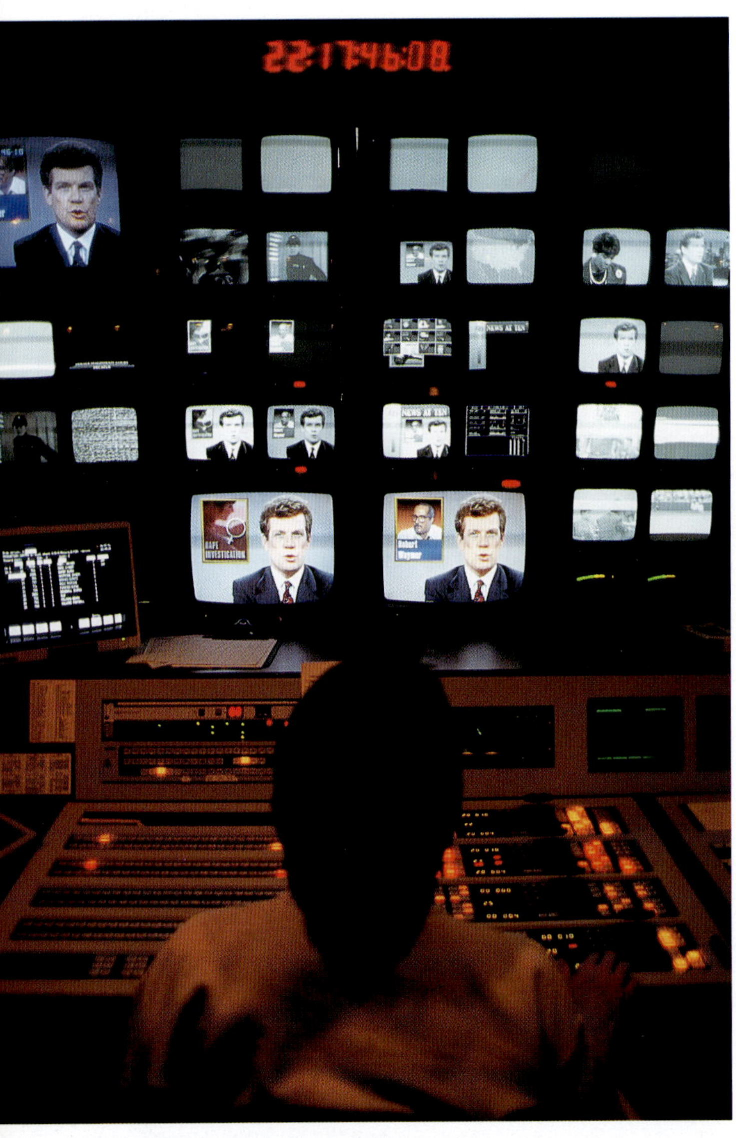

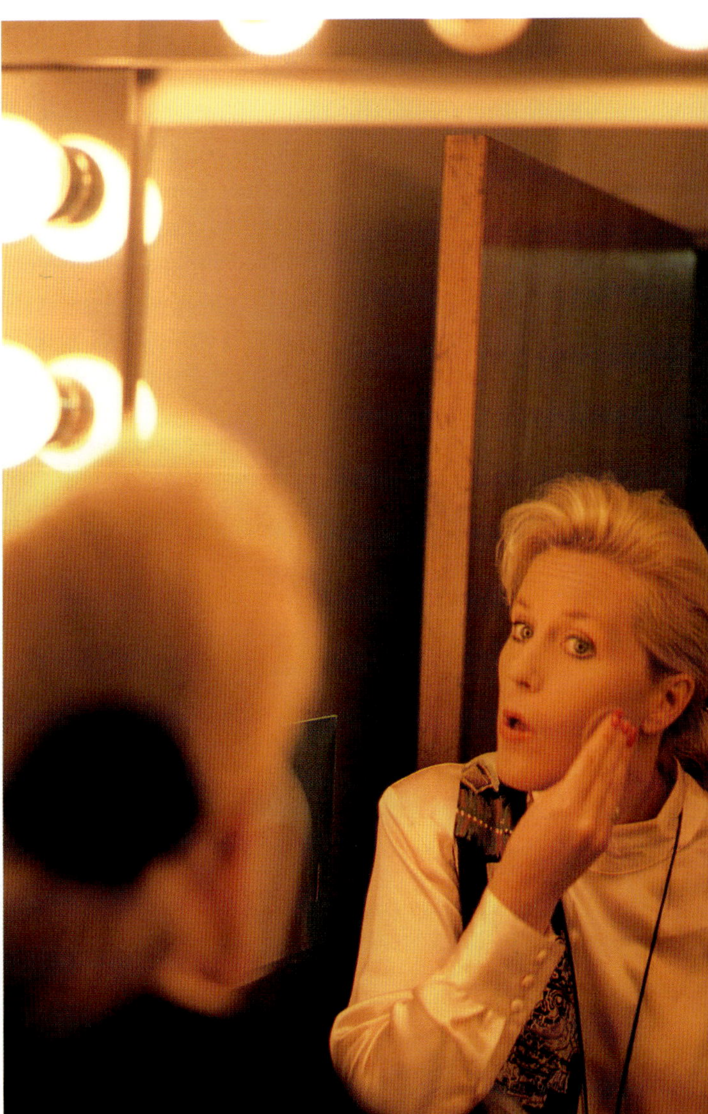

9:12 PM *The control room and studio set at WGNX-Channel 46 on Briarcliff Road are humming with pre-broadcast activity. Executive producer Mark Aldren is simultaneously editing stories, monitoring four television networks, talking on the phone and conferring with reporters, directors and technicians—all to the tune of nearby wire-service "tickers." Pictured here, Kathleen Kennedy puts on her make-up before taking her seat in front of the camera. Fifteen seconds before air time, all activity stops. Fourteen . . . thirteen . . . twelve . . . Co-anchors Kevin Cokely and Karyn Greer preside over a polished, hour-long television news broadcast. At one minute after 11* P.M., *it's over for another day.*

PHOTOS BY GREG FOSTER.

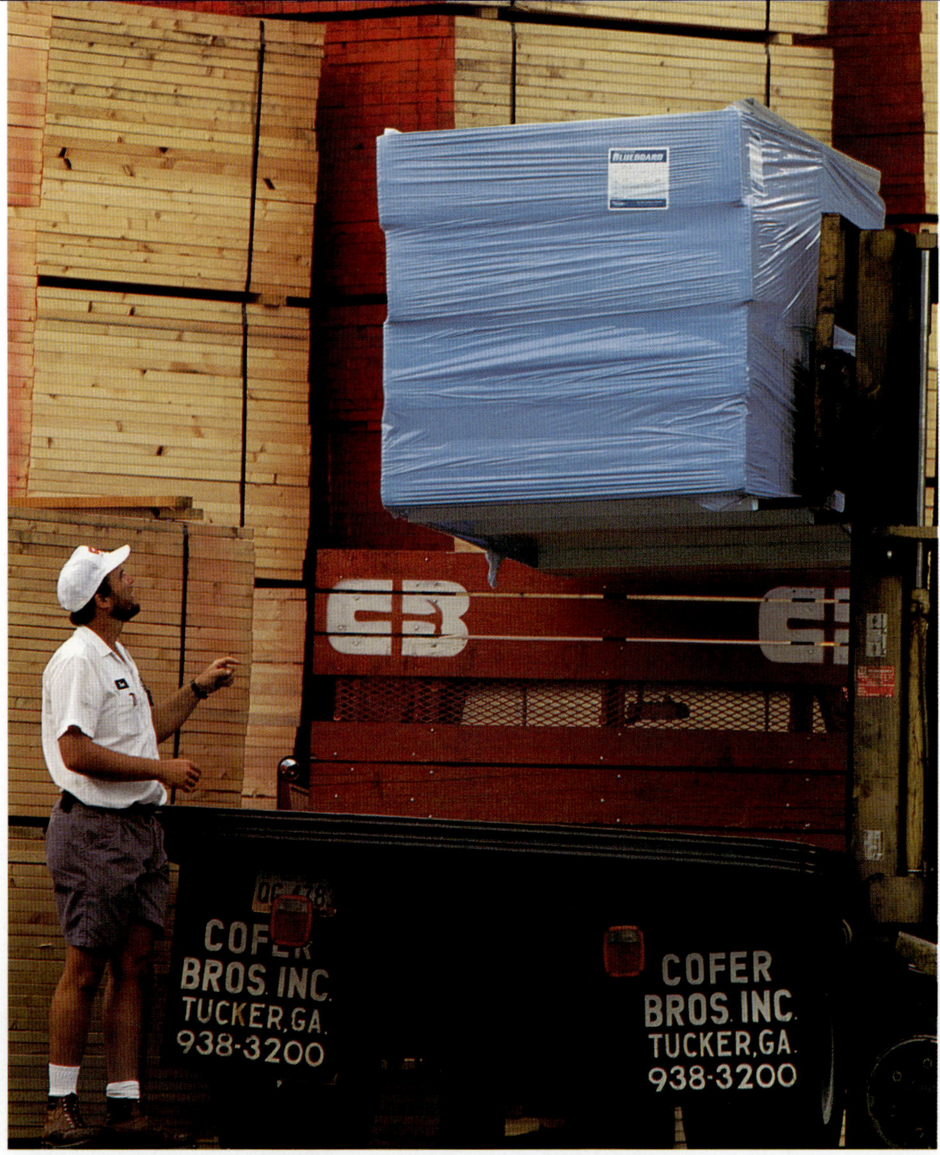

My grandfather, Reid, and his brother, Kelley, started this business as a general store in Tucker in 1919, selling goods and bartering for eggs, butter or whatever the customer had to trade. They then expanded into a grocery and dry goods store, and then added a department store. Building materials were added next, and at one time we had as many as seven stores. My father, Gene, who was Reid's son, became president in 1968. We closed our department stores in the early seventies, and gradually condensed everything back to one store in order to run a very tight operation in one location. ◆ "We are one of the last full-service building supply centers around. We offer high quality goods with high quality service, and we feel like that is our niche. I can't emphasize enough how loyal we want to be to our customers. We are as loyal to them as we want them to be to us. ◆ "In consideration of our customers, we took a real interesting stance when Hurricane Andrew hit the area, a little bit different from our competition. We didn't solicit any business from contractors going there. We didn't want to sell out or deplete our stock because we had an obligation to our customers here, to be fully supplied for them. ◆ "We place a real high premium on ethics and we don't compromise that for anything. We believe that whenever you come into our business, you should be able to talk to a family member. That's why we don't take lunch breaks or vacations at the same time. There is always a Cofer or someone in the family here to serve you. The buck can always stop somewhere at Cofer Brothers."

— Charles Reid Cofer
Executive Vice-President

COFER BROTHERS, INC.

Founded in 1919 by Reid and Kelley Cofer. A building supply business with over seventy employees.

"The Cofer family has been in business here since 1919, and we've got some people who have been here for forty years. Your life's blood is your employees, and we've got good employees. The market has changed in those seventy-four years, and because of the people who work for us, we have changed and hopefully moved with that market. ◆ "And we have loyal customers. We are a third-generation business, and we have third-generation customers. That's means a lot. Our watchwords? Service, service, service. Service to the customer and the community. ◆ "Because if there was no DeKalb County, we couldn't be here."

— Jim Wilson, Gene Cofer's Son-in-Law
Vice-President and Secretary

FRIDAY

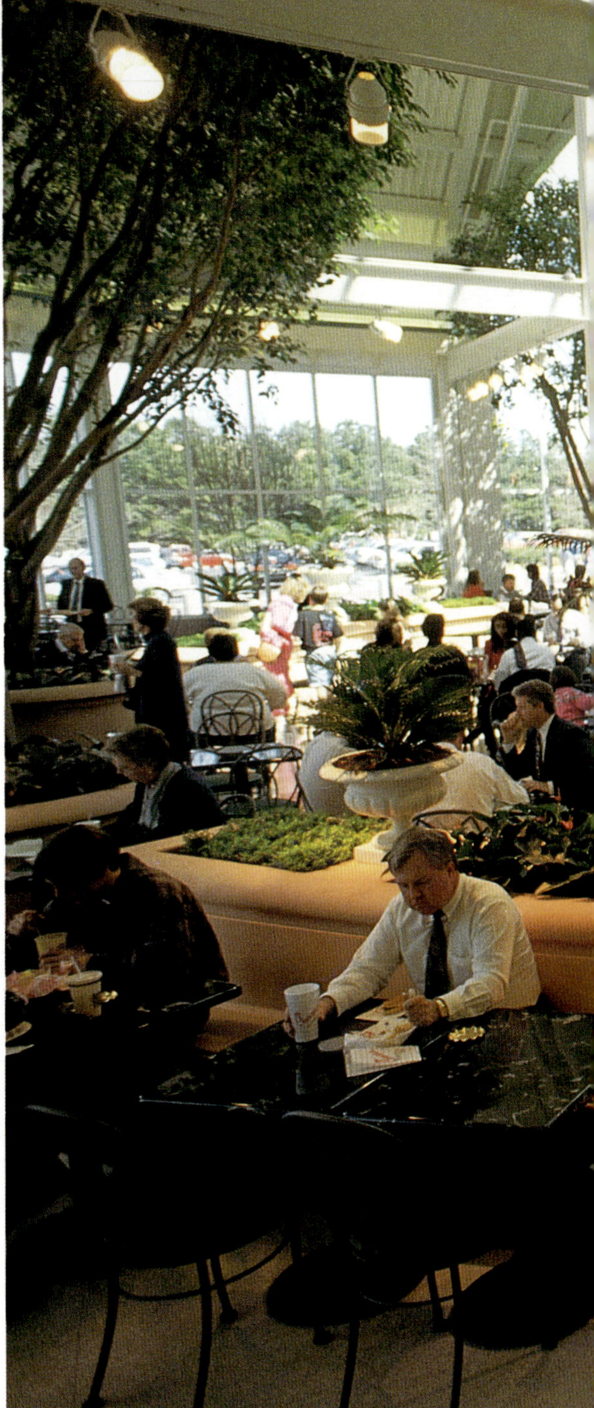

Definitely, we have generations of families shopping at Northlake Mall. We were really one of the first established businesses in the Northlake area of DeKalb and have grown to be a mainstay for Northeast Atlanta families. Our shoppers tell us they come here because they like the mall's friendly atmosphere, the customer service and the convenient location. ◆ "One of the ways we accommodate all of our shoppers is to take into account their particular needs. Our management has always been tuned into our customers. We continually ask them how we can be better for them. In response to their suggestions, we've made a lot of changes over the years to give them what they most desire in merchandise, service and a shopping environment. The Food Garden and Parisian are recent big wishes come true. ◆ "When The Food Garden opened in 1992, shoppers no longer had to leave the mall to get a good meal in a pleasurable atmosphere. And that's something all of our shoppers can really appreciate. We have a significant office population in the area, and more and more people are shopping on their lunch hour or before they go home. Shopping during the day can be less hectic if our older customers and our office shoppers can enjoy a nice meal in a beautiful place. And during the weeknights and the weekends, we cater more to families with activities planned just for children. At Northlake, we

NORTHLAKE MALL

125 stores

over 1,000,000 square feet

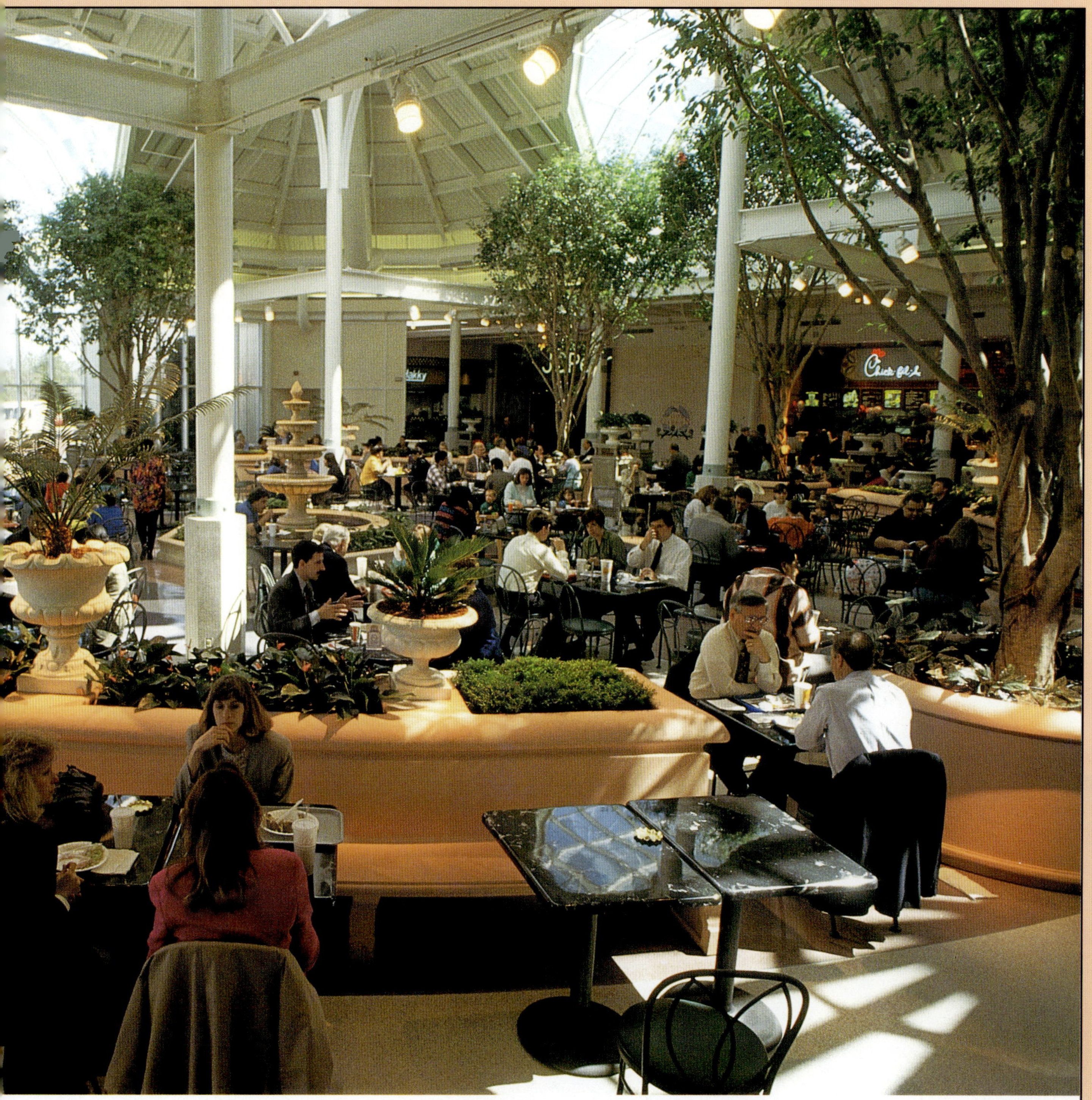

ALAN WEINER

appreciate the fact that if the children are happy, the whole family is happy. ◆ "And because we appreciate the sophistication of our shoppers, we are constantly upgrading our stores to meet their needs for both variety and value. The addition of Parisian, a specialty apparel department store, in 1994 will provide a whole new shopping experience at Northlake Mall and greatly enhance our selection of fashion merchandise. ◆ "Our customers are really interested in getting a good value. With the mix of stores, and the way we are merchandising today, good value is exactly what we deliver to our shoppers. I'm not talking about discounts and sales, but real customer value. We are less trendy and more value-oriented. Our retailers are smarter now. They are more focused on their particular niche. ◆ "Our goal at Northlake Mall is to be a mainstay for our community. And to do that, we will continue to address the needs, desires and wants of our shoppers."

— **Debra A. Lowrey,**
Marketing Director

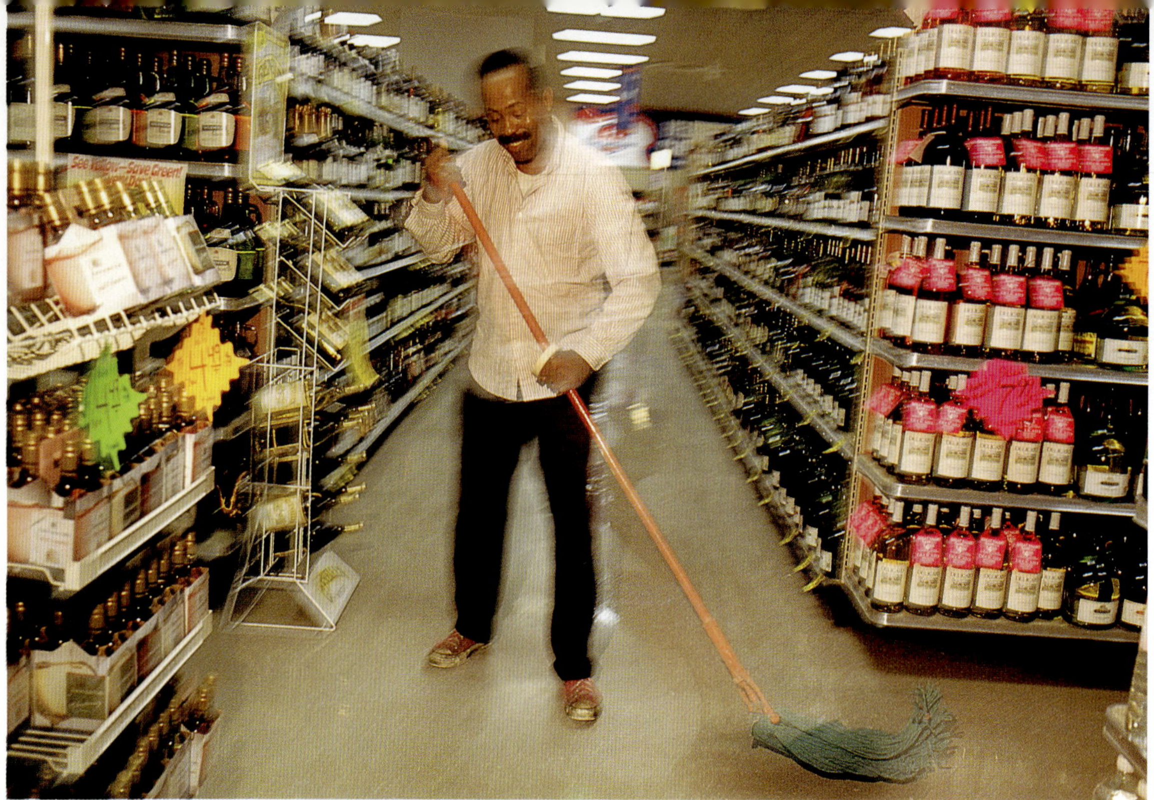

3:05 AM *DeKalb is fast becoming a community that never sleeps, and insomniacs and people who work odd hours know they can count on the Kroger at Toco Hills Shopping Center to be awake when they are. Manager Gary Libowsky said you'd be surprised how many people do their weekly shopping at 3 A.M. Stocking shelves, baking pastries and cleaning also are all in a night's work for Kroger employees.* PHOTO BY MARILYN FUTTERMAN.

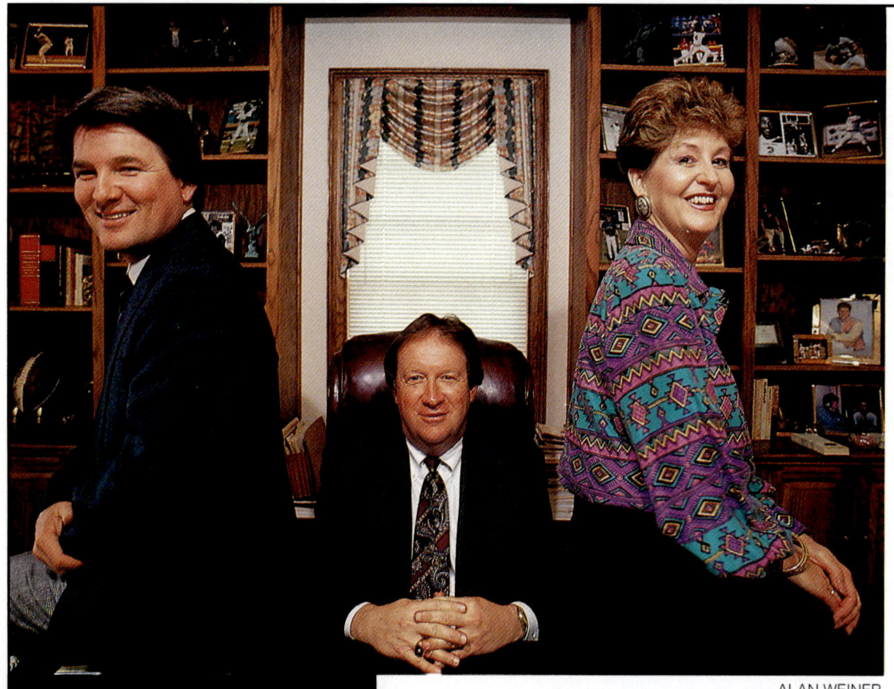

ALAN WEINER

MOUNTAIN NATIONAL BANK

First organized in 1987; opened in August 1988

I think people in general are leery of banking. But if someone lives in the community and they see me eating a hamburger or sitting down the street at Matthew's Cafeteria, I become a little more real to them. They are more comfortable coming into our bank. ◆ "Mountain National Bank was formed in the community by people who were interested in this community. The bank was formed to be a long-term player. And the fact that we have kept all of our original officers and directors and haven't had any division with the board since 1987 shows a consistency that I think people are really looking for. ◆ "It's important to Tucker, and to banking in general. People want to be treated like they are someone instead of being a number in a big bank. We're not a suburb branch of an Atlanta or regional bank. We know our community, and the customers we serve in DeKalb County. Our decisions are made locally by experienced bankers who have worked together for several years in this community. ◆ "To some extent, Tucker is a state of mind. Generations of people have lived here forever, with two and three generations of the same family going to Tucker High School. It's a little town that the city— and suburbia—just went past. ◆ "We have a lot of capital here, and once the economy is conducive to expansion, we will expand our market; however, we knew this was a good place to start our bank. We have a vested interest in working to make this bank and the community thrive. Regardless of where expansion leads us, Tucker is headquarters—this is home. ◆ "And we have tried, diligently, to put something back into the community that has given us a $65 million bank, that allowed us to be successful. That is really our philosophy."

— J. Randall Carroll, President

As Friday in DeKalb unveils itself over the next twenty-four hours, Judy Delany buys a house and the Curcios sell one. Dr. Cynthia K. Warner celebrates a laboratory victory while members of CANDID (Citizens Against Nude Dancing in DeKalb) pledge to keep fighting after being handed a setback in their battle against the dance clubs. Police nab the elusive "Fast Food Bandits" of DeKalb, but continue looking for suspects in a Tucker murder case. And while one of the county's oldest and most prominent financial institutions prepares to close its doors, Parker Hardy, president of the DeKalb Chamber of Commerce, sets in motion something new and exciting for DeKalb County.

6:33 AM *As president and chief executive officer of the DeKalb Chamber of Commerce, Parker Hardy is DeKalb County's chief business and development booster. Through its newest undertaking—the DeKalb Initiative—the Chamber is well on its way toward raising $1.9 million for projects in four areas: transportation, education, business expansion and an international village. The Chamber also currently is organizing several area councils, including one in South DeKalb where Hardy resides. Because of its proximity to transportation and its concentration of available land, South DeKalb, Hardy says, is where much of the county's future growth will occur.*
PHOTO BY GORDON JOFFRION.

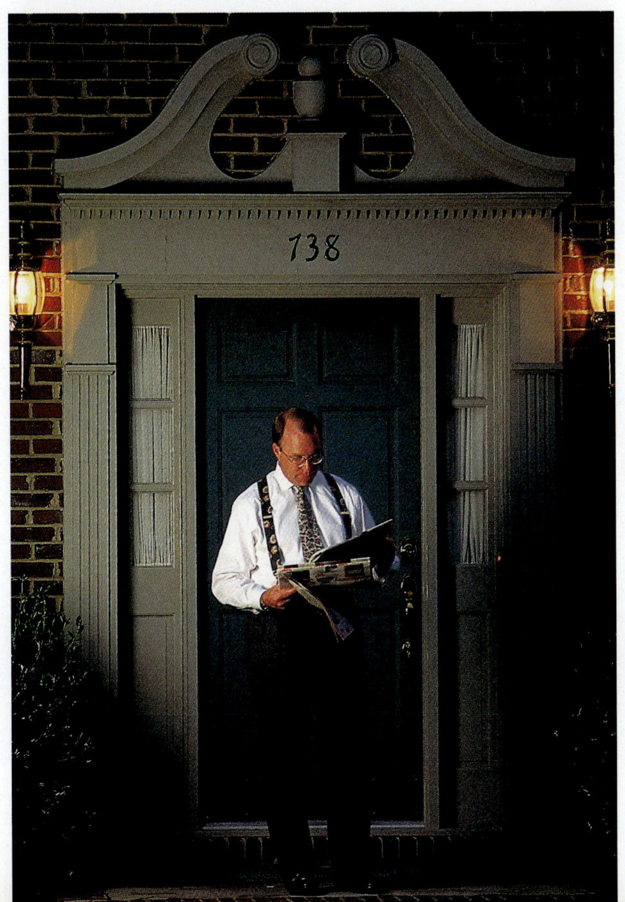

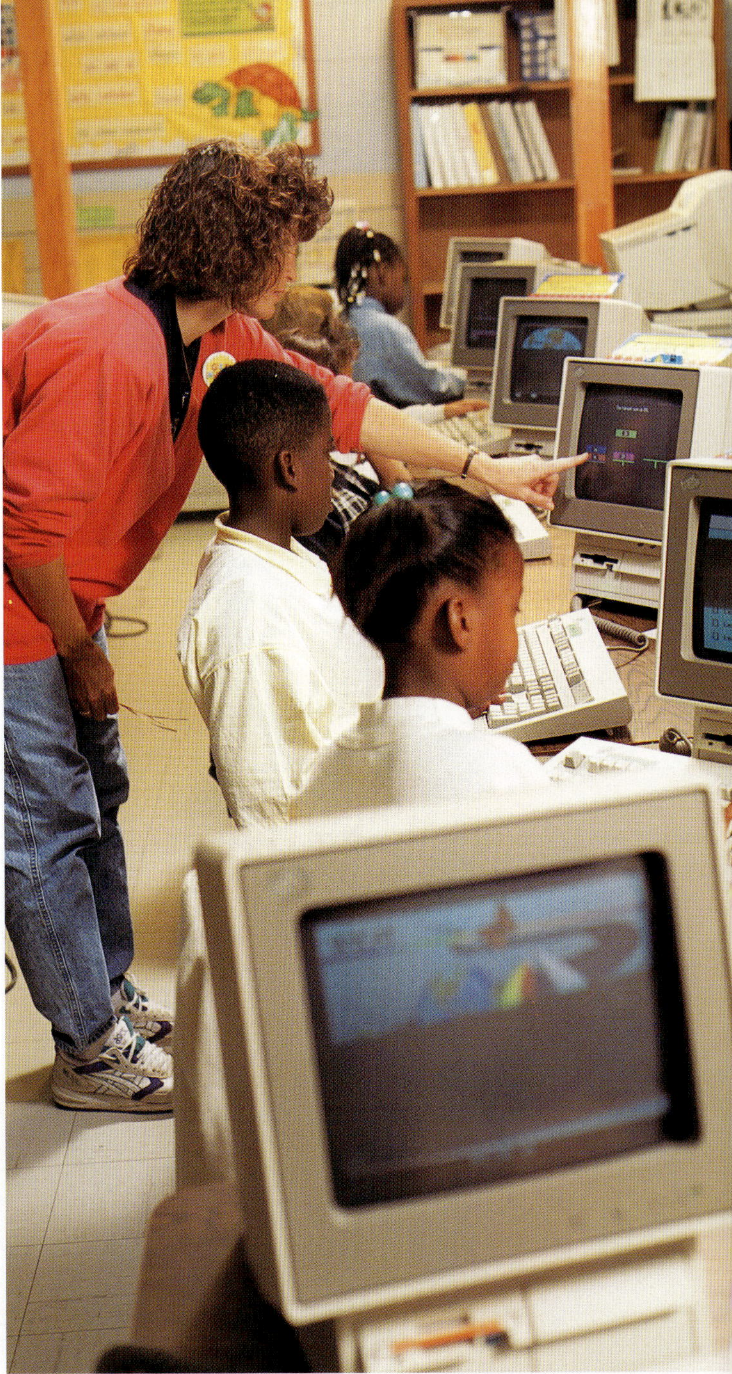

9:02 AM *The DeKalb County School System has one of the highest classroom ratios of computers to students in the country. Nowhere is the impact of computers in the classroom more evident than at Clifton Elementary School, which is the DeKalb system's magnet school for computer-technology education. At Clifton, each student has his own computer work station, where they learn how computers work, as well as the intricacies of word processing, desktop publishing, database and spreadsheet software.*
PHOTO BY TOM ENGLAND.

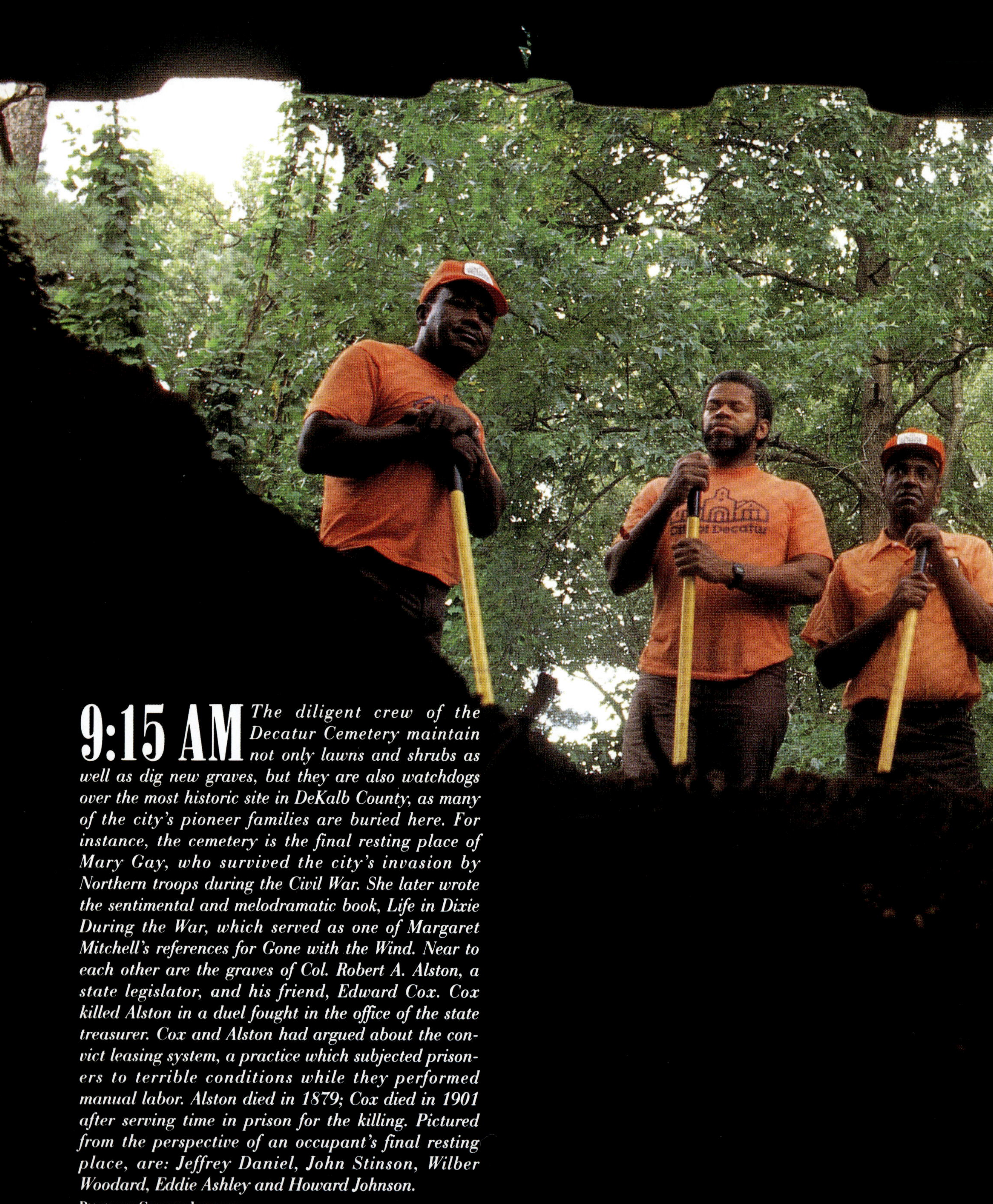

9:15 AM *The diligent crew of the Decatur Cemetery maintain not only lawns and shrubs as well as dig new graves, but they are also watchdogs over the most historic site in DeKalb County, as many of the city's pioneer families are buried here. For instance, the cemetery is the final resting place of Mary Gay, who survived the city's invasion by Northern troops during the Civil War. She later wrote the sentimental and melodramatic book, Life in Dixie During the War, which served as one of Margaret Mitchell's references for Gone with the Wind. Near to each other are the graves of Col. Robert A. Alston, a state legislator, and his friend, Edward Cox. Cox killed Alston in a duel fought in the office of the state treasurer. Cox and Alston had argued about the convict leasing system, a practice which subjected prisoners to terrible conditions while they performed manual labor. Alston died in 1879; Cox died in 1901 after serving time in prison for the killing. Pictured from the perspective of an occupant's final resting place, are: Jeffrey Daniel, John Stinson, Wilber Woodard, Eddie Ashley and Howard Johnson.*

PHOTO BY GORDON JOFFRION.

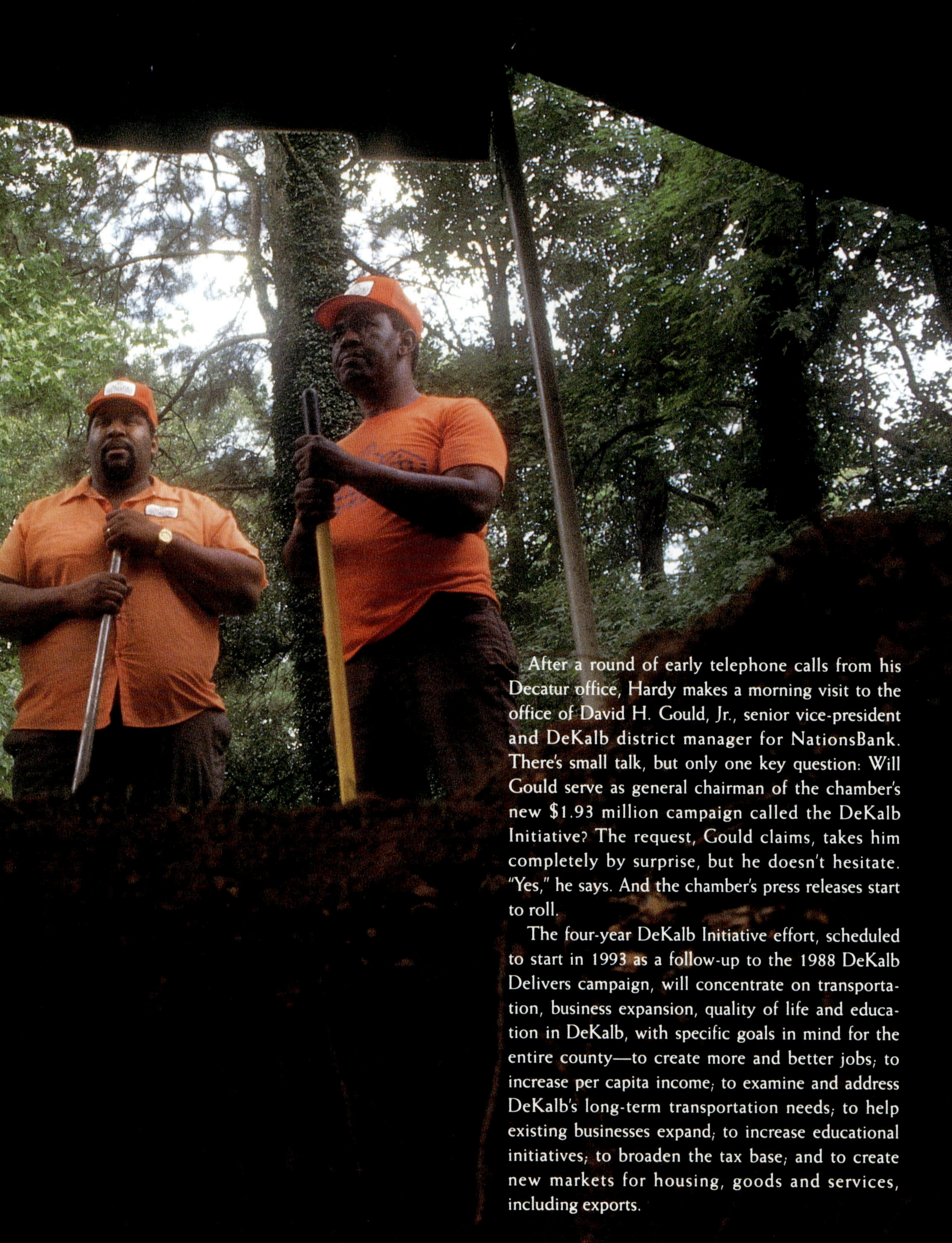

After a round of early telephone calls from his Decatur office, Hardy makes a morning visit to the office of David H. Gould, Jr., senior vice-president and DeKalb district manager for NationsBank. There's small talk, but only one key question: Will Gould serve as general chairman of the chamber's new $1.93 million campaign called the DeKalb Initiative? The request, Gould claims, takes him completely by surprise, but he doesn't hesitate. "Yes," he says. And the chamber's press releases start to roll.

The four-year DeKalb Initiative effort, scheduled to start in 1993 as a follow-up to the 1988 DeKalb Delivers campaign, will concentrate on transportation, business expansion, quality of life and education in DeKalb, with specific goals in mind for the entire county—to create more and better jobs; to increase per capita income; to examine and address DeKalb's long-term transportation needs; to help existing businesses expand; to increase educational initiatives; to broaden the tax base; and to create new markets for housing, goods and services, including exports.

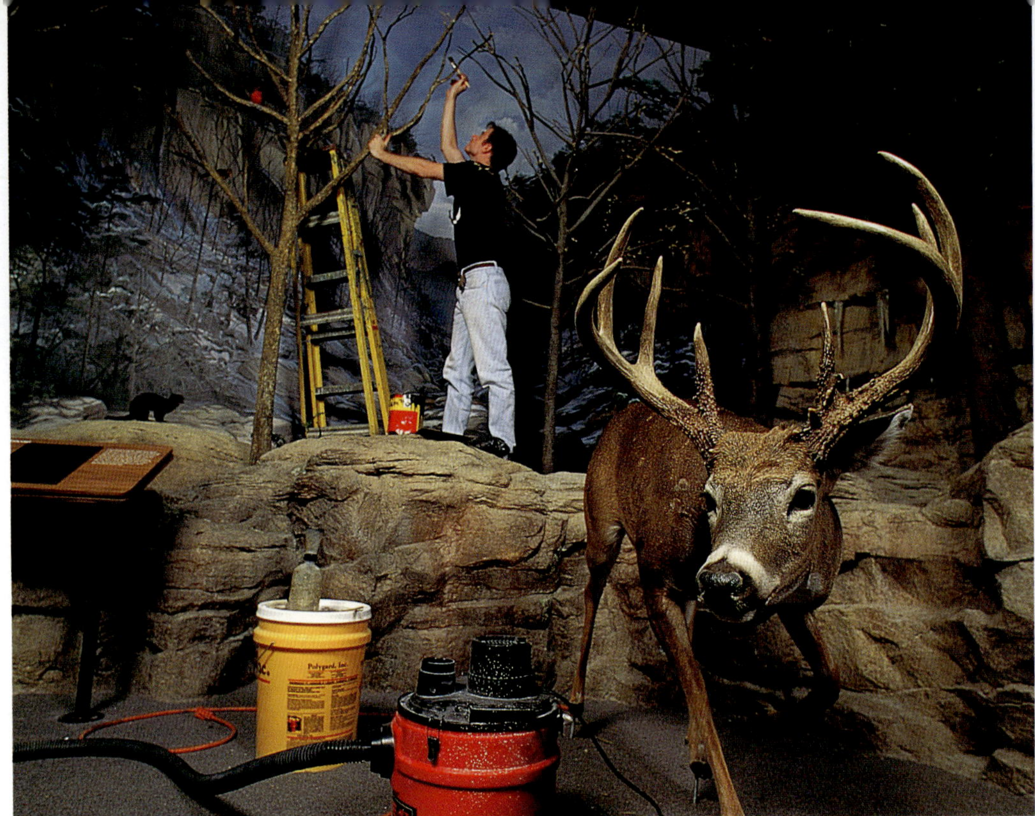

10:00 AM *Workmen rushed to put the finishing touches on the Fernbank Museum of Natural History before its opening in October. The largest museum of natural sciences south of the Smithsonian in Washington, D.C., Fernbank has 160,000 square feet of exhibit space, including 15,000 square feet for traveling exhibits like The Treasures of King Tut which have bypassed Atlanta in the past. Dinosaur Hall, shown here, is the highlight of the museum's permanent exhibit, A Walk Through Time in Georgia.* PHOTO BY ROB NELSON.

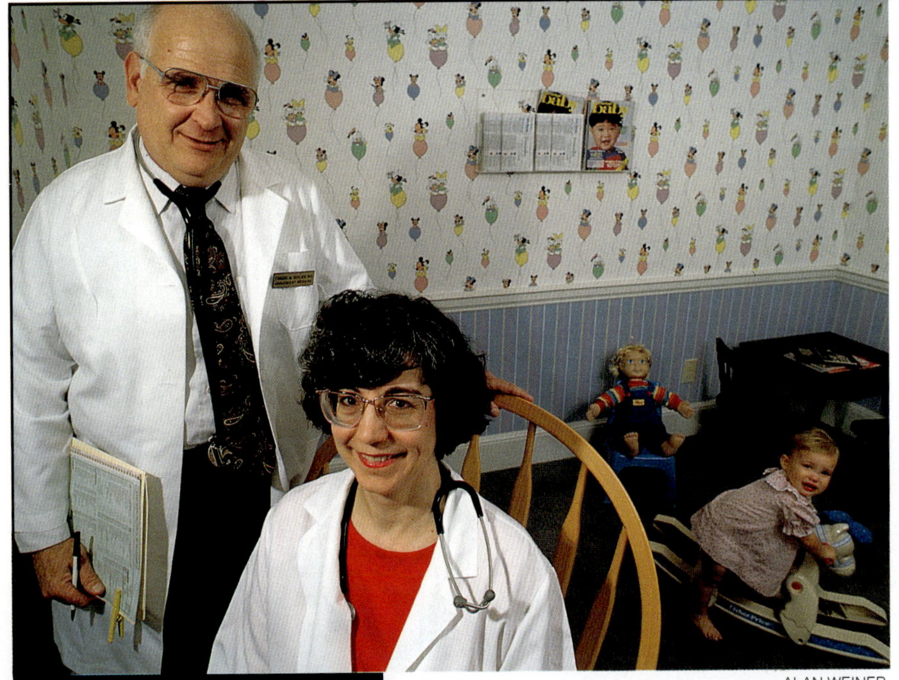

ALAN WEINER

THE PEDIATRIC CENTER

A private primary care and consultation facility
Established in 1976 by Drs. Edward M. and Jaquelin S. Gotlieb

The Pediatric Center offers a seamless approach to medical care for children—medical care that begins with newborns and their families and continues through adolescence. ◆ "From the first day, even before birth, we provide a lot of instruction to new parents, teaching them to help things along rather than trying to work in a way that goes against nature. ◆ "With toddlers, we help parents nurture independence, to see how they can give the child choices within the limits that the parents must set. ◆ "For the school-age child, we try to be very clear at the wellness checkups that school is a big part of a child's life. We ask about school, and focus on those issues that are a natural part of pediatrics and development. ◆ "And with adolescents, again, it's a matter of relationships—helping parents understand what is normal exploration, individuation or when it's going into rebellion, and learning how much to expect and what's reasonable. ◆ "Since 1976, we have offered private primary care and consultation and evaluation programs for children and adolescents. And while we both see all ages, I focus on infants and new families, and Ed specializes in adolescent medicine as well as pediatrics. We offer special evaluation programs for children with learning problems, and our counselor sees children of all ages. ◆ "At all stages, we focus on more than just the physical illnesses of children. We focus on the family relationships, on the psycho-social aspects of their lives, how they are developing and if they are meeting their developmental goals. We do this because so many of the problems of children are related to their development, to their family relationships and to their schools. ◆ "At the Pediatric Center, parents are always very involved—because we recognize that parents are who really care for their children."

— Dr. Jaquelin S. Gotlieb

And Hardy hopes to use the start of this four-year effort to put an end to what he calls the "Myths about DeKalb."

Number one on his myth list is that the "county is mature, that it's built up." In reality, county officials point out that in East and South DeKalb, there are approximately 6,000 acres available for future development. Based on the foresight of former county leaders, the infrastructure to support future development in these areas is already in place. Namely, more miles of interstate than any other metropolitan county (56.7 miles); rapid rail and bus service provided by the region's mass transit operations; and an extensive water and sewer system that's already in place, paid for, and designed to sustain capacity usage well into the next century. Another myth Hardy hopes to dispel concerns the county's educational system, whose image Hardy thinks has been somewhat tarnished by recent court battles over desegregation and the quality of county schools. The U.S. Supreme Court last year ruled that student assignment techniques in DeKalb meet the requirements of the Constitution. And while various issues like teacher assignments and student facilities still have to be reviewed, one thing is clear: there will be no forced busing in DeKalb County.

11:00 AM *As Pam Peel (left) and Aimee Fish can testify, a Friday-morning class on the lawn beats a classroom any day at Agnes Scott College.* PHOTO BY MICHAEL SCHWARZ.

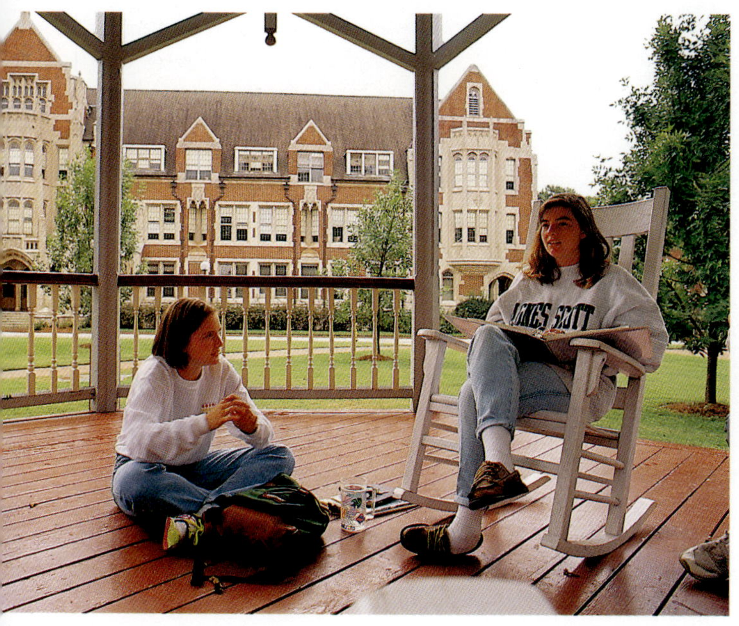

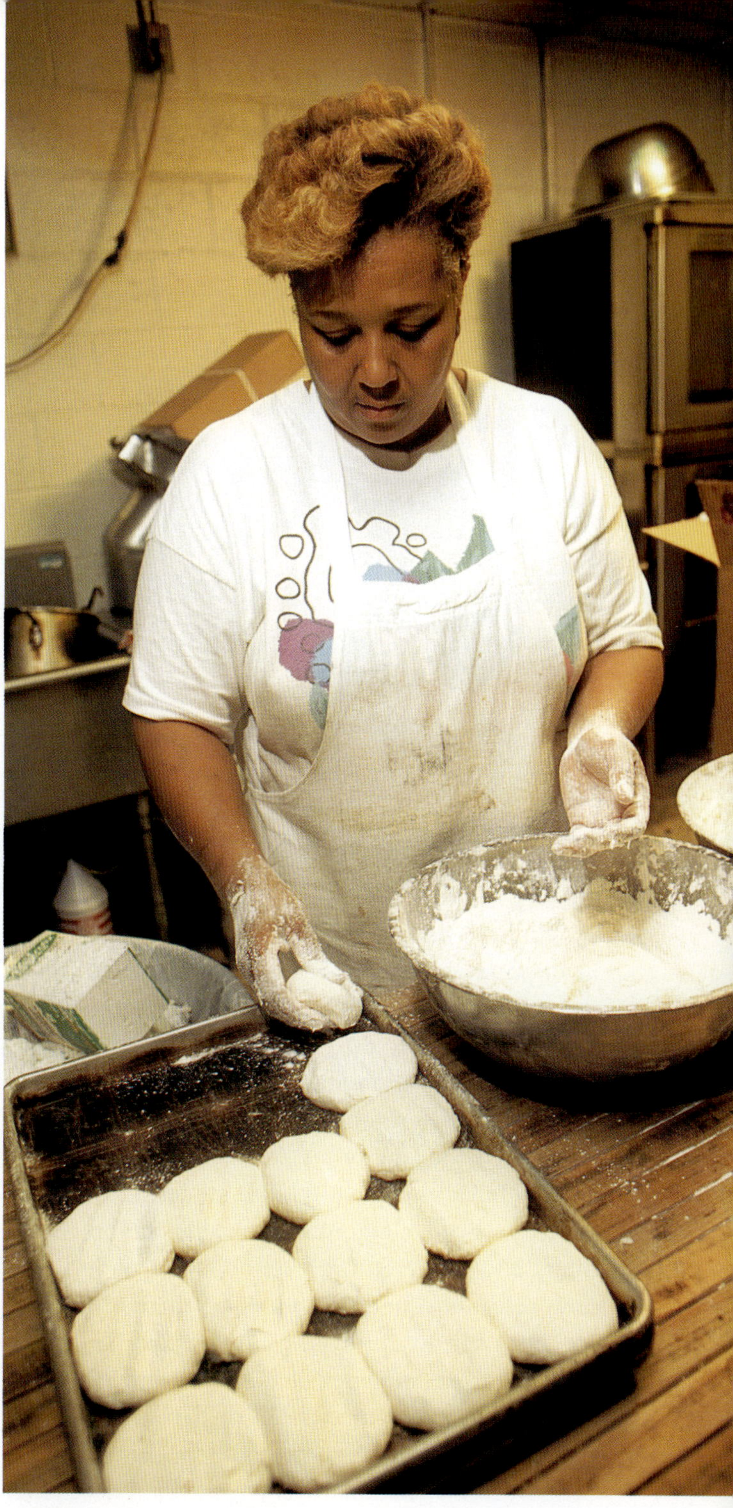

12:00 PM *Phil Howard and his family have operated Mamie's Kitchen in Lithonia for almost thirty years, so they know all the secrets of making perfect biscuits. There are some tips Phil is willing to share: never make biscuits with cold buttermilk (it should be room temperature); bake them only until the bottoms brown; never cut biscuits (shape them in the palms of your hands). The "ultra secret" to making perfect biscuits, Phil says, can't be taught. "It's in the hands of the breadmaker." Some of the famous techniques are being shown here by employee Doris Marshall.* PHOTO BY TOM ENGLAND.

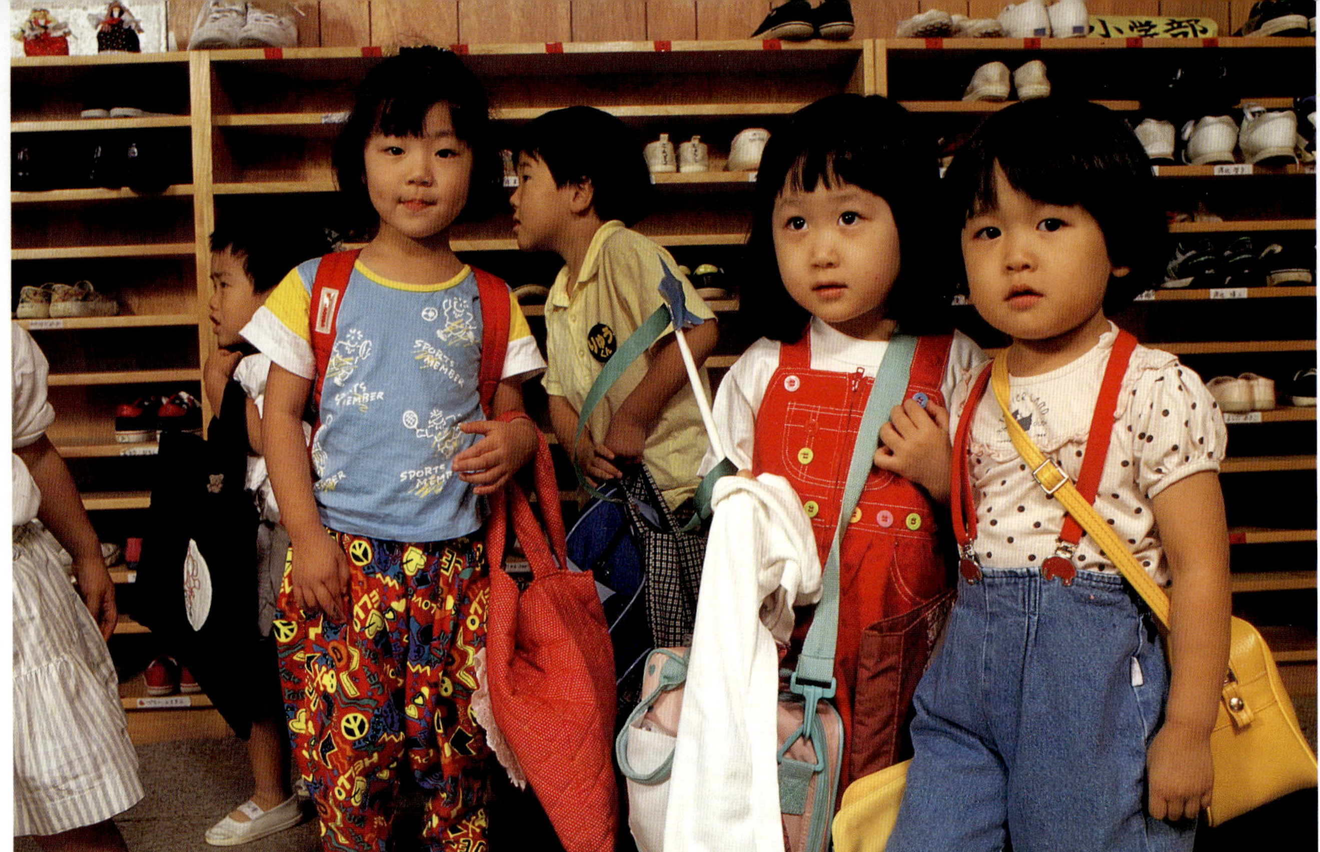

"We have one of the premiere education systems in the Southeast," Hardy argues. "It's the largest in the state, we have one of the lowest drop-out rates and approximately 80 percent of our students continue their education after high school. You can go from kindergarten to medical school in DeKalb and never leave the county."

For DeKalb's nearly 80,000 students, there are seventy-seven elementary schools, seven junior highs and nineteen high schools, with additional new schools scheduled to open throughout the 1992-93 school year (the independent Decatur School System provides nine schools for 2,200 students). Moreover, the school district operates the Fernbank Science Center, an Open Campus High School, an International Center, the DeKalb Center for the Performing Arts and numerous magnet school programs.

Clifton Elementary School is a computer magnet school in southwest DeKalb, a school that was once at the heart of the lengthy court battle. But there is no mention of court cases today as the PTA Fall Fund-raiser, an old-fashioned Southern barbecue, kicks into high gear on the front lawn. Inside the gymnasium, this year's safety patrol is sworn in as children and teachers everywhere wear Atlanta Braves paraphernalia to celebrate Braves Day. And

1:30 PM *Japanese children feel right at home at the Seigakuin Atlanta School near Oglethorpe University. Seigakuin provides a Japanese education for students ages three years through seventh grade, most of whom are children of parents temporarily in Atlanta. Following the guidelines of the Japanese minister of education, the school operates on the Japanese calendar (April to March) and teaches Japanese curriculum. Only Japanese is spoken. The Japanese school system of which Seigakuin is a part was started by American Christian missionaries. Seigakuin, says director Sherryl Lane, is "a mission returning to America."* PHOTO BY ALAN WEINER.

1:45 PM *At 107 years of age, Lillie Walton is thought to be DeKalb County's oldest citizen. Mrs. Walton never misses a day at the senior citizens' center in her Warren Street neighborhood and especially enjoys the exercise program and bingo games. The center is operated by the DeKalb Community Council on Aging, a private, nonprofit group which runs seven such centers, as well as countywide Meals on Wheels and Respite Aides programs. The Warren Street center also offers transportation, nutrition counseling, health checks, arts and crafts, Bible studies and field trips.* PHOTO BY ALAN WEINER.

students in Karen Boswell's fourth-grade magnet computer class couldn't be more excited about their projects: Andy has an idea for a computer-designed robot; Greer just wrote her first twelve-page book about Thanksgiving on the word-processing program; and Josh is creating his own computer-animation cartoon.

And if these children want to continue their education after high school, Parker Hardy is right. They don't have to leave the county to have their pick of a wide range of distinguished institutes of higher learning—Emory, Agnes Scott, Oglethorpe, Mercer, Columbia Theological Seminary, three campuses of DeKalb College, DeKalb Technical Institute and the DeVry Institute of Technology.

Under the DeKalb Initiative, Parker hopes to repackage and promote DeKalb's potential for business expansion in such areas as telecommunications, distribution facilities, manufacturing, and biomedical and biotechnical industries. Already, groups like the Georgia Biomedical Partnership, Inc. exist to promote the area's biomedical and technical advantages—ranging from a supportive business environment to some of the world's finest medical research facilities in Emory University's Rollins Research Facility, the national headquarters for the American Cancer Society and the internationally respected U.S. Centers for Disease Control and Prevention.

The CDC has already attracted 3,800 employees to the greater Atlanta area, nearly half of those to DeKalb's Clifton Road location. Two of these employees, Judy Delany and Dr. Cynthia Warner, don't know each other, but no matter. On this particular Friday, they both have reason to celebrate.

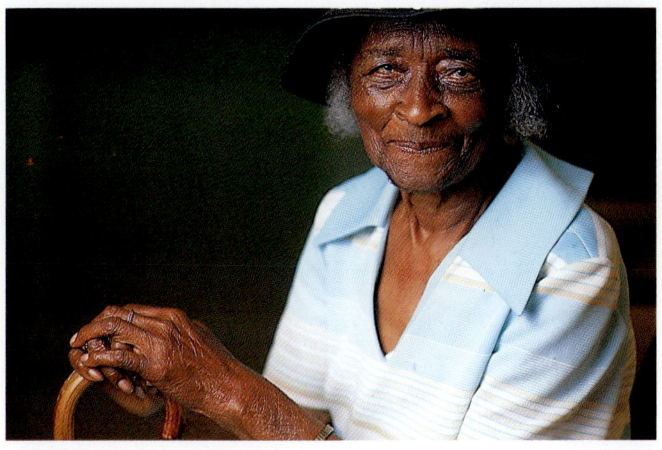

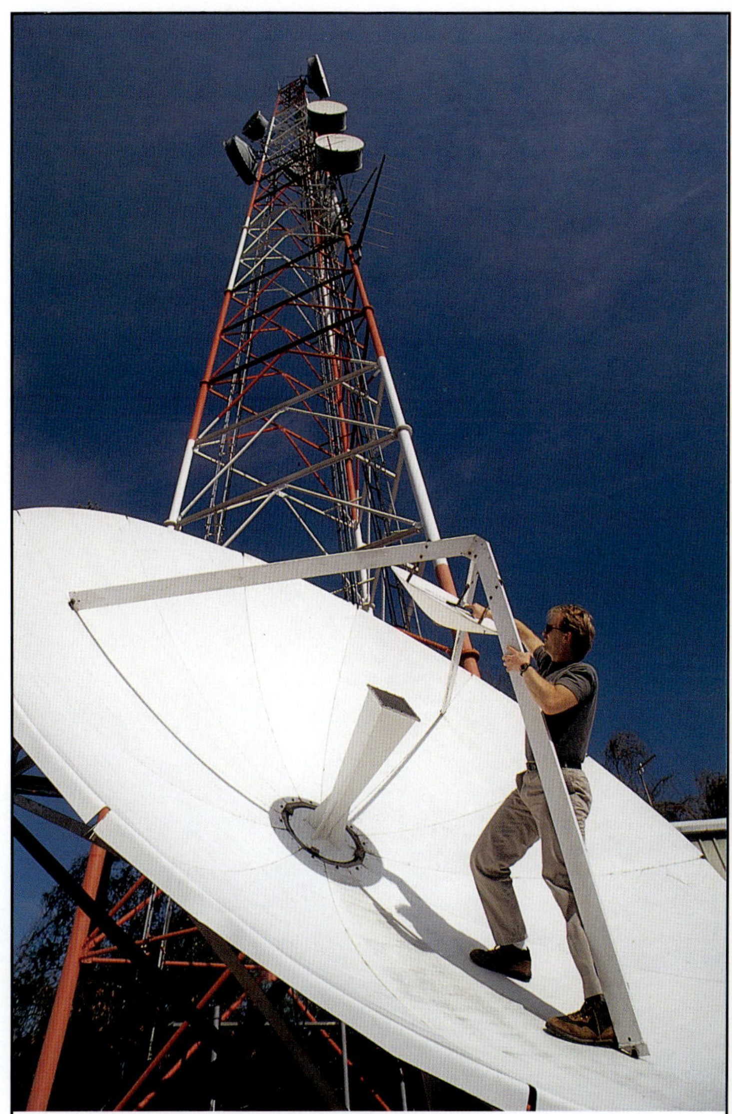

ALAN WEINER

At Georgia Cable TV & Communications, we view ourselves as being in the entertainment business. And what we have today is a niche in the market and the dollar. When you compare the high prices of a family of four going out to dinner or to the movies, a monthly subscription to our service is much less than those two. ◆ "I have five in my family, and we recently went to a matinee movie and then across the street for hamburgers and shakes. It cost us almost $70. And it just made me sit back and say, 'No wonder I'm in the cable business.' ◆ "We've been in DeKalb County for twelve years, and we are the original franchising cable company. Today, we have over 1,840 miles of cable that pass 165,000 homes in the county, and more than 50 percent or 85,000 of those homes are subscribers. For a metropolitan cable system, that is a somewhat higher than average subscription rate. ◆ "Our subscribers receive forty-two channels of basic services. Then we have six premium services including movie channels, and four pay-for-view channels that include first-run movies and special sporting events. Right now we are looking at new technologies like fiber optics and digital compression that will enable us to carry more than 125 channels in the future. ◆ "Even during the slow economic cycle, our business has continued to grow. We add about 3,000 subscribers a year. In addition to our broad selection of programs, we have an extremely focused and customer-conscious group. We take phone calls seven days a week until midnight, and we install in homes seven days a week. ◆ "As far as accessibility, we are 99.9 percent built out in DeKalb County. And when you consider that cable television is used an average of seven hours and twenty minutes a day, we think we offer a tremendous value."

— Ted Williams, General Manager

GEORGIA CABLE TV & COMMUNICATIONS

Established in 1980.
85,000 Subscribers,
100 Employees
in DeKalb County.

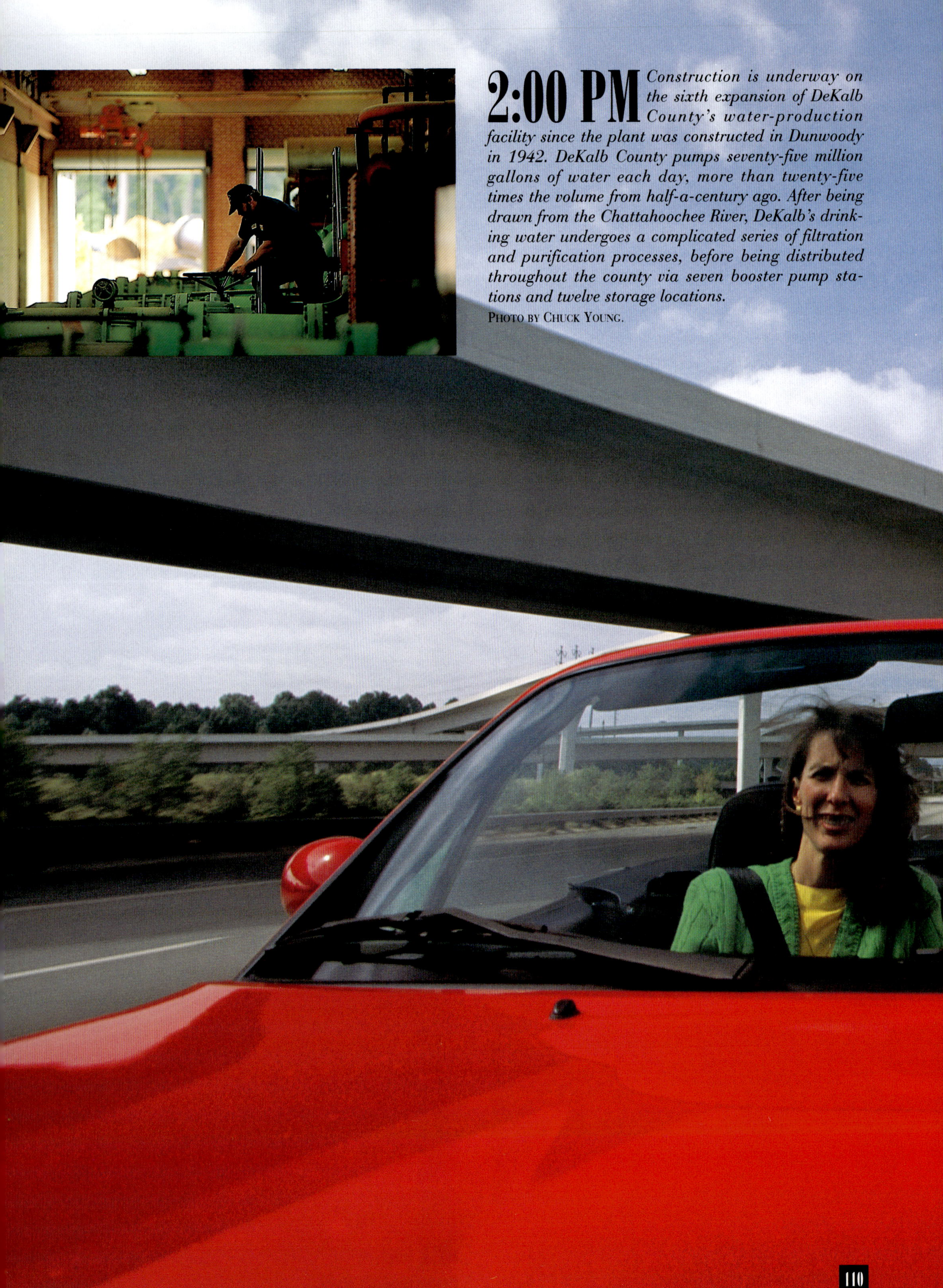

2:00 PM *Construction is underway on the sixth expansion of DeKalb County's water-production facility since the plant was constructed in Dunwoody in 1942. DeKalb County pumps seventy-five million gallons of water each day, more than twenty-five times the volume from half-a-century ago. After being drawn from the Chattahoochee River, DeKalb's drinking water undergoes a complicated series of filtration and purification processes, before being distributed throughout the county via seven booster pump stations and twelve storage locations.*

Photo by Chuck Young.

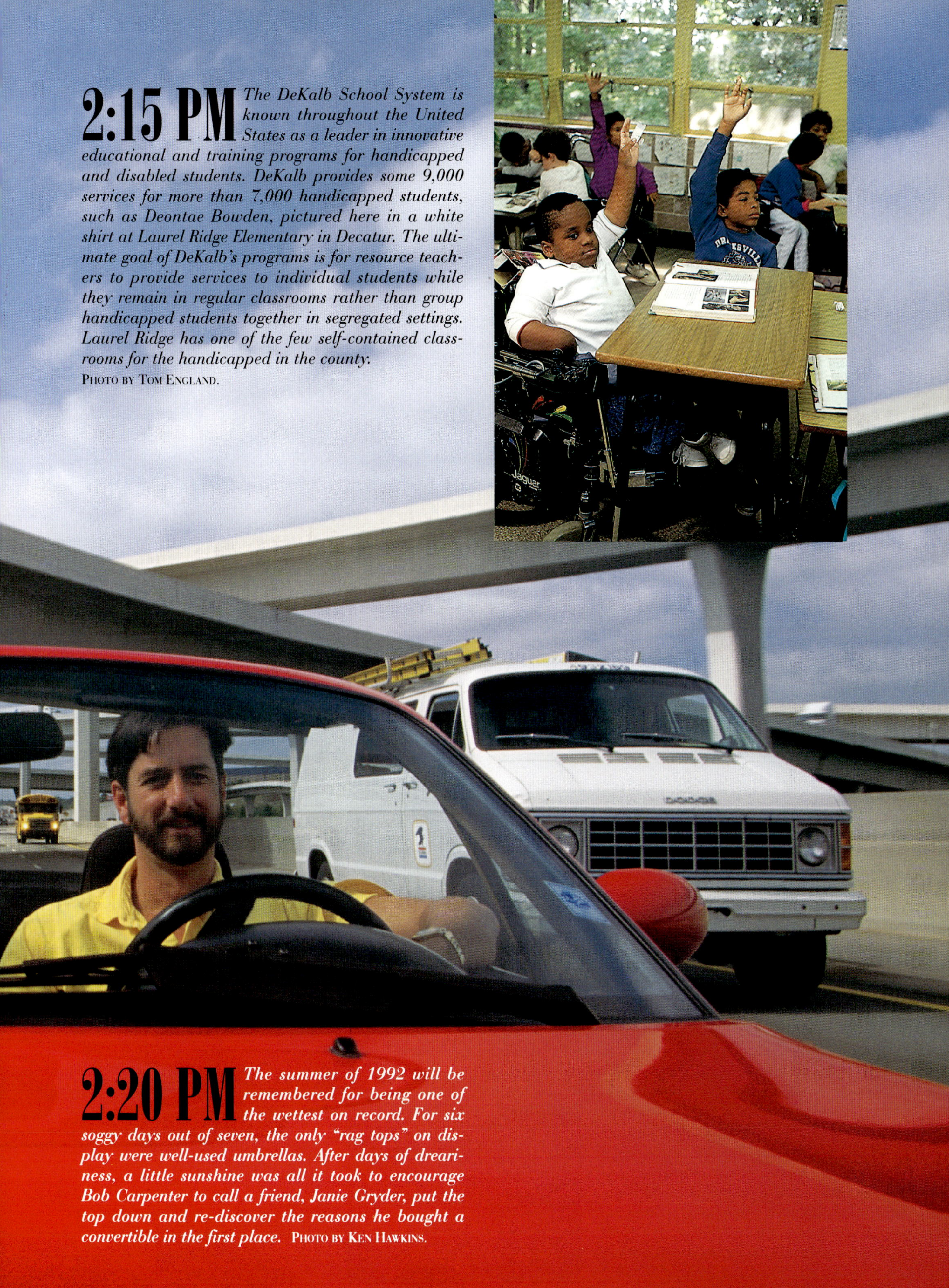

2:15 PM *The DeKalb School System is known throughout the United States as a leader in innovative educational and training programs for handicapped and disabled students. DeKalb provides some 9,000 services for more than 7,000 handicapped students, such as Deontae Bowden, pictured here in a white shirt at Laurel Ridge Elementary in Decatur. The ultimate goal of DeKalb's programs is for resource teachers to provide services to individual students while they remain in regular classrooms rather than group handicapped students together in segregated settings. Laurel Ridge has one of the few self-contained classrooms for the handicapped in the county.*

PHOTO BY TOM ENGLAND.

2:20 PM *The summer of 1992 will be remembered for being one of the wettest on record. For six soggy days out of seven, the only "rag tops" on display were well-used umbrellas. After days of dreariness, a little sunshine was all it took to encourage Bob Carpenter to call a friend, Janie Gryder, put the top down and re-discover the reasons he bought a convertible in the first place.* PHOTO BY KEN HAWKINS.

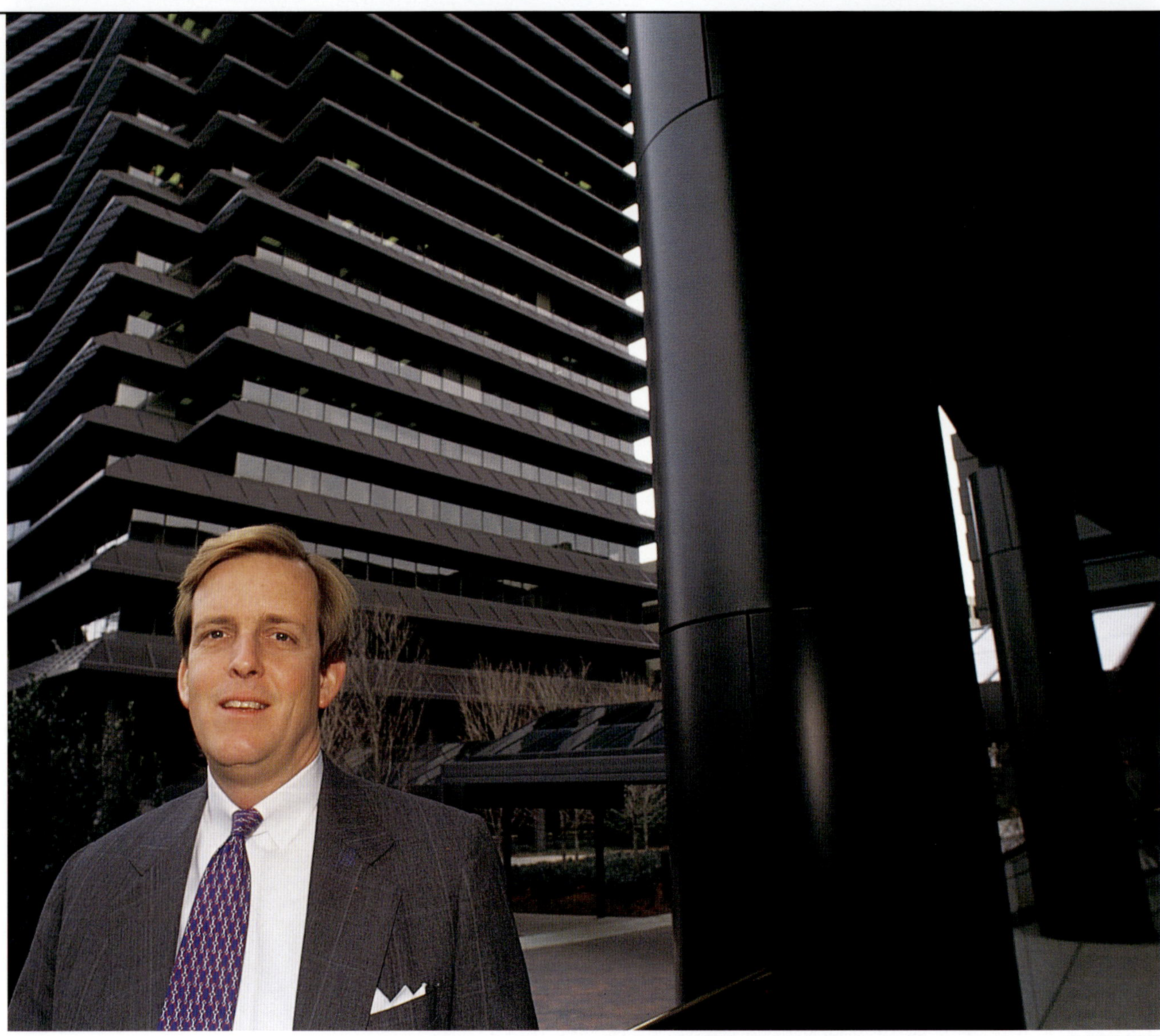

ALAN WEINER

There is no single word to describe the total environment of Ravinia, because it is just that. An environment. An environment that offers the highest quality suburban office address in the whole greater Atlanta area. An environment created to be sensitive to the community. And an environment of unique architecture that blends into, rather than competes with, its surroundings and natural landscape. ◆ "Ravinia is the name for an entire forty-two acre business center located in DeKalb County along the northeast corner of Interstate 285 and Ashford-Dunwoody Road. The name 'Ravinia' comes from a music and entertainment park located in suburban Chicago, the summer home of the Chicago Symphony Orchestra. It was a name suggested for the project by Kevin Roche, an internationally acclaimed architect who created the master plan for the entire complex. ◆ "At the heart of Ravinia, and one of the most significant things that we did during the development of this project, was to preserve a native, ten-acre hardwood forest within the property. Ravinia's three major office complexes all look inward into the forest. The buildings are designed with Oriental lines and reflective materials to relate to their surroundings, instead of standing out as urban office buildings in a suburban environment. They are hard to interpret—some people have called them the 'Darth Vader' buildings. But I think that when you see the buildings in context, they work wonderfully. This integration of architecture and environment is one of the hallmarks of Ravinia, and certainly the inimitable signature of Kevin Roche. ◆ "Our original ground breaking was in late 1983, and One Ravinia Drive opened in 1985. Two Ravinia Drive was delivered during 1987, and Three Ravinia opened in April 1991. Combined, they offer more than 1.5 million square feet of premiere office space and amenities, including the Holiday Inn Crowne Plaza at Ravinia; The Ravinia Club, a private dining and athletic club; and a full range of retail, financial and professional services to support the Ravinia business community—which includes roughly 5,000 people every day. ◆ "As a project of Hines Interests, Ravinia is somewhat unique in their portfolio, which has been dominated by central business district office towers. Ravinia is, in fact, one of Hines' favorite suburban office projects. And Hines, which has created more than 385 major office, retail and mixed-use projects around the country, envisions similar suburban projects like Ravinia in the late 1990s. ◆ "One of our major investors in this project, the Shell Pension Fund Foundation, has referred to Ravinia as their portfolio favorite. We couldn't agree more."

— Robert P. Voyles, Project Manager

HINES INTERESTS LIMITED PARTNERSHIP

Developers of Ravinia, a 1.5 million square foot complex for corporate and professional tenants

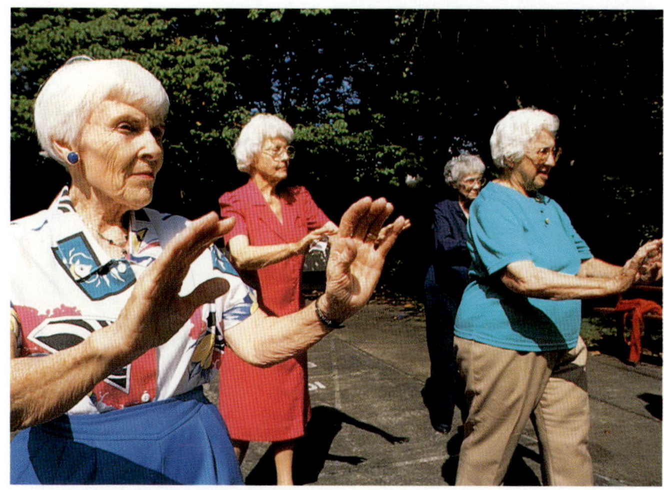

2:40 PM *At eighty-seven, Frances Pauley may be the oldest member of her tai chi class, but she also is one of the most energetic and well-known community activists in Atlanta. She is a powerful advocate for the poor, whether she is lobbying the Appropriations Committee of the Georgia House of Representatives or working with Open Door, a local community center for the homeless. Pauley lives at Wesley Woods, the community on the Emory University campus that includes two retirement centers, the Emory University outpatient Geriatric Center and Georgia's only hospital specializing in geriatrics. Left to right: Jean S. Nunn, Miriam Alexander, Frances Pauley and Dora Byron.* PHOTO BY DAVID MURRAY.

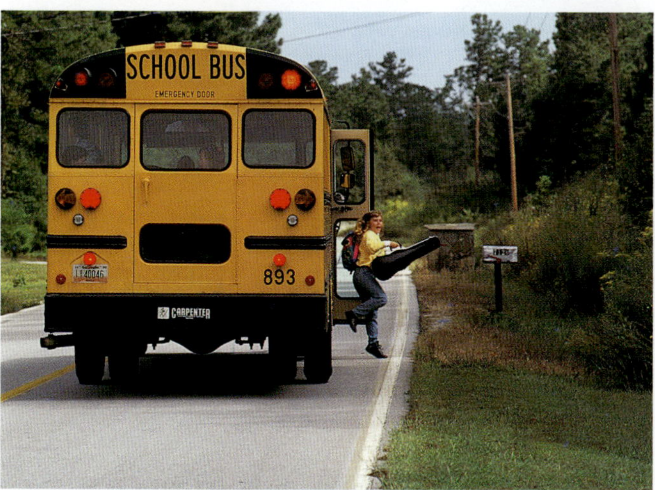

3:00 PM *Some 58,000 students daily ride 709 DeKalb School System buses to and from school. Bus drivers navigate 46,000 miles on 1,275 routes as demographically different as apartment-strewn Buford Highway and remote, rural southeast DeKalb, such as where this photo was taken.* PHOTO BY ROB NELSON.

Today, Judy Delany buys a new house and starts a new life. Recently promoted to training network coordinator for the CDC, Delany is moving from Nashville to a four-bedroom ranch in DeKalb's Henderson Mill area, one of nearly 150,000 single-family houses in the county. How did she find the house? Reba Tietjen, an agent with Northside Realty (they sell homes "DeKalb Style," according to their ads), worked with Delany for four weeks to find the right house, while Delany started a new job and sold her Nashville condo. Was it difficult? "It was a very stressful time," says Delany, who is divorced and the mother of three daughters, one in college in Knoxville and another at Mercer in Macon. What was she thinking about during her afternoon settlement? "I felt numb the whole time. Now, I am very excited and pleased. It is a big relief. After starting a new job, selling my house, getting my daughters off to college and moving, I am looking forward to relaxing in my peaceful backyard."

And today, after nearly eight months of continuous experimentation, molecular biologist Dr. Cynthia K. Warner sees a brown line on a white membrane in her laboratory in Building 15 at the CDC. A simple translation of her very complicated procedure is that an antibody recognized the protein, in this case a rabies protein. Application? A potentially new way of producing rabies vaccines. An even broader application, perhaps five to ten years down the road? "Rabies is frequently looked upon as a model for other viruses. I think if this works for rabies, the application could work with other viruses, too." To celebrate, Warner baked a dozen chocolate chip cookies and savored the moment. "I don't have this unmitigated, technical success every week," she says. "It has to be repeated, mind you, but in terms of my life in the lab, Friday was a very good day."

It was not such a good day for Robert C. McMahan, chairman and CEO of Decatur Federal Savings & Loan, a venerable financial institution in downtown Decatur that has been purchased by Charlotte-based First Union. With the merger less than one month away, Friday represented an uncertain time for nearly 1,000 employees; some will be hired by the new bank, others will be laid off. "We've produced four, maybe five, heads of the DeKalb Chamber of Commerce, more than any other institution has provided," says McMahan, sitting in his elaborately carved, wood-paneled office on Friday

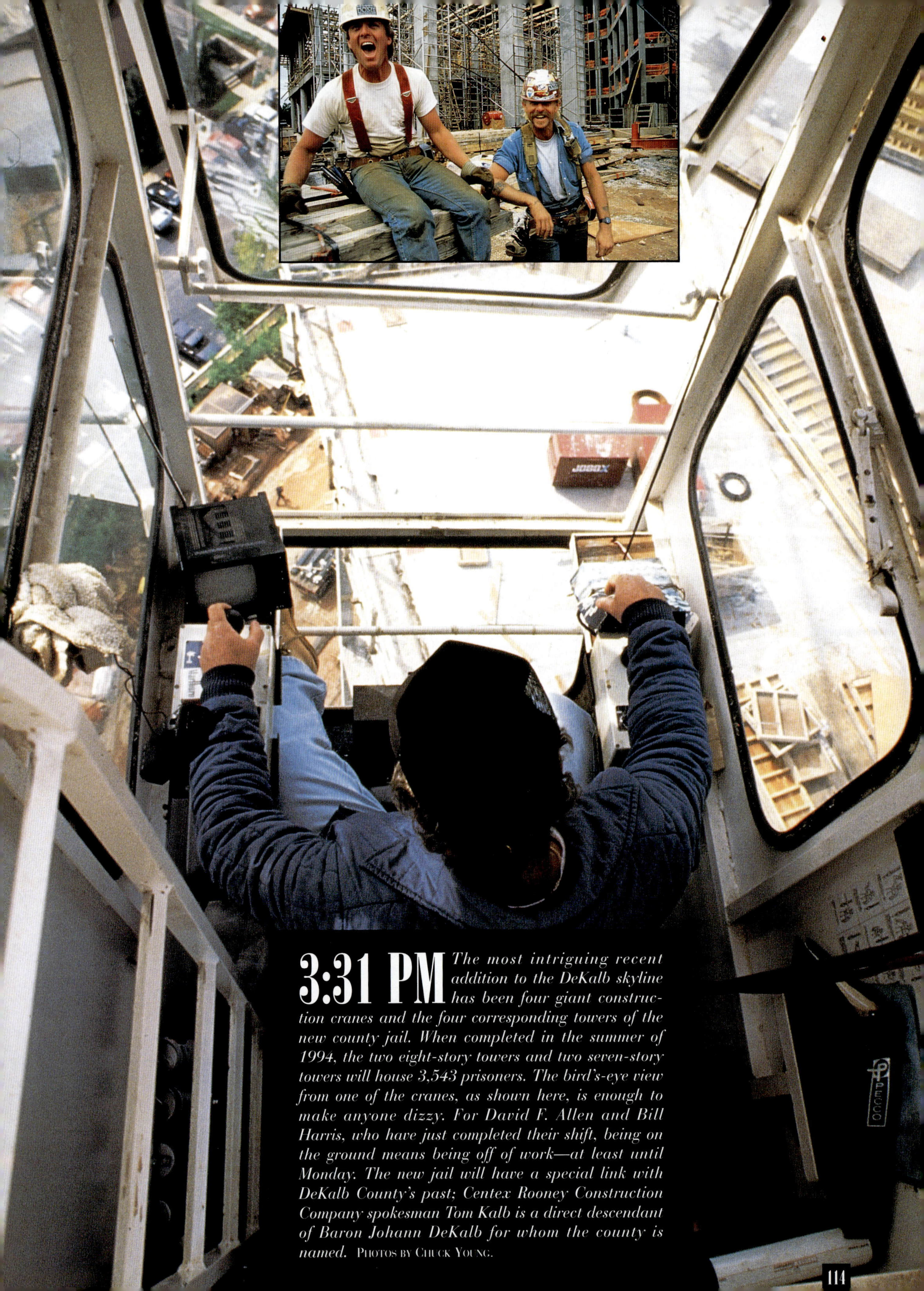

3:31 PM *The most intriguing recent addition to the DeKalb skyline has been four giant construction cranes and the four corresponding towers of the new county jail. When completed in the summer of 1994, the two eight-story towers and two seven-story towers will house 3,543 prisoners. The bird's-eye view from one of the cranes, as shown here, is enough to make anyone dizzy. For David F. Allen and Bill Harris, who have just completed their shift, being on the ground means being off of work—at least until Monday. The new jail will have a special link with DeKalb County's past; Centex Rooney Construction Company spokesman Tom Kalb is a direct descendant of Baron Johann DeKalb for whom the county is named.* PHOTOS BY CHUCK YOUNG.

afternoon, pointing out that the current chairman of the chamber is Decatur Federal President Wilbur G. Kurtz III. "We're going to leave a void in the community that others will have to fill."

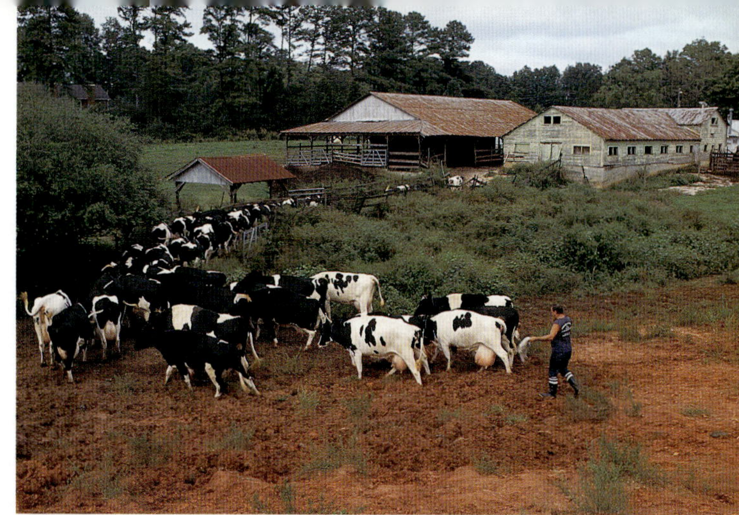

4:10 PM *Sheppard Brothers is the last working dairy farm in a county that had more dairies than any other area in the Southeast in the 1930s and 1940s. Milton Sheppard and his two sons, along with two hired hands, care for and sell milk from one hundred cows on the sixty-five-acre farm. The dairy has been in continuous operation on South Hairston Road in Stone Mountain since 1936. The biggest threat to the family farm is not the hard work or the long hours, it's the property taxes, according to Milton Sheppard. Here, Alvin McCullough herds the cattle in for the afternoon milking and then connects them to the machines that replaced stools and hands years ago.* PHOTOS BY ALAN WEINER.

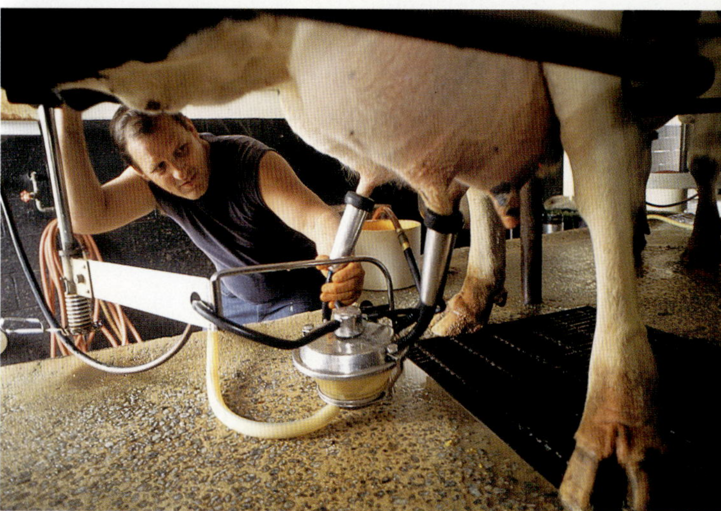

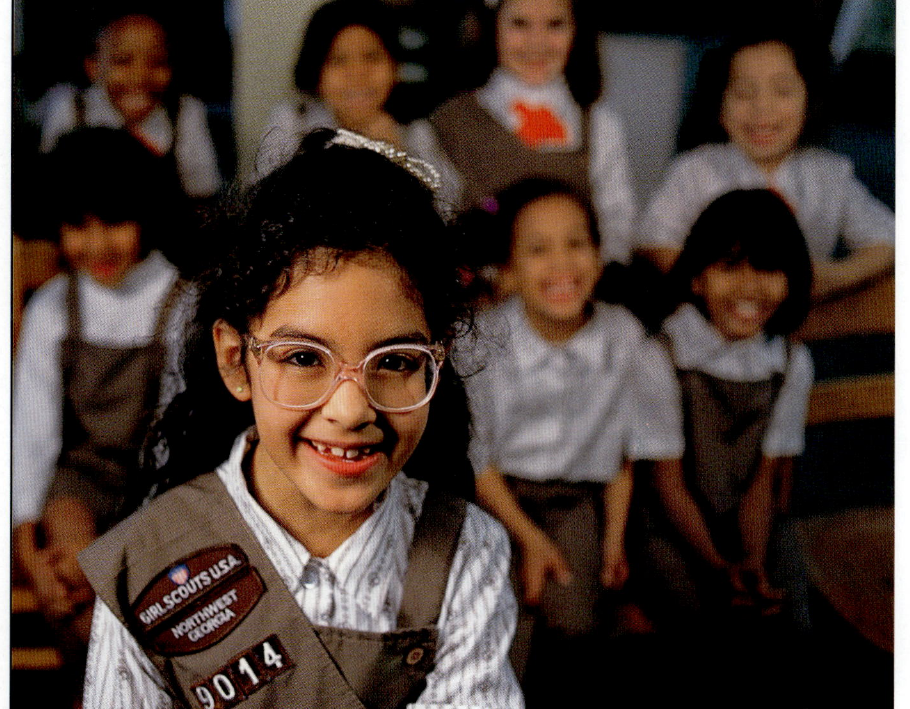

ALAN WEINER

NORTHWEST GEORGIA GIRL SCOUT COUNCIL, INC.

Incorporated on January 1, 1964
Over 4,500 Girl Scouts and nearly 2,000 Adults in DeKalb

I think the heart of Girl Scouting today is teaching girls to make decisions for themselves, to help them be independent and to have the kind of self-esteem they need to make their way in the world. ◆ "And in its own way, Girl Scouting is very different today. When we were in Scouting and earning badges, we were learning a lot of things about the world, but I don't think we had to make the kinds of choices that a lot of girls have to make today about careers. We are making girls aware of their options, and that they can do whatever they want to do. ◆ "Girls today are faced with life-preserving types of decisions — the kinds of decisions that are so difficult when placed before you by your peers. We hope that we are helping our young girls rely on themselves more and feel good about being able to stand up and do what they think is right. ◆ "Too, we serve all economic spectrums. We target girls from less fortunate backgrounds and from volatile living situations. We are trying to make sure that Scouting is an avenue that is consistent, something that is always going to be there and provide a safe haven for them. We know that a lot of the more affluent children have as basic a need for self-esteem in peer pressure situations as the child who has very little economically. ◆ "Our leaders use the broad outlines of Scouting to best serve the needs of their group. Whether it's taking trips together or earning badges, we are training our leaders to make the best decisions for the futures of our Girl Scouts."

— Susan M. Thigpen, President, NW Georgia Girl Scout Council, Inc.
Group Vice President, Trust Company Bank

SmithKline Beecham Clinical Laboratories bought the laboratory where I was working in 1981. At that time the lab was a pioneer in the laboratory industry. We were working on what was then state-of-the-art equipment. I'm amazed when I look back and see how far the industry's come. And it feels good to be part of a company that's stayed right at the leading edge of the industry. ◆ "My laboratory career began as a sixteen-year-old high-school student. I made tissue slides from surgical procedures. I continued to study and learn about all areas of the laboratory business. I've come a long way to become a member of the executive management team. Throughout my career I've been lucky; I've had technical, supervisory and managerial positions. ◆ "One of my most interesting positions was as operations manager of our drug testing laboratory. SmithKline's largest drug testing lab is in Atlanta. This is one of the industry's most challenging types of testing — it requires the highest level of accuracy and is of great value to society. ◆ "I've even worked as an operations manager in a local hospital. I'm currently a field operations manager, overseeing patient service and STAT labs. These are like mini-labs around metro Atlanta where tests come back without a long wait. ◆ "There's no doubt in my mind that SmithKline is the industry leader. Technology is available to any company. But what sets SmithKline apart is its drive to excel in quality, and more importantly, customer service. Even our new lab in DeKalb is one of the most modern lab facilities in the industry. We provide clinical laboratory testing for hospitals, physicians and industry. It's a role model for companies all over the world. ◆ "I think all of us in the health care industry realize we're doing something to help others. Sure, we concentrate on the technical aspect of the work — because laboratory testing is all about accuracy. But the data we track represents a real patient whose health depends on the work we do. Most of us got into this business because we care about other people. ◆ "I love my work, and I believe in this company. SmithKline may be a multinational corporation, but it provides a warm, personalized work environment. We have phenomenally high morale and many long-term, dedicated employees. Our values are definitely consistent with our mission statement: ◆ My goal is to earn your trust. ◆ My job is to meet your need. ◆ My commitment is 100 percent customer satisfaction.

— Patricia R. Ben-Dov
Field Operations Manager

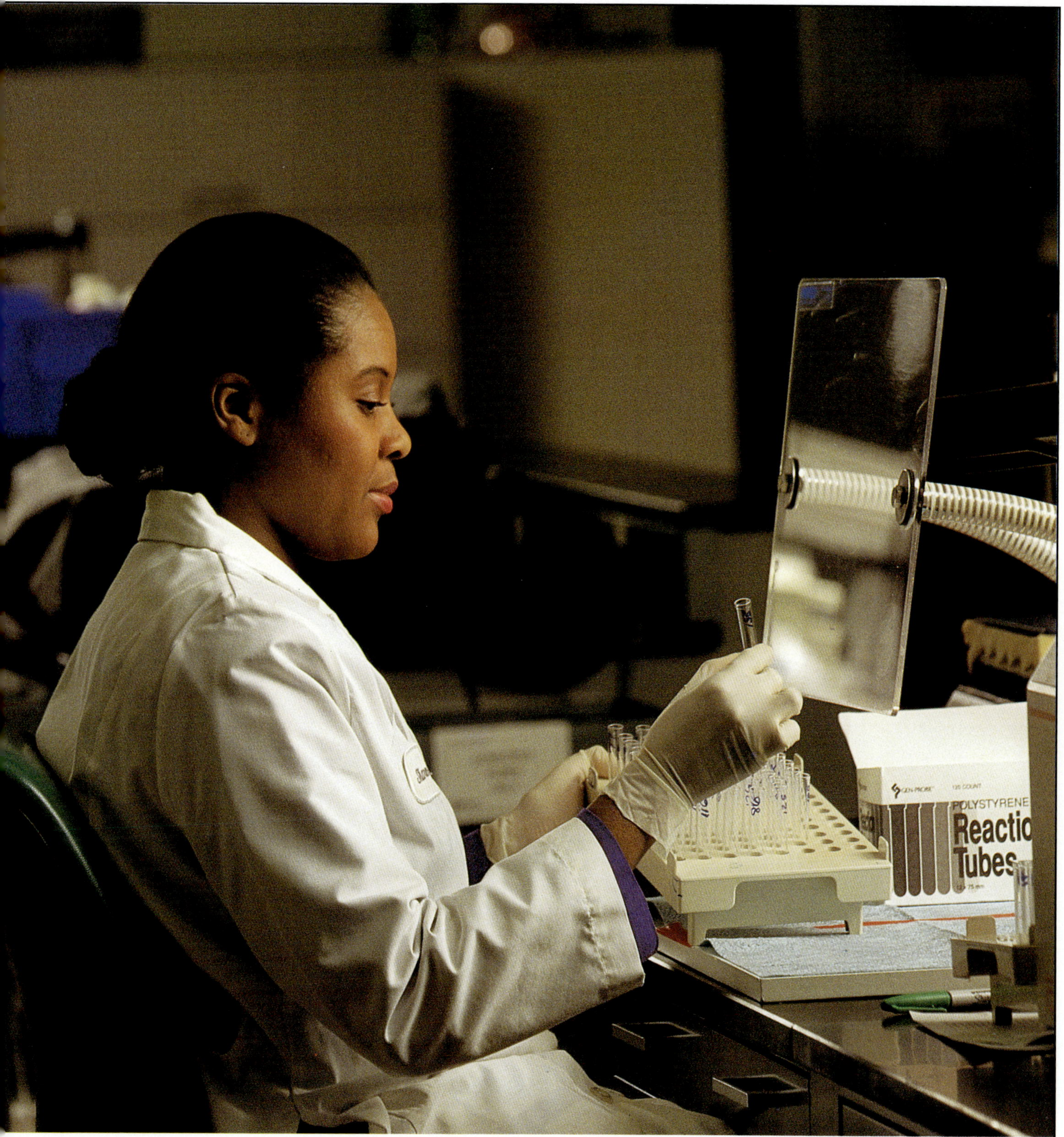

SCOTT ROBINSON

SMITHKLINE BEECHAM

One of the largest clinical laboratories under one roof.
1,000 employees testing for hospitals, physicians and industries.

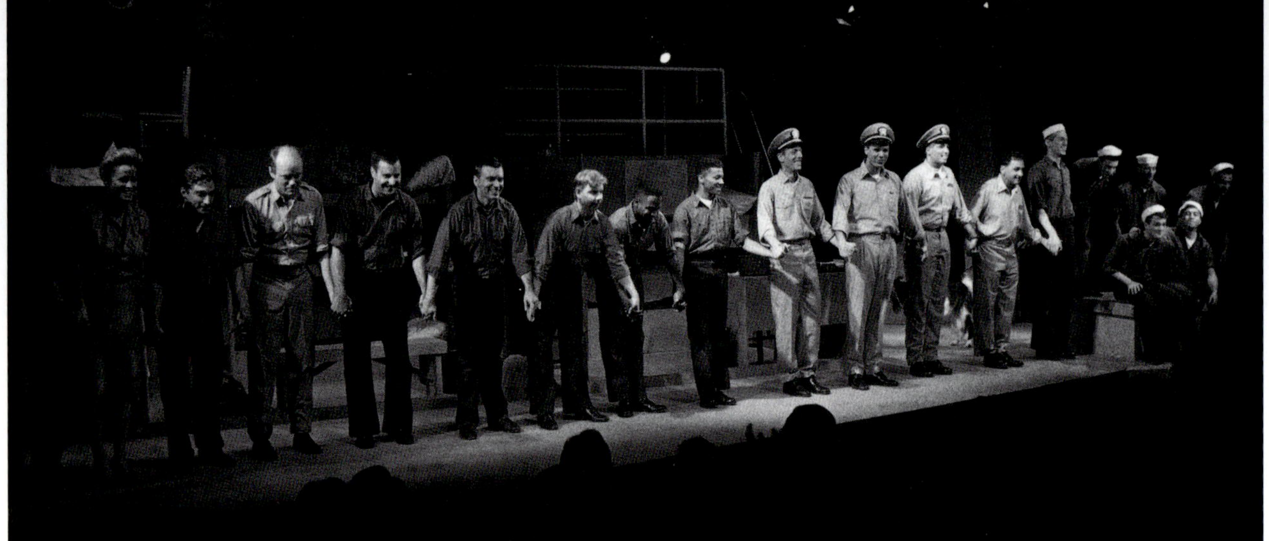

7:21 PM *Theater-goers relived scenes from World War II through the play, Mr. Roberts, staged by one of Atlanta's best community theater groups, the Neighborhood Playhouse. The classic U.S. Navy story was presented in the 170-seat theater housed in old City of Decatur elementary school which has been renovated into a community center. Here, Mario Cieri applies make-up for his role as Doc, a much-older character than the young actor. Afterwards, the cast comes stage front for the customary curtain call.*
PHOTOS BY MICHAEL SCHWARZ.

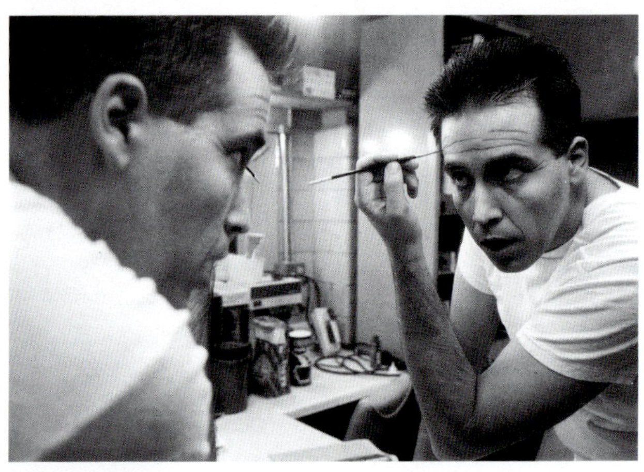

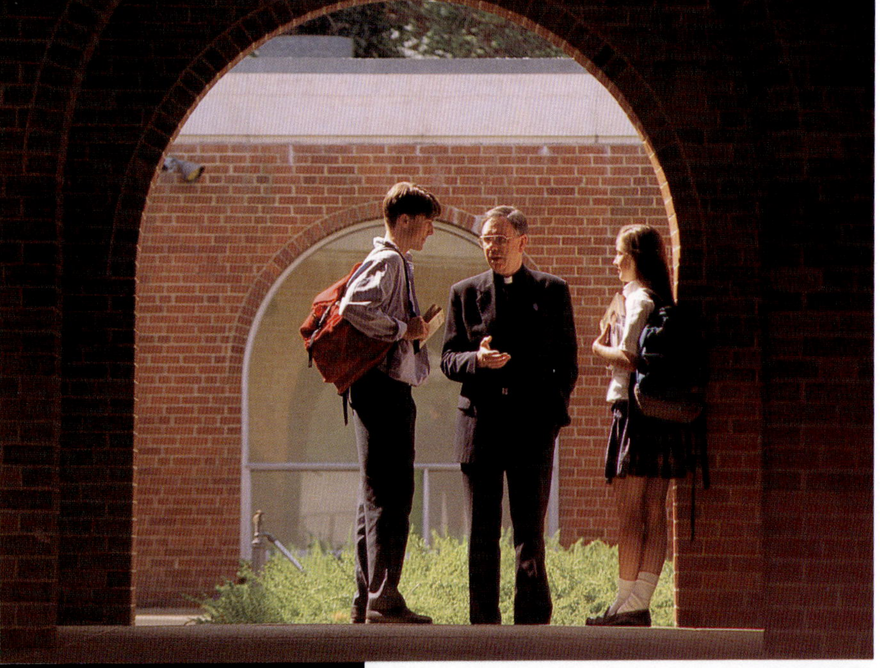

ALAN WEINER

Why is Marist a special school for Atlanta? I respond by explaining what we have in common with other schools and how we differ from them. Since 'school' is our last name, Marist does what schools do—provides a college preparatory program. That is what we have in common with other schools. ◆ "But our first name is Marist, and there is the difference. Marist, a Catholic school, is named for Mary, mother of Jesus. But for us at Marist, Mary is more than a mother, she is, in a certain sense, the first of her son's disciples. Disciples think differently as they reach out to embrace others. Marist is a school that teaches young people to think in a similar way. ◆ "We look at youngsters as individuals endowed by God with talents and abilities. Our goal at Marist is to teach them how to use those talents in and outside the classroom. ◆ "That goal is based on the very name of the school. Not only did Mary hear the Word of God, but she acted on it. That's what makes Marist different. The answer to 'Why am I learning?' is that I want to use my talents to advance myself and others. ◆ "Marist has its share of scholars, athletes and artists. But Marist is especially proud that it holds the first high-school charter for a Habitat for Humanity unit, that its students have been involved in soup kitchens and helping tutor inner-city children. ◆ "There's more to a name than meets the eye. When someone says 'Marist School,' I hope they grasp the full meaning of those words."

— **Father James L. Hartnett, S.M.**

MARIST SCHOOL
An Atlanta Tradition of Excellence
since 1901
1,000 Students in Grades 7 through 12
With a Professional Staff of 94

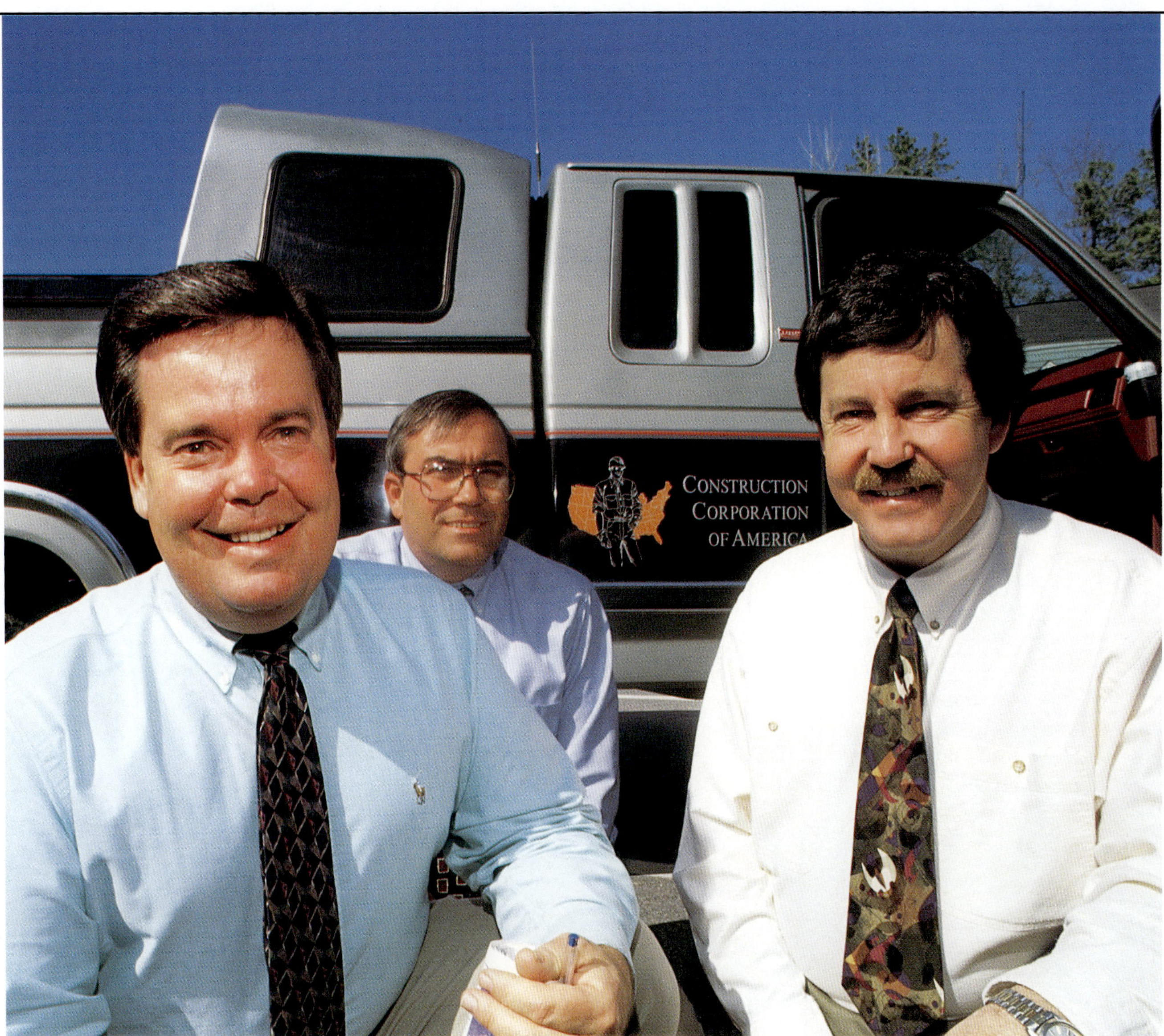

ALAN WEINER

Construction has been in our family history forever, focused primarily on grading and land contractors. But when my brother, Randy, and I started our company, we didn't pursue that angle. We ended up in multi-family renovations, and now that's all we do. ◆ "We work for syndicators, owners, developers and investors to renovate large apartment communities, primarily 180 units and up. When properties are allowed to go into disrepair, or when there has been a major fire, we bring the buildings back to a modern appearance. ◆ "It's exciting to see a cold, empty property changed into a nice, liveable space for someone to occupy. I'm not exaggerating when I say I've seen kudzu growing into the windows and along the walls of some of the properties we've renovated. ◆ "And it's interesting how this became our specialty. When we began, we were working for the federal government's Housing and Urban Development (HUD) program, repairing houses and bringing them up to minimum property standards. Then we were invited to look at HUD multi-family foreclosures and apartment buildings, and we worked on those in the late 1970s. Our business just evolved from there. We formed our own company in 1982 and kept going forward with multi-family projects. ◆ "As a result of tax law changes in 1986, a lot of changes were made regarding investments into multi-family communities, and a lot of tax credits and deductions were eliminated. Many of our customers had to rethink how they were going to pursue the multi-family market. To put it mildly, we suffered from 1987 to 1990, while everyone was trying to decide how to create a cash-producing property from a former cash-shelter property. "Now, we are seeing foreclosures slowing, and there are new owners coming into the arena with money to spend because properties were literally let go for so long. On the average, we have about six jobs going at once, with as many as 300 subcontractors on different jobs. We employ seven people, in strictly supervisory positions. ◆ "We really like the environment of DeKalb. We feel safe here. We think very highly of our police and fire protection. And Clarkston is like a home community. You know the mayor and the banker and the people at your post office. ◆ "It's a good area."

— **Steve Allgood, President**

CONSTRUCTION CORPORATION OF AMERICA

Steve Allgood, President
Randy Allgood, Vice-President
Multi-family renovations business

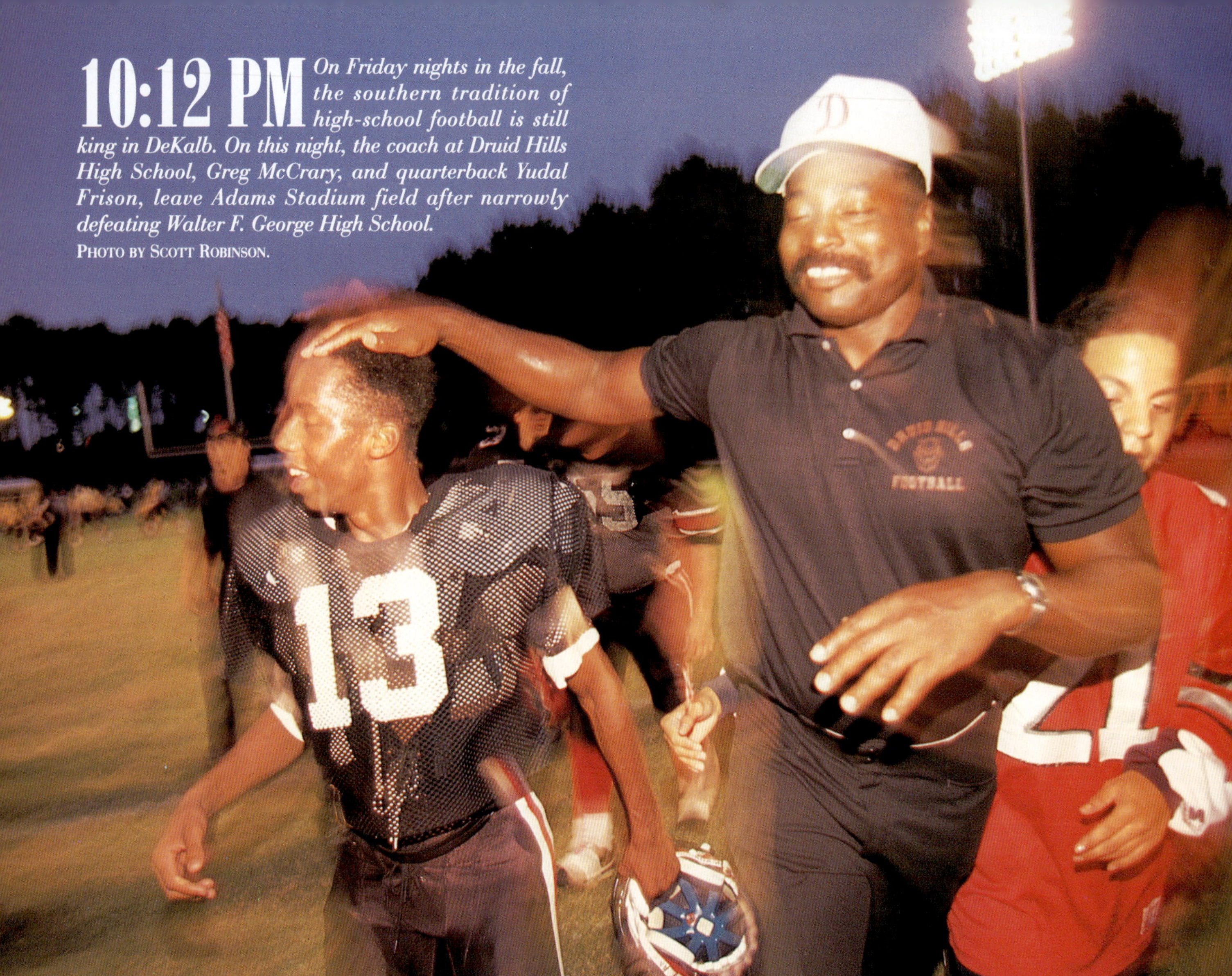

10:12 PM *On Friday nights in the fall, the southern tradition of high-school football is still king in DeKalb. On this night, the coach at Druid Hills High School, Greg McCrary, and quarterback Yudal Frison, leave Adams Stadium field after narrowly defeating Walter F. George High School.*
PHOTO BY SCOTT ROBINSON.

As Friday evening approaches, office politics, homework assignments, job anxiety and classroom angst of the past five days give way to the approaching weekend. For many DeKalb workers, their thoughts are already perhaps racing ahead to a weekend at Stone Mountain or some other activity. For others, such as parents working at SmithKline Beecham Clinical Laboratories, their thoughts are only minutes ahead as they leave work and walk the few steps next door to where their children are. SmithKline was one of the first DeKalb companies to implement on-site day care for the children of its employees. Built and operated by DeKalb-based AmeriCare Early Learning Centers, parents are able to work any shift and know their child is on site and in professional hands. They can even eat lunch together or use a video monitoring system to observe their children during activities.

Inside the Avondale Community Club, decorated with balloons and ribbons in the school colors of blue and white, the Avondale High School Class of 1954 celebrates its thirty-eighth class reunion. Why, there's Pat Ducote Dunklin, former cheerleader, handing out name badges! Buddy Hart, who played in the school band and helped win the state championship title his senior year! And former Principal J. E. Burgess, drama teacher Hilda Dykes and class salutatorian Laura Nickel Friedman, all the way from North Attleboro, Massachusetts! There's time for looking back, and appreciating what was. "It was a good time in life. It was a happy time," says Laura Friedman. "I'm so sorry that our children couldn't enjoy the same thing."

From the bleachers of Adams Stadium, former University of Georgia head cheerleader Gladys Phillips often uses binoculars to spot son, Britt, number eighty, a tight end and field-goal kicker playing for the Lithonia High School Bulldogs in tonight's Class AAA football showdown between archrivals Lakeside (4-0) and Lithonia (3-1). Tonight, there are seven high-school football games in DeKalb, and this one is the hottest. Seated with Britt's dad and grandparents, Gladys Phillips can hardly look as Britt attempts a thirty-seven-yard field goal with less than eight seconds to go in the first half. The kick is wide. "Oh, God, that's what they said in the newspapers," she half whispers, half laughs. "That the game might come down to a Britt Phillips' field goal." Final score: Lakeside 7, Lithonia 6.

In nightspots around the county, people who want to put the workweek behind them and pretend to be someone else can do just that. Freelance photographer Neal K. Matthews becomes a bodacious hunk named Bill Starbuck in the Stage Door Players' production of *The Rainmaker* at the North DeKalb Cultural Center. Backstage in Decatur's Neighborhood Playhouse, mortgage processor Nancy Conn gives an actor an eyebrow pencil to draw a seam up the back of her stockings for her role as Lt. Anne Girard in that classic World War II Navy play, *Mister Roberts*. Cynthia Cari Holloway and Robert Clark prepare for their roles as Elaine and Mortimer in the Saint Timothy United Methodist Church's production of *Arsenic and Old Lace*. And Rob Williams, who works for the DeKalb County Board of Health, teams up with Gwinnett County policewoman Nicole Downard to sing in a karaoke contest at Billy's in Decatur. After two years of karaoke, Williams declares, "It's very addictive." Tonight, appropriately, he sings "The Time of My Life."

But along Montreal Circle, there's no blurring reality with fantasy, no mixing pleasure with business. It's still a workday as the third shift begins at SmithKline Beecham, the largest laboratory in the country under one roof. From midnight to 8 A.M., 110 employees sort, sift, test and examine blood and urine specimens; the evening's 13,000 to 14,000 requisitions, or job descriptions, may require three or four tests of just one specimen. The weekend is another eight hours away as Idora Harris looks through her microscope, quietly investigating red and white blood cells. If someone's sick, she's usually the first to know.

11:30 PM *With 9,800 students, Emory University is a small city. And like a city, Emory has its "downtown"—Emory Village. The area is not a "village" in the traditional sense, but is a collection of businesses essential to the well-being of college students: a pharmacy, laundromat, gasoline station and pizza parlor. Emory Village provides a backdrop for the college's "Main Street," the place to be seen cruising to the Friday-night party at one of the school's twelve social fraternities or nine sororities.*
PHOTOS BY ROB NELSON.

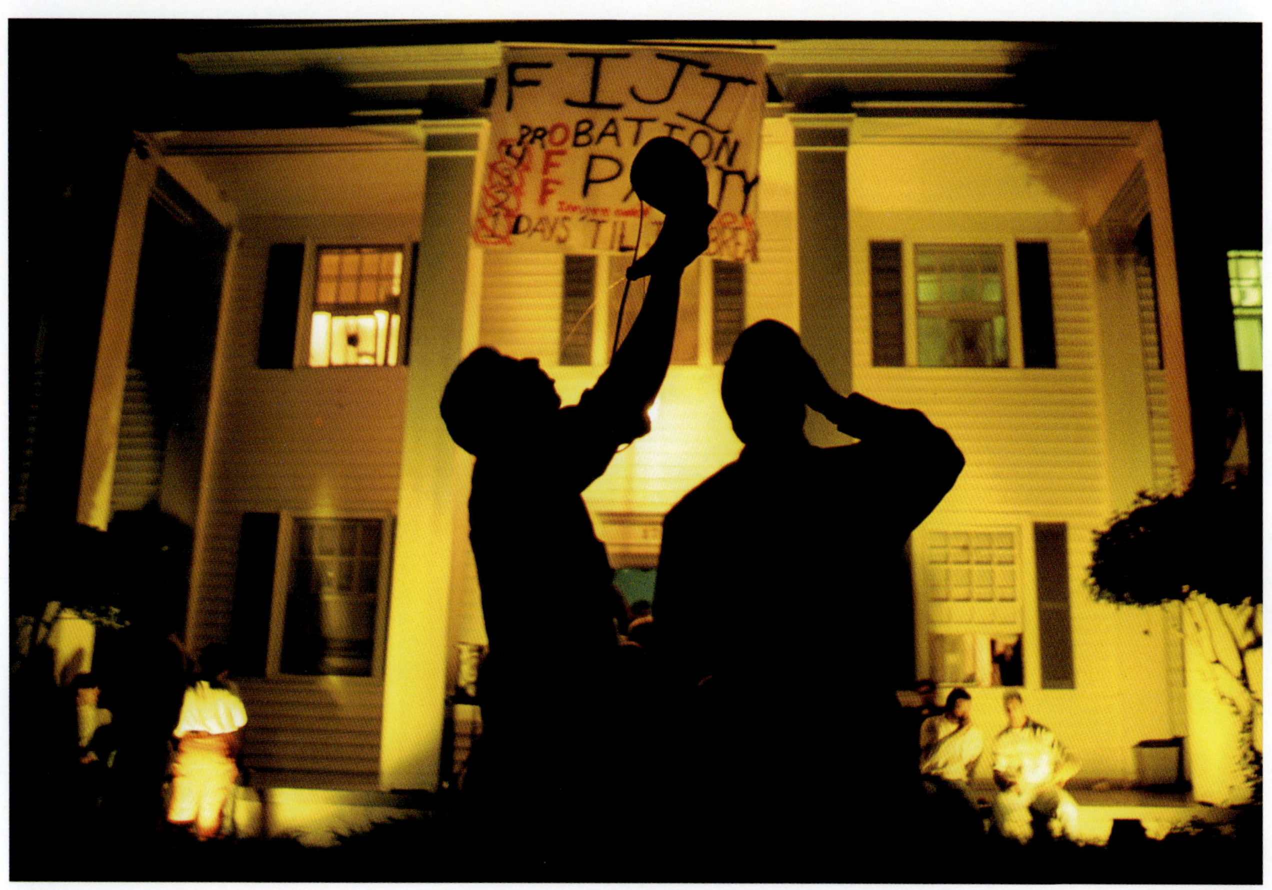

EGLESTON CHILDREN'S HOSPITAL AT EMORY UNIVERSITY

The Southeast's most comprehensive children's hospital, Egleston was founded in 1928 and is now serving more than 100,000 patients yearly.

I love working with children. As a pediatric nurse, you are the one who is always there. And at Egleston, nursing sick children does not mean just giving patients their medicine, or shots, or I.V.s. You have time when you can sit and hold them and rock them to sleep. You become part of their family. ◆ "When babies come into the hospital, everything around them is so unfamiliar to them. We want them to bring their own toys or special blankets or stuffed animals. Their toys provide security, something they know is theirs. And we want them to be babies — to be children, even in the hospital. If that means bringing their own toys and putting a blanket on the floor and letting them crawl around during a treatment, that's what we do. ◆ "I think these kids are special. Maybe it's because we spend more time with them. Our kids come in for chemotherapy, then they go home, and then they come back. You become very close to the families. The emotional bond that you have with families of children with cancer is something that you can never find anywhere else."

— Sally Plourde, Staff Nurse, IV Hematology/Oncology

"Before a child has surgery, one really important thing that we do is medical play. We use dolls to help explain the surgical procedures, and we have dolls that are made with G.I. tubes and I.V. lines and even a place where stitches go in and then come out. The children get to put on gowns and masks and gloves so they can dress up like the doctor, with a stethoscope around their necks. We talk about germs, which is the purpose of the special clothing. And later, when they are in the operating room, they will remember, 'Lynn told me the doctors and nurses would dress up like that because of germs.' ◆ "For all the children scheduled for surgery, we offer a tour of the hospital. We start by writing a book, similar to the book that the doctors will write about the patients on the day of their operation, including their names and how much they weigh. We ride the X-ray machine back and forth, and I tell them that all the machine does is take a picture of them. The children then know, 'I can handle this. We practiced this with Lynn.' I talk to them about getting sleepy air, and how it smells like bubble gum, and that they will take a nap and then they'll wake up. We explain how they'll feel when they wake up, and that we're all here to make children well. I tell all the children that everyone at Egleston is here getting something fixed. ◆ "When our tour and medical play are over, the children have their doctor's costume, a coloring book that outlines the procedure, and they also have the autographs of their new friends. They know that those new friends will be taking care of them. And they have some answers to their questions, some very honest, calm answers that communicate to a child, 'There is trust here. I don't have to be afraid.'"

— Lynn Elise Ney, Activities Coordinator, Child Life Department

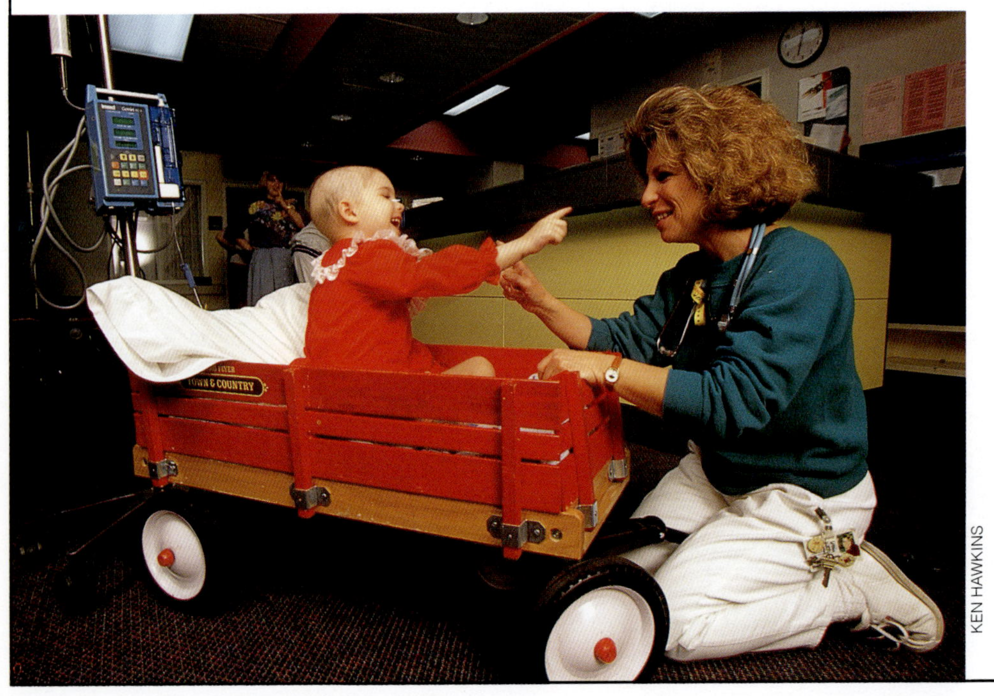

KEN HAWKINS

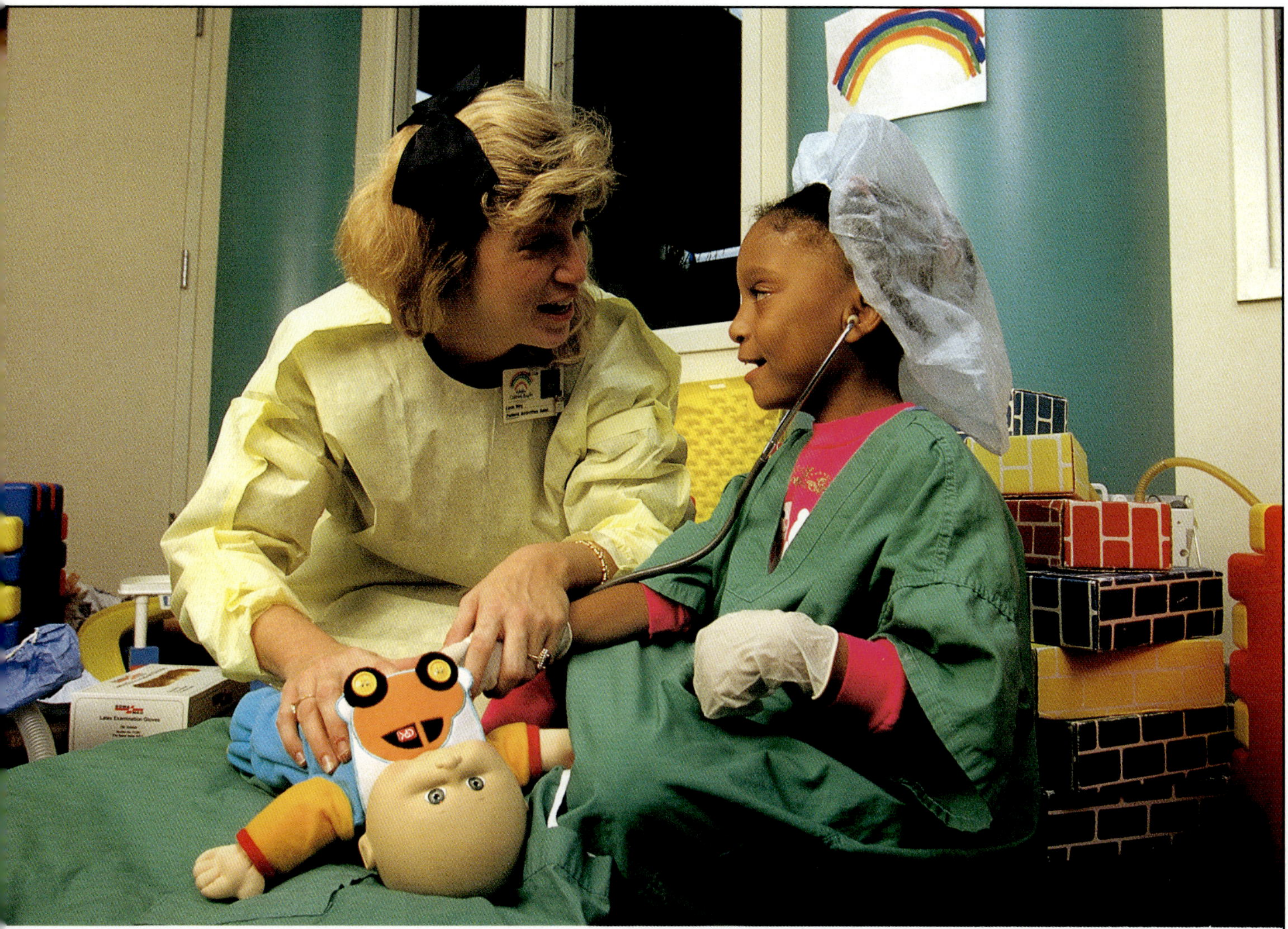

VKINS

"Children are so innocent, and they don't realize the severity of their illnesses. They trust you completely. And Egleston provides children with anything and everything that reminds them first and foremost that they are children and not just patients. ◆ "For instance, it's less scary for a child to ride in a wagon instead of a wheelchair to get a procedure done. By riding in that red wagon, they learn that along with the painful things they go through, there are some good things, too. That not everything we're going to do to them will hurt. It helps them mentally and physically. Consequently, it helps their parents. ◆ "I always try to make the children laugh. I just love them as much as I can. I feel fortunate that I can comfort them in some way and make their hospital stay a little easier. Because they go through so much. And they are so special."

— **Peggy Kerns, Staff Nurse, IV Hematology/Oncology**

KEN HAWKINS

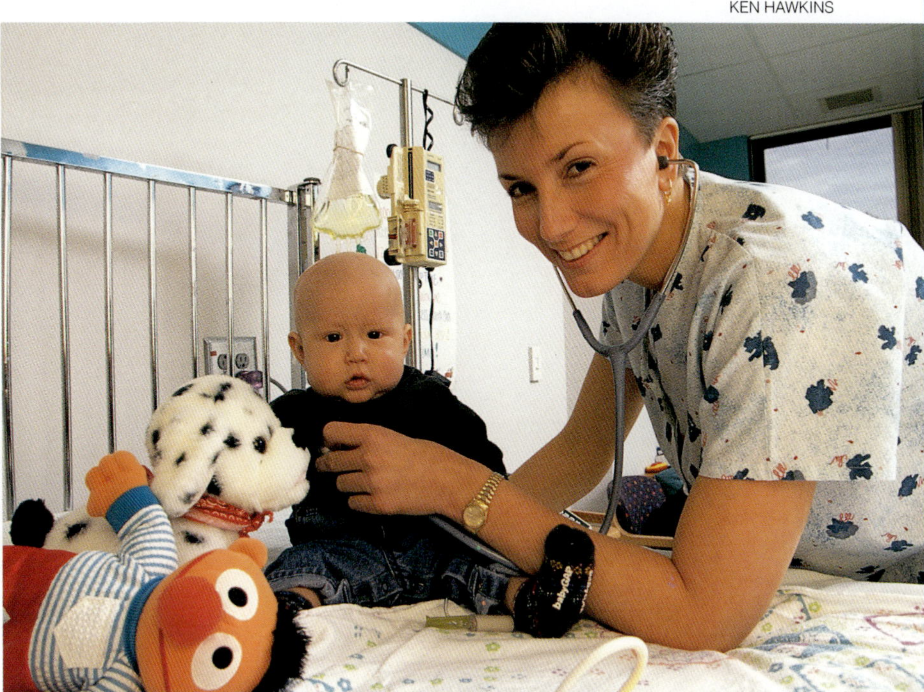

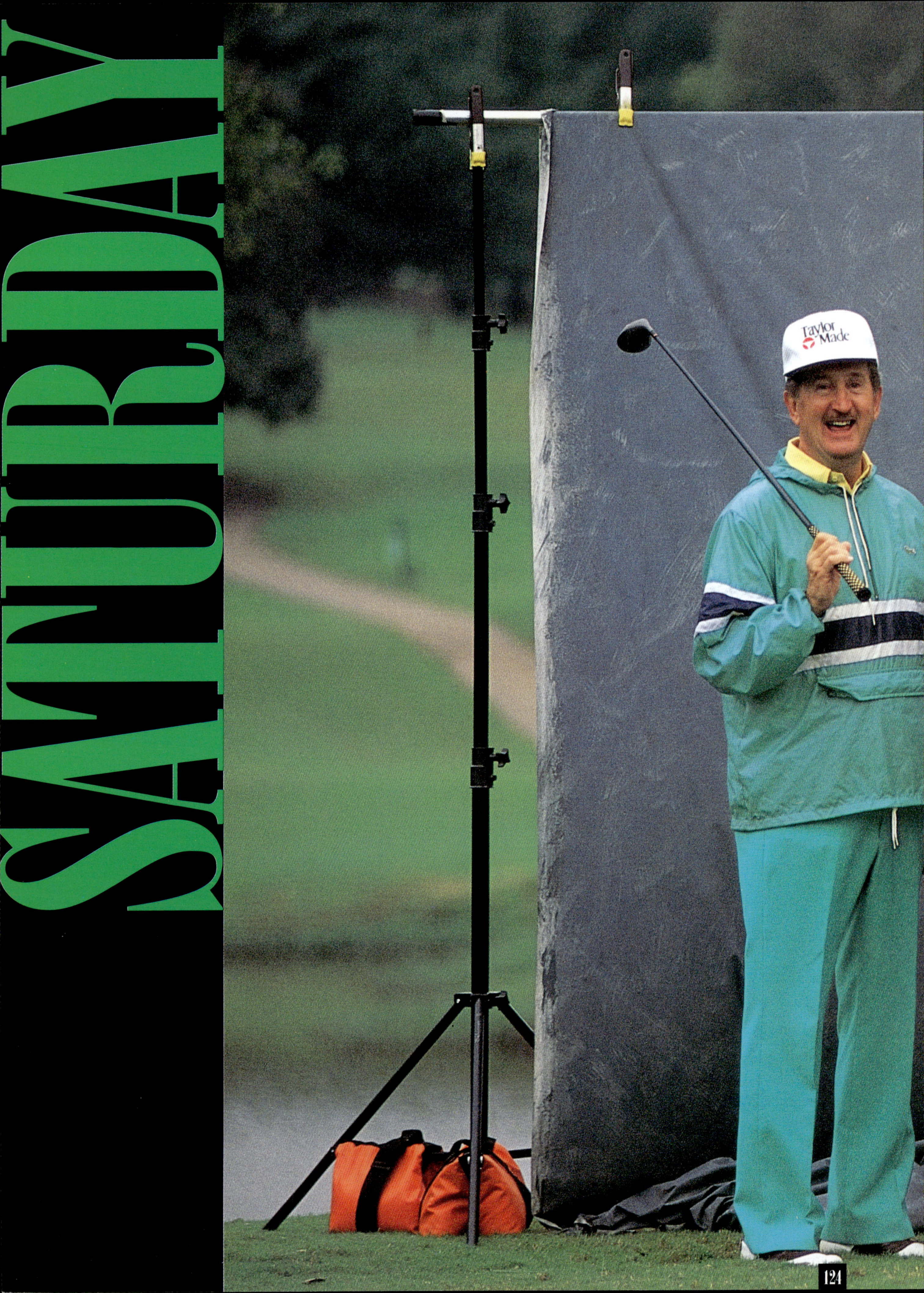
SATURDAY
Taylor Made

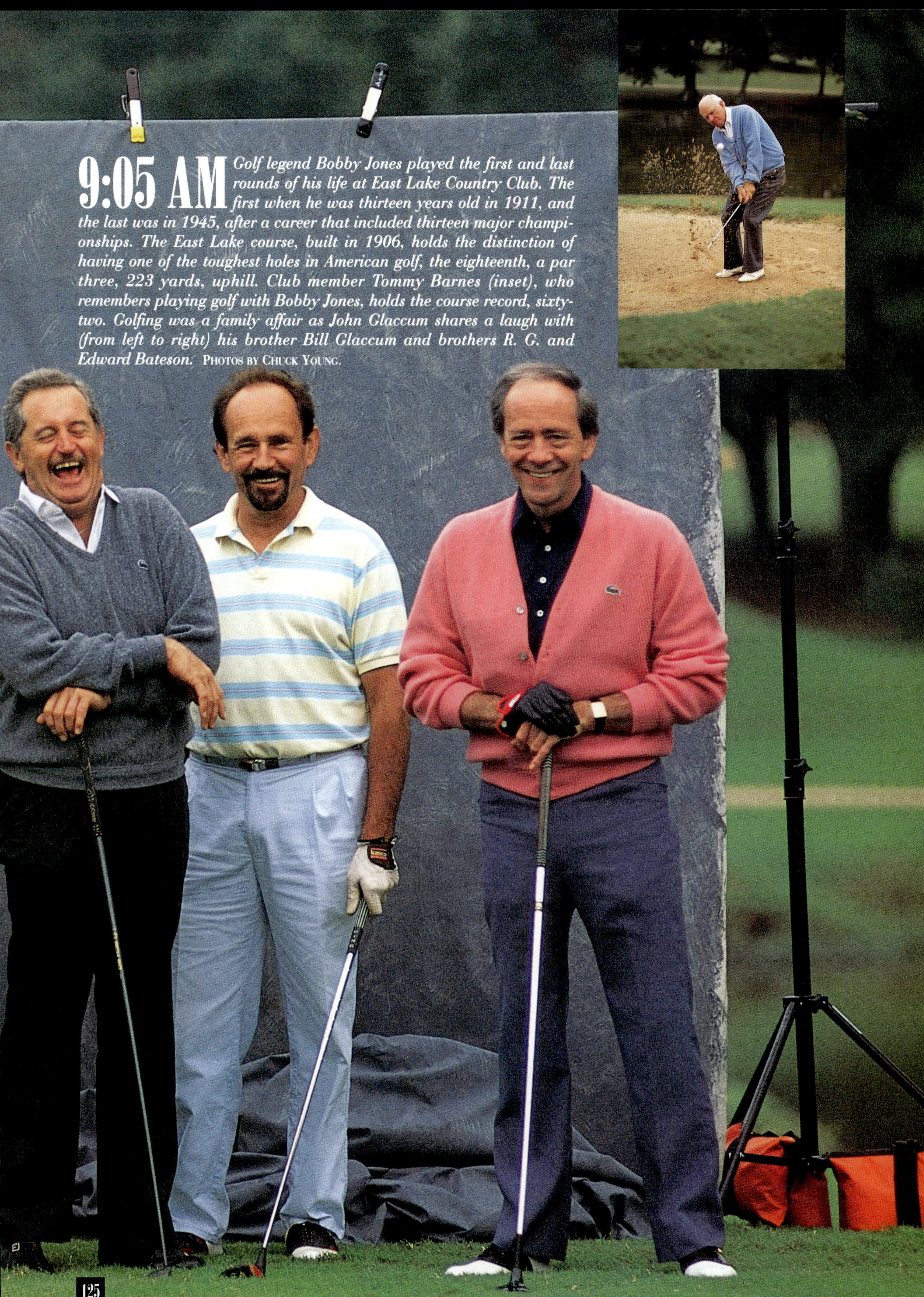

9:05 AM *Golf legend Bobby Jones played the first and last rounds of his life at East Lake Country Club. The first when he was thirteen years old in 1911, and the last was in 1945, after a career that included thirteen major championships. The East Lake course, built in 1906, holds the distinction of having one of the toughest holes in American golf, the eighteenth, a par three, 223 yards, uphill. Club member Tommy Barnes (inset), who remembers playing golf with Bobby Jones, holds the course record, sixty-two. Golfing was a family affair as John Glaccum shares a laugh with (from left to right) his brother Bill Glaccum and brothers R. G. and Edward Bateson.* PHOTOS BY CHUCK YOUNG.

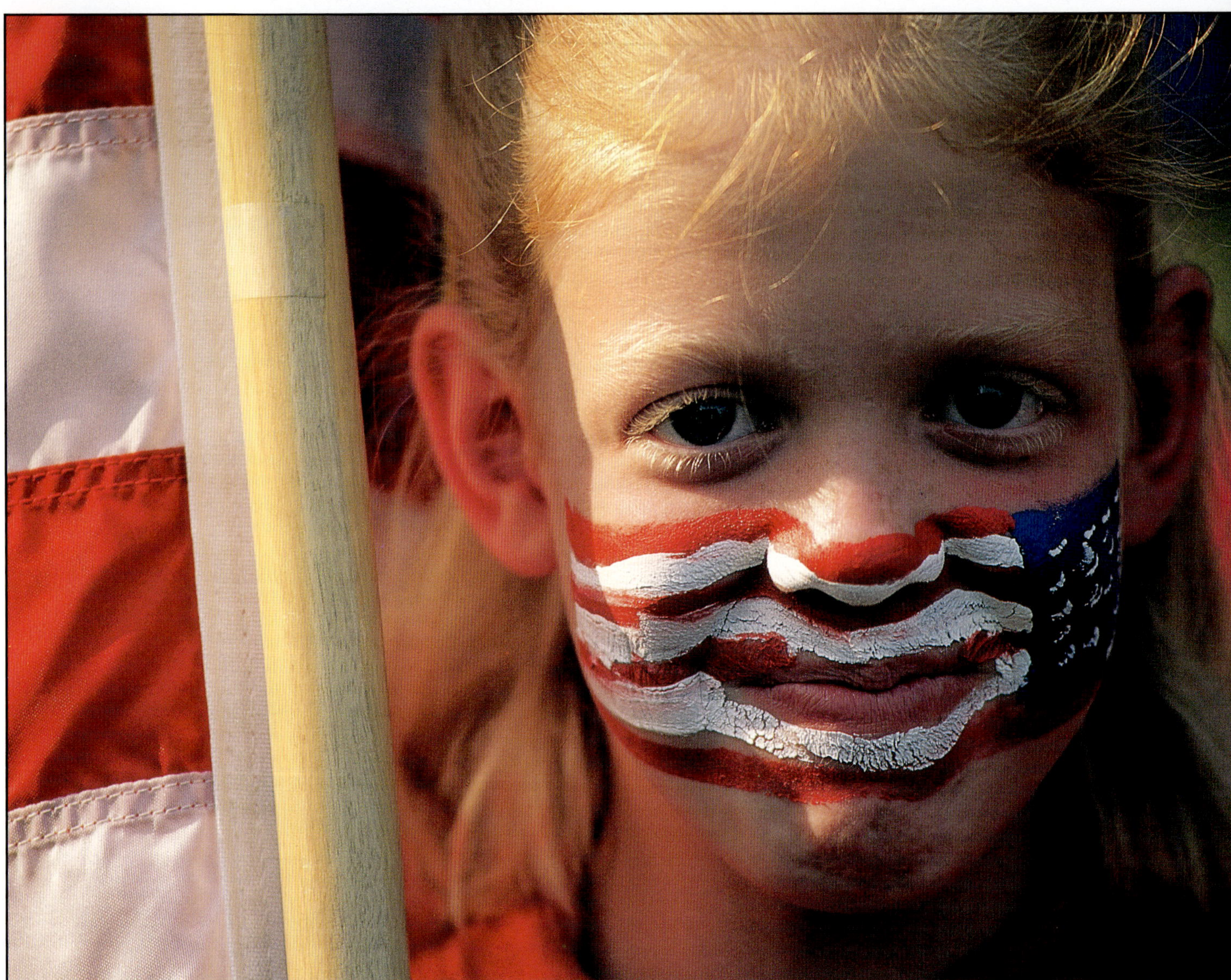

ALAN WEINER

I think we have worked real hard to build back a small town, a place called Decatur that isn't a little Atlanta but is instead a small town that recognizes the strengths that make it a unique small town. ◆ "The Decatur Downtown Development Authority grew out of a controversy over a development philosophy — with one group thinking that old is not good and everything needs to be new and better, and another group thinking that we should appreciate Decatur's older, historic qualities. ◆ "And in 1982, these two groups came to the table and developed the Decatur Town Center plan, creating the Downtown Development Authority to put this plan in operation. And everyone recognized that being a small town was Decatur's marketing niche. ◆ "What is a small town? It can be described in a couple of ways. There are those 'tangible' issues like design issues — with sidewalks and trees and buildings that respect the fabric and flavor of community. We encourage good contemporary architecture, but we want our buildings to have an urban, pedestrian feel that is welcoming and not overpowering. ◆ "And we work hard with the 'intangibles' of what the community is all about, a building up of community spirit and a sense of belonging. The Square surrounding the old Courthouse is what we describe as the 'Living Room of Decatur.' This is where the farmers used to come for the Farmers Market. This is where everyone came to be seen. And that's why we do our concerts and festivals on The Square. We want our residents and the people in the surrounding area to feel like there is something always going on. That this is a place where you can come with your family and have a positive, fun-filled experience. ◆ "This is very much a small town. And one of our important roles is to market Decatur as a self-contained town consisting of four square miles, a population of 17,800, an independent public school system and a full-service municipal government. All within the greater Atlanta metropolitan area. ◆ "Decatur is exactly what our motto implies — a family of homes, schools and places of worship."

— Evelyn W. Menne
Executive Director

DECATUR DOWNTOWN DEVELOPMENT AUTHORITY

A seven member board appointed by the Decatur City Commission, with two staff members. Redevelopment, economic, marketing and community activities.

On Saturday in DeKalb, much like Saturdays in communities all across the country, there's a whole lot of the ordinary going on.

Chores . . . Michael Frewer drags out kids' toys, old toasters and car seats for an early morning garage sale along Ponderosa Circle. *Fun* . . . The DeKalb Bulldog Club meets at Don and Kate Connelly's house in Avondale Estates, a lavish tailgate spread of French bread, brie, grapes, fried chicken, coleslaw, deviled eggs, beer, Bloody Marys and soda already packed for the trip to Athens to watch the University of Georgia take on Ole Miss. *Family* . . . Barbara and James Hickey visit with her father, the distinguished ninety-nine-year-old Philip K. Robinson, at his home in the King's Bridge Retirement Community. *Shopping* . . . Thousands of mallers shop till the bargains run out at Northlake Mall, where Becky Moore, a registered nurse at Egleston Children's Hospital, sits behind a children's health-fair table to explain why popcorn, balloons, quarters and peanuts are bad news for toddlers.

Sports . . . In a county with 102 public parks, take your pick: there's youth soccer at Henderson, youth football at Murphey Candler and fast-pitch girls softball at Wade-Walker. *Children* . . . Jerilyn Hardnett, thirteen, Jill Upchurch, thirteen, and Shanterri Hunter, sixteen, ballerinas all since the age of three, each dream of dancing the role of Clara in *The Nutcracker* after an afternoon at the *barre* at the Decatur School of Ballet. *Community* . . . There's a set of glass dessert bowls ($7) on sale at the Junior League Bargain Bazaar at the DeKalb County National Guard Armory—make that $3.50 when the security guard blows his whistle and Leaguer Karla Preston yells, "Everything is now half-price!" *Work* . . . Sgt. Frederick A. Woods, a twelve-year police veteran, patrols the North Precinct. "I like police work. I like feeling like I'm doing something to help, trying to deter crime and help young people who might go astray." *Relaxation* . . . After sunset at the I-85 Drive-in, Elaine Bailey, a 1968 graduate of St. Pius X High School, fondly remembers those yesteryear drive-in days when speakers full of static hung from car windows and there was an "aura of naughtiness in going to the drive-in with a date."

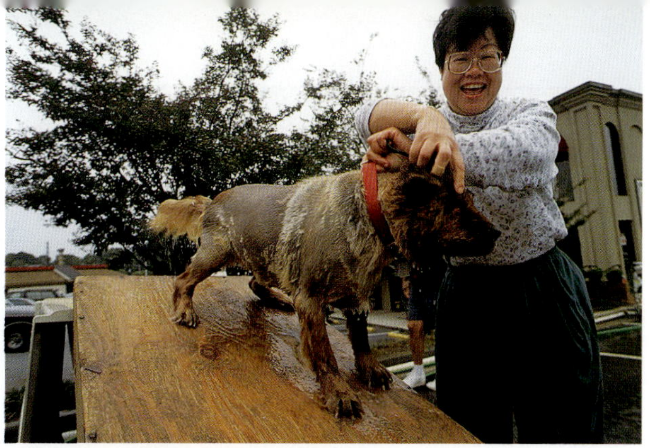

10:20 AM *Everybody—owners and pets alike—ends up wet when giving your favorite housemate a flea dip at the Cheshire Pet Supply at Toco Hill shopping center. The Saturday-morning affair is part ritual, part carnival.* PHOTO BY ALAN WEINER.

10:25 AM *Lisa Coleworthy and Lauren Burke became husband and wife in the garden of the gracious Houston Mill House at Emory University. Acquired by Emory in 1959, the facility is now used by Emory and the community as a hospitality center and as headquarters for the Emory University Women's Club. The house was first the home of Maj. Washington J. Houston who operated a water-powered mill on the South Fork of Peachtree Creek nearby. As a result of mill-generated electricity, in 1906 Major Houston's was the first home in the county to have electric lights.* PHOTO BY SCOTT ROBINSON.

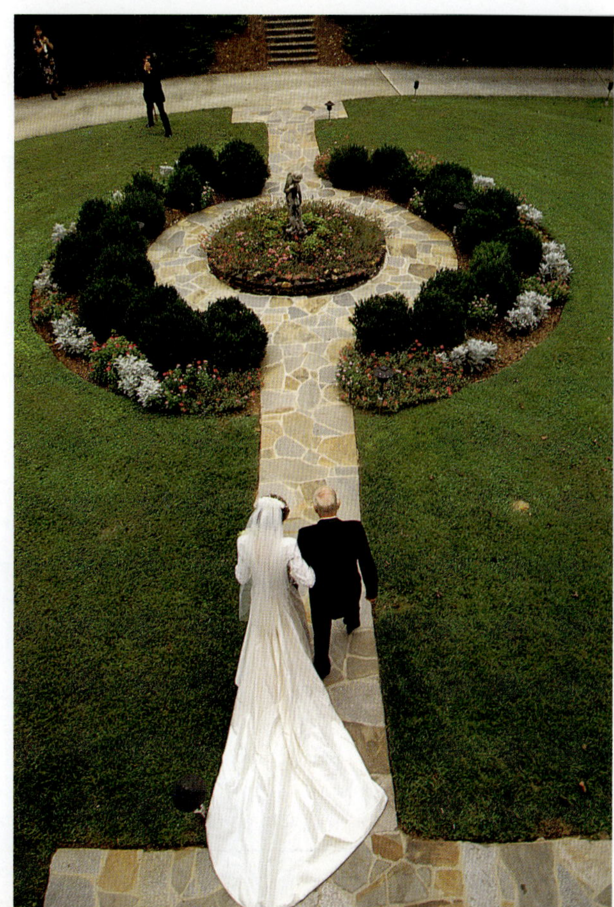

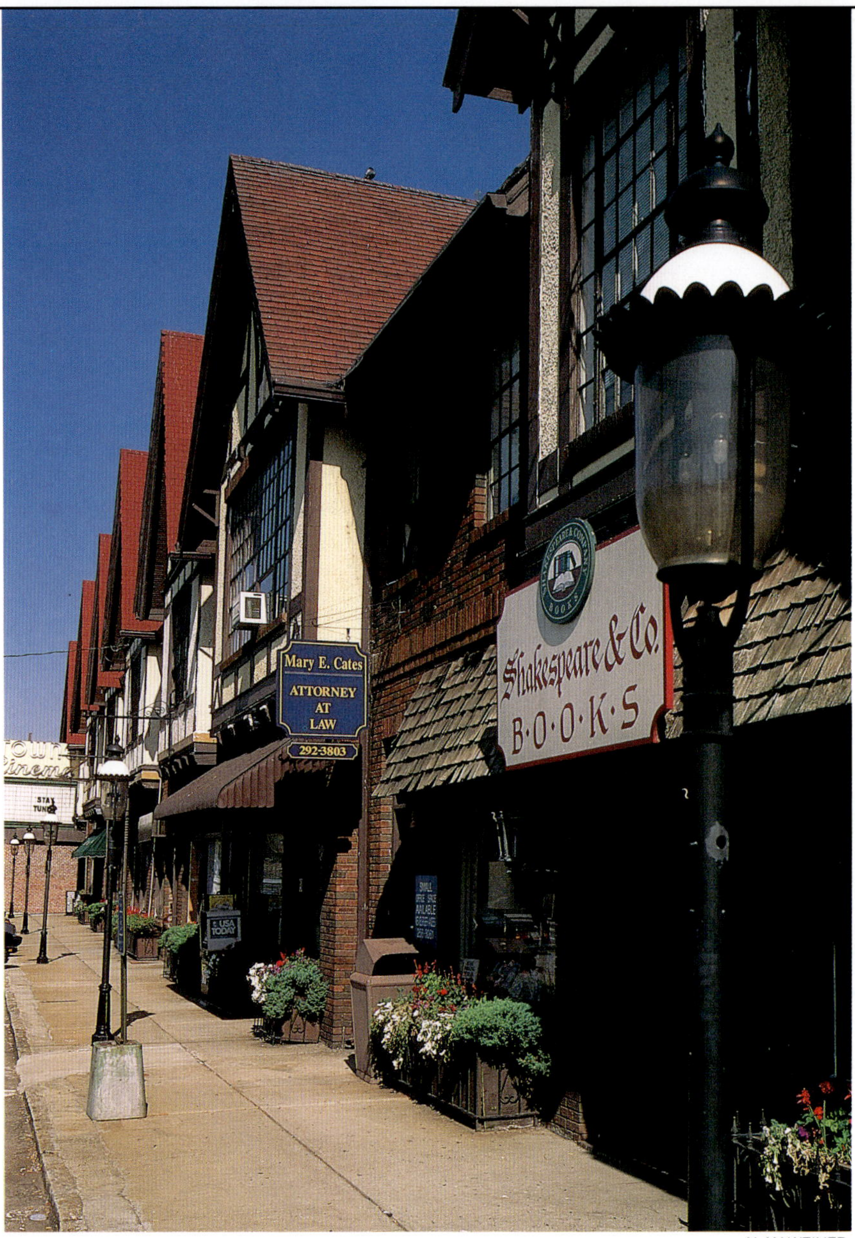

ALAN WEINER

Avondale Estates is a unique community. We're a Norman Rockwell, *Saturday Evening Post* cover come to life. ◆ "With only 2,400 people here, you know almost everyone. You can hop on your bike, jog down the street or walk on the sidewalk. We are a safe community, something our citizens demand. I think we have the highest ratio of police protection per citizen of any town in the state. And we have trees and parks and gracious homes, a surprising amount of character and a quiet kind of wealth. And while we are only sixty-five years old, Avondale Estates has the character of some of those English villages that are 200 years old or older. ◆ "We are a good anchor for central DeKalb, and we have a large impact both politically and economically. We are the only city in Georgia with its own film commission. Part of 'I'll Fly Away' was filmed here and 'The Traveling Man' was filmed here, too. Macy's uses our lake for some of their advertisements. It's great public relations for our community. ◆ "And what's unusual about our small town is all its different organizations. We have a swim and tennis club, a retired men's club, a community club, two garden clubs, a business association, a historic preservation commission, a women's club, Boy Scouts and Girl Scouts, a community action group and development authority. ◆ "And for a small community, we have a tremendous number of facilities and activities — a new City Hall, community club house, Olympic pool, tennis courts, parks, gazebo, clock tower, Christmas and Halloween decorating contests, July 4th fireworks, Labor Day Road Race, moonlight concerts Easter egg hunts, fishing derby at the lake, a citywide flea market in the fall, not to mention our community newsletter. ◆ "We want to maintain our small town integrity, but we have room to grow, too. We like to think we are the Georgetown of Atlanta, because the residential area is pretty substantial. We are in the midst of doing some redevelopment in our business area, and we would like to develop a commercial artist center in our Tudor village. ◆ "We are only six miles from Atlanta, but you might as well be seventy-five miles and fifty years away. We still have such a small town feel, which is unique, and we have three and four generations of families who live here.

— Allan A. Kirwan,
City Commissioner

CITY OF AVONDALE ESTATES

2,400 Population

Six miles east of Atlanta, one mile inside the Perimeter

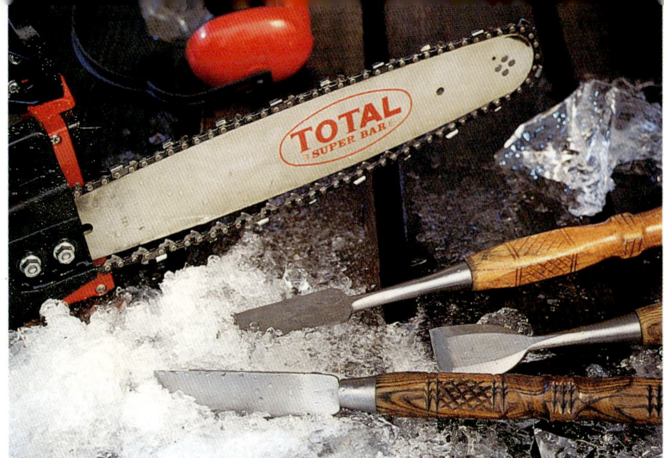

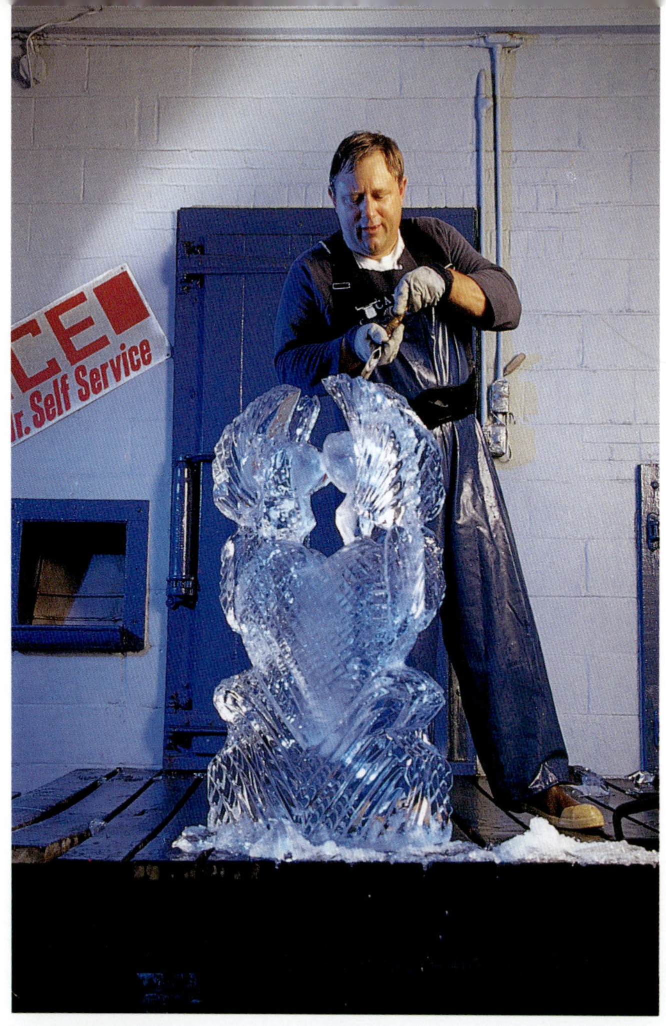

10:30 AM *Goree Ice is DeKalb's only business specializing in ice carving, delivering as many as 200 carvings and carving blocks each week to Atlanta's hotels, clubs and restaurants. Goree carvers create Easter bunnies, Thanksgiving turkeys, Christmas reindeer and swans for June weddings, and claim they can reproduce absolutely anything in ice. The carvings they're asked to create for bachelor parties truly stretch the imagination. Goree was the first business in Doraville—opening in 1945—and has long been known for the adjacent eclectic store where you could stop for everything you'd need for a day on the lake—from outboard motor fuel to fishing licenses to tins of Vienna sausage to fish bait to ice for the cooler.* PHOTOS BY KEN HAWKINS.

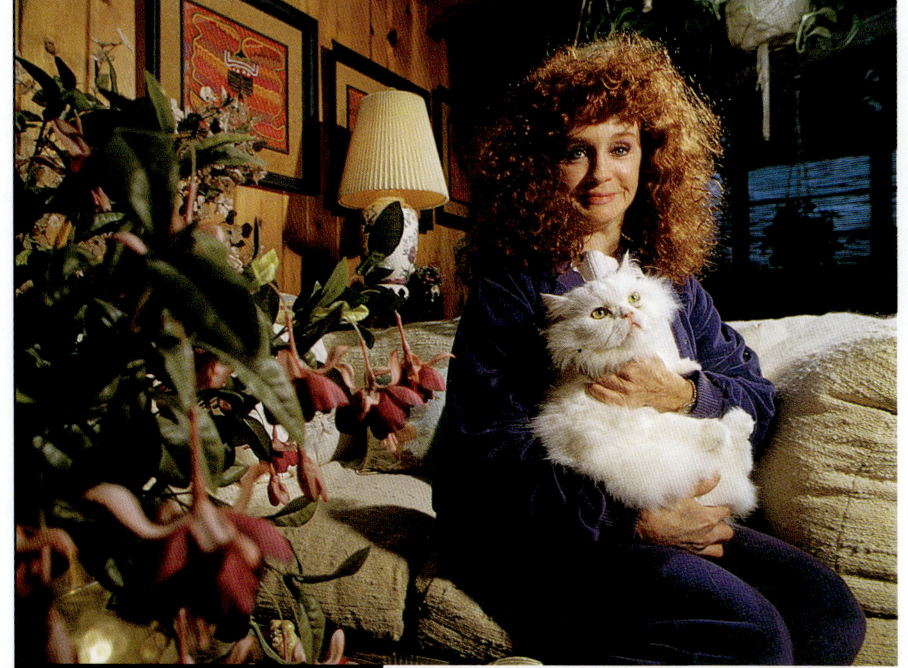

ALAN WEINER

I'm an electrologist. Basically, I remove superfluous and unwanted hair. Sometimes that hair is in discreet areas, and sometimes it's not. ◆ "In this area, my customers are mostly women. I don't know if they can cut bathing suits any smaller, but it's sure been great for business! I get a lot of referrals from doctors. And some wives bring in their husbands who have hair in their ears, and the barbers have been making it grow stronger and longer all these years by cutting it out. ◆ "I went to electrologist school at Forty-second Street and Broadway, twenty-four years ago. The business has changed since then, and they have come up with a bunch of new stuff. I keep going around to see if it's any better, but it's not as good. This is the oldest method on the market and it's the best. ◆ "Most electrologists don't hold out for this long. It's kind of boring. It's not brain-taxing, you just pump the pedal with your foot. You're pumping the electricity. We remove the hair follicle, period. We call it dissolving. ◆ "Waxing? That's a no-no! It stimulates the hair growth. There are a possible 1,500 hairs in a square inch, and it takes thirteen weeks for each to go through a cycle. When you tweeze and take out an unwanted hair, you'd swear it's the same spot, but it's not. And it's not the same hair. ◆ "I've been doing this for twenty-four years. I like people and I can make them feel good, and I can give them new confidence. I'm an electrologist, but I'm really a cheap psychiatrist!"

— Learita Lear, Owner

LEARITA
ELECTROLOGIST

Member of the Chamber of Commerce, local Civitan Club

But in a county that likes to call itself "Atlanta's Leading Edge," imagine what Saturday might be like when stripped of its ordinary weekend veneer.

Imagine spending time in a county that claims the largest collection of antique shops in the Southeast as well as the most ethnically diverse neighborhood in the state (Chamblee); the largest bas relief carving in the world (Stone Mountain); the largest museum of natural sciences south of the Smithsonian (Fernbank's Museum of Natural History); and a private golf course where the first and only grand slam winner in golf history once played (golf legend Bobby Jones played at the venerable East Lake Country Club, where he and local golfer Tommy Barnes jointly hold the course record).

Not to mention thirty Civil War battlefield site markers (two-thirds of the Battle of Atlanta took place in DeKalb); a farmers market called "The United Nations of Fresh Food" (buffalo carp, yellow fin grouper and common jack on sale today at the DeKalb Farmers Market); the Softball Country Club (nine meticulously manicured softball fields, out-

10:45 AM *Neighborhood kids take to the hoops for a morning in Dunwoody.*

PHOTO BY DAVID MURRAY.

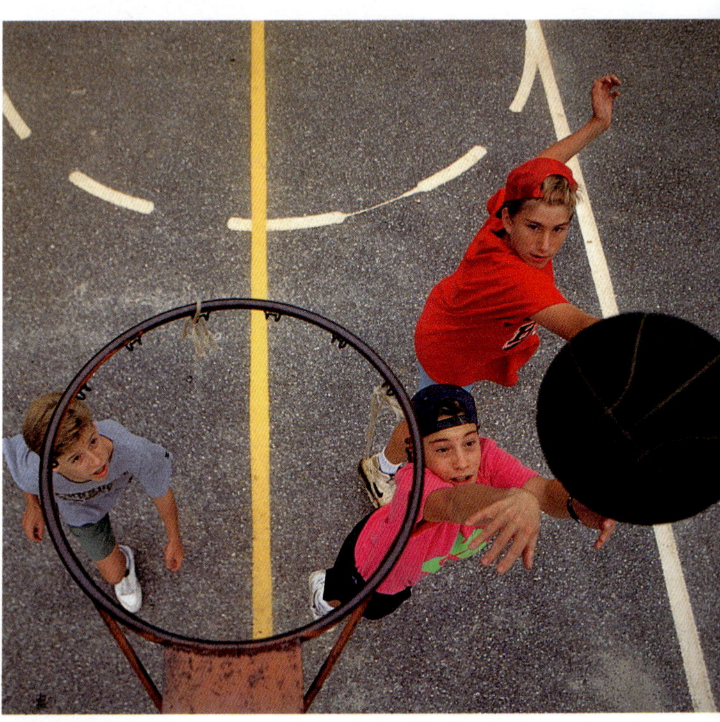

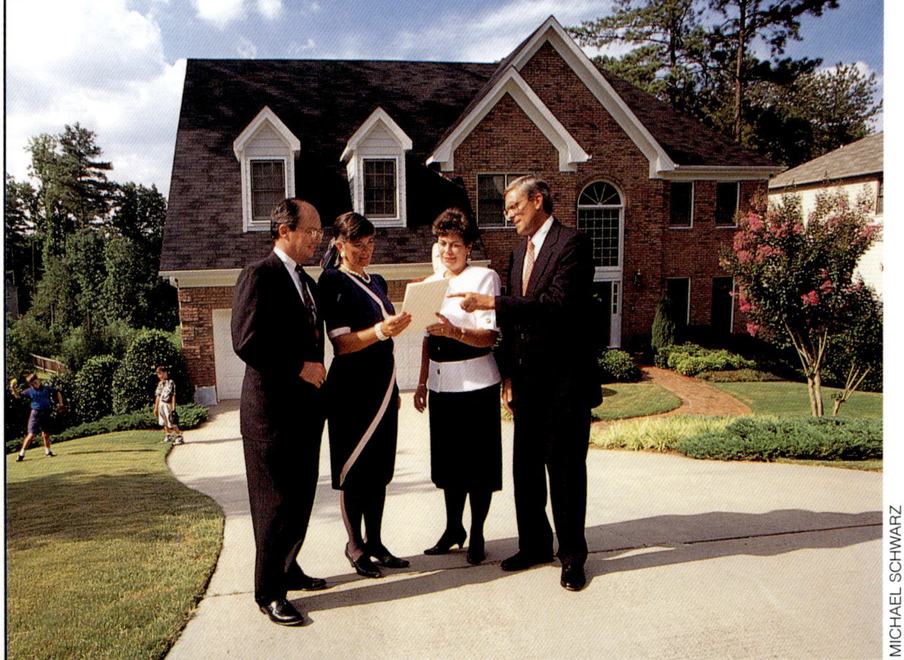

MICHAEL SCHWARZ

The DeKalb Board of REALTORS is a local Board of REALTORS chartered under the National Association of REALTORS, which is the largest trade organization in the world. The purpose of the National Association is to enhance the ability and opportunity of its members to conduct their business successfully and ethically, and to promote the right to own, transfer and use real property. ◆ "While there are plenty of real estate professionals to choose from, a good bet in terms of ethical, efficient and reliable service is a REALTOR. Unlike many real estate brokers and sales-associates who are simply licensed by their state to do business, REALTORS have taken additional steps to become members of the local board of REALTORS, and have agreed to adhere to a strict Code of Ethics. This membership obligates them to be fair to all parties involved in a transaction, be it buyer, seller or cooperating agent. ◆ "Our DeKalb Board of REALTORS is thirty-six years old, and with 1,500 members, it is the third largest local board in the state. ◆ "We have twenty-nine standing committees that handle everything from professional standards and monitoring legislation on all levels, to coordination with the Georgia Association of REALTORS. And a big part of our mission at the DeKalb Board of REALTORS involves committees with the function of education, where we try to keep our membership up to date on industry-related matters, and make sure we are the most professional real estate people in the business. ◆ "We are proud to be a part of the DeKalb County community. Our doors are open to the public. We want people to visit us anytime, or call on us for real estate help or real estate information."

— Jim Thibadeau, President
DeKalb Board of REALTORS
Principal, Thibadeau-Burton, Realtors

THE DEKALB BOARD OF REALTORS

A Professional Organization of 1,500 Members in DeKalb County

11:48 AM *Don and Kate Connelly and Red and Sidney Murphey see red every Saturday during football season—red clothes, red pompons, red football players. They are University of Georgia alums and members of the DeKalb Bulldog Club. Properly fortified with a tailgate spread of fried chicken, deviled eggs, French bread, brie and Bloody Marys, they prepare for an afternoon in Athens as the Bulldogs take on Ole Miss.* PHOTO BY DAVID MURRAY.

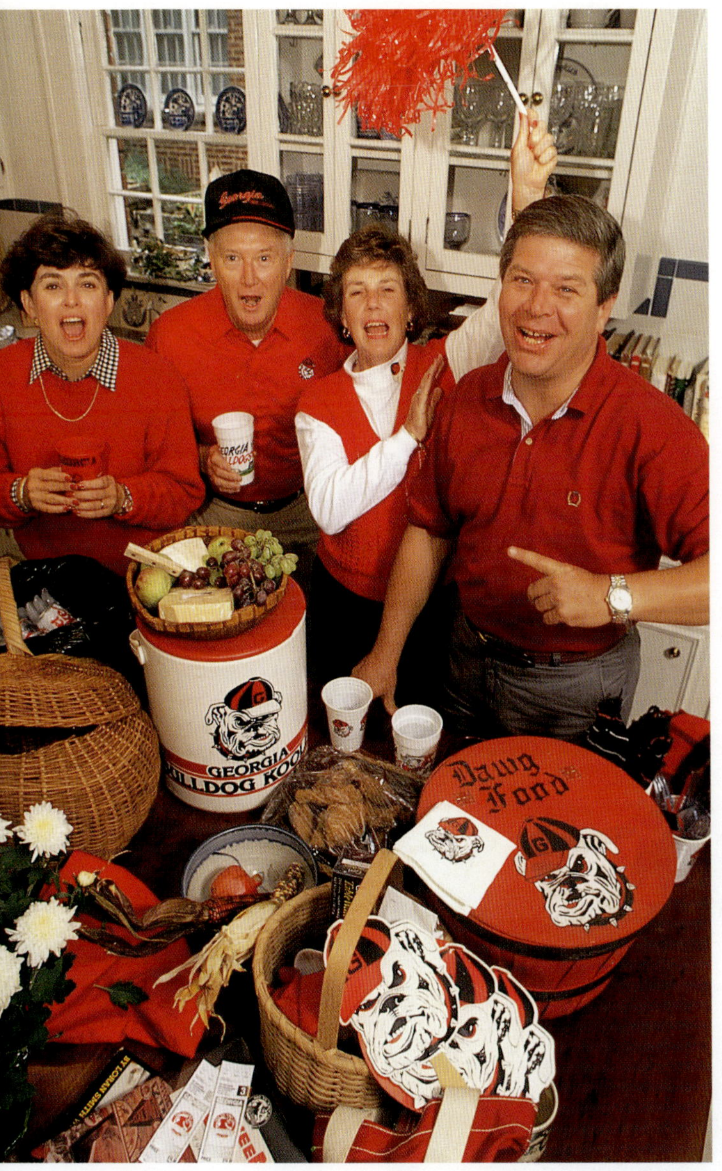

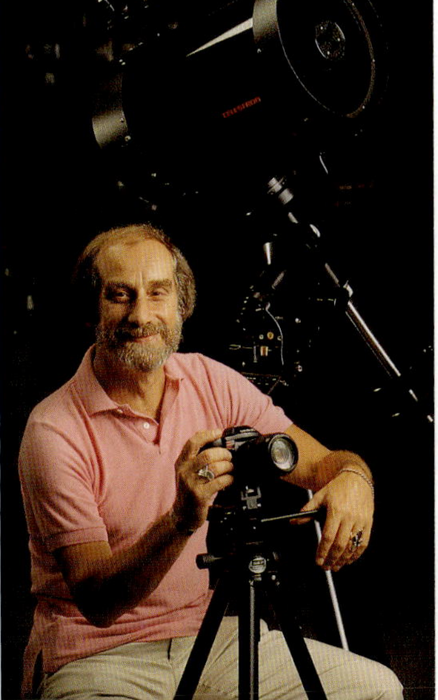

SCOTT ROBINSON

We're a full service photography center two miles away from The Southeast Center for the Photographic Arts, with Emory University right at our back door. We are so involved in helping teach people about photography that we feel very lucky to be in this location. ◆ "We recently renovated our store. I like to say that we leaped out of the sixties and into the nineties. We have a cleaner, uncluttered look. We put in a photo-finishing lab, and a full framing department, all designed to provide quality services to our customers. ◆ "In addition to film processing, and the sale of film and equipment, we do a lot of training. Medical students don't know that much about photography, but they are going to be using photography throughout their careers, for patients or for teaching, and they turn to us for advice. ◆ "Photography students come to us for advice about cameras, equipment and darkroom facilities. It's such a pleasure working with them over the years, and watching their expertise and their skills develop. ◆ "For our corporate accounts, we provide practically anything related to photography — processing, film, equipment. And we are uniquely familiar with their needs because the people employed in The Camera Bug have been here virtually all of their adult lives. We don't have a high turnover rate for our staff. ◆ "We've made a lot of friends here over the years. It's just a good feeling being settled in DeKalb County."

— Larry Fruwirth, Owner

THE CAMERA BUG, LTD.
Opened in 1980, eight employees
Processing, Equipment, Framing, Film

fields sodded with Tifway Bermuda!); the only government-operated firing range in the metro-Atlanta area (open to the public on Saturdays); the Atlanta Greek Festival (eighteen years of baklava, flogheres, galaktobouriko and strifta); and a country music dance floor big enough to hold 1,000 synchronized bodies lined up shoulder-to-shoulder for the South Side Hustle (get your boots on, sweetheart, it's Mama's Country Showcase!).

And today in DeKalb, who *didn't* dial 1-800-326-4000 in a mad scramble for Braves playoff tickets?

Picture all of these out-of-the-ordinary opportunities, and that's DeKalb County, too. And each year this rather extraordinary side of DeKalb generates over $700 million in local tourism and hospitality dollars, accounting for more than 16,000 jobs throughout the county. Which just goes to show that what seems an ordinary Saturday in DeKalb isn't necessarily so.

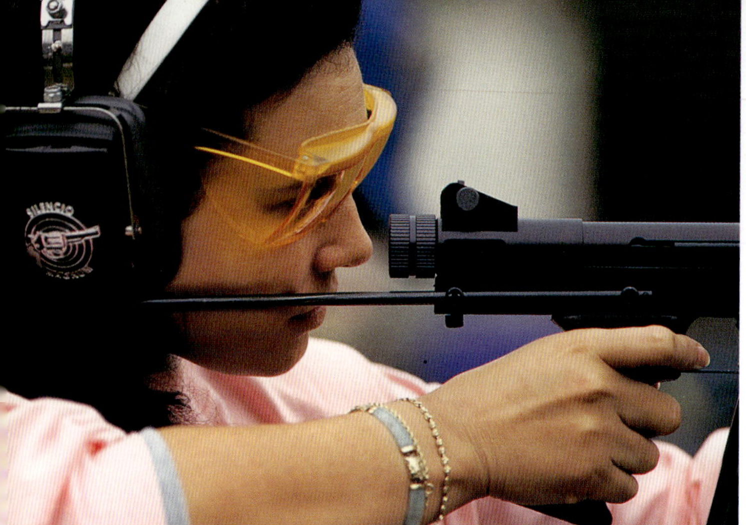

12:30 PM *DeKalb County has the only public, outdoor firing range in Atlanta. Shooters, such as Lori Maddock, from all over the state come on Saturdays to practice at the sixty-acre facility. Operated by the DeKalb Public Safety Department, the complex also serves as a firearms training site for police officers.* PHOTO BY KEN HAWKINS.

1:45 PM *No one in the 160-member Jaguar Club of Atlanta, based in DeKalb County, owns one of the new XJ220 models, billed as the world's fastest production car with a top speed of 200 miles per hour . . . yet. Government regulations prohibit the car's sale in the United States, but club spokesman Allan Talbott predicted if anyone can find a way to modify the car enough to get it into the country, it will be an Atlanta club member. In addition to meetings and tech sessions, the club participates in shows and driving tours of the north Georgia mountains and other destinations. Pictured here are Graeme Goodall, Terry Girone, Marlene Cox, Warren Fox, Pete Scarborough, Allan Talbott, Frank Coleman, Roy Cleveland, Steve Unti, Gary Morgan, Richard Sims, Randy Ficklim and Terry Hulsey.* PHOTO BY ROB NELSON.

Today, 200 member-dealers in "the Antique Paradise of the South" along Peachtree Road in Chamblee offer everything from vintage clothing to antique toys and trains to old-fashioned appliances at Rust N' Dust, where Shirley and Gerry Maddox often rent stuff to movie and television producers. Just this week, producers for the television series "I'll Fly Away," which is filmed in the Atlanta area, walked into Rust N' Dust and rented a 1950s television set. Says Shirley Maddox: "Once there was a list of thirteen movies being made here in town and we were working on twelve of the thirteen. And the one we weren't involved with was a Japanese science fiction movie."

Rust N' Dust is a just a half-block away from Chamblee City Hall, a single-story, red brick building where Mayor Johnson W. "Dub" Brown has presided for four terms. In many ways, the sixty-two-year-old mayor seems part of the past (he even has a girlie calendar from Chamblee's Pierce Oil Company on his office wall, circa 1962), but the city he runs is anything but. Gone are Chamblee's days as a town of factories and dairy farms alongside the rail line that connected it to downtown Atlanta. Today, Chamblee is a city of contrasts, home to the most ethnically diverse community in all of Georgia.

According to the 1990 census, DeKalb County has 25,885 Asian and Hispanic residents, with a rich mix of Chinese, Korean, Vietnamese and Hispanic businesses, financial institutions, restaurants, churches and community centers. Many of these are concentrated in Chinatown on New Peachtree Road through Chamblee and Koreatown on Buford Highway in Doraville.

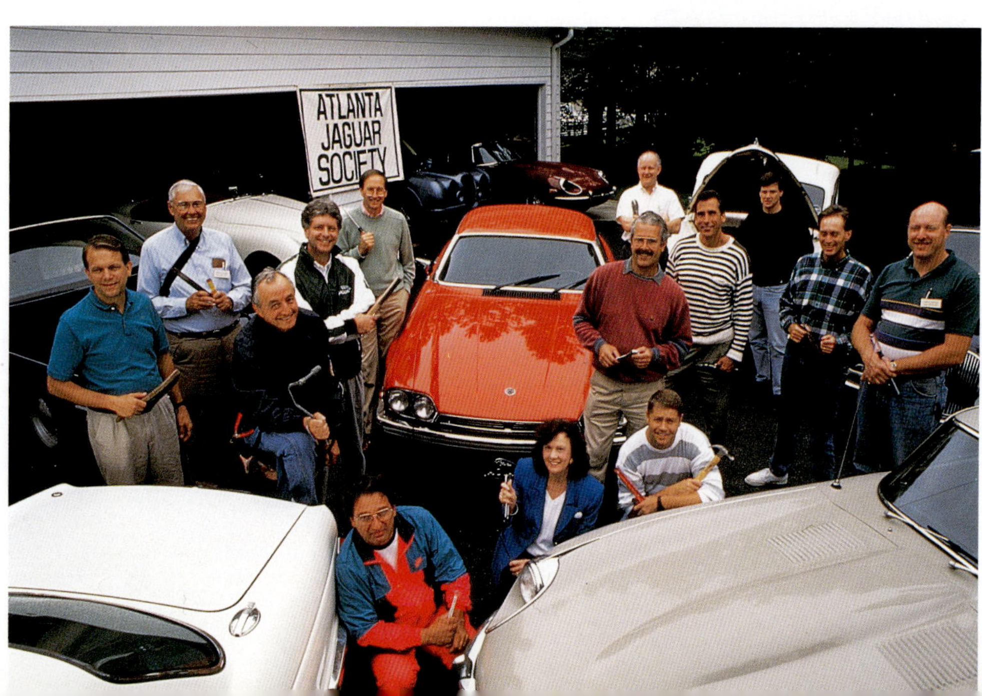

Chinese throughout the area come to Chamblee's Chinatown, a pagoda-topped complex that contains more than forty businesses and the Chinese Community Center. Inside the center today, Carolyn Schiffman, a Chinese-born teacher who is married to an American, leads a class of Chinese-American children in discussing the phonetics of the Chinese alphabet that few of the children know. "They're good students," she says. "They're learning their culture, which isn't easy. Chinese is a hard language to learn."

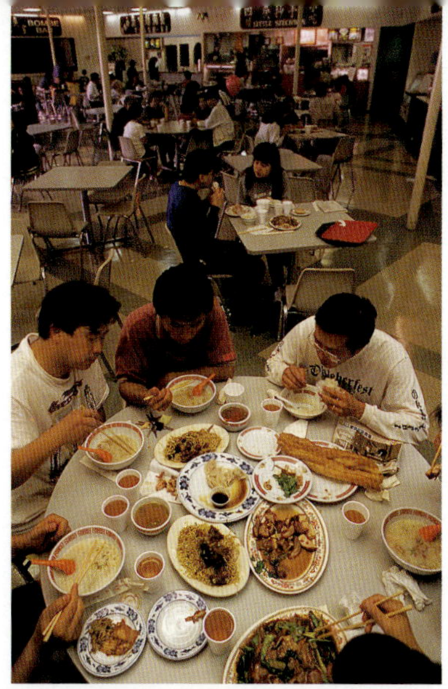

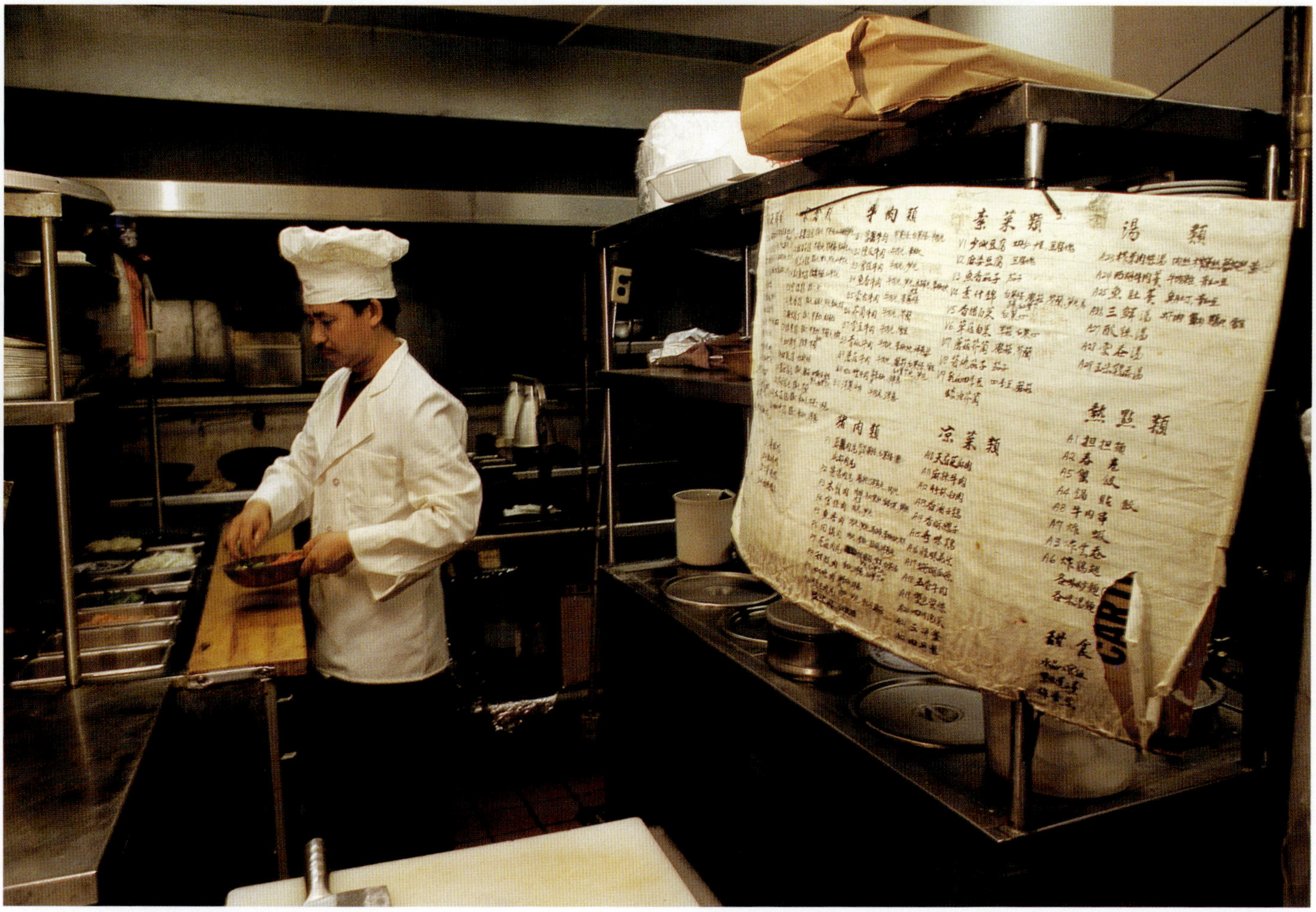

2:15 PM *Nowhere is the changing culture of DeKalb County more evident than at the Chinatown Square mall in Chamblee. Anchored by a 20,000-square-foot Chinese grocery store, the mall features twenty Asian retail stores, eight restaurants and Summit National Bank, where twelve languages are spoken in-house. Chinatown's Chinese Community Center houses amenities including Chinese language classes for American-born Chinese children. Nearby locations offer English-as-second-language classes. The Chamblee-Doraville area has become a focal point for other Asians, as well as Hispanic immigrants from every Central American country from Mexico to Panama. In these photos, Lung-Fai Wong, Le Chiem and Chee-Kiong Tan enjoy a meal in the food court, while chef Xiao Zhong Hu prepares beef with orange flavoring.*

PHOTOS BY MICHAEL SCHWARZ.

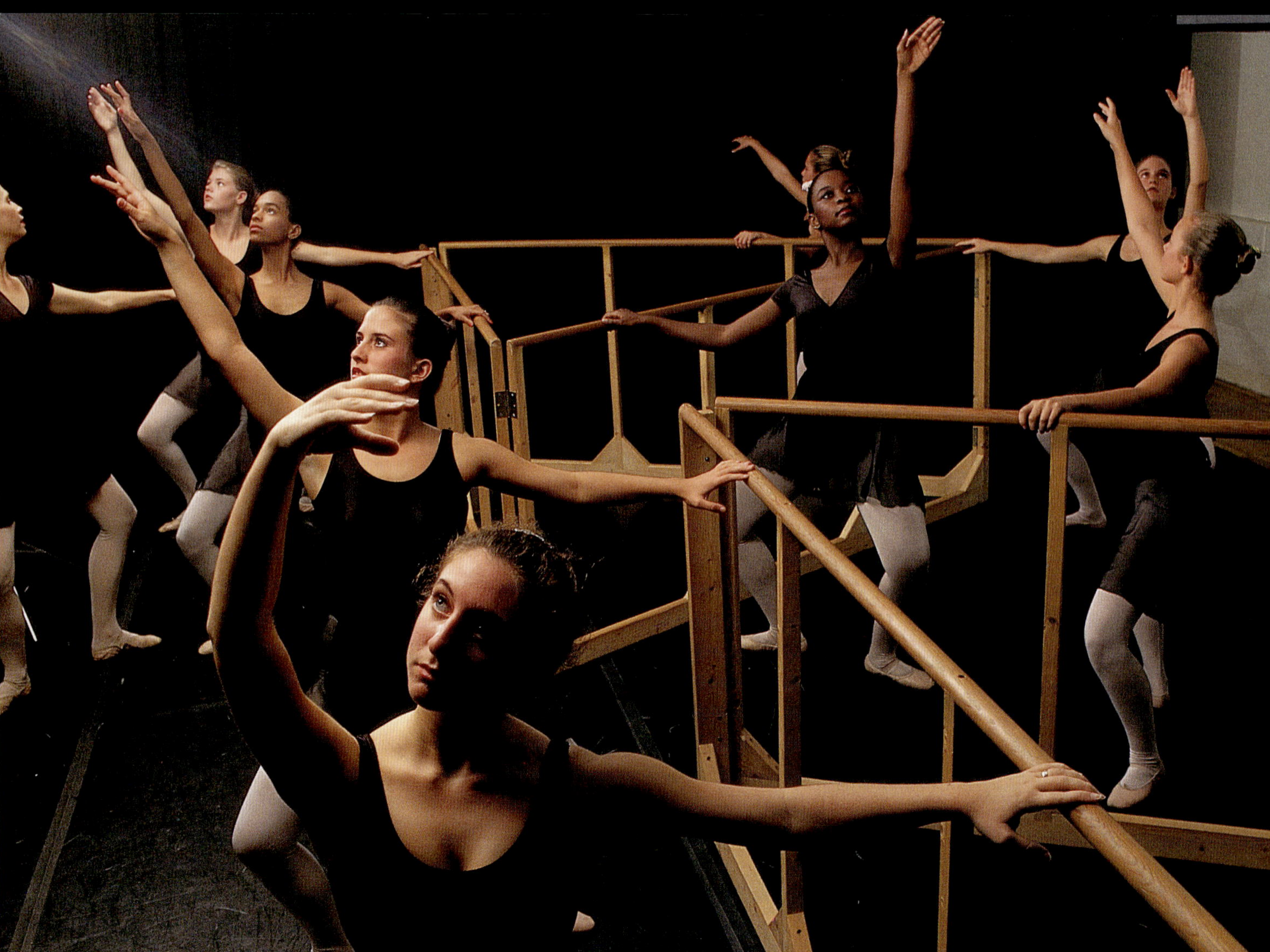

2:30 PM *"Plie, one, two, three. Lift in your abdominals. Feel the rotation. Demi arm, front and stretch. Grande plie, tendu and pour de ras. Balance. Shoulders down. More energy in your fingers, please, ladies. Pleasant faces." Eleven young girls are put through their paces at the Decatur School of Ballet. The school, housed at the Beacon Hill Arts Center, has 400 students ranging in age from three years to grandmothers.* PHOTO BY ALAN WEINER.

Dr. Mikel Richardson, with Adult Education programs at DeKalb Tech, says DeKalb has experienced a "dramatic increase in its foreign-born population over the last ten years. We're servicing about 6,800 adults a year in our English-as-second-language programs, but if you go back to 1980, there were 1,500 to 1,600 a year." And according to recent studies, 45 percent of the non-English-speaking population in the five-county region live in DeKalb.

The changing cultural and ethnic pattern in DeKalb has created some concerns for the county, but it's also led many to dream of developing an International Village here, a place where the county's ethnic groups could live and work and educate citizens and tourists alike about their different cultures. Indeed, the recently announced DeKalb Initiative will study such a village and how it might showcase DeKalb in time for the '96 Olympic Games.

With all the changes taking place in DeKalb, there's something totally predictable (dare we say rock solid?) about the granite monolith that looms two miles long and a quarter of a mile high in the eastern part of the county, where the chiseled faces of Robert E. Lee, Stonewall Jackson and Jefferson Davis stand guard over the 3,200-acre park known as Stone Mountain. Hundreds of thousands of tourists and DeKalb citizens visit here each year, while only a fraction visit another granite park that lies due south of this famous landmark. Namely, Arabia State Park.

3:15 PM *There are swim teams, and then there are the Dolphins. DeKalb County's only African-American swim team has been undefeated the last three years and at the time of this photo held seven county team records and fourteen individual records. Some of the team members include, left to right: Allana Jackson, Charles Saxon, Torrence Ford, Ayana King, Brandon Little and Carmen Sulton, and John Davis who is treading water. The team hosts meets frequently during the summer at the Brook Glen subdivision pool in South DeKalb. There are no public pools in the predominantly black area south of I-20.*
PHOTO BY SCOTT ROBINSON.

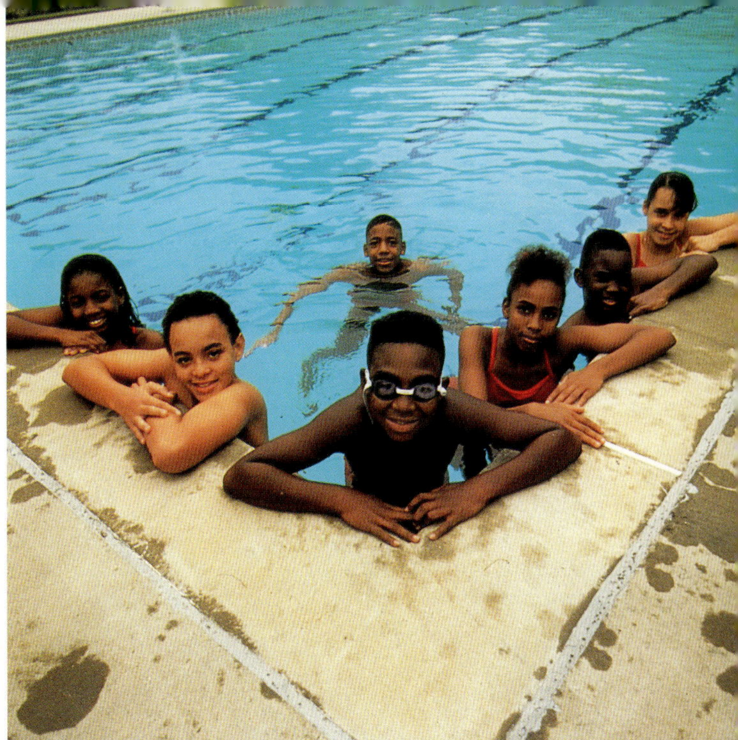

In the southeastern reaches of DeKalb, this 500-acre park surrounds a granite outcropping known as Arabia Mountain. Cut in half by Klondike Road, Arabia State Park is peaceful and empty today, the starkness of the area interrupted by clumps of Confederate daisies protruding from the granite crevices. Less than a mile into the park, Goddard Road enters from the west. Follow this road for about a mile and all quiet ends. That's the sound of gunfire at the DeKalb County Firing Range, an enclosed sixty-acre compound that is a training ground for DeKalb's 639 sworn police officers and, on Saturdays, it's open to the public.

From 3 P.M. to 11 P.M. today, Phillip S. Cunningham, the chief financial officer with Lithonia's First Southern Bank, interrupts his Saturday routine to see firsthand what the life of a DeKalb police officer must be like. For an entire shift, he rides in the patrol car with Sgt. James L. Goodrum, responding to two domestic calls, a stolen car rammed into an apartment building, a potential robbery in progress and other miscellaneous calls throughout the South Precinct. The experience—coordinated by the Chamber of Commerce's Leadership DeKalb program to give different professionals a look at each other—gives Cunningham a "new-found respect for the police profession," says the young banker, who's also a member of 100 Black Men of DeKalb County, an organization designed to provide positive role models for young black men and women. "They never know what is going to happen on a given night. There is a high level of stress, and they have to be able to deal with that. These guys go out every day and put their lives on the line."

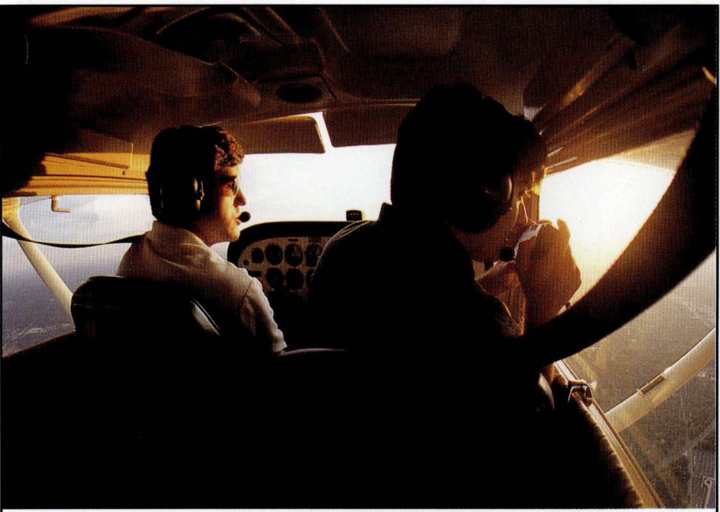

SCOTT ROBINSON

3:30 PM *With more shops than anywhere else in the Southeast, Chamblee is an antique-lover's dream come true. Nowhere else are you likely to find such treasures as lifesize Remington western figures on horseback and a bright red horsedrawn sleigh that seats four, casually packed in among the old advertising signs, bedsteads, walking canes, quilts, seventy-eight records, andirons and kitchenware. Even the buildings that house the shops are antiques, like the old Chamblee Methodist Church building, where Biggars Antiques is today.* PHOTO BY GORDON JOFFRION.

3:35 PM *The territory covered by DeKalb Police Sgt. Frederick A. Woods is as divergent as any in the Atlanta area. Posh Dunwoody residential streets, the black, low-income Lynwood Park neighborhood and Shallowford Road apartment complexes populated by Hispanic immigrants all are covered by the North DeKalb Precinct across from Perimeter Mall. The calls Sergeant Woods answers are just as varied: a check forgery by a man dressed in drag, a leaf blower stolen from a Dunwoody yard, young people breaking into a vacant apartment to have a party, shoplifting at Rich's.* PHOTO BY TOM ENGLAND.

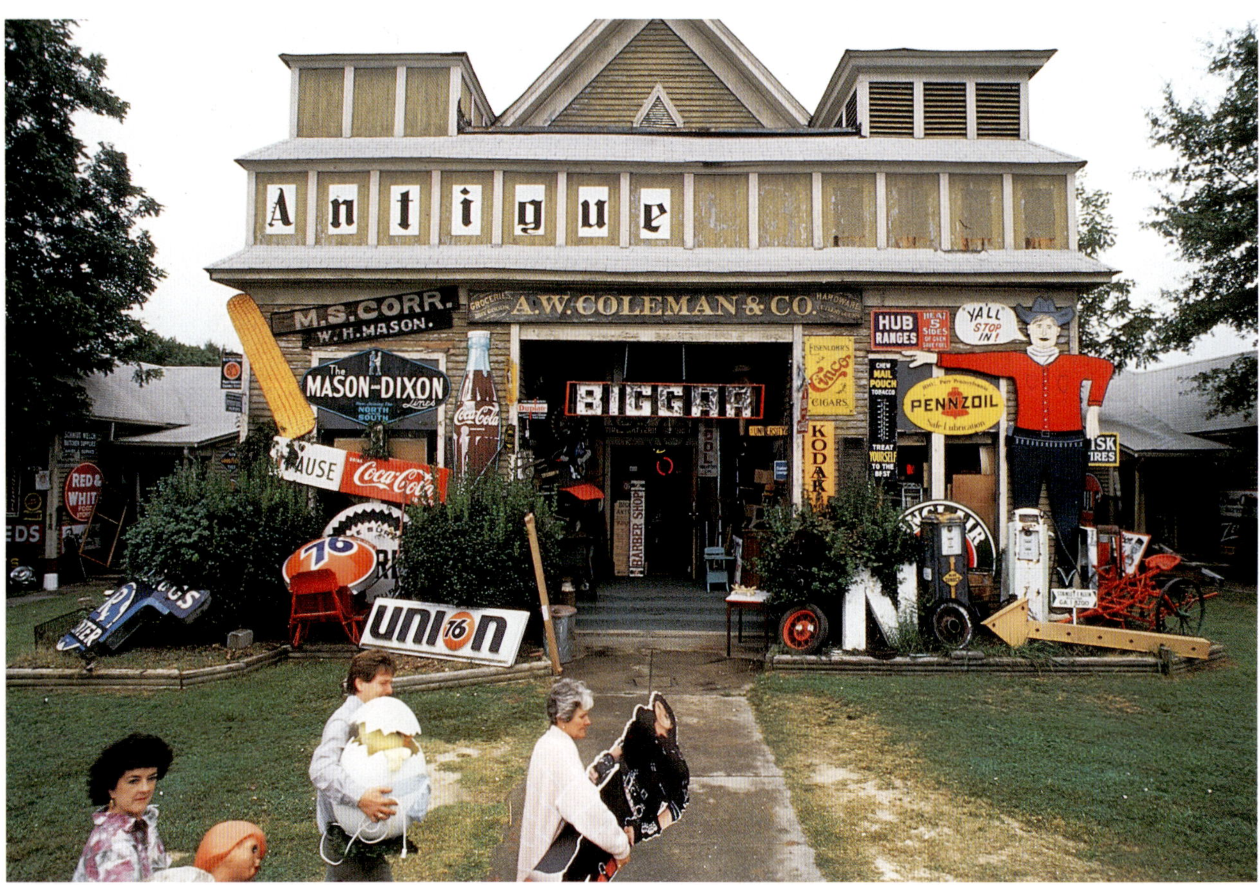

After promising her son that they'll go to a movie tonight, Donna D. Mancini slips a bit of her workweek back into her weekend. There's a meeting late this afternoon of The Friends of the Library at the Scott Candler Branch in South DeKalb, and Mancini can't resist addressing even a small crowd that's interested in libraries. As director of the DeKalb County Public Library system, she's recently completed a $33 million expansion program that doubled the number of libraries throughout the county and brought millions of books into neighborhoods that never even had libraries before. "Flat Shoals—there was no library there. Now there is!" says Mancini, holding high a report called "Focus on the Future." "But none of this will be any good if we don't have a plan for how it's all going to work. And *this* is that plan."

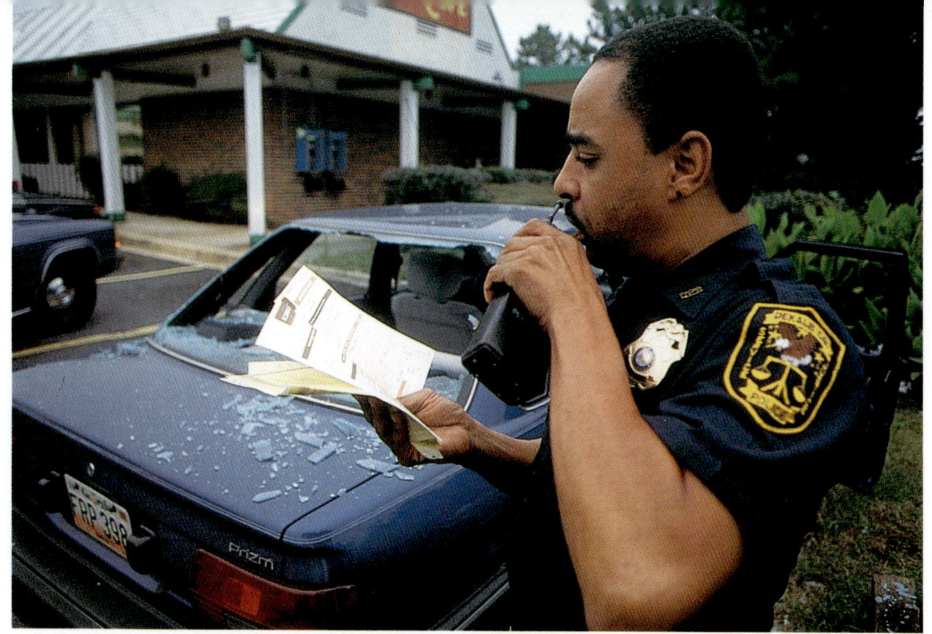

3:45 PM *John Matthews, seventy-three, began building his fire-engine red Marquart Charger biplane when he was fifty-five, and promptly made Stone Mountain a favorite destination. He is not alone, as man has been fascinated by Stone Mountain since he first set foot in what would become DeKalb County. Artifacts show that aboriginal Indians lived in the area 5,000 years ago. Their descendants, the Creek Indians used the mountain as a military outpost. Spanish explorers first marveled at the sight in the sixteenth century. Aaron Cloud, who built a tower atop the mountain in 1838, was the first to realize the mountain's potential as a tourist attraction. And religious ceremonies have been conducted on the mountaintop for 200 years—from Indian ceremonies to Christian Easter sunrise services.* PHOTO BY KEN HAWKINS.

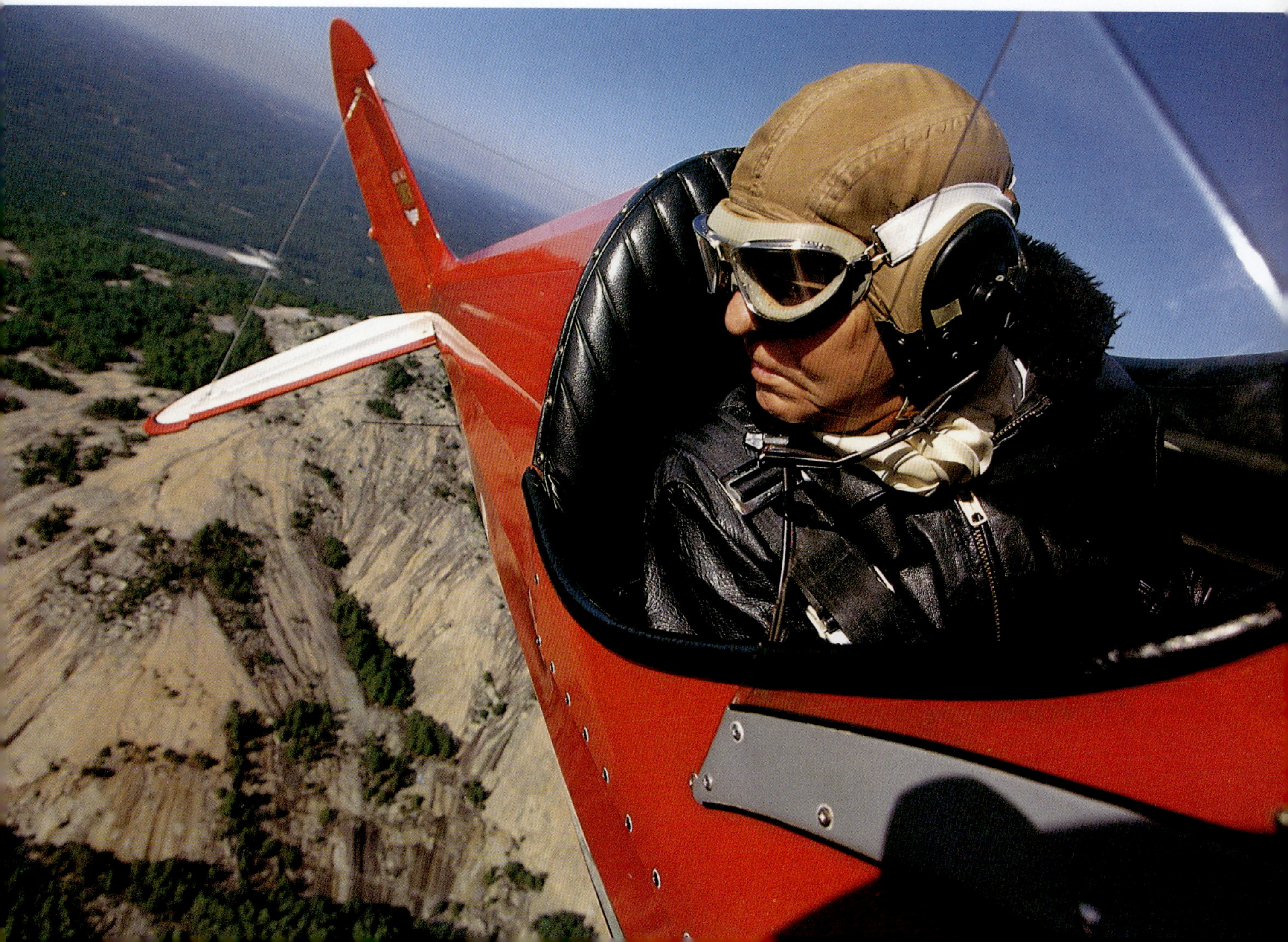

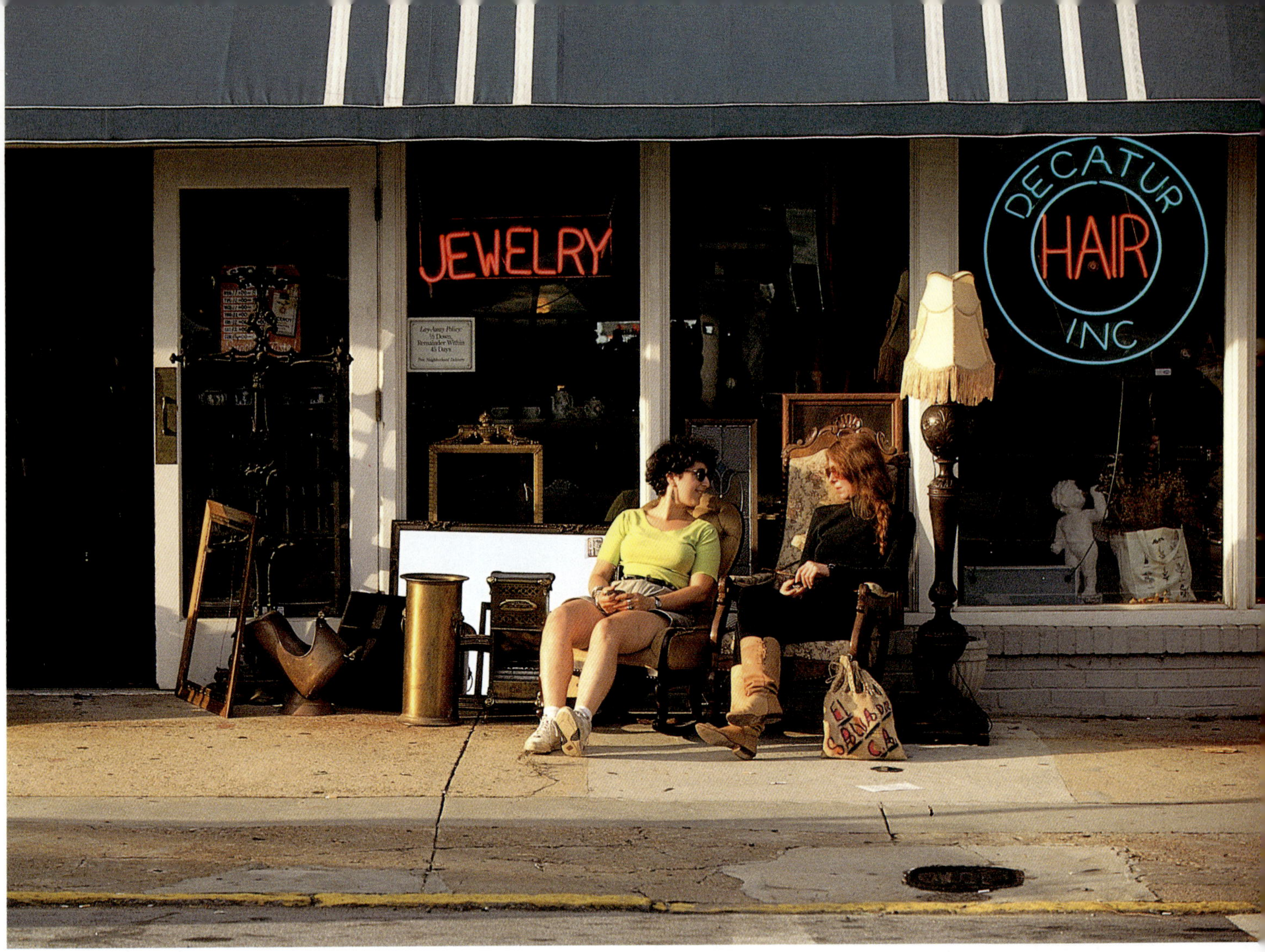

3:50 PM *"I just love Decatur," says Lisa Cohen. "It's a great place to do business, to socialize and to live." Lisa's shop, The Family Jewels, is one of many lining the Square in Decatur that specialize in what Lisa calls "neat stuff." A leisurely afternoon of shopping in Decatur can yield such unusual treasures as a bronze lamp in the shape of a languid cat, an antique violin, an eight-foot-tall tree fern, a Beatrix Potter doll and an autographed copy of a local author's book.* PHOTO BY SCOTT ROBINSON.

4:02 PM *For most of DeKalb's working citizens, Saturday is a day spent running errands. You drive to the grocery store, to the dry cleaners, to the hardware store and the pharmacy. You indulge yourself with a frozen yogurt along the way. And sooner or later, it's inevitable, you will spend a Saturday getting tires put on your car.* PHOTO BY ALAN WEINER.

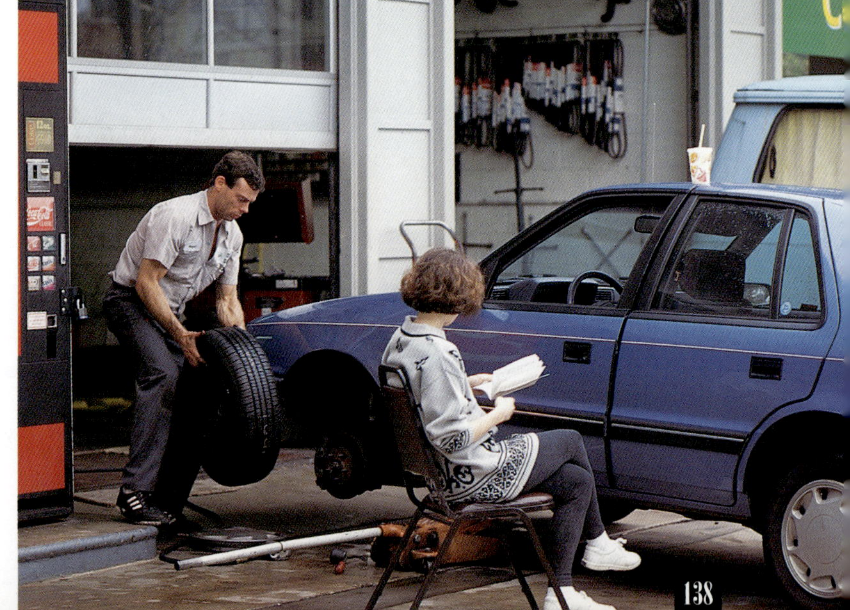

4:20 PM *DeKalb County has its own "field of dreams" in the forty-seven-acre Softball Country Club in Scottdale. The best facility of its kind in the state, the Softball Country Club annually hosts the Flag City Shootout, the largest softball tournament in the world. With its manicured fields, clubhouse, covered bleachers and pro shop, the Softball Country Club could pass for a major-league spring training complex.* PHOTO BY ROB NELSON.

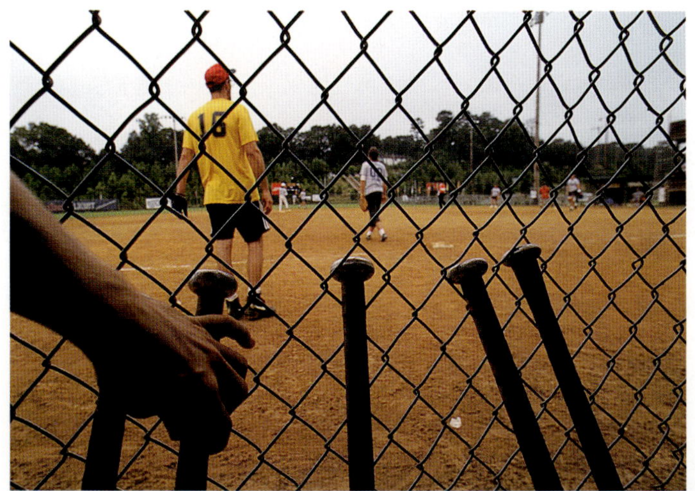

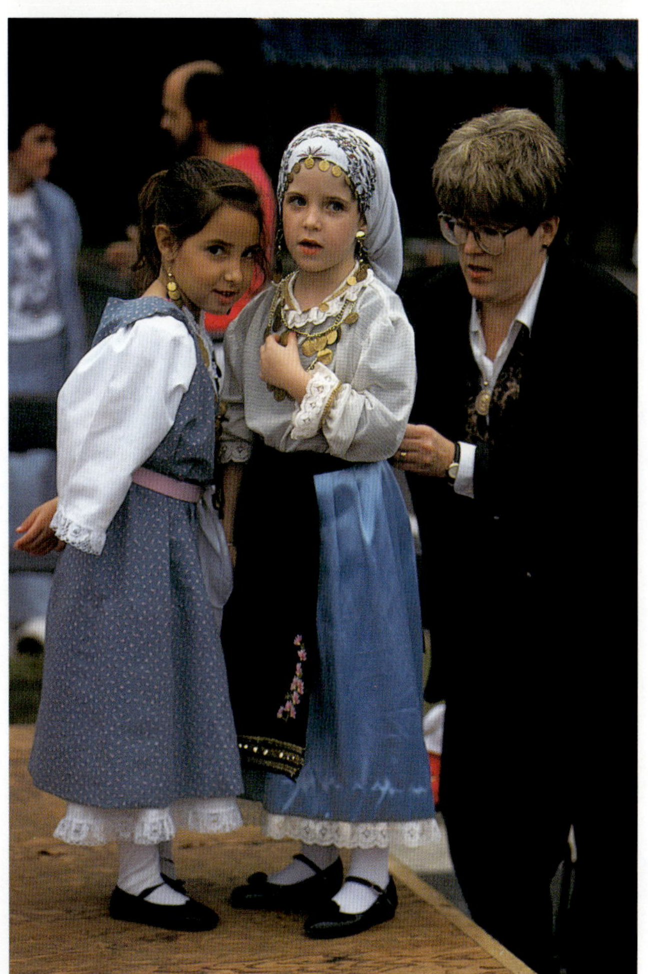

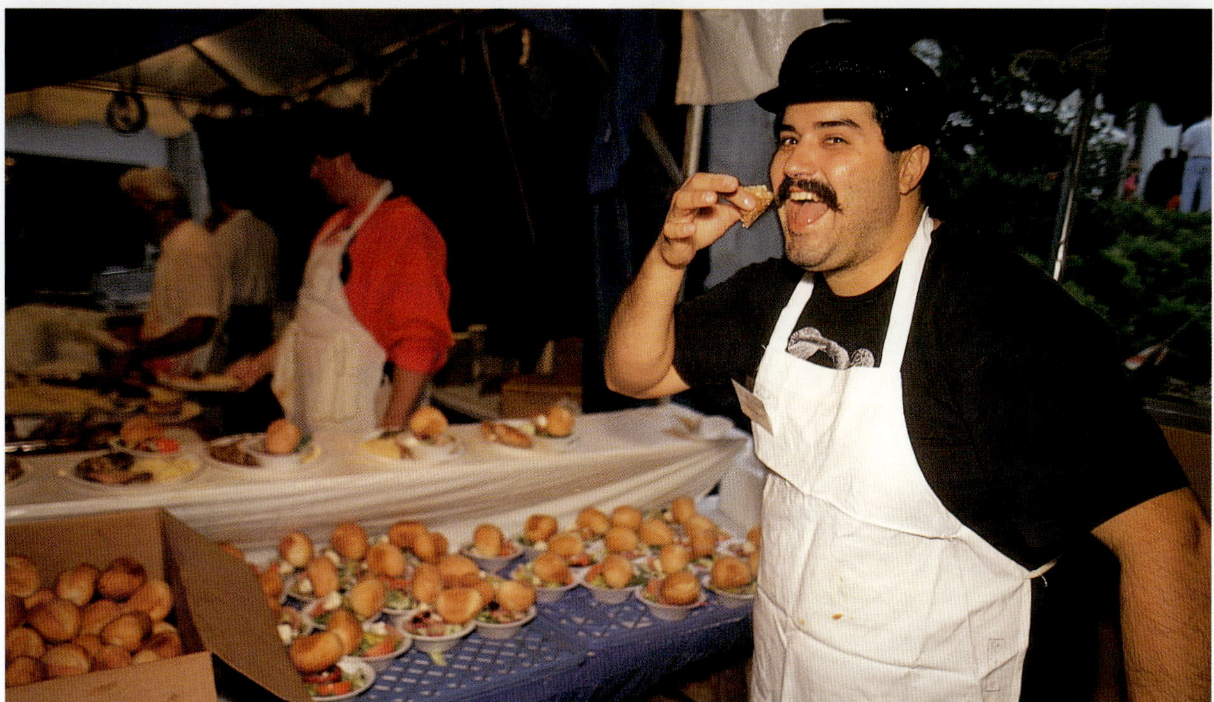

5:45 PM *"Opa!" is the traditional greeting in DeKalb County during Greek Festival days. The four-day event is DeKalb's largest festival, drawing as many as 40,000 visitors to the Greek Orthodox Cathedral on Clairmont Road. For seven months, 1,000 volunteers get ready; many are church women who handmake the mouthwatering Greek pastries like baklava, a honey-drenched triangle of layered phyllo dough and walnuts. Visitors are treated to dinners of fragrant lamb roasted outdoors in earthen pits, exuberant dancing and singing, displays of handicrafts and tours of the church sanctuary with its spectacular religious mosaics.* PHOTOS BY DAVID MURRAY.

6:00 PM *A single picture fails to tell the entire story of John and Mary Huntz's departure for the Garden of Eden benefit ball at the Atlanta Botanical Garden. The Huntzes daughter, Megan, was the first to request a photo of her elegantly dressed parents at their home near Emory University. Photographer Ken Hawkins took this picture of Megan taking a picture of her parents. WGNX-TV cameramen took a picture of Hawkins taking a picture of Megan taking a picture of her parents. The WGNX footage was part of a news segment on the shooting of 7 Days in DeKalb.* Photo by Ken Hawkins.

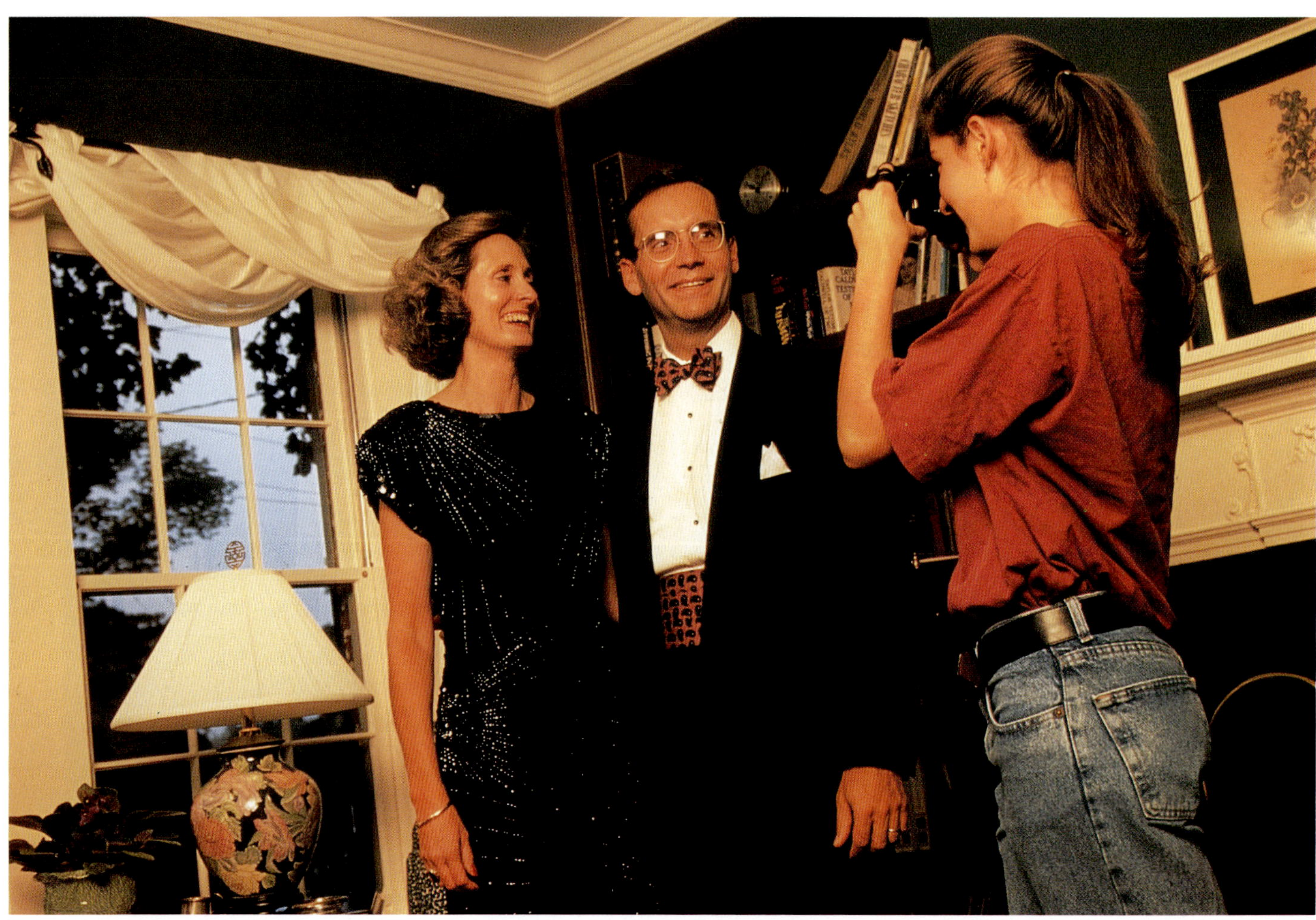

The elements of past, present and future intermingle in Decatur tonight as a lacy, wet mist slips in over the town's historic center Square, just before dark. In front of the Old Courthouse, potential donors to the courthouse renovation campaign are courted with candlelight, wine, and pink and beige dinner baskets filled with crudities, spicy mango mayonnaise, Greek chicken in pita bread and luscious desserts from Lisa Turner's Hawthorne Cottage Tea Room. Across the Square, there's the promise of music as the Bill Patton "Big Chill" Band prepares for its last Big Chill concert of the season. Oblivious to the night's dark clouds, slowly, into the Square, they come—families with fried chicken picnics, babies asleep in strollers, couples with silver candlesticks and carafes of Chablis. But before the music starts, Evelyn Menne, executive director of the Decatur Downtown Development Authority, and Mayor Mike Mears, have an announcement to make. That hideous MARTA bubble, long a design thorn in the sides of those who love the otherwise picturesque Square will soon be replaced by a Victorian-era bandstand. Everyone cheers!

Which reminds us. Today, just an ordinary Saturday for thousands in DeKalb, was a very special day for Lisa Coleworthy and Loren Burke. It's their wedding day. Congratulations, folks.

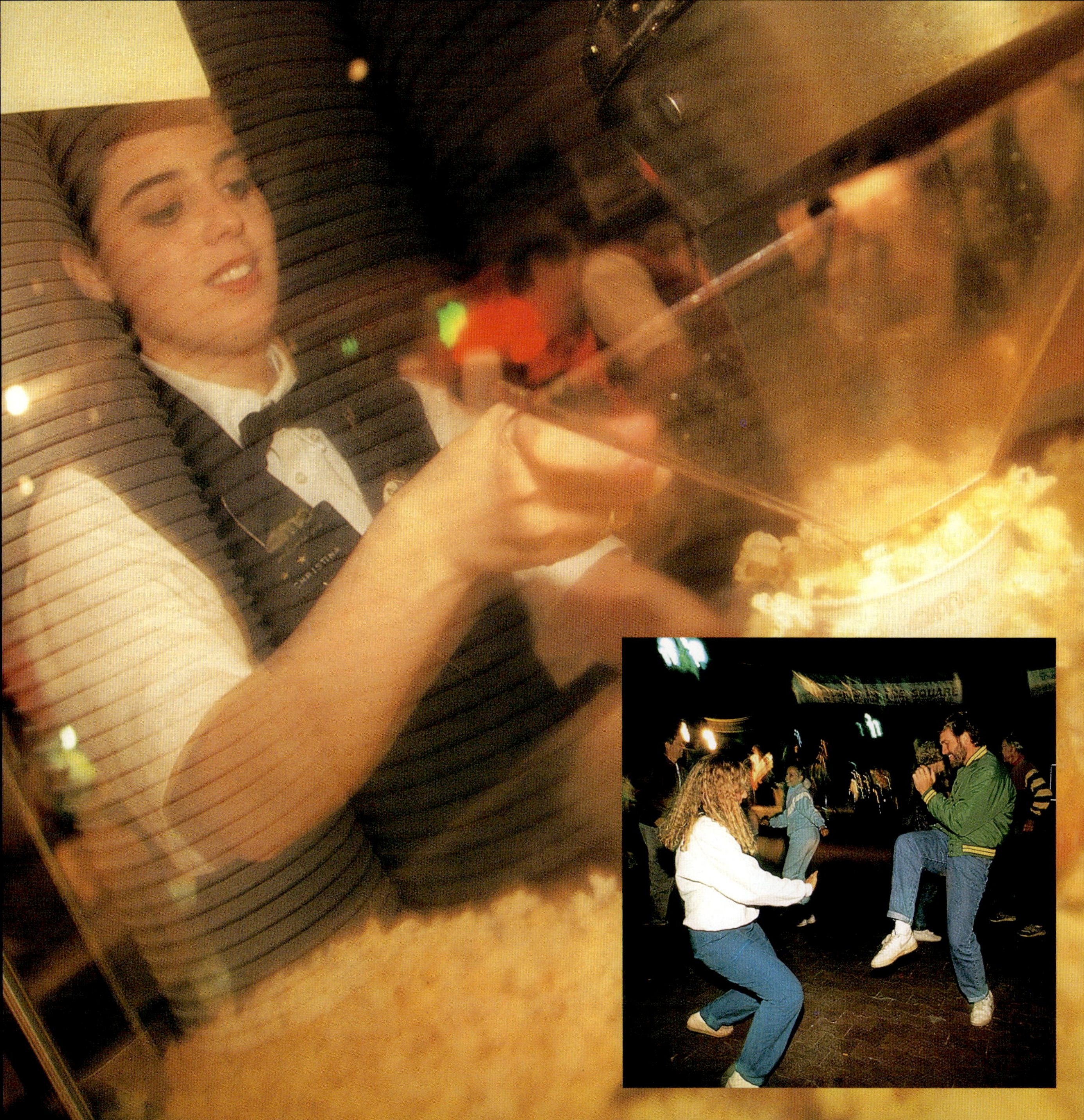

7:30 PM *Some things—like Saturday night at the movies—haven't changed in generations. If you were going to the Northlake Festival Theaters on the last Saturday night in September, chances were you saw Whoopi Goldberg. She was the only film star in two movies that week: Sister Act and Sarafina, the dramatic story of a black South African girl. Also playing were Honeymoon in Vegas, Last of the Mohicans, Innocent Blood, Husbands and Wives, Captain Ron and School Ties. And Christina Rinaldi was there to serve them all popcorn.*
PHOTO BY KEN HAWKINS.

9:25 PM *Just as the bandstand in the park in years gone by was the neighborhood gathering place so has the Square in Decatur become DeKalb's primary location for community activities. The Big Chill Concert invited all-comers to dance to nostalgic tunes from the '50s, '60s and '70s played by the Bill Patton Band. The lawn around the Old Courthouse is the site of lunchtime, evening and weekend concerts during warm-weather months, as well as the springtime Decatur Beach Party and the Fourth of July celebration.* PHOTO BY ROB NELSON.

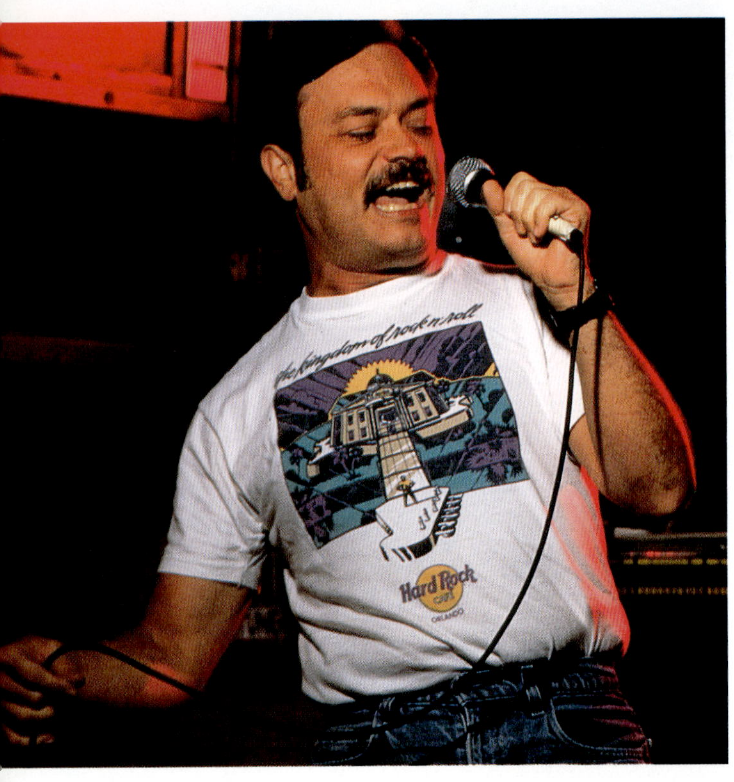

10:37 PM *Singers heretofore confined to the shower become momentary stars on karaoke night at Billy's restaurant in Decatur. Normally reserved, would-be entertainers take to the stage, microphone in hand, and sing along with their favorite music videos in front of a roomful of other restaurant patrons. "New York, New York," "Crazy" and "It's Now or Never" are said to be Atlanta's top karaoke songs. The songs have one thing in common: the singers who originally made them famous are not around to witness the spectacle.*

Photo by Michael Schwarz.

11:55 PM *Texas has nothing on DeKalb when it comes to big. Mama's Country Showcase on Covington Highway is Atlanta's biggest nightspot, with ten bars dispensing 350 cases of beer every week and all presided over by Reba McEntire, Travis Tritt, Alan Jackson and Garth Brooks, who peer down from a seventy-foot-long mural.*

Photo by Scott Robinson.

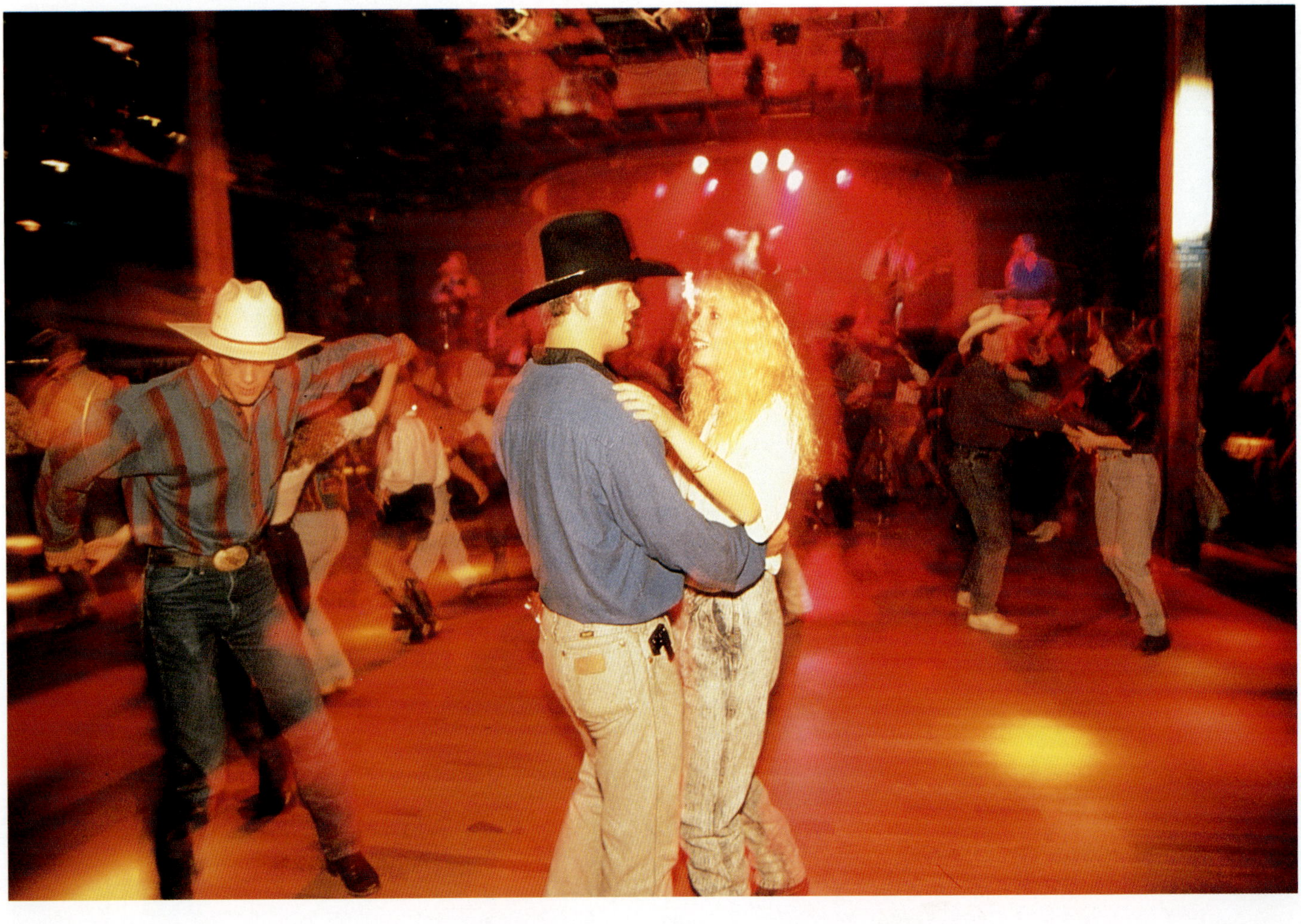

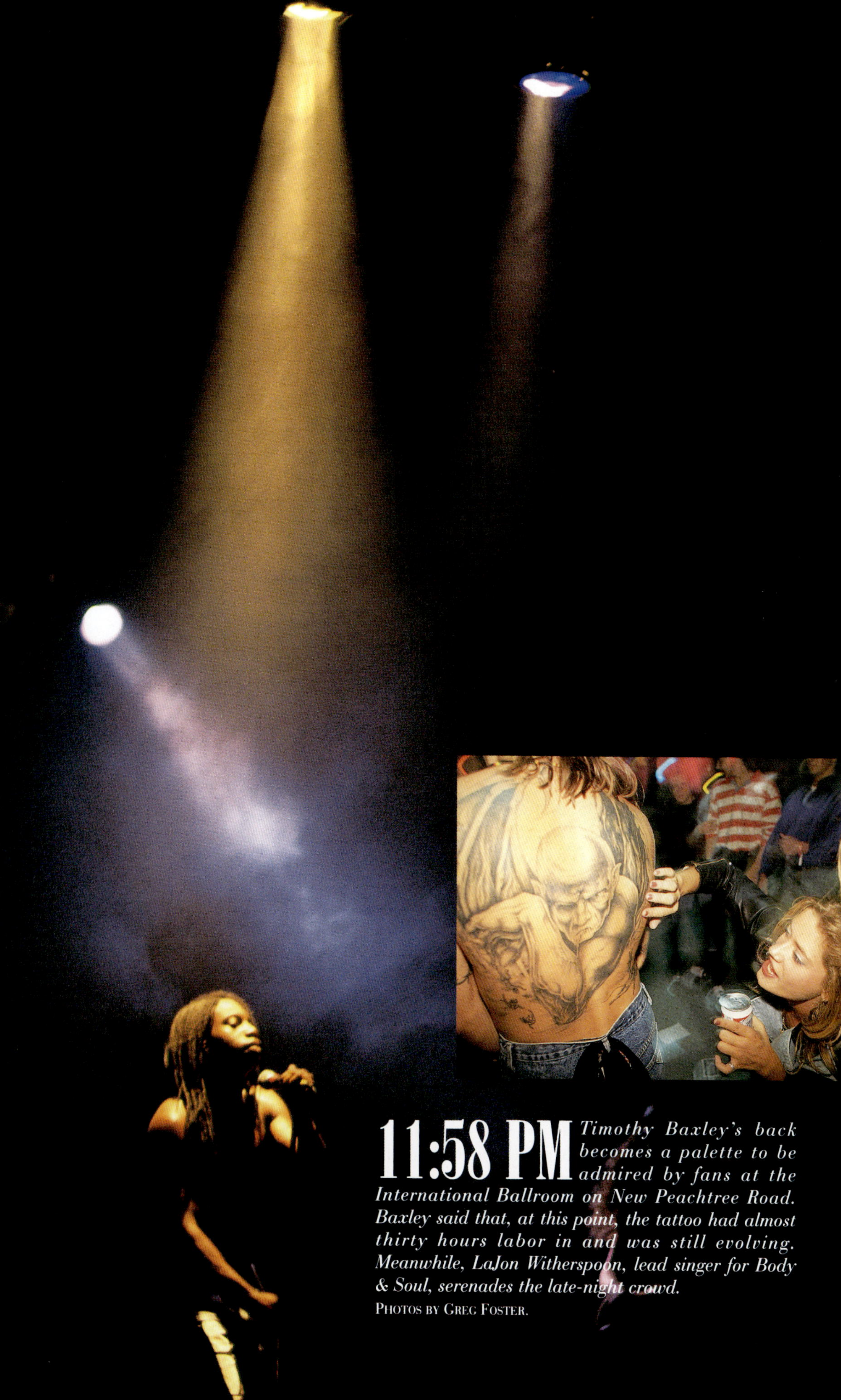

11:58 PM *Timothy Baxley's back becomes a palette to be admired by fans at the International Ballroom on New Peachtree Road. Baxley said that, at this point, the tattoo had almost thirty hours labor in and was still evolving. Meanwhile, LaJon Witherspoon, lead singer for Body & Soul, serenades the late-night crowd.*

PHOTOS BY GREG FOSTER.

Taylor & Mathis is one of the largest developers of top quality high-rise office buildings, office parks and mixed-used communities in the United States, including the award-winning Perimeter Center in DeKalb County. Since 1972, Taylor & Mathis has enjoyed a close association with Metropolitan Life Insurance Company, which is one of the world's largest financial services organizations, with nearly $25 billion invested in real estate throughout the country. The unique aspects of these two companies and their close association were discussed frankly by C. Mack Taylor, chairman of Taylor & Mathis, and William A. Worthington, assistant vice-president and regional manager, Atlanta office, Metropolitan Life. ◆ Mr. Taylor: "Perimeter Center is certainly our cornerstone, the most important project completed by Taylor & Mathis to date. But I want to be fair. When we started Perimeter Center, Harvey Mathis and myself were partners with Mike Gearon in the Gearon Company. The initial land acquisition and the initial buildings out here were done under the Gearon Company. In 1972, we purchased Gearon's interests, and at that point the company became Taylor & Mathis. ◆ "Perimeter Center has 400 acres of offices, shopping, professional services and entertainment. The Terraces, which is part of Perimeter Center North, is probably the finest thing we've built. It's big, it's innovative — with a lake, a suspension bridge connecting the two buildings, with ten-story high atriums. ◆ "When we began Perimeter Center, Interstate 285 was not completed. But we knew the highway was going to create an explosively growing place due to the incredible access it would provide to DeKalb and Cobb counties. We felt that the Perimeter area would be the place of the future, in terms of where companies would want to locate their offices. ◆ "Without Met, I don't think we could have built all of this. They are visionary people. They are astute real estate people. They have been a great partner, a help to us other than a tremendous financial power. We have learned a lot from them." ◆ Mr. Worthington: "Met Life has enjoyed a tremendous relationship with Taylor & Mathis. They are jointly involved with us in the management, leasing or ownership of projects throughout the Southeast. And while we hire the best people in the industry to help us with our real estate assets, I do believe that it's true and safe in saying that there is not another company that we rely on more than Taylor & Mathis. We have a quote: Some may equal, but none excel. I feel safe in saying that about Taylor & Mathis. ◆ "They (Taylor & Mathis) are truly experts in the real estate industry. They have the finest professionals in the industry working for them. They understand clearly who the clients are. I have had people in my office who ask for my opinion about business. My recommendation is that they get to know whoever they can within Taylor & Mathis. They recognize that you can't have weak links in the organization." ◆ Mr. Taylor: "The loss of Harvey Mathis was terrible. I don't think this company would be a shadow of what it is today without Harvey's participation all those years. He was a wonderful businessman, and we still miss him. But a lot of our top young people were trained by him and that had a lot to do with their development. He left a legacy beyond his name to this company. We still feel his presence." ◆ Mr. Worthington: "Harvey used to tell me that you don't have a very solid organization if it can't run without you. I think the biggest testament to Harvey Mathis and Mack Taylor is that when Harvey died suddenly, they lost an extremely valuable asset to the organization, and yet the organization skipped a half a beat the day he was buried but that was all."

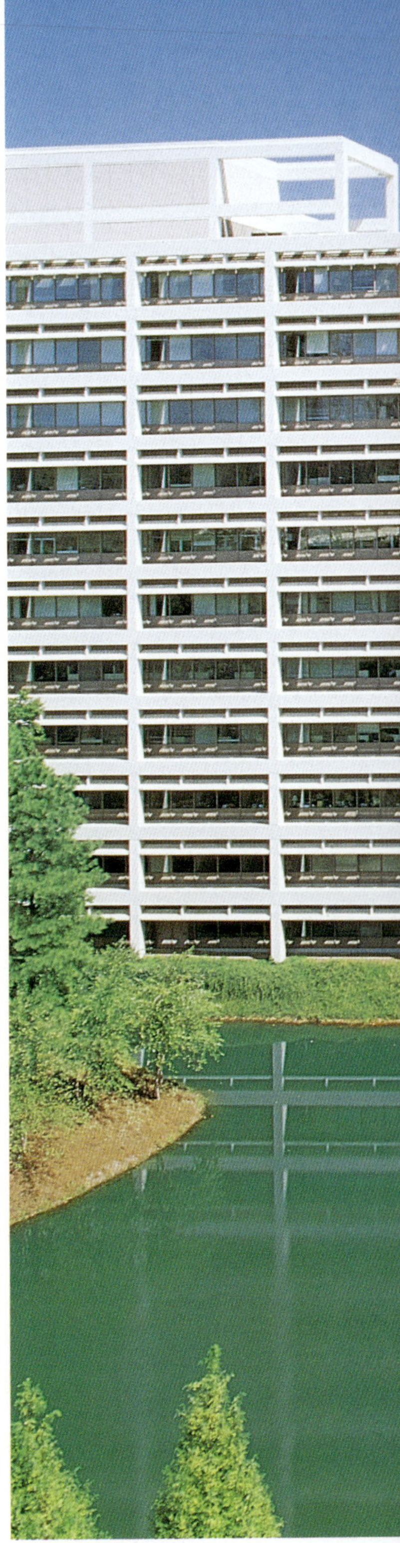

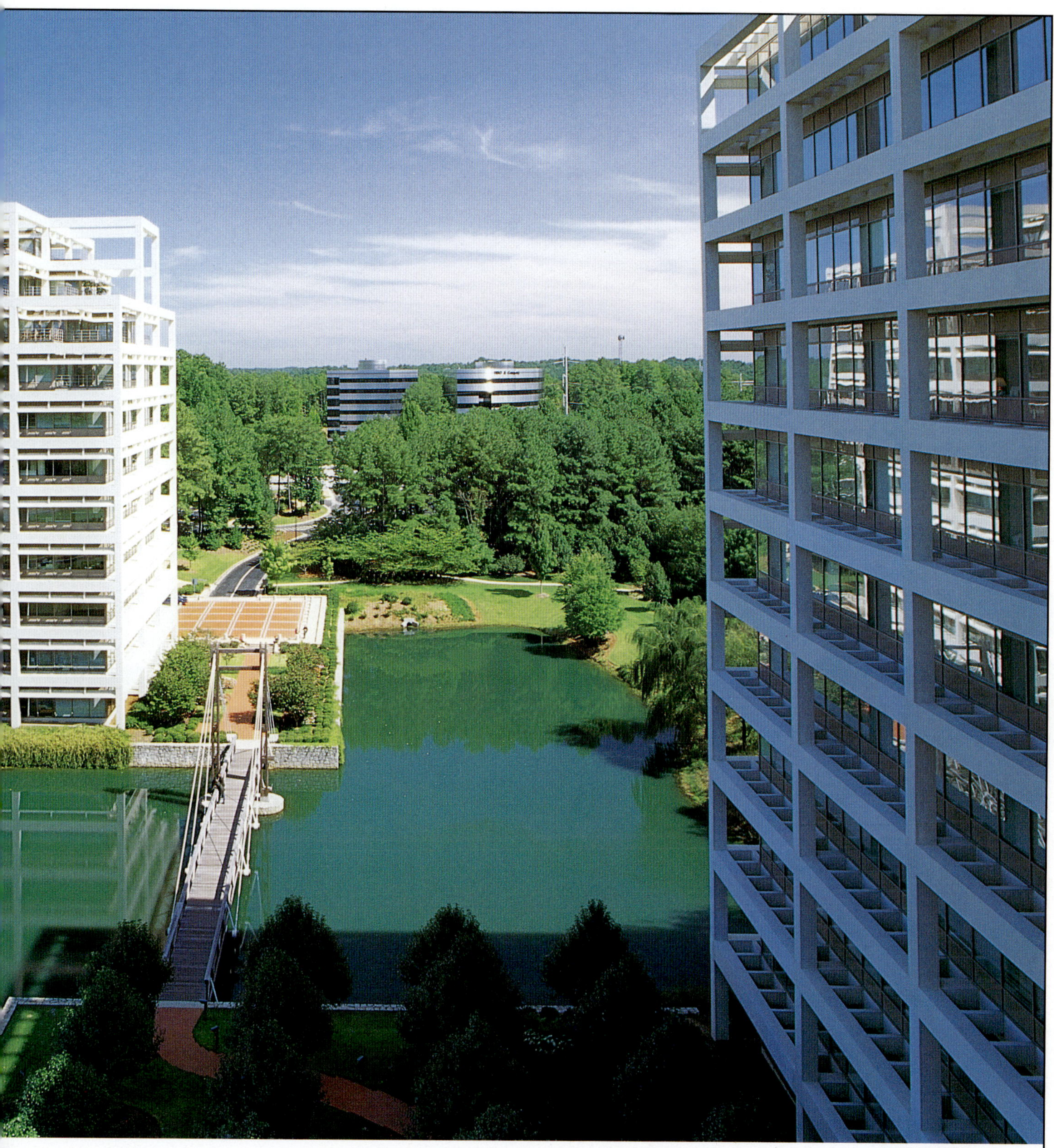

SCOTT ROBINSON

TAYLOR & MATHIS

Atlanta, Georgia

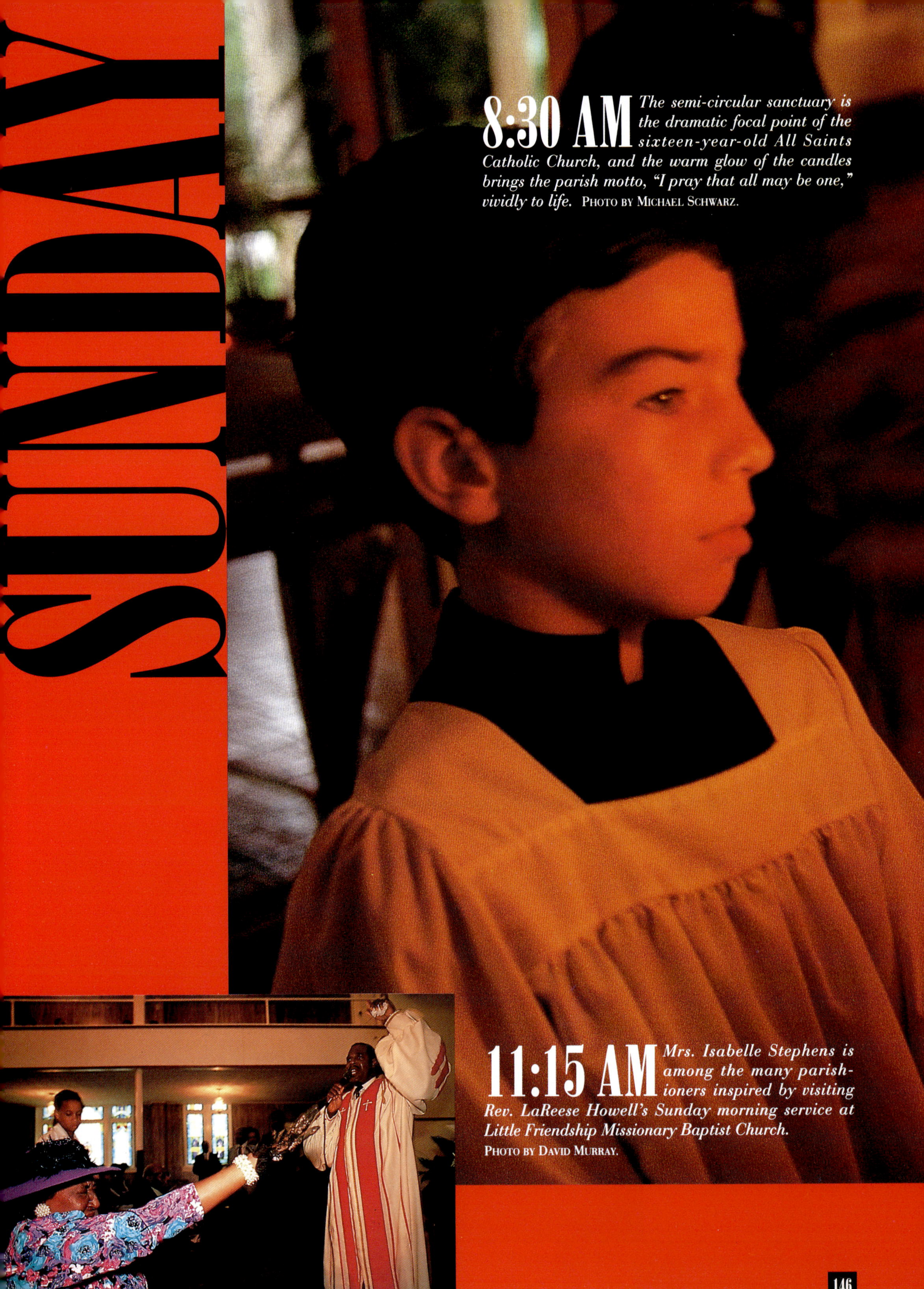

8:30 AM *The semi-circular sanctuary is the dramatic focal point of the sixteen-year-old All Saints Catholic Church, and the warm glow of the candles brings the parish motto, "I pray that all may be one," vividly to life.* PHOTO BY MICHAEL SCHWARZ.

11:15 AM *Mrs. Isabelle Stephens is among the many parishioners inspired by visiting Rev. LaReese Howell's Sunday morning service at Little Friendship Missionary Baptist Church.* PHOTO BY DAVID MURRAY.

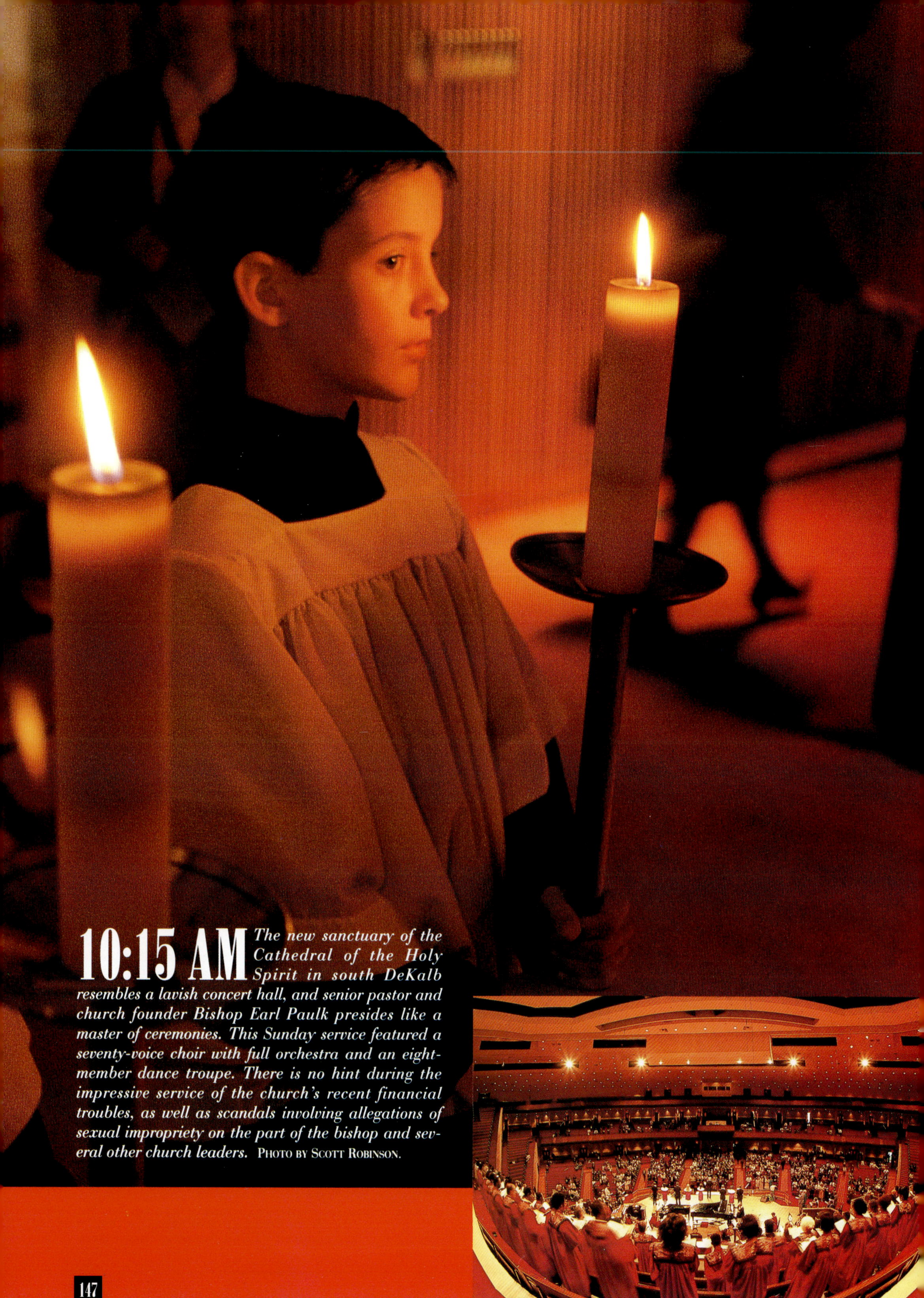

10:15 AM *The new sanctuary of the Cathedral of the Holy Spirit in south DeKalb resembles a lavish concert hall, and senior pastor and church founder Bishop Earl Paulk presides like a master of ceremonies. This Sunday service featured a seventy-voice choir with full orchestra and an eight-member dance troupe. There is no hint during the impressive service of the church's recent financial troubles, as well as scandals involving allegations of sexual impropriety on the part of the bishop and several other church leaders.* PHOTO BY SCOTT ROBINSON.

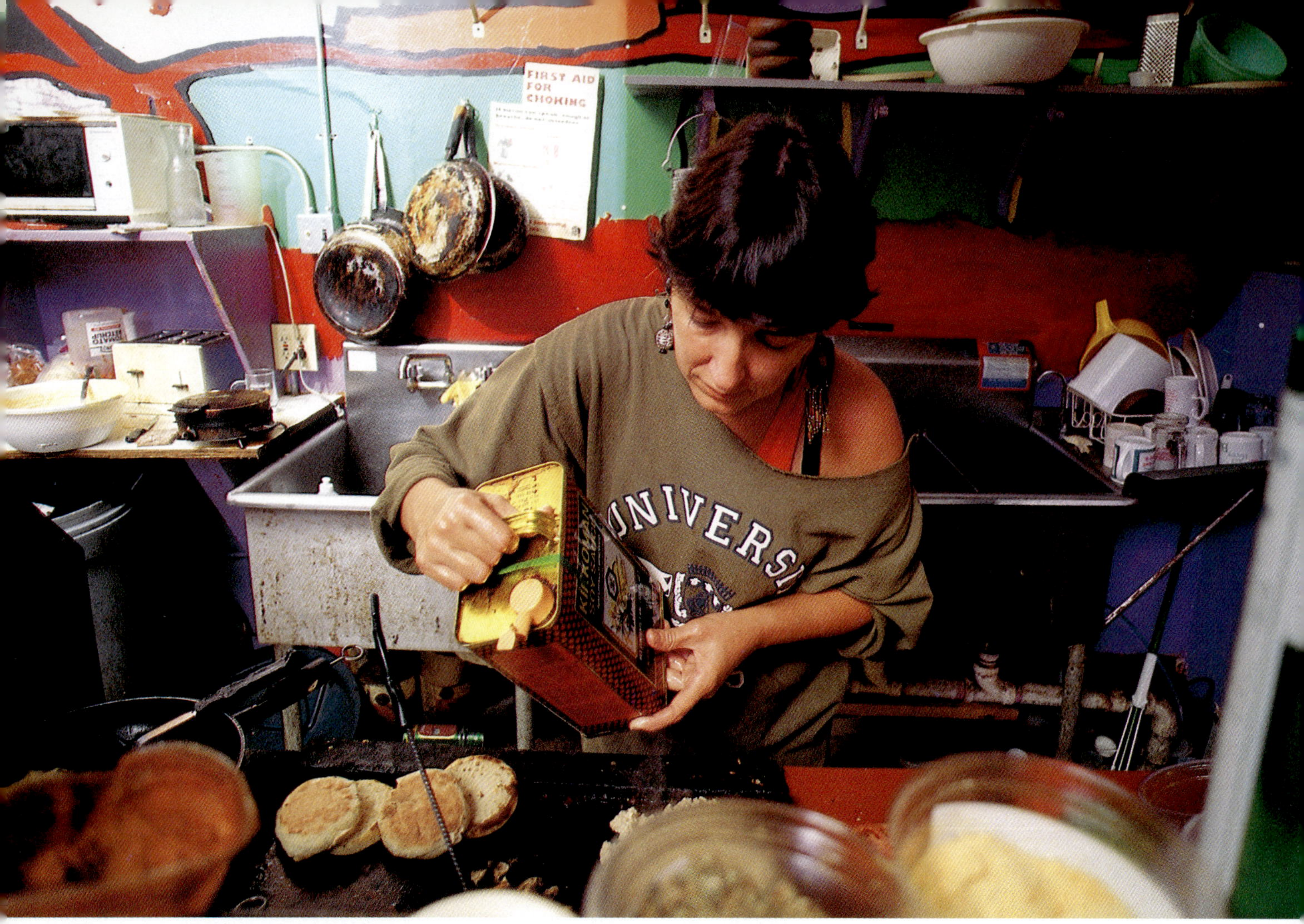

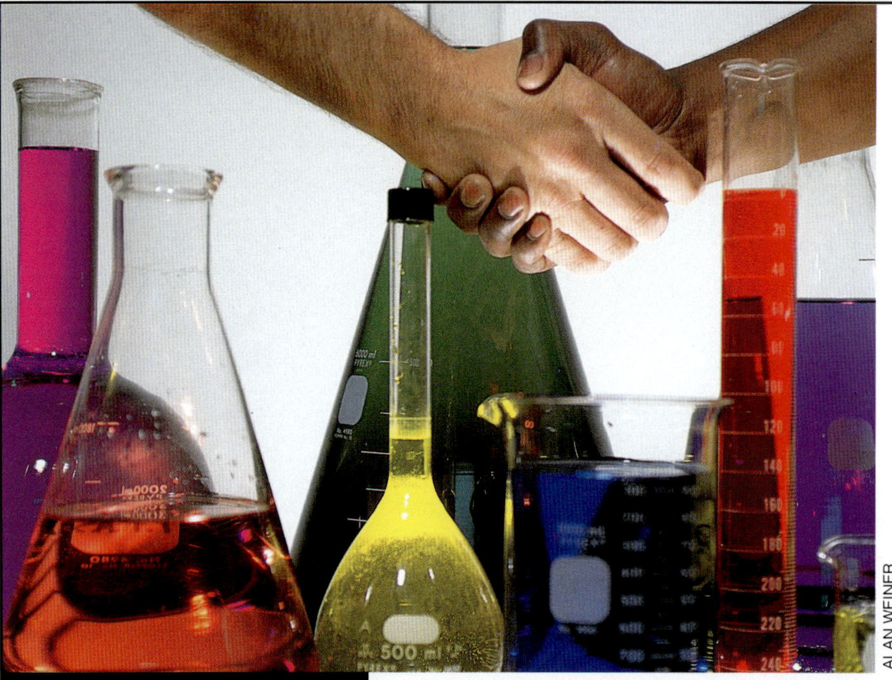

ALAN WEINER

GEORGIA BIOMEDICAL PARTNERSHIP, INC.

A nonprofit organization designed to promote Georgia's Biomedical Industry and Resources

The genesis for the Georgia Biomedical Partnership began when the American Cancer Society decided to relocate to the Atlanta area. The people who were successful in that recruitment process realized what tremendous resources Georgia offered as a center for biomedical research, development, manufacturing and related industry—and we were chartered in November 1989. ◆ "And while there are eighty-six biotech-related centers in the United States, this one is unique. Our partnership, which has over 150 members with combined research budgets over $1 billion, combines a major federal laboratory, public and private research universities, and the corporate and government communities working together for the common purpose to develop the biomedical R and D industry in Georgia. ◆ "Our services are diverse: technology transfer, resource marketing and economic development, biomedical networking, and public information. And in addition to the state's positive economic environment, we offer supportive, pro-business government and a moderate cost of living and doing business. ◆ "In a very short time, we have become the biomedical industry's catalyst—the vital link among businesses, academic and government sectors throughout the state. And some of the strongest assets of our partnership are institutions based in DeKalb County. To name a few, the American Cancer Society, The Centers for Disease Control, Emory University and related medical schools, hospitals and clinics, Yerkes Regional Primate Research Center and Wesley Woods Geriatric Center. ◆ "Georgia and DeKalb County have all the assets necessary to support individual companies within the biomedical industry. Our job is to make sure that this burgeoning industry recognizes the unique and powerful mix of biomedical resources our area has to offer."

— R. Eric Greene, Partnership Executive Director
Director of CDC's Technology Transfer Office

Sunday in DeKalb begins with a promise of renewal and the guarantee of redemption. But like a Sunday anywhere in the South, politics and fried chicken are sure things, as well.

From her pew inside Decatur First United Methodist Church, Mrs. Ouida Allison holds her breath as Senior Minister Rev. Bill Edwards mentions politics. She's afraid his sermon might venture into the proposed lottery, which she opposes, and she's relieved when it doesn't. "Besides," she thinks to herself, "the United Methodist Women will surely bring it up at their meeting Tuesday."

Four women and three men receive a spiritual baptism at the Atlanta Unity Church on Chamblee-Dunwoody Road, but there's no water, no hallelujahs. Instead, Minister Albert Wingate exhorts the candidates three times to "receive ye the Holy Spirit."

11:30 AM *Sylvia Cross describes her Atomic Cafe as "beyond the parameters of normal." The tiny cafe in Candler Park caters to an offbeat crowd with early morning and late night breakfasts, "bizarre" dinners, local musicians, storytelling, puppetry and parties, sometimes for special people like the woman who decorated the cafe bathroom and sometimes for special causes, like raising money for someone's home down payment. Sylvia's menu ranges from an Atomic variation on Eggs Benedict called "Eggsplosion" to heavenly fruit pancakes to tofu burritos. Decor ranges mismatched tablecloths to a mural of an "abstracted bird-egg thing."*

Photo by Gordon Joffrion.

11:40 AM *The Druid Hills Golf Club is more than a place to play eighteen holes. It is one of only a handful of clubs in the city where generations of the same families go to maintain the traditions of genteel life in old Atlanta. The Sunday brunch menu at the venerable, eighty-year-old club consists of roast beef—being served here by Shari Bernecky—fried chicken, blackeyed peas, coleslaw, macaroni and cheese and plenty of iced tea.*

Photo by Greg Foster.

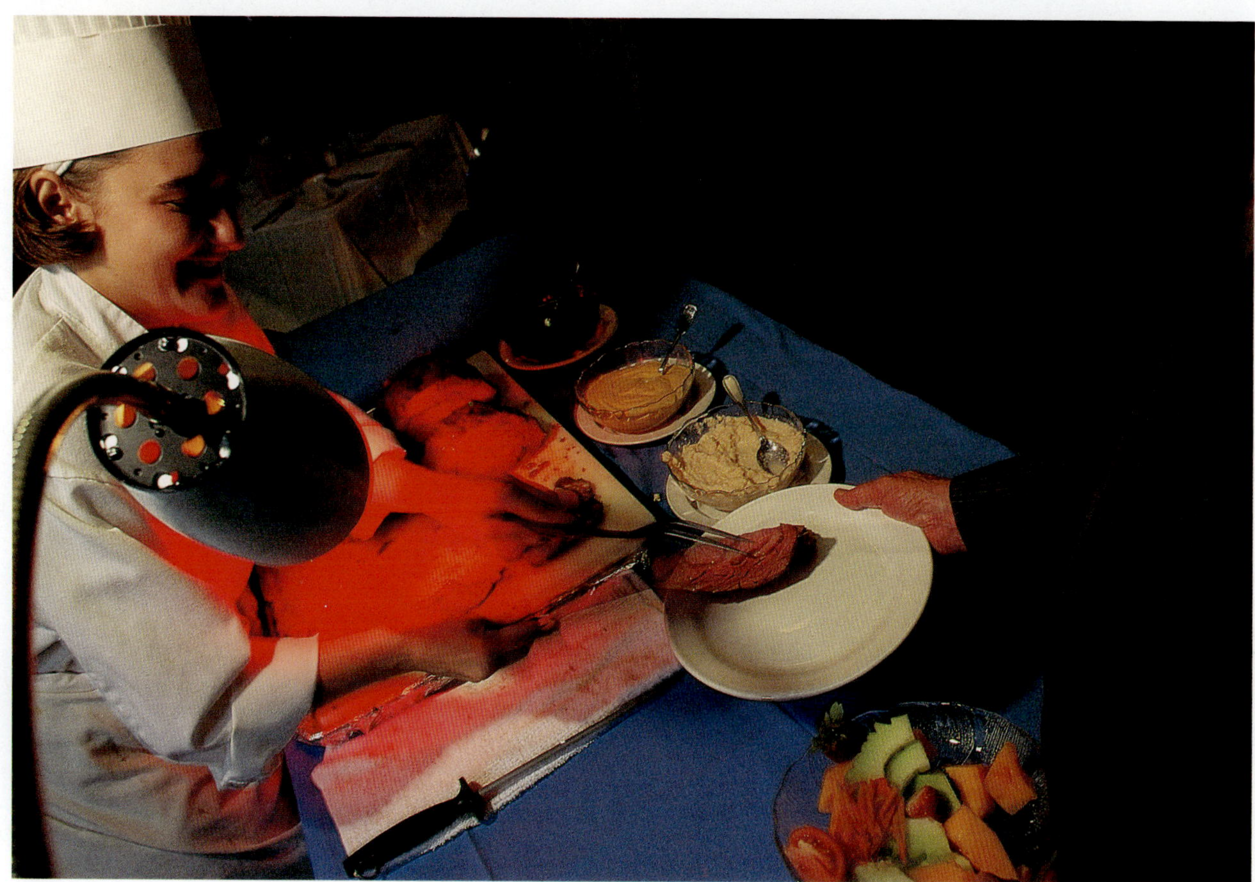

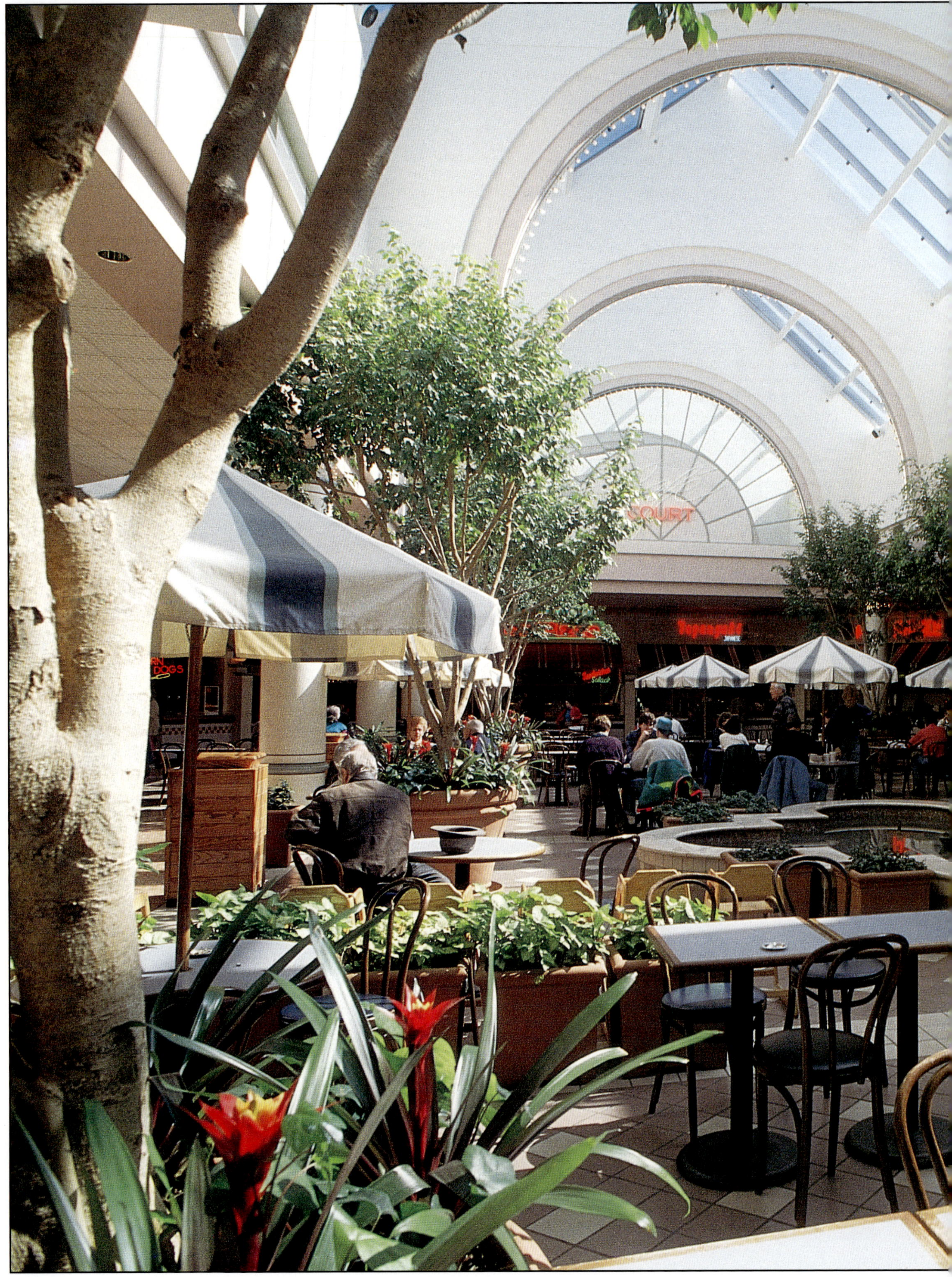
COURT

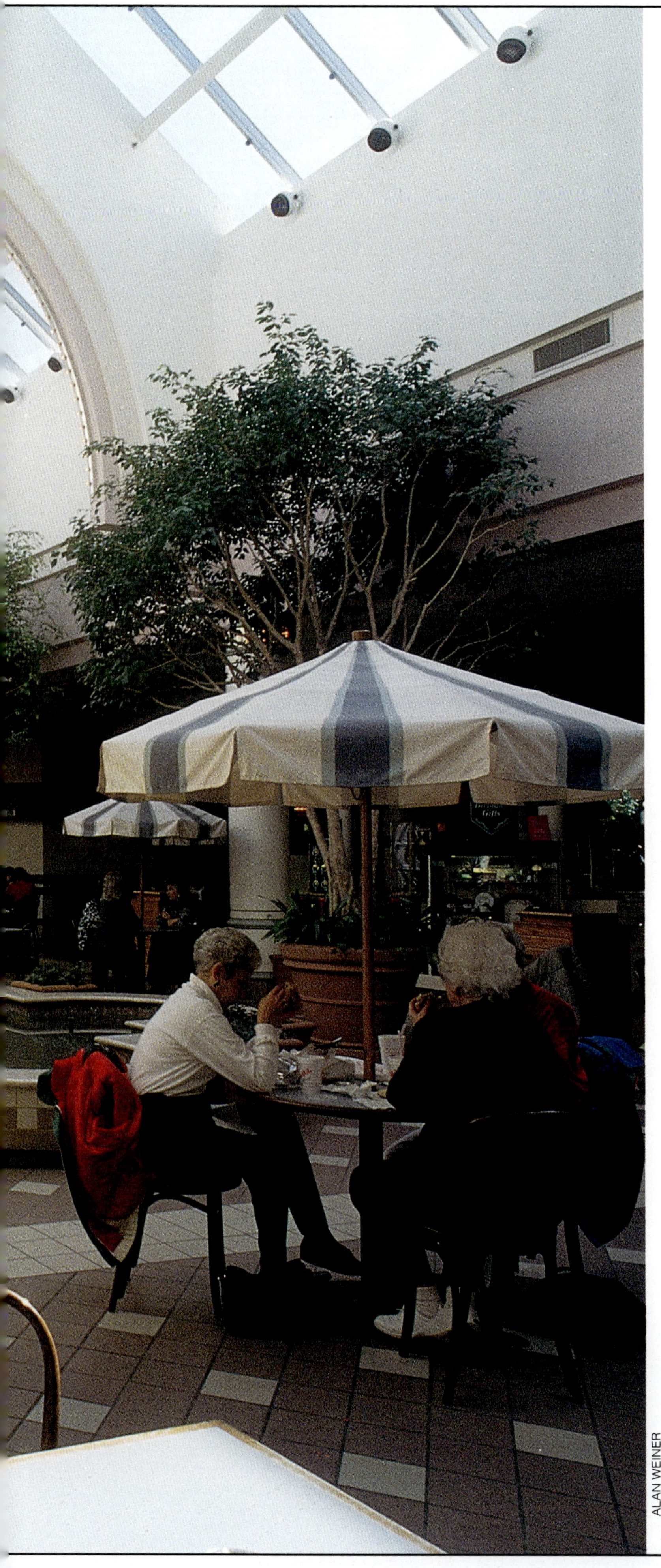

ALAN WEINER

I think what makes Marketsquare special is the ambience of the center: the skylights, marble floors, park-style benches and greenery, all provide a bright, cheerful atmosphere for everyone from the browser to the serious shopper. ◆ "We were Atlanta's first enclosed regional shopping center. And when developer Scott Hudgens cut the ribbon on July 29, 1965, what was then the North DeKalb Center had the largest Rich's Department Store in DeKalb County. The original advertising campaign, 'Leave Your Umbrella at Home,' introduced climate controlled shopping convenience to metroAtlanta. ◆ "Today, after a complete renovation in 1986, we offer shoppers a variety of stores with something for every budget and style. A four screen movie theater, banking services and our food court round out the selection. ◆ "We are located at the intersections of Lawrenceville Highway, North Druid Hills Road, and the Stone Mountain Freeway, and we are committed to creating a friendly, safe shopping environment. We have experienced, dedicated employees who provide information, security and maintenance throughout the center. Mall management encourages stores and their employees to provide friendly service to our customers. ◆ "We also strive to be a committed partner in the community. This is one of the most important things we do. We work with the county by keeping recycling bins on the property for glass, newspapers, aluminum and telephone books, and every year in January, we collect over 30,000 Christmas trees which are recycled into mulch for the county park system. It's a tremendous event! ◆ "Senior citizens are a big part of not only our community but of our mall. Each Valentine's Day, our unique 'Salute to Seniority' program does just that. Seniors model in a fashion show, provide entertainment, enjoy refreshments, prizes, honors, flowers and a classic film. During the day-long celebration, an Outstanding Senior DeKalb County Volunteer is honored. ◆ "Each morning we open our doors to the mall walkers, an estimated 300 to 400 exercise enthusiasts, some members of the Feets of Fitness Club and others on their own. They have specific walking patterns and hit every corner of the mall. Twice a week a registered nurse leads an exercise program at the Clock Court. Afterwards the walkers gather for refreshments, good conversation and even some shopping. We've had two couples, who met while walking, decide to get married, and of course they continue to be a part of the walking program. ◆ "Our food court is the focal point of the mall, with seating for 400 and a variety of food choices, all under a huge skylight. Birthday parties are held here and at anytime during the day and evening, you'll see people enjoying not only food but friends and conversation. ◆ "We are a friendly, convenient, community mall with stores and services to meet the needs of every shopper. And as we approach our thirtieth birthday in 1995, that's how we plan to continue."

— Ronald E. Duguay, General Manager

MARKETSQUARE AT NORTH DEKALB

Featuring Rich's, Mervyn's, Stein Mart, Cineplex Odeon Theaters, The Cafe Court and ninety stores and services

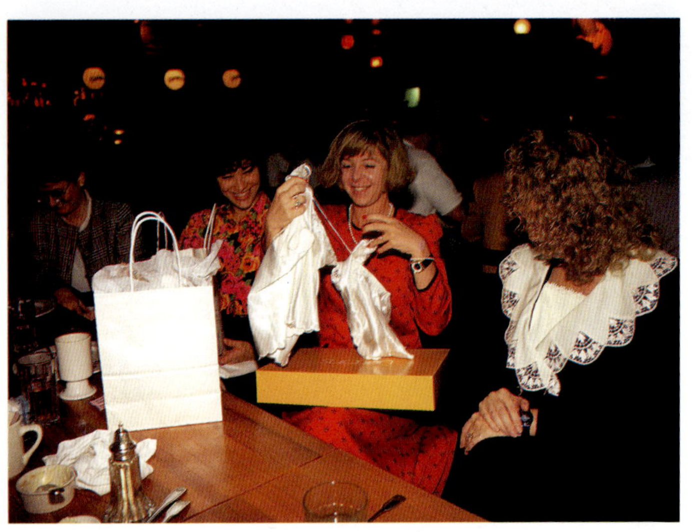

12:15 PM *Chequers Bar and Grill in Dunwoody is popular spot for Sunday brunch. In addition to traditional breakfast fare, omelets, ham, pancakes, fresh fruit and waffles, the restaurant serves such exotic specialties as spiced shrimp, crab and shrimp souffle and smoked salmon. This Sunday found Chequers hosting a sorority bridal shower, in addition to the weekly after-church families and couples out for a special treat.* PHOTO BY ROB NELSON.

12:40 PM *Lazy Sunday afternoons are even more relaxing when you don't have to leave your own backyard to enjoy the scenic view across a tranquil lake. Hala and Christopher Carlton and their small son Shawn live on Kingsley Lake in Dunwoody.* PHOTO BY KEN HAWKINS.

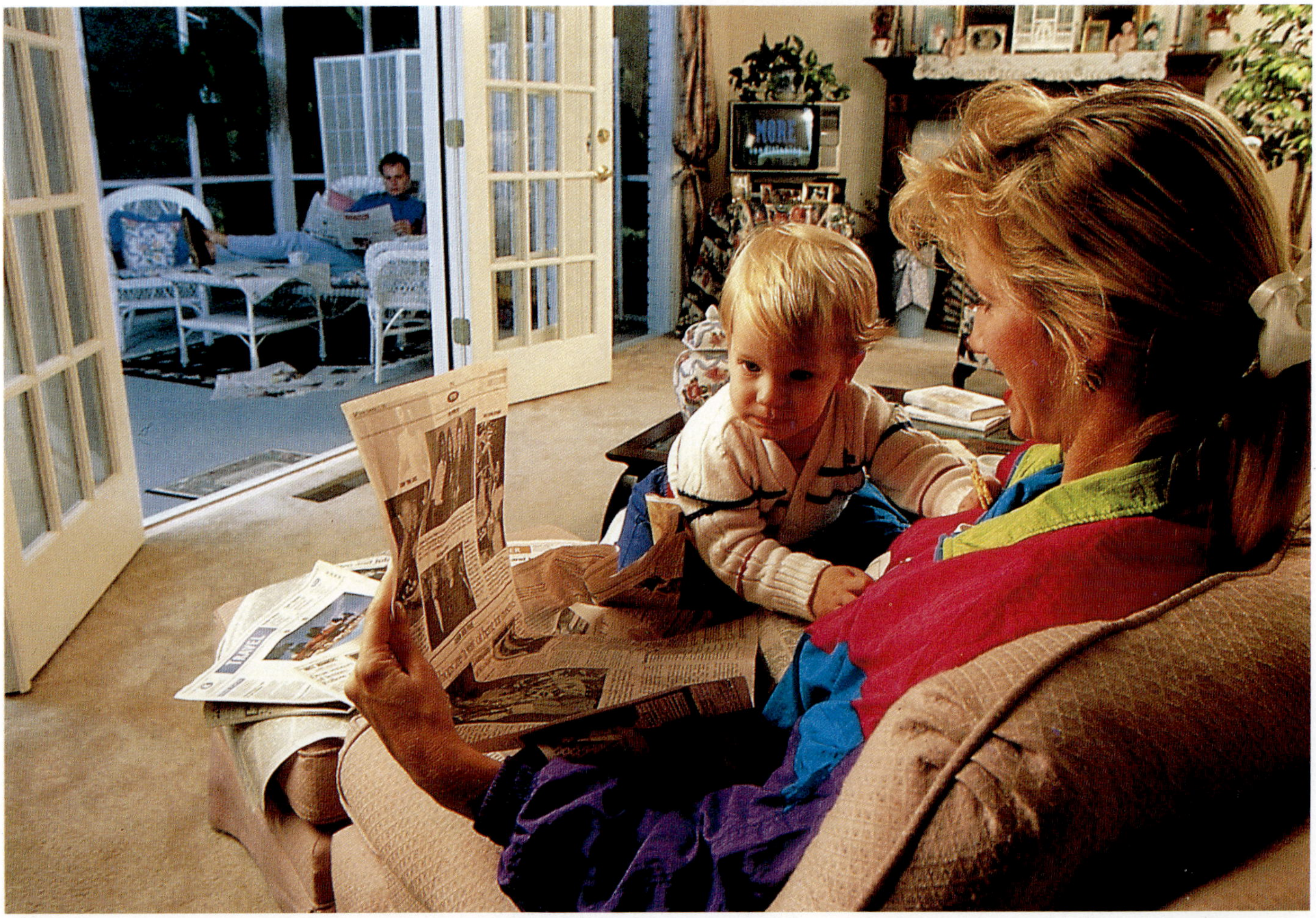

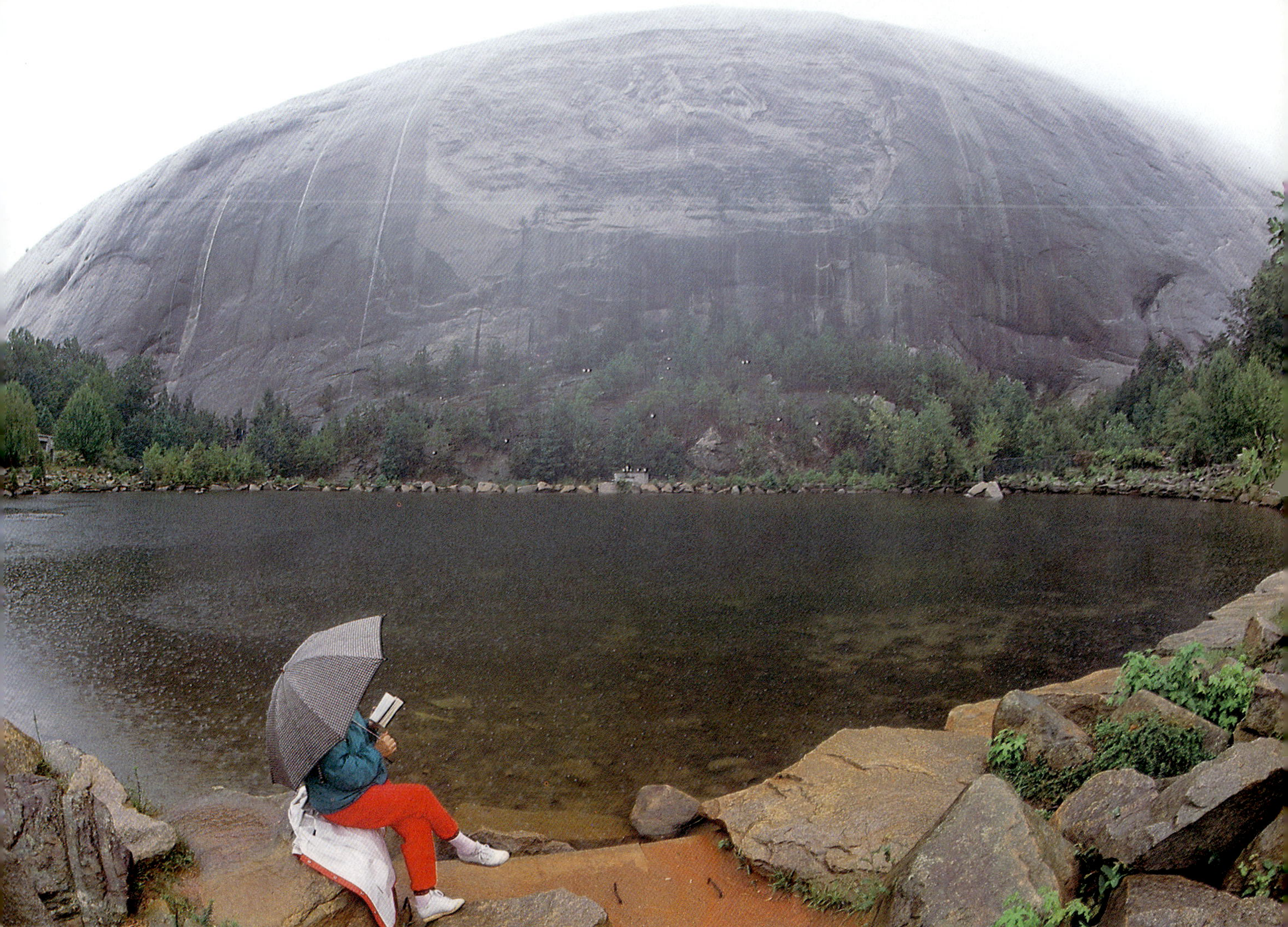

2:15 PM *Even on a rainy Sunday afternoon, Dolores Rehonic finds time and a place to read at Stone Mountain Park. More visitors come to the park than to any other attraction in the Southeast, with the exception of Disney World. They come to view the world's largest bas relief carving on the side of the mountain, to learn about the historic South, to attend year-round festivals and to enjoy the scenic natural beauty of the park. The park will be the site of several events during the 1996 Olympics.* PHOTO BY ALAN WEINER.

And at Little Friendship Missionary Baptist Church in Decatur, five members of the Nurses' Guild sit in the front row, their uniforms white and starched, their white hats pinned to their hair. In this "Friendly Church with a Personal Touch," these women assist worshipers who are overcome with emotion during the upcoming sermon, fanning them with folded programs and taking their blood pressure. With a church goal of winning over five hundred souls for Christ before the end of the year, today's emotion-packed sermon does not fail to deliver. "I'm coming home!" a woman cries out, walking to the front of the church after ninety-five minutes of hearing Satan admonished, Evil denounced and the Savior praised. "I'm coming home!"

It is Sunday in DeKalb, and all is not quiet.

The sights and sounds of more than fifty religions and denominations can be found throughout the county today, from early morning Mass at All Saints Catholic Church to sunset services celebrating Rosh

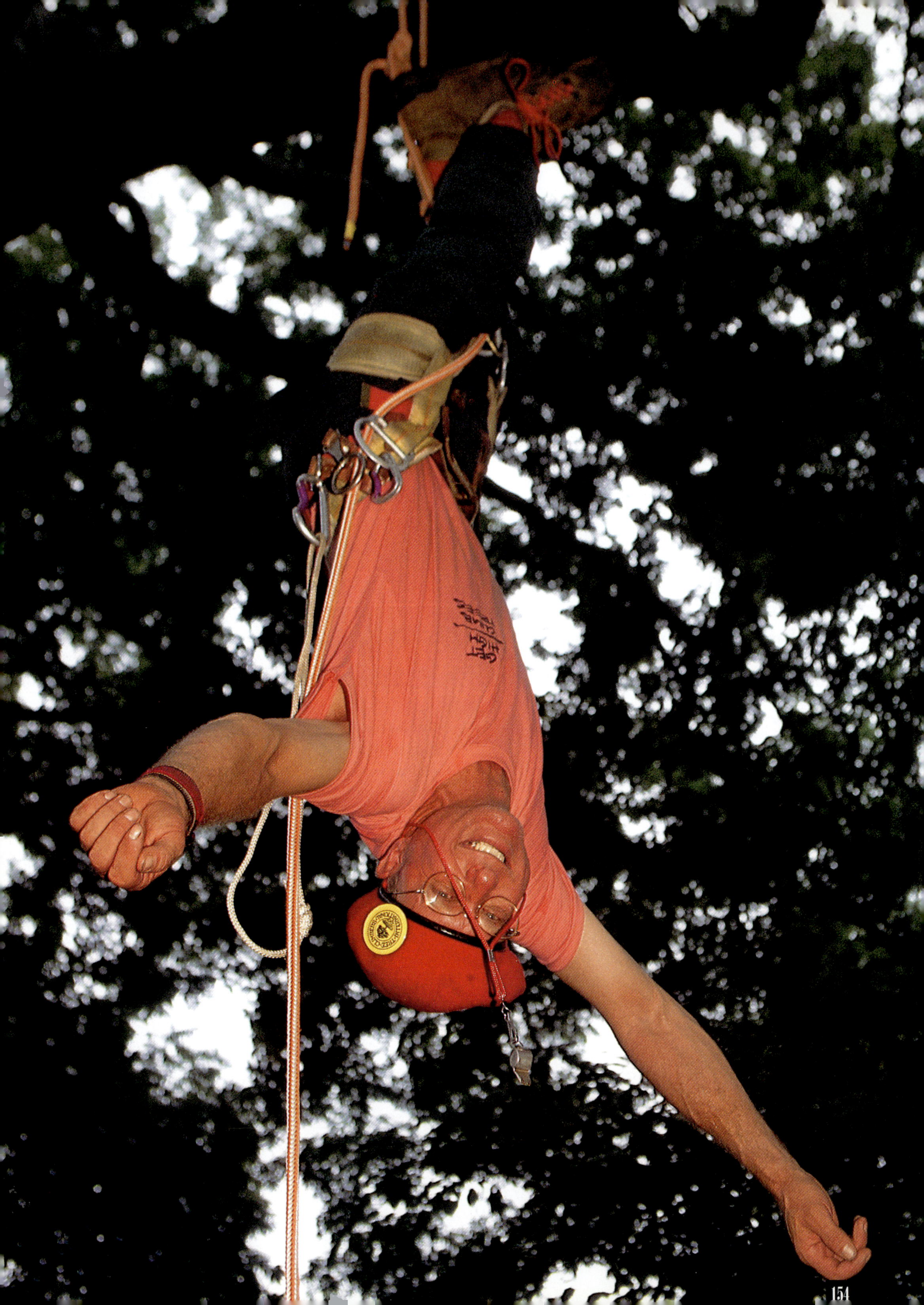

3:10 PM *Peter Jenkins sees nothing wrong with getting high; in fact, he encourages it. Jenkins is the founder of Tree Climbers International. On Sundays, members gather at a vacant lot in Candler Park to climb two huge white oak trees named Nimrod and Diane. Jenkins climbs trees for fun. A former carpenter, he is now an arborist by trade.*
PHOTO BY DAVID MURRAY.

Hashanah, the Jewish New Year. And within the boundaries of this particular Sunday, when things religious and decidedly otherwise occur from Browns Mill Road in the southeast to Mill Shire Lane in the northwest, DeKalb County prepares to bring the week to a close.

It's noon, but this is not the usual corporate and business lunch crowd at Chequers Bar and Grill, across from Perimeter Mall. Ready for their turn at the $12.95 brunch buffet is the dressed-in-Sunday-best crowd, families with children, retirees and even a table of sorority sisters hosting a bridal shower. Waitress Denise Hatmaker, whose husband works at nearby Houlihan's, glances out the window. "When it rains, it brings people out," she says, smiling. "They don't like to sit at home on rainy days."

Tradition, not weather, pervades Druid Hills Golf Club, even for Sunday brunch. When Jerry Fischetti, a Long Island native and the club's food and beverage director, tried to update the menu, the membership was less than enthusiastic about fresh salmon and shitake mushrooms on Sunday. So Fischetti scratched his notions of nouvelle cuisine and brought back perfectly fried chicken, peppery blackeyed peas, cole slaw, new potato salad, macaroni and cheese—timeless Southern recipes steeped in tradition, which club members Mamie and Rick Bell of Decatur certainly seem to appreciate. Rick, whose father was a member of the eighty-year-old club where his own two sons now romp, explains that tradition is a way of life in the South. "It's one of those things you can't escape, even if you wanted to."

For many in DeKalb, Sunday means a trip to the Atlanta Antique Center & Flea Market in Chamblee, once described by the *New York Times* as one of the top ten flea markets in the country. Everyone knows that the stuffed moose in the center aisle is not for sale, but $3,000 will buy the turn-of-the-century oak wardrobe at Trader Doys and $3 takes home the Deion Sanders baseball card ($4.50 for the Deion rookie card). In this huge brick warehouse, there are spaces for 150 booths. "Sundays are the biggest crowd," says Carl Davis, one of the owners, as people wander the aisles aimlessly, looking at everything and nothing in particular. "During the Democratic National Convention, Bryant Gumbel came in and bought an Oriental rug and had it shipped to New York. It got to be that this is the place to be seen in Atlanta."

By early afternoon, DeKalb chapter members of the American Red Cross are concluding their thirteenth blood drive of the week, over at St. Timothy's in Stone Mountain. An unusual site for a Sunday? Not when you consider that the Atlanta region covers eighty-two counties and requires eighteen blood drives a day to collect the 900 units of blood needed daily for over 100 hospitals in the region, including the seven general and ten specialized hospitals in DeKalb.

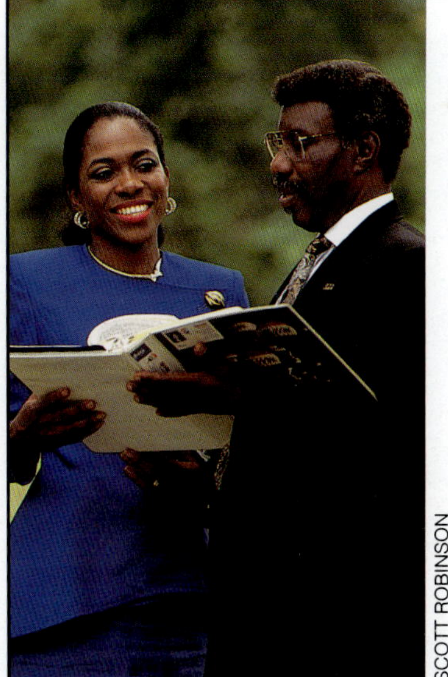

SCOTT ROBINSON

Buying a home is a very emotional decision. In a lifetime, it is probably the largest purchase people will make. And what I like most about being in the real estate profession is providing my buyers and sellers with as much information as possible about today's market. The challenge is to match the right buyer with the right home. ◆ "We are a full-service company. Our services include commercial, residential sales, both new and resales, relocations and property management. At RE/MAX Pacesetters, our motto is 'professionalism is a matter of excellent service' and I'm proud of that. ◆ "As a broker, I feel it's very important to understand the needs of the purchaser and the seller in order to give them the very best service. Metro Atlanta is our service area, although our area of concentration is DeKalb County. DeKalb County offers today's purchasers an excellent selection of new and resale homes. We at RE/MAX Pacesetters look forward to continuing to offer the very best service to the community we serve."

— Connie Stokes
Associate Broker/Owner

RE/MAX PACESETTERS
James A. Stokes and Connie Stokes, Brokers and Owners

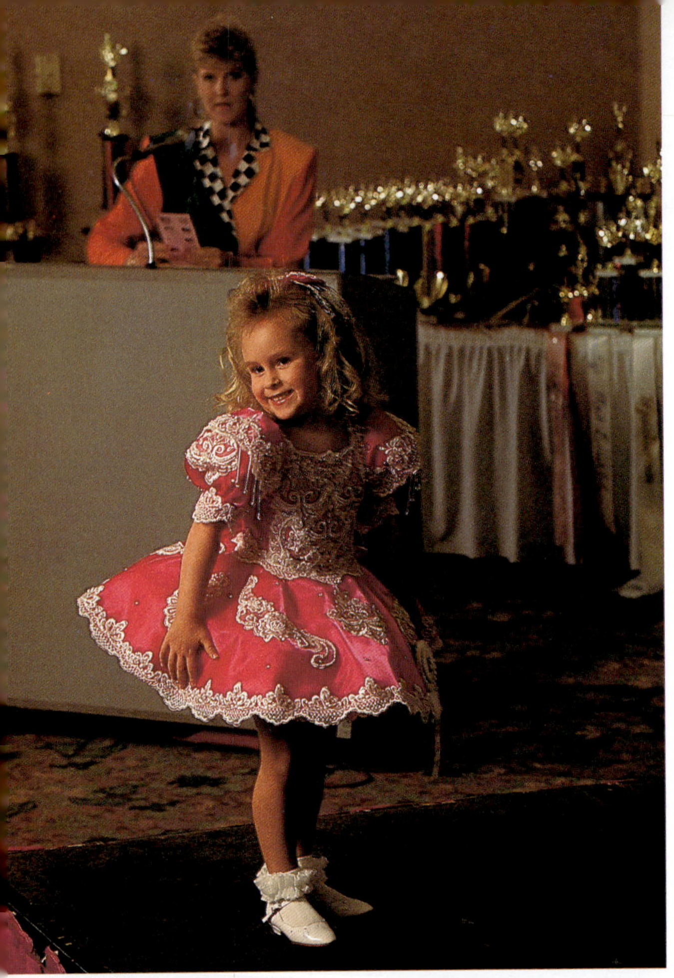

4:00 PM *A children's talent show can be exciting, traumatic, stressful, depressing and exhilarating. And that's if you are the parent. For this girl, in a Prestige Pageant held at the Perimeter North Inn, it was mostly a fun afternoon, a chance to show some poise and a $300 sequined gown.* Photo by Scott Robinson.

4:01 PM *Liane Levetan, campaigning here at the Greek Festival, ventured on in the November elections to become DeKalb County's first female chief executive officer, replacing three-term CEO Manuel Maloof. A former county commissioner, Levetan once was Maloof's political enemy, trying unsuccessfully to unseat him in a bitter contest in 1988. One of the strengths of her current campaign was Maloof's support. Levetan came to the United States as a child after her family fled their native Austria during Hitler's reign.* Photo by Tom England.

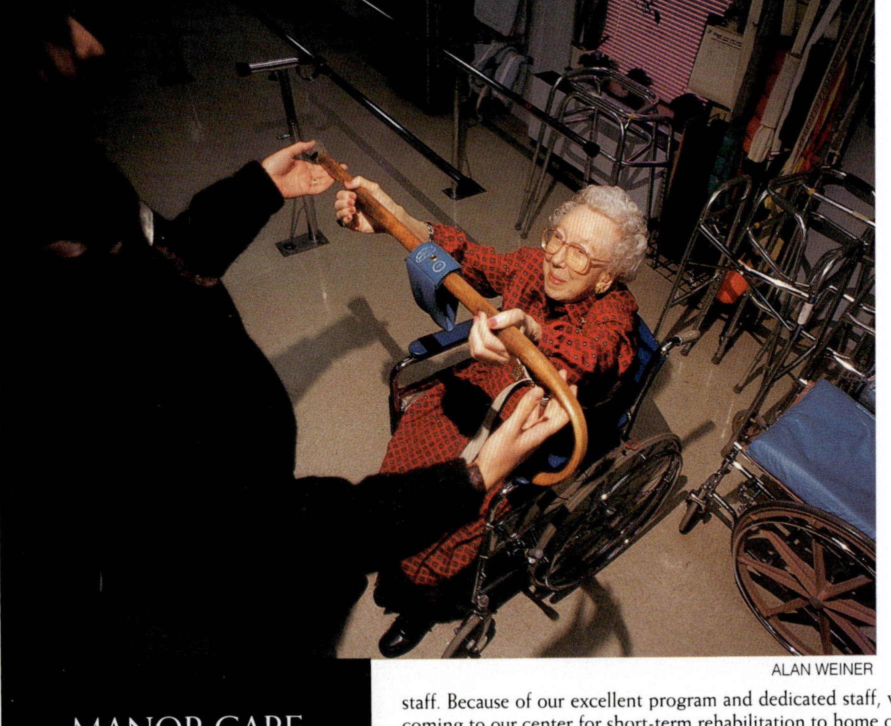

ALAN WEINER

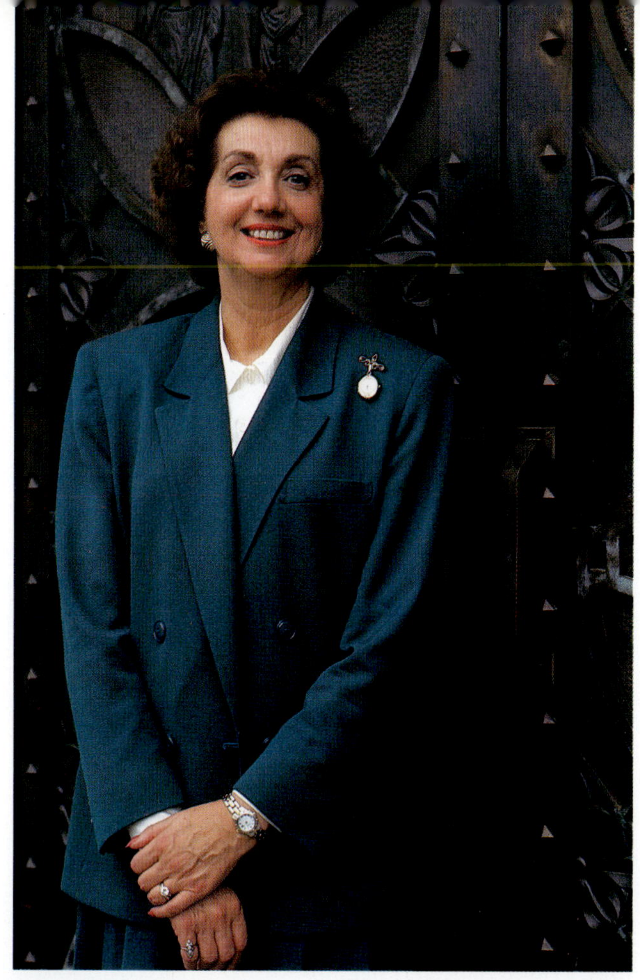

4:10 PM *The DeKalb Farmers Market is more than just a neighborhood produce market. It is a tourist attraction visited by more than two million people every year. Opened in 1977 in a 7,500-square-foot building, the market now is housed in a state-of-the-art facility almost twenty times that size. More than one million pounds of produce are sold every week. Wares come from all over the world: pears from Japan, salmon from Norway, octopus tentacles from Chile, tomato sauce from Italy, figs from Greece, orchids from Thailand, coffee beans alone from more than half a dozen countries. Flags from 174 nations of the world fly inside the market, and employees represent thirty-five different countries.*

PHOTOS BY ALAN WEINER.

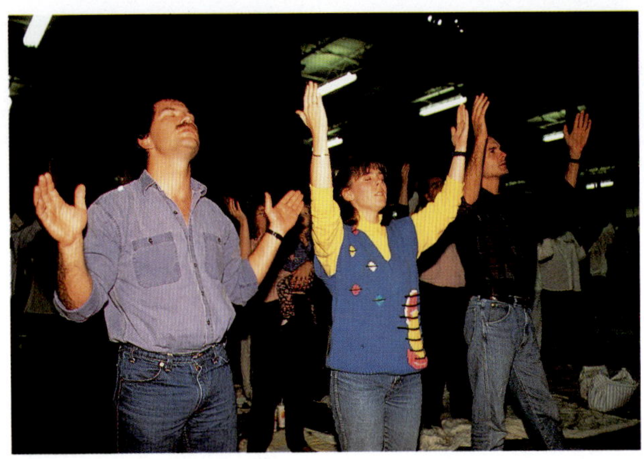

4:45 PM *More than one thousand members of the First Baptist Church of Atlanta congregation had planned a picnic, and a picnic they had—despite the persistent rain. There was plenty of room for hampers, lawn chairs, quilts and children in the giant warehouse that once housed the Avon cosmetics company. The 12,500-member church moved from its Midtown Atlanta location to build a $25 million sanctuary on the Dunwoody site. The picnic was a dual celebration of the move and of Pastor Emeritus Charles Stanley's sixtieth birthday.* PHOTO BY ROB NELSON.

Today, Stone Mountain Mayor Patricia Wheeler makes plans to attend an afternoon preview party at Fernbank's new natural history museum. She's been away at a conference all week, and is anxious to catch up. But for Mike Gardner, people and activity are not what he has in mind.

A painter for DeKalb County who lives in the Village, Gardner sits alone, in a secluded corner of Stone Mountain Park where a thin spit of forest floats into the mountain lake. It's a solitary spot, just right for fishing, for listening to the ethereal, melancholy sound of the park's carillon bells drifting out over the water. Hunched inside his yellow slicker, with a casual eye toward his three fishing poles, Gardner seems content just to listen . . . first "April Showers," then "Singing in the Rain," the same songs Mabel Sansing Sharp has played on her carillon bell tower keyboard for the past sixteen years. Gardner never tires of the sound. "I just throw back whatever I catch, anyway," he says. "But I love being out here, under these bells and fishing."

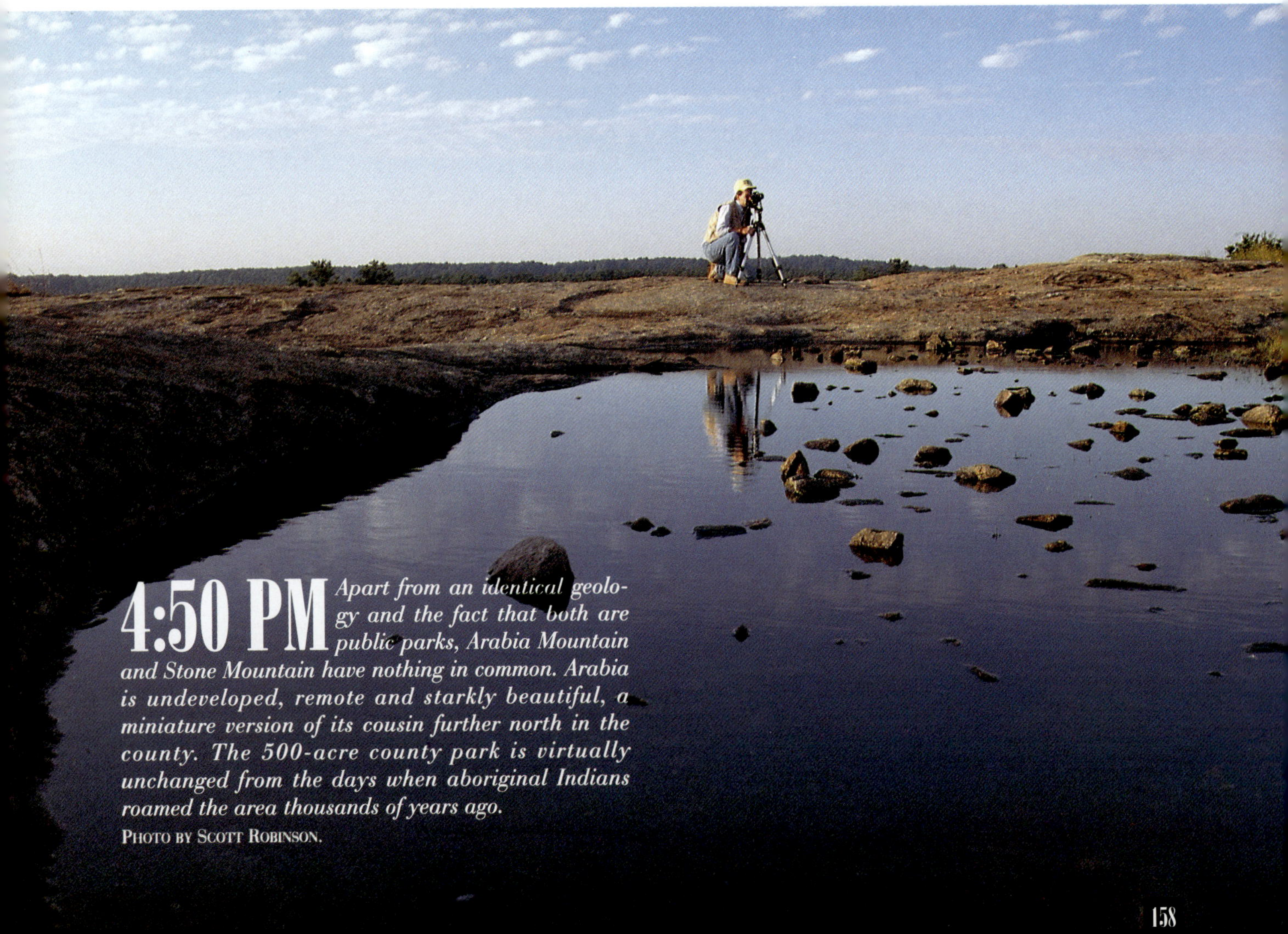

4:50 PM *Apart from an identical geology and the fact that both are public parks, Arabia Mountain and Stone Mountain have nothing in common. Arabia is undeveloped, remote and starkly beautiful, a miniature version of its cousin further north in the county. The 500-acre county park is virtually unchanged from the days when aboriginal Indians roamed the area thousands of years ago.*
PHOTO BY SCOTT ROBINSON.

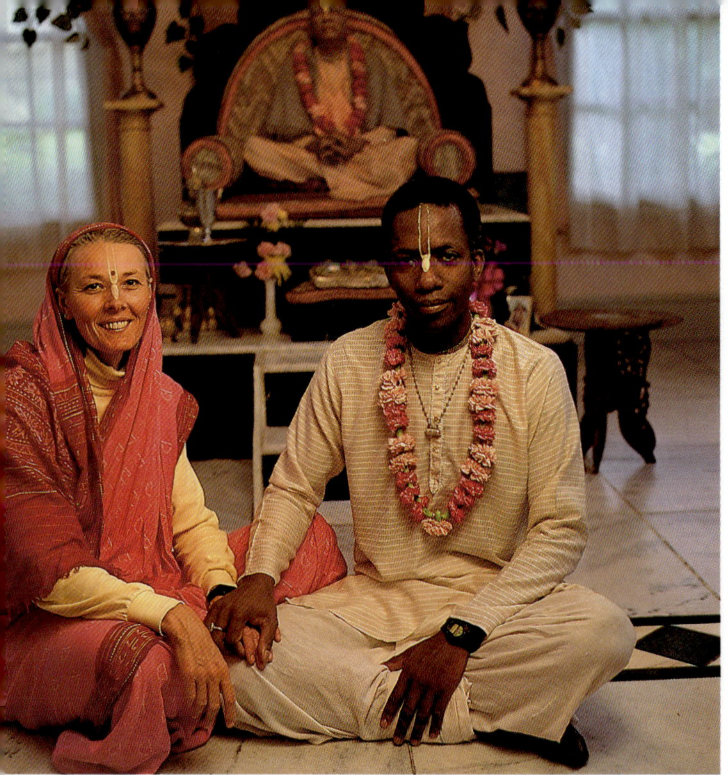

And while the afternoon's weather keeps members of the Tree Climbers International Club indoors, nothing keeps club director Peter Jenkins out of a tree—particularly those two enormous, century-old white oaks that stand side-by-side on a vacant lot owned by Jenkins in Candler Park. Wearing a red beret, a whistle around his neck and a salmon-colored T-shirt that says "Get High: Climb Trees," Jenkins uses various ropes and a harness to get to the top of one of the ninety-foot-tall trees. "We can get anybody up a tree," he says, noting that tree climbing is "the eco-sport of the future. Tree climbing is the only vertical climb suitable for the masses. There aren't too many rocks or caves, but trees are everywhere."

5:00 PM *Three houses on South Ponce de Leon in the Druid Hills community serve as home, business and place of worship for members of the International Society for Krishna Consciousness, an orthodox sect of Hinduism. The Krishnas hold their first prayer service daily at 4:30 A.M. and spend their days worshiping and telling others about Krishna, tending their greenhouses and gardens, and selling books, incense and clothing. Their religion forbids illicit sex, alcohol, drugs, caffeine, gambling and eating meat, fish or eggs.* PHOTO BY MARILYN FUTTERMAN.

5:30 PM *The oldtime hardware isn't the same anymore, not since The Home Depot was invented. One of the fastest-growing and most successful companies in America, the Atlanta-based company has transformed thousands of couch potatoes into enthusiastic do-it-yourselfers. One of them is Arthur Robinson, pictured here at the Memorial Drive store, The Home Depot chain's first outlet. Robinson is searching for supplies to renovate his recreation room.* PHOTO BY MICHAEL SCHWARZ.

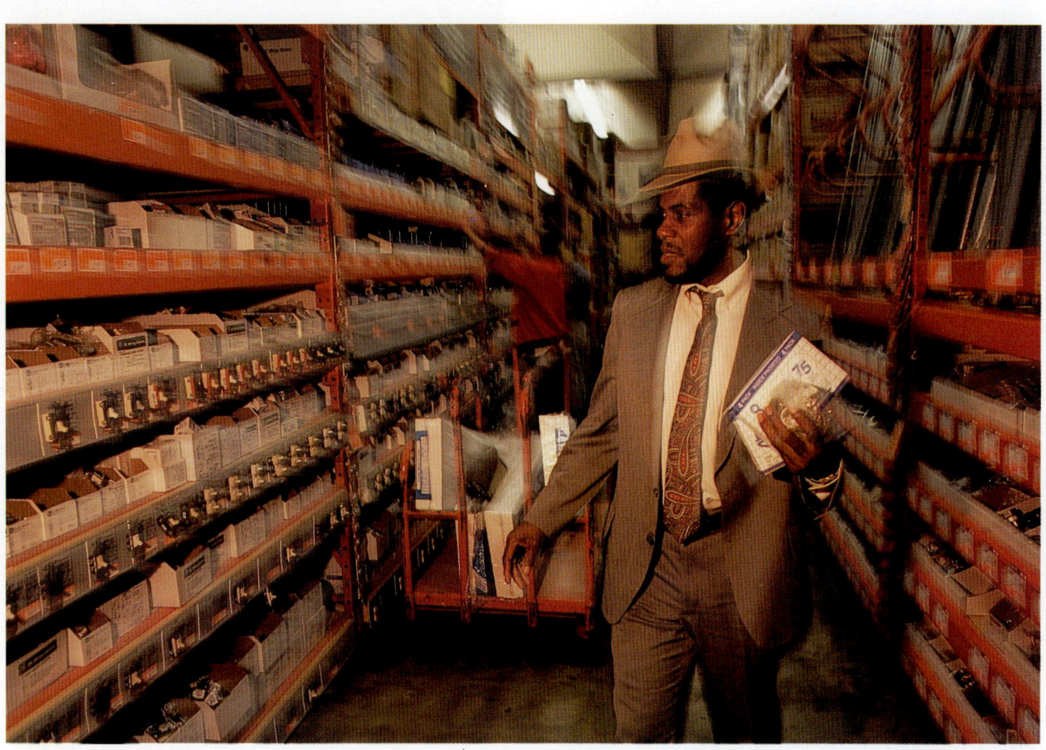

5:50 PM *In increasingly dense, almost urban DeKalb, Louis and Margaret Sansalone are the only petitioners ever to request that the zoning designation of their property revert to agricultural. The Sansalones asked that their five acres in South DeKalb be rezoned from single-family residential so the couple can operate a truck farm. Louis Sansalone says the land reminds him of his native Italy.*
PHOTO BY KEN HAWKINS.

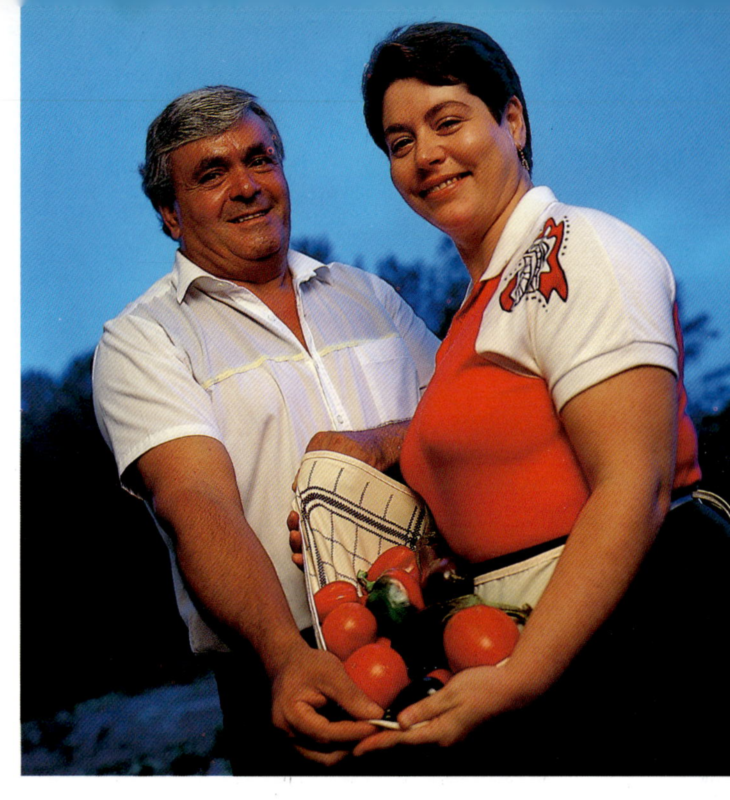

6:15 PM *DeKalb's Jewish citizens, like ten-year-old Jordan Rodbell, gathered at neighborhood synagogues on Sunday to celebrate Rosh Hashana, the Jewish New Year, which began at sunset. Members of Congregation Beth Jacob on Lavista Road described Rosh Hashana as an occasion of solemnity and joy, a time of judgment, repentance and forgiveness of sins.*
PHOTO BY ALAN WEINER.

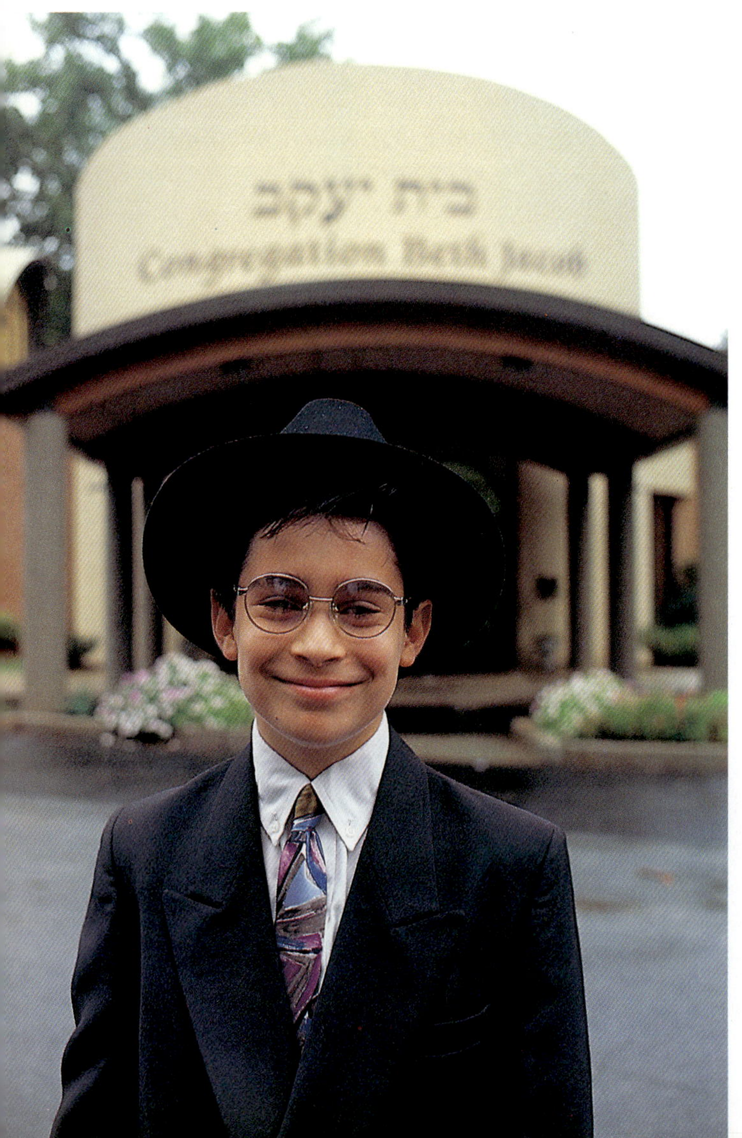

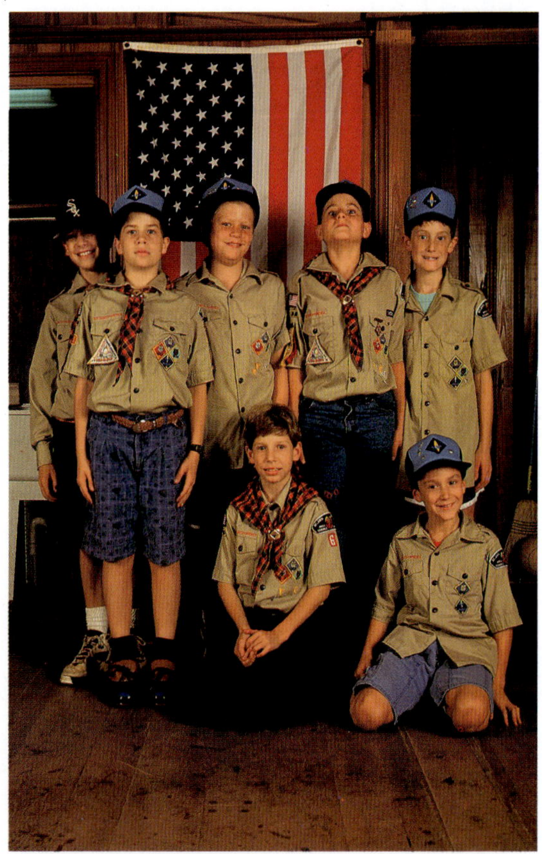

6:12 PM *Den 7, Pack 6 convenes at attention—sort of—at its weekly meeting at the Venetian Pool club house on Ponce de Leon. Pictured are Chris McClure, Ben Sitter, Alex Cheek, David Berger, Graham Carsson, Josh Goldman and Matthew Young.*
PHOTO BY CHUCK YOUNG.

As the afternoon gives way to early evening, a disparate array of activities comes to an end.

A trio of characters named Dinky, Ollie and Miz Mattie take their final bows in today's performance of Eudora Welty's *Why I Live at the P.O.*, staged by Southern Fried Productions at Mercer's Fine Arts Building Auditorium; down the hall, the production company's Susie Caldwell helps out during auditions for Southern Fried's next play, *Crimes of the Heart*.

In a former Avon warehouse in Dunwoody, members of the First Baptist Church of Atlanta gather to celebrate the church's future $25 million sanctuary, as well as Rev. Charles Stanley's sixtieth birthday. Although his son Andy leads the suburban home of the church, Charles Stanley remains the guiding light for the congregation of 12,500. Today, before a congregation-style picnic, Stanley asks his flock to kneel and pray together for the strength to raise the building program's first $7 million.

DeKalb County will soon elect its first female chief executive officer but, alas, there are still beauty pageants for little girls—Prestige Pageants, to be

7:10 PM *Richard and Vanessa Clark and their children, Richard and Alexandria, settle in for a Sunday-evening dinner of broiled salmon steaks, rice and cabbage, before seeing what's on TV for the night and getting ready for Monday. Everyone has their assignment—even Alexandria, three, must be sure her tap shoes are in their carrying case, ready for her dancing class in the morning.* PHOTO BY MICHAEL SCHWARZ.

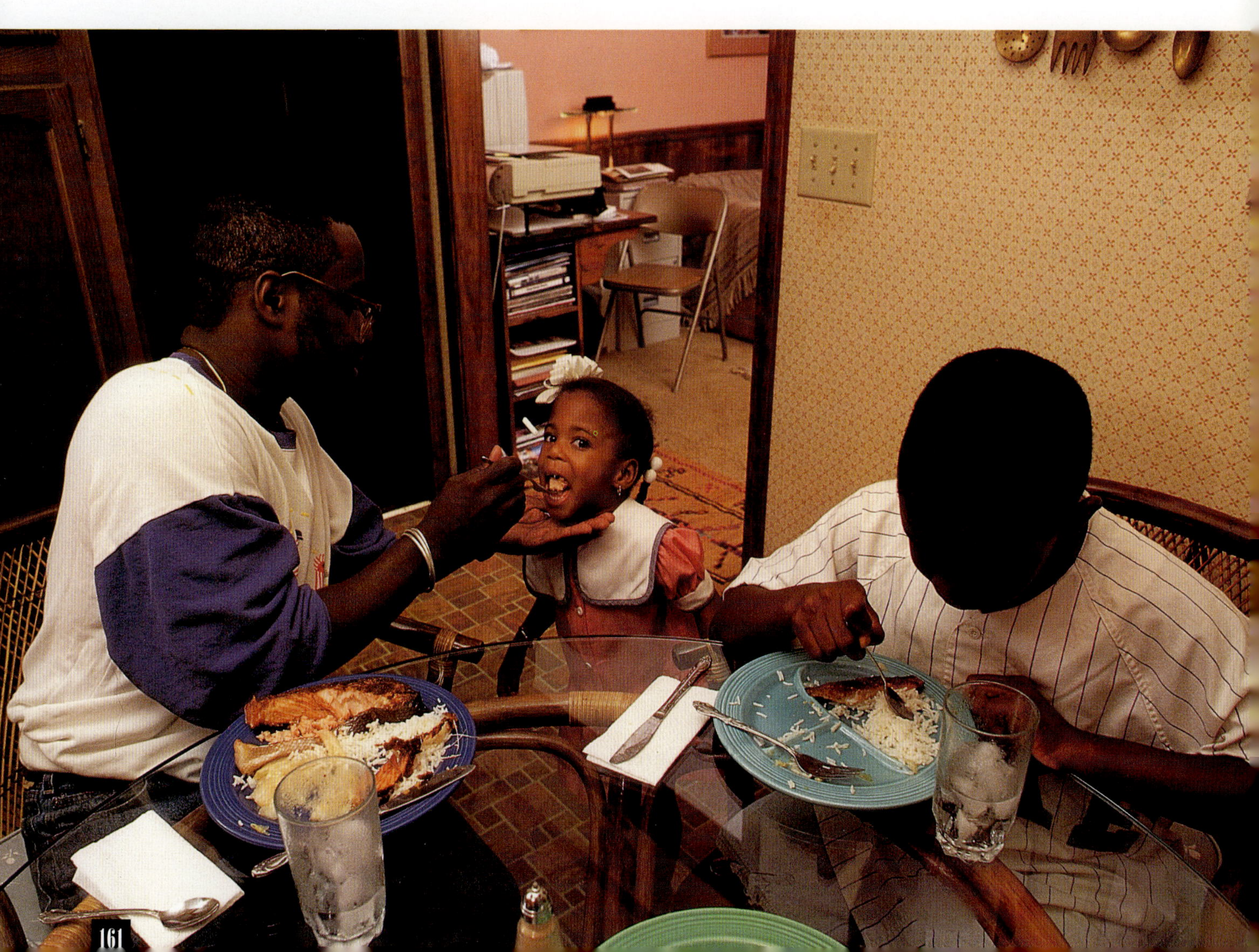

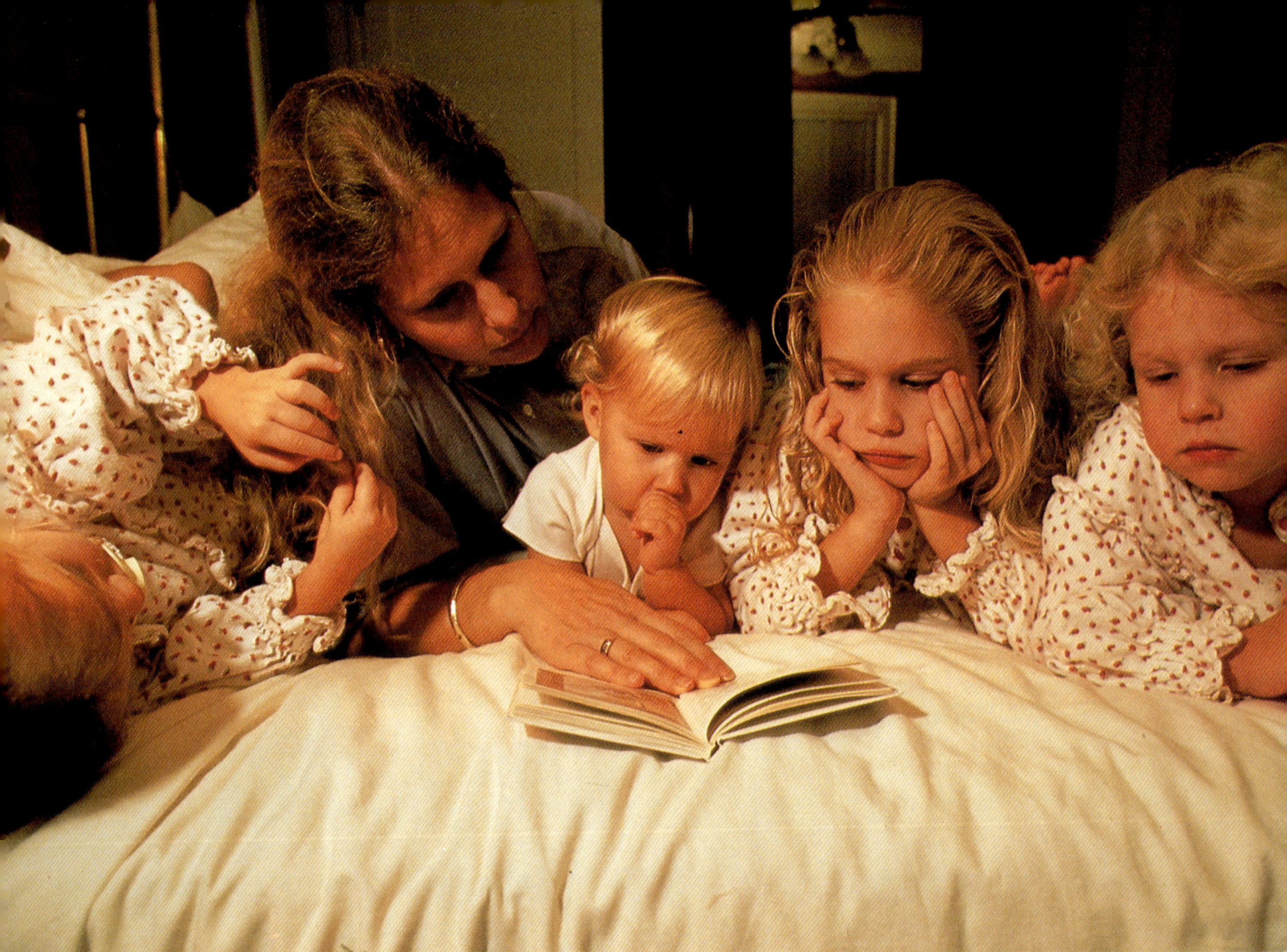

exact, where a five-year-old named Brittany Denise Haney wears a coquettish smile, a touch of make-up and a $300 sequined gown on her way to being crowned Most Beautiful, Most Photogenic, Best Sportswear and Most Talented in a room filled with parents and grandparents at the Perimeter North Inn. Says her beaming mother, Elizabeth Haney, "We do it for her confidence."

At Congregation Beth Jacob, an Orthodox synagogue on Lavista Road, the approaching sunset signals not only the end of a day but the beginning of a new year for Paul Rodbell and his ten-year-old son Jordan as they prepare to celebrate Rosh Hashanah. Says Rodbell, "I will pray for a year of good health and success for all."

And, finally, it's time for supper. Vanessa Clark of Decatur prepares broiled salmon steaks, rice and cabbage for her husband Richard and two children, Richard, nine, and Alexandria, three. A communal meal is served at the Atlanta Temple of the International Society for Krishna Consciousness on South Ponce de Leon Avenue, where devotees bless their vegetarian portions of puri, rice, pakoda and subji to the glory of Krishna before eating. The picnicking Baptists munch on Mrs. Winner's fried chicken. And Bernie Idov, who claims to run the only kosher bakery in the Atlanta area, is delighted to know that his raspberry nut cakes, almond tortes and taiglech (little nuggets of dough boiled in honey) will be part of tonight's Jewish New Year celebrations. "You're supposed to eat sweet things," says Idov, owner of Bernie the Baker in Toco Hills Mall, "so you'll have a good, sweet year." It is Sunday in DeKalb, and all is nearly quiet. For in the homes of over half a million citizens, it is time to end one week and simultaneously prepare for another.

7:30 PM *A busy, working mom, Lisa Turner makes sure she has time for what's most important: intimate intervals with daughters Catherine, Sarah, Rebecca and Elizabeth. Sharing a bedtime story brings to a sleepy conclusion a hectic week for the Decatur family.* PHOTO BY GREG FOSTER.

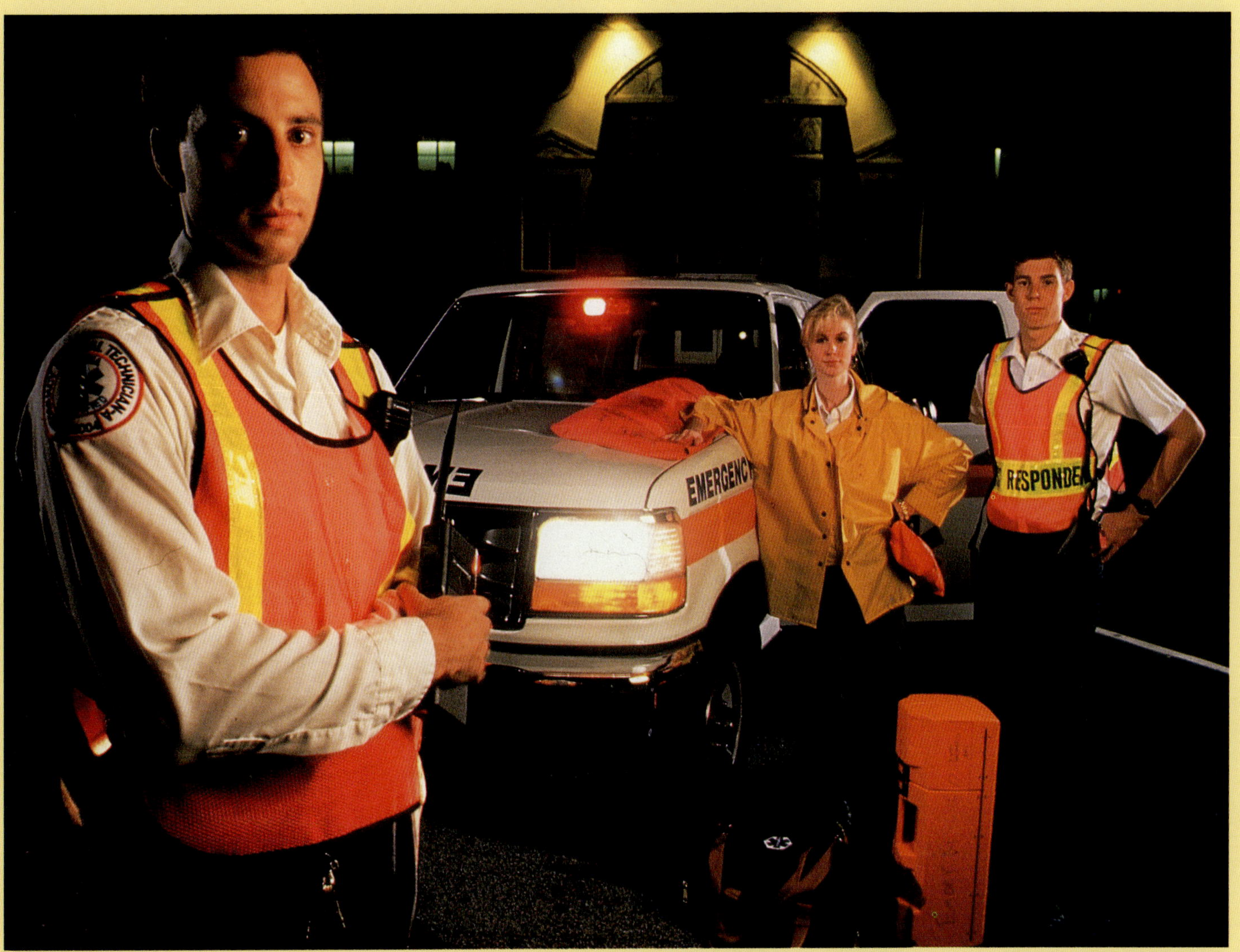

10:00 PM *Emory University's First Responder Unit was only one month old when this photo was taken, and already it is being called by some the finest organization on campus. Law student Roger Neustadt, pictured here with colleagues Kim Williams and Matthew Tucker—organized the ambulance unit which is made up of student volunteers who pay for their own medical emergency training and uniforms.* PHOTO BY ROB NELSON.

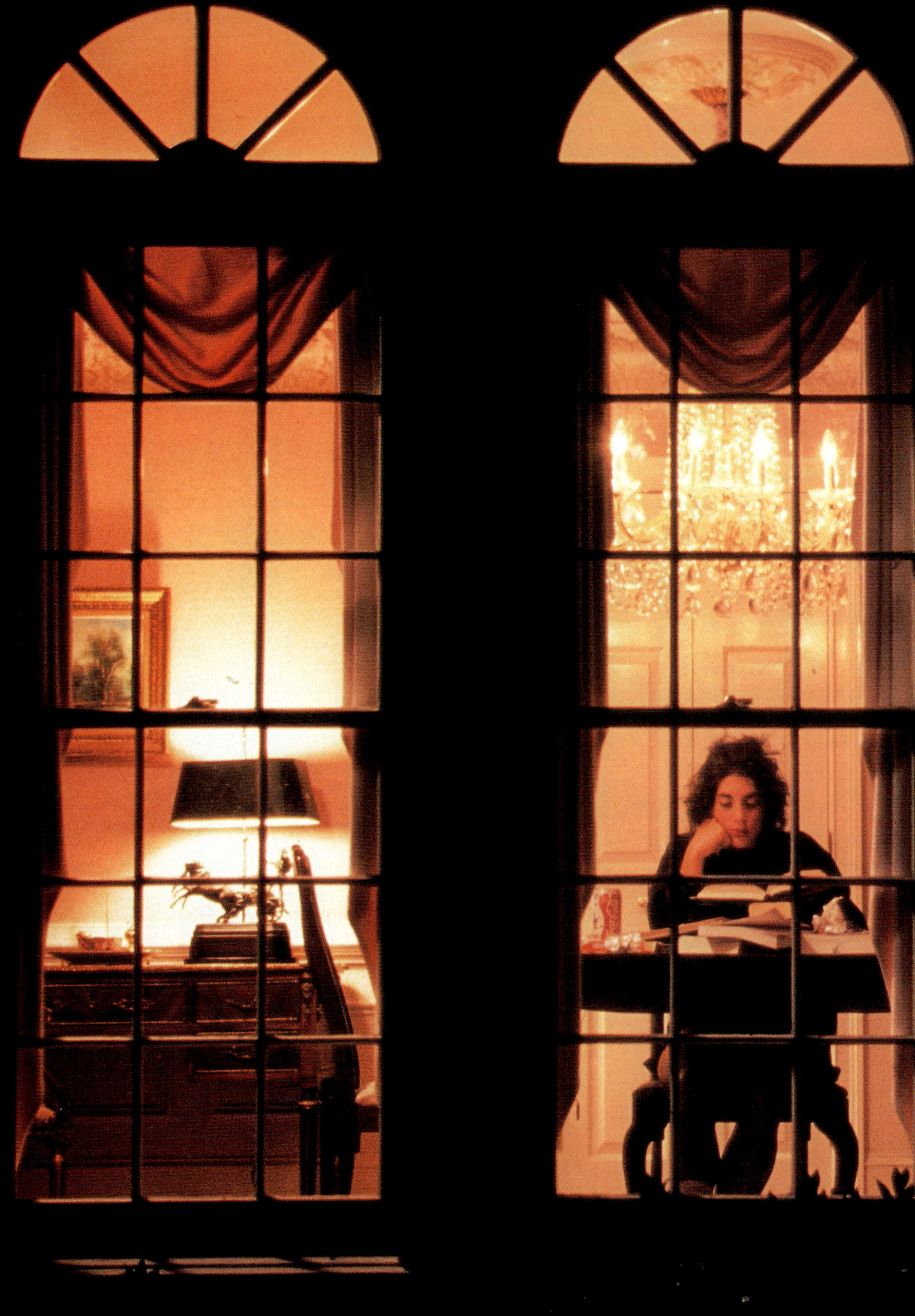

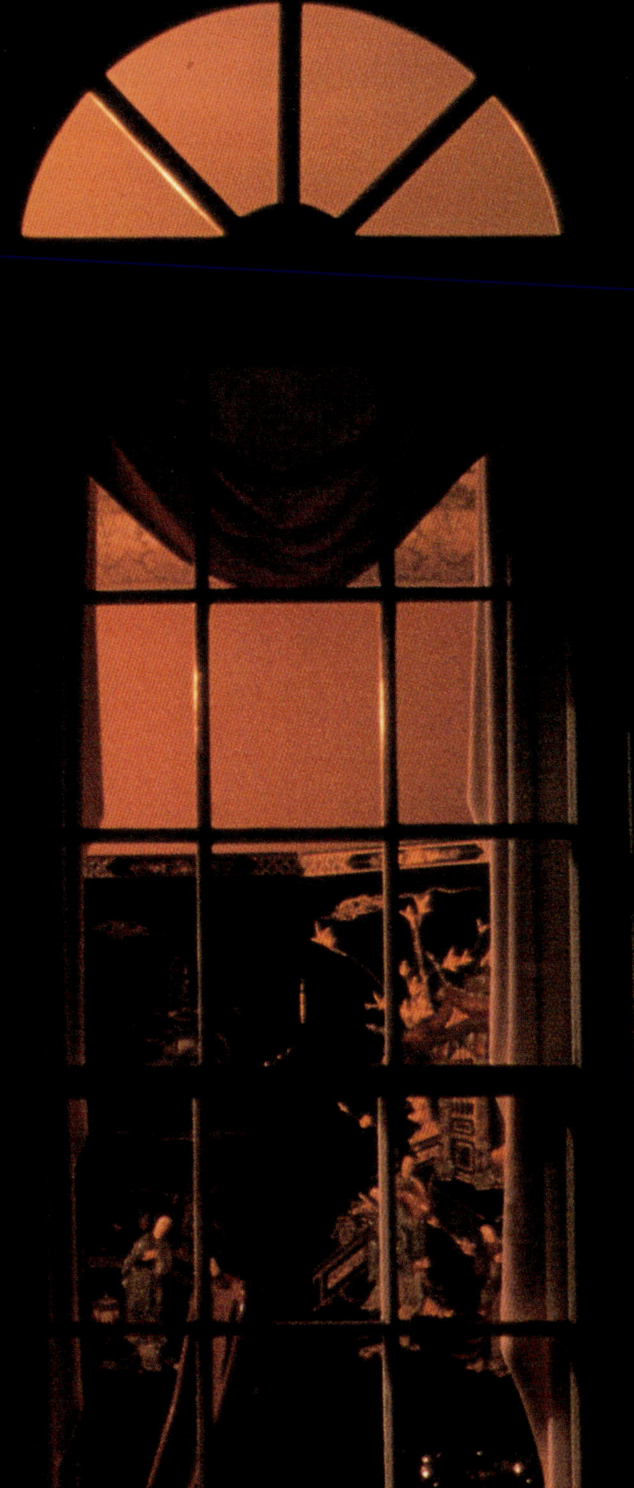

Which means that it's bath night for the Turner girls, before they snuggle up with mom and dad to read their favorite nighttime stories, while students must settle in and finish homework due Monday morning. While real estate agent Reba Tietjen bundles up 350 of her neighborhood newsletters called "Right Off Briarcliff," ready to deliver them first thing tomorrow, football player Britt Phillips puts Friday night's defeat behind him and starts to think about next Friday's game. And as musical director Mary Root sits at her dining room table, reviewing a score by Atlanta composer Tristan Foison in preparation for Monday night's rehearsal of the DeKalb Choral Guild, people like Lithonia Mayor Harold King, Jr., banker Phillip Cunningham, Scottdale day-care director Audrey Collier, Korean business owner Sarah Bayaona, newspaper distributor Albert Davis, state employee Sheila Yarn and Principal Virginia Davis get ready to go back to work.

Because tomorrow, DeKalb County, Georgia, dawns again.

10:45 PM *Rene Latone spends Sunday night getting ready for the coming week at school. The senior at St. Pius X High School is studying to take the SAT test, in preparation to attend Auburn University. Rene says her best subject is math, but she plans to major in radio broadcasting.*
Photo by Ken Hawkins.

PHOTOGRAPHERS

Thomas England
People, National Geographic Publications, *Time*, and various books
Decatur, GA

Greg Foster
Former staff photographer at *The National Sports Daily*; *Sports Illustrated*, *LA Times*, *NY Times*; as well as many corporate clients
Atlanta, GA

Marilyn Suriani Futterman
Dancing Naked in the Material World, *Atlanta Magazine*; corporate clients include Coca-Cola, Carter Center; a member of Nexus Studio Artist Program; work has been exhibited locally, nationally, and internationally
Atlanta, GA

Ken Hawkins
Photo editor/principal photographer at *Georgia Trend*, *Time*; Sygma (photo agency based in Paris) Photo editor of *7 Days in DeKalb*.
Atlanta, GA

Gordon Joffrion/Egami Media
Town & Country, *Travel & Leisure*, *Sport*, *Inc.*, Financial World
Ponte Vedra Beach, FL

David Murray, Jr.
Pulitzer Prize finalist in 1981 for spot news, *Life*
Atlanta, GA

Rob Nelson
Newsweek, Black Star, *Business Week*, *LA Times*, recent projects include *Hong Kong: Here Be Dragons*, a photojournalistic essay.
Atlanta, GA

Scott Robinson
Sports Illustrated, *Time*, *Newsweek*, *Premiere*
Los Angeles, CA

Michael A. Schwarz
U.S. News and World Report, *Fortune*, *NY Times*, *The Power to Heal*
Atlanta, GA

Ann States
Forbes, *People*, *NY Times Sunday Magazine*, *Time*
Atlanta, GA

Chuck Young/Chuck Young Photography, Inc.
Corporate Stories, Ltd., Coca-Cola, IBM, NationsBank, BellSouth
Atlanta, GA

Alan S. Weiner
NY Times contract photographer, *Forbes*, Gamma-Liaison (a Paris-based agency), and many corporate clients
Atlanta, GA

Jim Cook, Jr.
Decatur News Publishing
Decatur, GA

WRITERS

Margaret O. Kirk
Philadelphia Inquirer Sunday Magazine, *Philadelphia Magazine*, *USAir Magazine*, the *New York Times*, *Money*.
Philadelphia, PA

Linda Patillo
Atlanta Bureau of ABC News
Atlanta, GA

Don Winbush
Former Atlanta Bureau Chief, *Time*
Atlanta, GA

Terry Wells
Former reporter for the *Atlanta Constitution*, and nationally recognized writer specializing in the technology and telecommunications fields.

Steve Frandzel
Businesss Atlanta, *American Health Magazine*, *Medical Tribune*
Atlanta, GA

Leslie Bayor
LIFE, *Advertising Age*, *Conde Nast Traveler*
Marietta, GA

Cheryl Crockett
Business Atlanta, *National Real Estate Investor*, *Business Edition Network*; corporate clients IBM and Georgia-Pacific and is president of Write Now!
Atlanta, GA

Michael Pousner
The *Atlanta Constitution*, *Penthouse*, the *New York Daily News*. Nominated for Pulitzer Prize in local reporting.
Atlanta, GA

Charles Yoder
Has written for the University of Michigan, University of Chicago, Tennessee State University and the Great Lakes Basin Commission.
Decatur, GA

Vivian Price
Special Sections Editor at the *DeKalb News-Sun*, and numerous magazines and newspapers.
Chamblee, GA

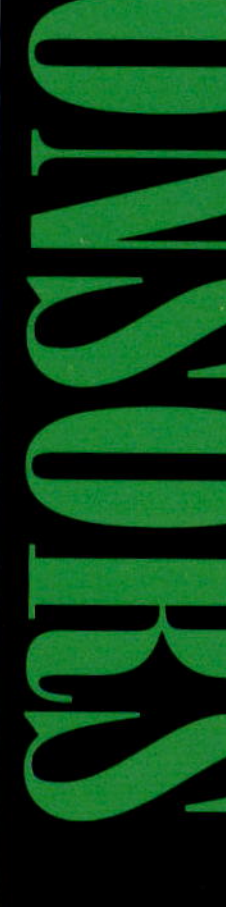

A.C.S.S.
1880 Forge Street
Tucker, GA 30084

Agnes Scott College
141 East College Avenue
Decatur, GA 30030

Air BP Atlanta
DeKalb-Peachtree Airport
1 Corsair Drive
Atlanta, GA 30341

American Prosthetics, Inc.
2754 North Decatur Road, Suite 102
Decatur, GA 30033

AmeriCare Development, Inc.
1587 NE Expressway Access Road, Suite 180
Atlanta, GA 30329-2401

Camera Bug, Ltd.
1799 Briarcliff Road
Atlanta, GA 30306

Centers for Disease Control and Prevention
1600 Clifton Road, NE
Atlanta, GA 30333

City of Avondale Estates
21 North Avondale Plaza
Avondale Estates, GA 30002

Cofer Brothers, Inc.
2300 Main Street
Tucker, GA 30084

Construction Corporation of America
3729 Church Street
Clarkston, GA 30021

The Davison School, Inc.
1500 North Decatur Road, NE
Atlanta, GA 30306

Decatur Downtown Development Authority
P.O. Box 220
Decatur, GA 30031

Decatur Hospital
450 North Candler Street
Decatur, GA 30030

DeKalb Board of REALTORS
1414 Montreal Road
Tucker, GA 30084-8115

DeKalb College
3251 Panthersville Road
Decatur, GA 30034

DeKalb County EOA, Inc.
3597 Covington Highway
Decatur, GA 30032

DeKalb County Public Library
215 Sycamore
Decatur, GA 30030

DeKalb Private Industry Council, Inc.
750 Commerce Drive, Suite 202
Decatur, GA 30030

DeKalb Technical Institute
495 North Indian Creek Drive
Clarkston, GA 30021

Egleston Children's Hospital at Emory University
1405 Clifton Road, NE
Atlanta, GA 30322-1101

G.C.T.V.
1038 W. Peachtree Street
Atlanta, GA 30309

Georgia Biomedical Partnership
P.O. Box 54151
Atlanta, GA 30308-4151

Georgia Power Company
1790 Montreal Circle
Tucker, GA 30084

Gladney & Hemrick, P.C.
2250 North Druid Hills Road, Suite 228
Atlanta, GA 30329

Grace Community Church
1983 Brockett Road
Tucker, GA 30084

The Hawes Company
2370 Main Street, Suite B
Tucker, GA 30084

Hines Interests Limited Partnership
Three Ravinia Drive, Suite 1430
Atlanta, GA 30346-2131

Historic Air Tours
P.O. Box 88423
Dunwoody, GA 30356

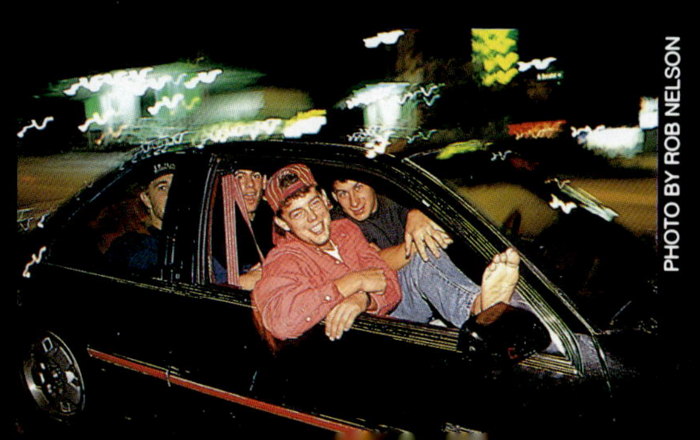
PHOTO BY ROB NELSON

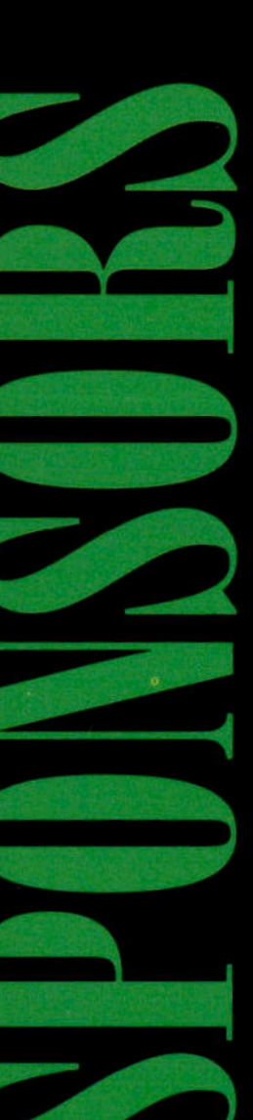

Kings Bridge Retirement Home
3055 Briarcliff Road, NE
Atlanta, GA 30329

Learita Electrologist
1411 Clairmont Road
Decatur, GA 30033

Lullwater School
705 South Candler Street
Decatur, GA 30030

Manor Care
2722 North Decatur Road
Decatur, GA 30033

Marist School
3790 Ashford Dunwoody Road, NE
Atlanta, GA 30319

Marketsquare at North DeKalb
2050 Lawrenceville Highway
Decatur, GA 30033

Mountain National Bank
5100 Lavista Road
Tucker, GA 30085-0049

NationsBank
600 Peachtree Street
3 NationsBank Plaza
Atlanta, GA 30308

Northlake Mall
1000 Northlake Mall
Atlanta, GA 30345

NW Georgia Girl Scout Council
100 Edgewood Avenue, Suite 1100
Atlanta, GA 30335

The Pediatric Center
5405-D Memorial Drive
Stone Mountain, GA 30083

Rehab Orthopedic Medicine
1452 Church Street
Decatur, GA 30030

REMAX Pacesetters
5353 Fairington Road
Lithonia, GA 30038

SmithKline Beecham Clinical Laboratories
1777 Montreal Circle
Tucker, GA 30084

South DeKalb Mall
2853 Candler Road, Suite 5
Decatur, GA 30034

Spruill Center for the Arts
5339 Chamblee Dunwoody Road
Atlanta, GA 30338

T. H. Mize Electric Company
123 N. Clarendon Avenue
Avondale Estates, GA 30002

Taylor & Mathis / Metropolitan Life
115 Perimeter Center Place, Suite 200
Atlanta, GA 30346

Tib's Electrical Service Company
178 Laredo Drive
Decatur, GA 30030

Weekes & Candler
1 Decatur Town Center, Suite 100
Decatur, GA 30030

Zachary & Segraves
1000 Commerce Drive
Decatur, GA 30030

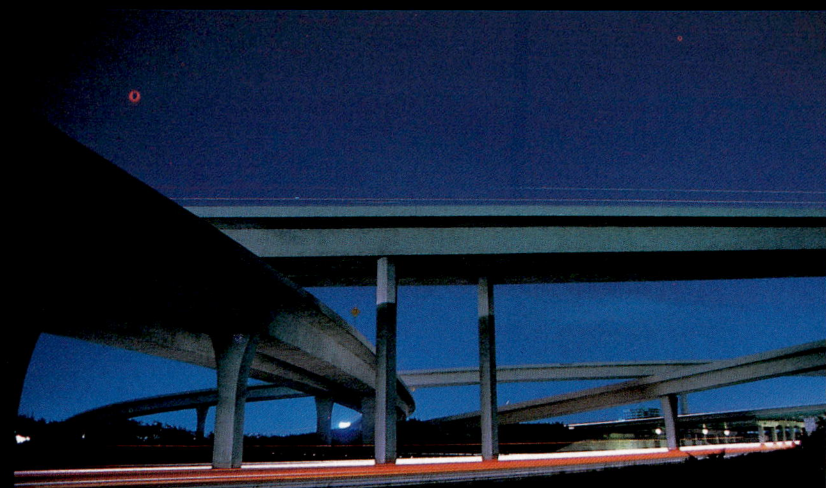

PHOTO BY SCOTT ROBINS